THE WHOLE IS GREATER THAN ITS PARTS

THE WHOLE IS GREATER THAN ITS PARTS

ENCOUNTERING THE INTERRELIGIOUS
AND ECUMENICAL OTHER
IN THE AGE OF POPE FRANCIS

EDITED BY
PETER CASARELLA
AND
GABRIEL REYNOLDS

A Herder & Herder Book
The Crossroad Publishing Company
New York

A Herder & Herder Book
The Crossroad Publishing Company
www.crossroadpublishing.com

© 2020 by Peter Casarella and Gabriel Reynolds.

Crossroad, Herder & Herder, and the crossed C logo/colophon are registered trademarks of The Crossroad Publishing Company.

All rights reserved. No part of this book may be copied, scanned, reproduced in any way, or stored in a retrieval system, or transmitted, in any form or by any means, electronic, mechanical, photocopying, recording, or otherwise, without the written permission of The Crossroad Publishing Company. For permission please write to rights@crossroadpublishing.com.

In continuation of our 200-year tradition of independent publishing, The Crossroad Publishing Company proudly offers a variety of books with strong, original voices and diverse perspectives. The viewpoints expressed in our books are not necessarily those of The Crossroad Publishing Company, any of its imprints or of its employees, executives, or owners. Although the author and publisher have made every effort to ensure that the information in this book was correct at press time, the author and publisher do not assume and hereby disclaim any liability to any party for any loss, damage, or disruption caused by errors or omissions, whether such errors or omissions result from negligence, accident, or any other cause. No claims are made or responsibility assumed for any health or other benefits.

The text of this book is set in 12/15 Adobe Garamond Pro.

Composition by Sophie Appel
Cover design by Sophie Appel
Cover image by Jakub Gojda Photography

Library of Congress Cataloging-in-Publication Data
available upon request from the Library of Congress.
ISBN 978-0-8245-9713-9 paperback
ISBN 978-0-8245-9803-7 cloth
ISBN 978-0-8245-9804-4 ePub
ISBN 978-0-8245-9805-1 mobi

Books published by The Crossroad Publishing Company may be purchased at special quantity discount rates for classes and institutional use. For information, please e-mail sales@crossroadpublishing.com.

CONTENTS

A Note on Transliteration and Translation — ix

Preface: Spreading the Gospel of Peace (Eph 6:15):
Christian Unity and Interreligious Encounter
According to *Evangelii Gaudium* — xi
WALTER CARDINAL KASPER

Introduction — 1
PETER CASARELLA and GABRIEL SAID REYNOLDS

INTERSECTIONS AND CONVERGENCES

1. Christian Unity and Interreligious
Encounter Today: The Nigerian Experience — 17
JOHN CARDINAL ONAIYEKAN, Archbishop of Abuja, Nigeria

2. Whole and Parts:
Ecumenism and Interreligious Encounters
in Pope Francis's *Teología del Pueblo* — 31
PETER CASARELLA

3. Hindu, Christian, Catholic: Four Western Jesuits in India
and the Balance They Achieved — 71
FRANCIS X. CLOONEY, S.J.

4. The Relationship between Ecumenism
and Interreligious Dialogue: Insights from
the Catholic Evangelization of Eastern Africa — 95
PAUL KOLLMAN, CSC

CHRISTIAN UNITY IN THE AGE OF GLOBAL ENCOUNTERS

1. Ecumenism from the Viewpoint of the
   Pontifical Council for Promoting Christian Unity   129
   BISHOP BRIAN FARRELL

2. Revitalizing the Fading of Ecumenical Memory
   and Reenergizing the Promise of Our Ecumenical
   Future: Can Ecumenism Be Taught?   141
   J. JAYAKIRAN SEBASTIAN

3. An Initial Schism between the Synagogue
   and the Church? Some Implications
   of an Ancient Debate for Ecumenism Today   157
   MARIE-HÉLÈNE ROBERT

THEOLOGY OF RELIGIONS AND INTERRELIGIOUS LEARNING

1. Towards a Tentative Catholic Zionism:
   The Trajectory after *Nostra Aetate*?   185
   GAVIN D'COSTA

2. The Way Forward   211
   ABRAHAM SKORKA

3. Reading Qur'anic Verses on Other Religions: Modern
   Exegetical Approaches   223
   MUN'IM SIRRY

4. Scripture Speaking about Itself:
   The Self-Referentiality of the Qur'an
   and Christian-Muslim Dialogue   259
   DAVID MARSHALL

5. The Best of Schemers:
   Divine Plotting in the Bible and the Qur'an   281
   GABRIEL SAID REYNOLDS

6. "In Them Ye Have Benefits for a Term Appointed"
   (Q: 22:33). A Girardian Perspective
   on the Origin of Islam   305
   MARTINO DIEZ

7. Towards a Communion of All Things beyond
   Anthropocentrism and Biocentrism:
   A Catholic-Confucian Dialogue on Social Justice
   and Ecology   329
   ANSELM MIN

   Afterword: The Truth Shall Set You Free!   357
   ROBERT CARDINAL SARAH

   Index   360

A NOTE ON TRANSLITERATION AND TRANSLATION

Transliterations of Arabic follow the system utilized by the *International Journal of Middle Eastern Studies* (IJMES) (https://ijmes.chass.ncsu.edu/docs/TransChart.pdf). Different English Qur'an translations have been used in this volume depending on each contributor's preference. Some contributors may have used their own translation or a particular Qur'ān translation with some modifications.

PREFACE

Spreading the Gospel of Peace (Eph 6:15): Christian Unity and Interreligious Encounter According to *Evangelii Gaudium*

Walter Cardinal Kasper, Rome

Peace is humanity's highest good and God's fundamental promise. Ecumenical and interreligious dialogue are indispensable contributions to peace. Without peace in the Church and peace among religions, there can be no peace in the world. Before we enter into the many individual questions here, this preface aims to answer the following questions: What does the Gospel of peace tell us? What and how can ecumenical and interreligious dialogue contribute to peace?

I.

The Second Vatican Council (1962–65) inaugurated a new epoch in the history of the Church, which Pope Paul VI summarized with the following formula in 1975, at the Council's tenth anniversary: "to make the Church of the twentieth century ever better fitted for proclaiming the Gospel to the people of the twentieth century"

(EN 2).¹ With these words, Paul VI, one of the greatest reformer popes in the history of the Church, moved those fundamental biblical words, *euangelion* (Gospel) and evangelization, back into center focus. His two successors, John Paul II and Benedict XVI, followed him in this respect and took up the new evangelization as a central program.² Pope Francis took the name of Francis with an eye toward Francis of Assisi, who in front of Pope Innocent III said that together with his brothers, he wanted to return to the Gospel and live it *sine glossa*. And Francis set down his first apostolic letter under the programmatic title *Evangelii gaudium* (2013) in order, as he put it, to introduce a new stage of evangelization with the joyful message of the Gospel (EG 1).

In the Bible, the Gospel is the good news of the coming of the universal, messianic kingdom of peace, which was already promised by the prophets, and which has come into the world for good with the coming of Jesus Christ, his death, and his resurrection. It is not merely the historical message of Jesus of Nazareth. According to Paul, it is written on the hearts of the faithful in the Holy Spirit (2 Cor 3:2f.) (EG 37).³ The faithful themselves are the Gospel

---

1. For the sake of convenience and brevity, the following abbreviations will be used throughout the paper when referring to Church documents:
    AG – Second Vatican Council, *Ad gentes* decree
    EG – Pope Francis, *Evangelii gaudium* encyclical
    EN – Paul VI, *Evangelii nuntiandi* encyclical
    GS – Second Vatican Council, Pastoral Constitution *Gaudium et spes*
    LG – Second Vatican Council, Dogmatic Constitution *Lumen gentium*
    NA – Second Vatican Council, *Nostra aetate* declaration
    UR – John Paul II, *Unitatis redintegratio* encyclical
2. Pontificium Consilium De Nova Evangelizatione Promovenda, *Enchiridion Della Nuova Evangelizzazione: Testi Del Magistero Pontificio E Conciliare, 1939–2012* (Città Del Vaticano: Libreria Editrice Vaticana, 2012).
3. Pope Francis explicitly refers to Thomas Aquinas (*S.Th.* I/II q. 108 a.1), whose theology in general is often an important point of reference for him.

epistle; they all have the *sensus fidei*. The whole people of God is for this reason the bearer of the mission to evangelize (EG 119; 139).[4]

Thus, the Gospel of Joy and Peace is no abstract edifice of teachings. The one message of Jesus Christ, who "is our peace" (Eph 2:14), is passed on in the Holy Spirit in human language, by people, always in specific situations. This transmission takes place in dialogue, by our contemplating the historical situation in the light provided by faith (EG 238). It does not mean a relativistic and syncretistic adaptation to the spirit of the times; on the contrary, the message about the eternal newness of God (EG 11; 272) frees us from being blinded by opinions contingent on our times, and from being fixated on the going templates. It helps us to see the signs of the times communally, in the spirit of God (EG 14).[5]

It is a sign of our times, according to the Second Vatican Council, that today, in a dramatic "crisis of growth" (GS 4f.; 77), human beings are growing together in increasing "interdependence…one on the other" from day to day (GS 23; NA 1). In Jesus Christ, the Church is a sign and an instrument for union (LG 1; GS 42); she is supposed to be the salt of the earth and the light of the world (AG 1). Her calling is not to provide solutions to specific political, economic, and social questions; rather, she is to be light and strength (GS 42f.), with her gaze on Jesus Christ, who is the alpha and the omega of all history, and who in the fullness of time will gather everything into one (Eph 1:10) (GS 45).

It is in this sense that Pope Francis speaks of the transformative power of the Gospel. It does not reverse the identity of different nations' cultures and does not seek to impose a uniform cultural model on them. Rather, the Church shows its authentic catholicity

---

4. See LG 12; International Theological Commission, *Sensus Fidei in the Life of the Church* (2014).

5. The understanding of the Gospel as a prophetic interpretation of the signs of the times was adopted from French theology already by John XXIII (*Pacem in terris*, 1963), by the Second Vatican Council (GS 40, 92, among others), by Paul VI (*Ecclesiam suam*, 1964), and finally, by Pope Francis.

by introducing nations and their cultures into her community through the inculturation of the Gospel, in the course of which she herself is enriched (EG 116). In this comprehensive sense, the Gospel is a Gospel of peace (Eph 6:15), which inspires all the baptized to be—just as in Francis of Assisi's famous prayer—instruments of peace (EG 239).

Out of that spirit, Pope Francis formulates the following principle: "Unity prevails over conflict" (EG 226–30). To him, this principle is essential for ecumenical and interreligious dialogue, the two fundamental aspects of his program of evangelization.

II.

The ecumenical movement of the twentieth century understood itself from its beginning, at the world mission conference in Edinburgh (1910), as a movement which seeks to overcome the divisions in Christendom in the interest of global mission. The Second Vatican Council took up this concern; it was aware of the fact that, as a scandal for the world and as something damaging to the holy purpose of proclaiming the Gospel, the division between Christians contradicts the will of Jesus "that they may all be one" (Jn 17:21) (UR 1; AG 6).[6] In *Evangelii gaudium*, too, ecumenism is a contribution to the unity of the family of humankind (EG 245). It is no mere diplomacy or forced fulfillment of duties, but the unavoidable path of evangelization (EG 246). The shared path of evangelization is also the ecumenical path. To walk on this path is a matter of our credibility as Christians (EG 244–46).

What is new about ecumenical dialogue is that it does not start out from the things that separate us but rather from the grounds that unite us: our confession of faith in Jesus Christ, into whom we are baptized in one baptism, and through whom we are delivered

---

6. An important continuation of this theme can be found in John Paul II, *Ut unum sint* (1995).

by grace alone into the freedom of the children of God. In this dialogue, Pope Francis' outlook is first and foremost not directed backwards towards the past, with the aim of reprocessing the existing divisions. Francis looks ahead. To him, ecumenism means walking a path together in order to find peace in the face of the one God. On this path—he is convinced—we will find common forms of witness and of service, and we will learn from one other. The goal is not a uniform Church but a Church of reconciled diversity, which we can only receive as a gift from the spirit.[7]

III.

The dialogue with Judaism occupies a unique position in interreligious dialogue. The foundation for it was laid by the Second Vatican Council in the declaration *Nostra aetate* (4), after a long history of alienation. Pope Francis also takes up statements by John Paul II, which go beyond *Nostra aetate*. Judaism is no foreign religion to Christians; Christianity considers Judaism as its holy root (Rom 11:16–18). God's covenant with the people was never revoked. For this reason, dialogue and friendship with the children of Israel are part of the life of Jesus' disciples.

Evangelii gaudium goes even one step further. Francis not only takes into account the common origin of Christianity and Judaism, but also looks to current, postbiblical Judaism. God continues to dwell and to work in the people of the Old Covenant. Thus, a treasury of wisdom has developed there, which springs from the encounter with the divine word, and which is enriching for the Church as well. There is a rich complementarity which allows us the read the texts of the Hebrew Bible together and to help one other to plumb the riches of the word of God, as well as to share with one

---

7. Pope Francis early on adopted the idea of reconciled diversity from the reformed exegete Oscar Cullmann, an ecumenical observer at the Second Vatican Council and friend of Paul VI.

another many ethical convictions as well as the common concern for justice and for the development of nations (EG 347–349).[8]

IV.

In contrast to ecumenical dialogue and the dialogue with Judaism, dialogue with other religions cannot build on shared sacred texts. The meeting point with the other religions is human conscience.[9] For if members of other religions hear the voice of God in their conscience and follow it (Rom 2:14f.), they are following the fundamental law of love, and with the Golden Rule they fulfill the demands of the law and the prophets (Mt 7:12; 22:40).[10] All human beings are created in the image of God, who is love (Gen 1:27); everything is created in and for Christ (1 Cor 8:6; Col 1:16f.). Christ illumines every person who comes into this world (Jn 1:8), and through the Holy Spirit, he works in the hearts of all human beings, in all cultures and religions. Thus, non-Christians, too, are joined to the paschal mystery by listening to their consciences; they are included in God's walking with humans, and they can attain salvation. They do not belong to the external, institutional body of the Church, but they certainly belong to the heart of the Church (EG 254).[11]

Such common ground does not establish any sort of syncretism, which would essentially be a kind of totalitarianism that presumes

---

8. Pontifical Biblical Commission, *Le people juif et ses Saintes Écritures dans la Bible chrétienne* (2001).
9. Pope Francis refers to the International Theological Commission, *Christianity and the World Religions* (1997).
10. The thesis that natural law contains the law of the Golden Rule goes back to the *Decretum Gratiani* (1119–ca. 1140) and became fundamental to scholastic natural law.
11. Pope Francis is able to build on the teaching of the Second Vatican Council (LG 16; GS 16, 22) as well as on John Paul II's *Redemptoris missio* (1990), 28, 55f.

to disregard those values which surpass it and which are not its possessions. Rather, what belongs to interreligious dialogue are identity and openness, the readiness on both sides for both purification and enrichment, while all forms of fundamentalism have to be put aside (EG 250f.). The various cultures and religions interpret the holiness of God and of human beings, heard in one's conscience, in different ways. In interreligious conversation, wherever there are points of connection with these other interpretations, theology will correct, as well as surpass them in light of her understanding of God. But theology, too, will be purified by the dialogue and will be more deeply initiated into all truth (Jn 16:13); theology, too, must always be open in its history to the ever greater eternal newness of God (EG 11; 273).

V.

In the more than fifty years since the Second Vatican Council, the situation of interreligious dialogue has changed dramatically. Today, problems are re-emerging which were believed to have been long overcome. A new kind of nationalism and racism is arising in combination with a hostility towards foreigners exacerbated by the worldwide phenomenon of migration. Likewise, a new fundamentalism both inside and outside of the Church is emerging (EG 63; 250). Identitarian movements seek identity through exclusion instead of through integration. All these factors are becoming a threat to world peace. The rejection of all forms of exclusion of human beings, which runs like a golden thread through *Evangelii gaudium*, is for this reason highly topical (EG 53f.; 59f.; 186f.).

The contention is most of all with terrorist Islamism; *Evangelii gaudium* calls for religious freedom and mutual respect (EG

252–53).[12] Regarding the relationship with Muslims, the Council already recommended working together with Muslims for justice and peace in the world (NA 3). Of course, it would be naive to look to Islam only. *Evangelii gaudium* essentially makes clear that mission does not take place by proselytizing, but by attraction (EG 15); the "dialogue of life" is most essential (EG 250; 255f.). Based on the example of Charles de Foucauld (d. 1916), such dialogue can be attainable even in countries where open Christian witness is not a possibility. It can, of course, lead to martyrdom, as shown by the martyr monks of Tibhirine (murdered in April 1996) and many other martyrs of the twentieth and twenty-first centuries.

There are martyrs—true martyrs, not suicide assassins! —in all denominations and religions. There are also holy pagans. The same thing is true of them: "Blessed are the peacemakers" (Mt 5:9). This ecumenism of blood connects us across denominational and religious boundaries. We may hope that, through this ecumenism, a new form of Christianity is growing and ripening in the third millennium: a worldwide network of diverse Christian communities, in a fraternal bond, who peacefully coexist with all human beings of good will and of other religions, and who work together with them as peacemakers. It is my wish that in our peaceless world, this volume might be a contribution to the spreading of the Gospel of peace.

---

12. *Evangelii gaudium* says of Islam that it is of great importance today, that the Qur'an contains elements of Christian teaching, and that Islam deserves respect. But it avoids a fundamental theological categorization. Since Islam is a post-Christian religion, it is difficult to place it alongside, for example, Hinduism and Buddhism; of course, it is contested whether or not Islam can be categorized as one of the three Abrahamic religions, together with Judaism and Christianity.

INTRODUCTION
Peter Casarella and Gabriel Said Reynolds

The present book emerged from a conference organized by Notre Dame's World Religions & World Church program that took place from January 8 to 10, 2018. That conference, held at Notre Dame's Rome Global Gateway on Via Ostilia near the Coliseum, brought together Church leaders and theologians from different denominations and religious traditions to discuss ecumenical and interreligious dialogue. The conference organizers invited participants to consider what is particular and what is common to the Church's engagement in these two forms of dialogue and to assess current challenges and opportunities for these dialogues, especially in light of Pope Francis's vision for a Church that "goes forth."[1] As the World Religions & World Church program is particularly dedicated to bringing together the study of religions and cultures, the conference also involved discussions regarding interreligious and ecumenical dialogue in particular contexts, notably Africa and China.[2]

As editors we intend *The Whole Is Greater Than Its Parts* to be more than acts of a conference. The proceedings form just one part of what we have put together here, for the present volume includes a number of additional contributions from scholars and Church leaders who were not with us in Rome but are leading figures in

---

1. *Evangelii Gaudium* paras. 20–24.
2. We invite those who are interested in more detail on the Rome conference to consult the "Conference Report." See on-line: https://www.academia.edu/35700977/Conference_Report_The_Whole_is_Greater_Than_its_Parts_Christian_Unity_and_Interreligious_Encounter_Today_Jan_8-10_2018_

interreligious and ecumenical dialogue. Together the authors represent a conversation between the Church and the academy. The resulting volume is inspired in part by Pope Francis' *Evangelii Gaudium* (whence the title has been taken). But we also recognize the irreversible steps forward taken by Saint John XXIII, Paul VI, Saint John Paul II, and Benedict XVI in this regard as well. The search for unity never compromises the search for the truth about humanity. Proclamation and dialogue reinforce one another, to the same degree that Christian unity and interreligious understanding are complementary goals.[3] This book seeks to nourish friendships across denominations and religions even as it models a faithful and rigorous study of the sources of Christian revelation on the part of the Christian authors.

This book is divided into three sections. The first section, "Intersections and Convergences," is dedicated to a consideration of ways in which ecumenism and interreligious dialogue are related. It opens with a contribution from John Cardinal Onaiyekan, Archbishop of Abuja, Nigeria, on "Christian Unity and Interreligious Encounter Today: The Nigerian Experience." Therein Cardinal Onaiyekan notes the struggles of Christians to achieve greater unity in Nigeria and the challenges which extremism of all forms poses to interreligious dialogue. Nevertheless, Cardinal Onaiyekan offers hope that certain essential principles, including a belief in the oneness of God, along with a humble disposition, can bring an array of Christians as well as Muslims in his country closer together.

The next chapter looks directly at the teaching of Pope Francis and offers a hermeneutic for looking at and comprehending the subtle and differentiated relationship between different forms of dialogue. Peter Casarella's "Whole and Parts: Ecumenism and Interreligious Encounters in Pope Francis's *Teología del Pueblo*" is a

---

3. See, for example, the talk given in 2003 by Cardinal Nasrallah Pierre Sfeir on "Ecumenism in the Thought of Pope John Paul II," available on-line at https://www.ewtn.com/catholicism/library/ecumenism-in-the-pontificate-of-john-paul-ii-2258.

study of how the metaphors relating to wholes and parts function in Francis's pre-pontifical and pontifical writings. Pope Francis often uses related metaphors to talk about wholes and parts; one of the most recurrent ones is that of the polyhedron. The polyhedron is a unity in which the parts are organized in a different relationship to the center. Unity born of a polyhedron preserves difference, and unity born of the sphere reinforces homogeneity. He has utilized this metaphor to make two points. First, the epoch of globalization commends us to think about the cultural and economic exchanges in the world today in such way that difference is never abandoned for the sake of wanton hegemony and, thus, radical inequality is never left unchallenged. Second, the unity of charisms in the Church can be understood polyhedrically, for the Church in its essence is a differentiated unity greater than the sum of its homogenized parts. This chapter explores the polyhedric unity that underlies both ecumenical and interreligious dialogue according to Pope Francis and consists of four parts. In the first part, Casarella demonstrates that the roots of this type of thinking extend back to his time in Argentina, for the Argentine *teología del pueblo* is also a mode of reflection about wholes and parts. The second part is an examination of the roots of Pope Francis's thinking about wholes and parts in his own Ignatian spirituality of unity. In the third part, Casarella offers an overview of how the Pope, especially in his Apostolic Exhortation *Evangelii Gaudium*, has applied this polyhedric notion of encounter to the questions of ecumenism and interreligious dialogue. In sum, Casarella argues that God's love is the cause of the good in the other and the impetus for dialogue with the other. This formulation is a re-statement of the Bergoglian articulation of the idea that the whole is greater than the sum of its parts. God can elect Jews and Gentiles not out of a human kind of partiality but only out of a truly divine love. Inspired by this impartial and essentially "in-different" love of God for his creatures, Christians can be goaded not only to seek greater unity amongst themselves but also to witness to their faith.

The final two articles in this section consider the intersections of ecumenism and interreligious relations in two new contexts. Frank Clooney, in "Ecumenism, Global Christianity, and Interreligious Dialogue in Tension: Three Jesuit Examples in India," discusses particular cases of Jesuit priests who worked in India, and whose interreligious work was inflected by debates among Catholics and Protestants in their day. He also discusses how a certain ecumenism and disposition in favor of interreligious dialogue in the West may complicate, or even impede, deeper conversations with Christians in the global south, especially those living as minorities. For his part, Paul Kollman, author of "The Relationship between Ecumenism and Interreligious Dialogue: Insights from the Catholic Evangelization of Eastern Africa," studies the history of Catholic missionaries in Eastern Africa, their engagement with Protestant missionaries with a diverse sense of mission, and their work among non-Christians. Kollman notes that in the unfolding of these relationships Catholic missionaries dialogued directly with the other, including other Christian missionaries and notably the Muslim Sultan of Zanzibar. He also observes that in their zeal to make converts, some Catholic missionaries, although not all, failed to be attentive to the diversity among local followers of African traditional religions.

The second section of *The Whole Is Greater Than Its Parts* is entitled "Christian Unity in the Age of Global Encounters." This section is dedicated to Christian unity in the contemporary world, marked by globalization and new challenges, including the presence of intercultural and interreligious dynamics that were previously ignored. Bishop Brian Farrell ("Ecumenism from the Viewpoint of the Pontifical Council for Promoting Christian Unity") offers insight on the vision of Pope Francis for advancing ecumenism. The Holy Father seeks to shift the emphasis of the ecumenical movement from notional agreements to a practice of "life together." This involves both an appreciation for commonalities among Christians along with a disposition of respect for differences that complement but do not contradict each other. At the same time, he underlines real accomplishments in dialogues with both the Orthodox and Protestants.

Jayakiran Sebastian ("Revitalizing the Fading of Ecumenical Memory and Reenergizing the Promise of Our Ecumenical Future: Can Ecumenism Be Taught?") makes an energetic argument from a Protestant perspective that recent dialogues offer hope for advancing Christian unity. His contribution advances the conversation ecumenically, interreligiously, and interculturally. He underlines the importance of ecumenical documents including *Baptism, Eucharist, and Ministry* (1982) and *The Church: Towards a Common Vision* (2013) produced by the Faith and Order Commission of the World Council of Churches. He also emphasizes the obligation of ecumenical dialogue for believers, writing: "Christianity without dialogue is like a road with a map, a quest without a destination, a journey without a goal."

Finally, Marie-Hélène Robert sheds new light on the Jewish-Christian dialogue while developing her own idea of polyhedric unity. She argues from a Catholic perspective in "An Initial Schism between the Synagogue and the Church? Some Implications of an Ancient Debate for Ecumenism Today," that the ancient and foundational debate about whether the earliest Christians were permitted to be included in Jewish worship services can be revisited today in a fruitful way. She therefore speaks about the "initial schism" rather than an "original schism" in order to steer clear of the separation between Jews and Christians in its exclusively polemical dimension. She also wants to avoid the a-historical approach of those who claim that any mention of a schism in the past is detrimental to dialogue. The separation between Christians in the East (the Orthodox Church) and Christians in the West (the Roman Catholic Church) cannot in effect be confused with the separation between Jews and Christians. Given the importance of Christology to both forms of separation, the division between Christians would come from the initial schism and would not be capable of being resolved except through the reunification of Israel and the Church.[4] This hope for reunion on both ecumenical and interreligious levels comes from the recognition of a common origin before the initial schism, but also from the one sole people of God in spite of the schism, and therefore of even one eschatological hope whereby the schism will be reabsorbed at the time of the reintegration foreseen by Paul in Romans 11:11–32. The initial schism had dramatic consequences for the internal unity of the Church and in the history of the Jewish people. In general, the work on the historical problem has been approached from only one of the two sides of the division. This essay seeks to bring those two lines of reflection closer to one another so that ecumenists focused on letting the Church breathe with both its lungs (East and West) and practitioners of the Jewish-Catholic dialogue can draw from the same well of knowledge, practical experience, and Biblical wisdom.

The final section of *The Whole Is Greater Than Its Parts* addresses "Theology of Religions and Interreligious Learning." The contributors to this section address the relationship between Christianity and Judaism, Islam, and Confucianism. Gavin D'Costa carefully considers the Church's relationship to Zionism in light of her theological and social justice commitments in his article "Towards a Tentative Catholic Zionism: the Trajectory after *Nostra Aetate*?" D'Costa observes that the Church, in *Nostra Aetate* and other documents, recognizes the irrevocable covenant that God made with Israel, and that this covenant in the Old Testament / Hebrew Bible is connected to the land (he also argues that Zionism need not betray "the legitimate claims made by Palestinians to their own State"). D'Costa then investigates to what degree this recognition involves also a certain regard for Jewish practices among Hebrew Catholics. Abraham Skorka, in "The Way Forward," presents likewise the author's work in Jewish-Catholic dialogue in Argentina through the years, addressing the impact of the Shoah on his commitment to interreligious relations and telling the story of his friendship with

---

4. Paul Démann, "Israel and the Unity of the Church," *Cahiers sioniens* 1 (Mars 1953), 1–24.

Introduction 7

Jorge Mario Bergoglio, the former Archbishop of Buenos Aires and now Bishop of Rome. Rabbi Skorka notes that the tragedy of the Shoah can lead one to seek defense against hatred and aggression but might also inspire one to work towards changing the "status quo," transforming culture so that such tragedies are not repeated. Rabbi Skorka's conviction is that this hard work of reconciliation can be achieved through dialogue.

Four different chapters in the third section of *The Whole Is Greater Than Its Parts* address Muslim-Christian relations. Mun'im Sirry ("Reading Qur'anic Verses on Other Religions: Modern Exegetical Approaches") investigates Qur'anic passages on non-Islamic religions, especially those passages that address Christianity. He develops an exegesis of the Qur'an that involves a careful consideration of the sectarian tensions that marked the context of the Qur'an's initial proclamation, and of the imperative to advance friendship between believers today. This method, which has been worked out by a number of modern Muslim exegetes, offers a path to promoting peaceful interreligious relations. For his part David Marshall ("Scripture Speaking about Itself: The Self-Referentiality of the Qur'an and Christian-Muslim Dialogue") addresses a feature of the Qur'an—its frequent references to its own revealed nature and qualities—that has attracted attention in recent scholarship. Marshall sees the Qur'an's "self-referentiality" as a sign of its salient concern with how its audience responds to its claims of divine authorship. By contrast, the Bible is minimally invested in self-referentiality. This contrast is decisive both for Muslim views of the Bible and Christian views of the Qur'an. Marshall insightfully reflects towards the end of his article: "The only real analogy in Christianity to the self-referentiality of the Qur'an is the self-referentiality of Jesus, notably in the 'I am' sayings in John's Gospel."[5]

Gabriel Said Reynolds, in his chapter "The Best of Schemers: Divine Plotting in the Bible and the Qur'an," analyzes the richness

---

5. See below in Marshall's article.

of language affirming God's ability to scheme against, deceive, or trick the unbelievers. This, Reynolds argues, reflects the Qur'an's vision of God as a personal deity who is committed to rewarding and guiding His people, the believers, and taking vengeance on those who refuse His call to belief and obedience. God, as the Qur'an puts it (Q 3:68), is the "protecting guardian" or "ally of the believers." Reynolds also explores the subtext for this notion of divine scheming in the Bible, including in the drama of the crucifixion and resurrection of Christ. Finally, Martino Diez ("'In Them Ye Have Benefits for a Term Appointed' (Q 22:33): A Girardian Perspective on the Origin of Islam"), analyzes the Qur'an in the light of the theories of the Catholic literary critic and religious scholar René Girard (d. 2015), and in particular the ways in which the rites of the pilgrimage, especially the sacrifice therein, can be understood as part of a Girardian "sacrificial order." At the same time, Diez notes that the Qur'an critiques this order with its emphasis on the avoiding of sacrifice in the story of Abraham and his son.[6]

The last article in the final section of *The Whole Is Greater Than Its Parts* concerns a non-Abrahamic tradition in recognition of the need to expand our reflections beyond Christianity, Judaism, and Islam. Anselm Min ("Towards a Communion of All Things beyond Anthropocentrism and Biocentrism: A Catholic-Confucian Dialogue on Social Justice and Ecology") addresses in particular how recent teachings of the Catholic Church, notably the 2015 papal encyclical *Laudato Si'*, advance an ecological teaching which is close to that of the Confucian tradition. He notes that both Pope Francis and Confucian tradition offer a vision according to which humans are not distinct from nature, or masters of it, but rather joined to it.

Before concluding, let us offer some final reflections in the view of the whole about the complementarity of the two forms of dialogue. How, then, is ecumenical dialogue enriched by open-

---

6. Sura 37.

ing up one's eyes to the presence of the interreligious other?[7] Pope Francis has broadened the category of ecumenism in three ways: through an ecumenism of blood, an ecumenism of the poor, and an ecumenism of mission. Each of these new forms of ecumenical understanding demand an attentiveness to the interreligious other.[8] In fact, each of these three forms of witnessing were present in the earliest Christian community in Rome, and the participants in the conference were able to reflect upon that fact because of their proximity to the Coliseum. So Pope Francis's principles represent not a break with any tradition of the past but rather a renewed understanding (in line with the aforementioned reflection of Marie-Hélène Robert) of how the ecclesial unity and form of life prior to the present hardened divisions into Eastern and Western and Catholic, Reformation, and the non-denominational, can spur Christians all over the globe to recover the unity that Christ himself sought and seeks even now for the Church. A Church that goes forth cannot but seek to recover this original unity to which the earliest Christians testified in word and deed.

In general, one must avoid the defensive stance of seeking to form a Christian coalition simply to fight militant and unreasonable forms of belief that lie outside the Christian confession of faith. Furthermore, it is important not to confuse the two modes of discourse. Blind spots held in common by Christians can be erased or modified by allowing a non-Christian partner to illuminate the matter at hand, whether that be a doctrinal point of dispute within Christian discourse or a program for social action. Concerning the latter, the possibilities for collaborative work on peace and reconciliation are immense. In his address to the U.S. Congress, Pope Francis included Dr. Martin Luther King in a list of four witnesses

---

7. Santiago Madrigal Terrazas, *L'unità prevale sul conflitto. L'ecumenismo di Papa Francesco* (Vatican City: Libreria Editrice Vaticana, 2017).
8. See "Pope in Bulgaria," *Vatican News*, May 5, 2019, available on-line at https://www.vaticannews.va/en/pope/news/2019-05/pope-francis-bulgaria-apostolic-visit-orthodox-church-synod.html.

to the truth who could animate politicians in the U.S. to recover Biblical values from within the narration of the struggle of our own people.[9] Dr. Martin Luther King, for example, enjoyed a broad ecumenical coalition of partners in his fight for civil and human rights, but the real inspiration for his spirituality of non-violence came from Mahatma Gandhi, and Gandhi's vision in part was inspired by Tolstoy. To see Dr. King's triumph (as well as the ongoing challenge of living up to his ideal of a beloved community) in exclusively Christian terms is a truncation of the reality of that situation. Today we live in a much more globalized world than Dr. King and face new challenges. He offered relevant moral and spiritual lessons regarding Christian witness, even unto death, and the fostering of dialogue for the common good.

How, if at all, is interreligious dialogue enriched by a consideration of ecumenism and/or the challenge of Christian unity? First of all, there is no point to fusing the two tasks. Their aims are clearly distinct, and the procedures can also differ in both degree and in kind. Perhaps here is where we need to think more about the relationship between the interreligious and the intercultural and the different ways in which pluralism is experienced and expressed on different parts of the globe. In a globalized world it becomes difficult to carry out a dialogue between Christians and non-Christians in a manner that ignores the diversity of expressions of Christianity on the globe or the different experiences of pluralism. A Catholic, for example, in a country in Southeast Asia with a very small percentage of Christians and a high percentage of Buddhists is going to have a very different experience of the Catholic-Buddhist dialogue than someone with the same national heritage but who grew up in California as a disciple of Masao Abe, an American who practices

---

9. See Peter Casarella, "Pope Francis, Theology of the People, and the Church in the United States," in *Discovering Pope Francis: The Roots of Jorge Mario Bergoglio's Thinking*, eds. Brian Y. Lee and Rev. Thomas L. Knoebel (Collegeville, MN: Liturgical Press, 2019), 177–208.

Introduction

Zen Buddhism in a distinctively pluralist context.[10] Lamin Sanneh, a Muslim who grew up in Ghana, converted to Catholicism and became the Professor of Global Christianity at Yale Divinity School until his sudden death in 2019. He was known and even at times criticized for his insistence on the need not to abandon the missionary quest that helped Christianity in its origins to spread to through Asia Minor and later to Africa. At the same time, he was a voice who was nurtured by and lent support to ecumenical and interreligious efforts in the contemporary world.[11]

This volume opens with a foreword by Walter Cardinal Kasper and closes with an afterword by Robert Cardinal Sarah, both of whom offer readers a vision of the Church's commitment to both ecumenical and interreligious dialogue. The contributions to this volume suggest in myriad ways and enriched by diverse standpoints that each dialogue has its particular goals.

Yet both ecumenical and interreligious dialogue ultimately find their inspiration in the divine. There is no effective dialogue without prayer. Standing before the Absolute and acknowledging our yearning for union with a mystery and personal beckoning that fulfills our desire for salvation is essential for any effective and authentic dialogue, ecumenical or interreligious. Hearkening to a voice of an Other is also a plea to allow more voices—from East, West, North, and South—to participate in these dialogues. Too often in the past the dialogues have been too Western, too Abrahamic, and too focused on a narrow set of issues.

We live in a world where the local is increasingly global, which is not in any way an endorsement of a secular declension of unrestricted "globalism." U.S. Catholics who traveled to countries in Latin America with large indigenous populations like Bolivia might actually return to the U.S. to teach inculturation of the

---

10. David Tracy, *Dialogue with the Other: The Inter-Religious Dialogue* (Louvain: Peeters, 1990).
11. This report from the Ethiopian Graduate School of Theology confirms Sanneh's ecumenical and global outreach: https://egst.edu.et/?p=4002.

faith and a chastened and culturally sensitive science of development in an ecumenical or interreligious setting.[12] At the very least, the dynamics of the ecumenical encounter bleed into the interreligious experiences at many levels and in many different contexts. The tasks of ecumenism and interreligious encounter complement one another. This means that they are distinct but still should not be pursued in complete isolation from one another. Today in our globalized world communities seeking Christian unity dwell in the midst of communities seeking a new peace of faith among the religions (and vice versa). The questions and challenges from the ecumenical domain can find their way into global encounters that at first glance seem to be primarily or exclusively interreligious. In general, we need to rethink the categories of dialogue that we are using, and the contributions of this book can be read as a first step in that direction.

The title of this book is not a slogan or a mantra. In the actual experience of believers, there is no tangible whole that literally contains within it all the parts to which we have referred in this introduction. Unity in diversity is finally a divine attribute that makes itself present to sustained reflection and practical life by analogy to an unfathomable whole that belies all creaturely senses of pre-containing our ideologies of unity into one that is of our own invention. In the actual sense of believers, interreligious and ecumenical relationships nonetheless might advance their vocation to love God and love neighbor. The sense of polyhedric unity that we are suggesting for consideration in this volume is therefore one that maintains unity in diversity as a norm in the light of the analogy of unity between divine love and the human search for

---

12. The work of anthropologist Kevin Healy is a good example in this regard. See his book *Llamas, Weavings and Organic Chocolate: Multicultural Grassroots Development in the Andes and Amazon of Bolivia* (Notre Dame: University of Notre Dame Press, 1990), a study that features grassroots development stories with which he has been associated.

one family that includes all of humanity.[13] The experience of the "Whole" in this manner can outstrip any sense of isolation undergone by an individual or a religious body. As Rabbi Skorka fittingly reminds us in his essay: "The Voice that seeks to dialogue with us also intends for us to dialogue with each other."[14]

---

13. Cf. Henri de Lubac, *Catholicisme* (Paris: Aubier, 1940); *Catholicism* (San Francisco: Ignatius Press, 1988).
14. See the essay by Rabbi Skorka in this volume.

INTERSECTIONS AND CONVERGENCES

Chapter One

CHRISTIAN UNITY AND INTERRELIGIOUS ENCOUNTER TODAY: THE NIGERIAN EXPERIENCE

John Cardinal Onaiyekan, Archbishop of Abuja, Nigeria

Introduction

It is indeed a great honor for me to be invited to participate in this very important conference, but especially to be given this special slot for a keynote address. I have decided to adopt the theme of the conference as the title for my address. The only addition is that I shall reflect on this theme based on my Nigerian experience.

I am convinced that in these matters—whether they pertain to ecumenism, interreligious dialogue, or perhaps the interaction between both—my country Nigeria is well placed to offer to the world a number of important insights. For one thing, our country is known to be very religious. Christianity has come to us in many forms, just as Islam has been very much a part of our religious national culture. It is important that, from the point of view of demography, the more than 180 million Nigerians are almost equally divided among these two major religions. We can therefore say that more or less every Nigerian belongs to one or the other religion. In this sense, Nigeria is a good case of a situation wherein Christianity and Islam try to live peacefully together in a state of relative equality. This is why I believe that addressing the Nigerian experience in a conference of this nature will be found quite relevant for all who have shown interest in this World Conference.

In what follows, I will divide my reflections into three parts. The first part will look at the ecumenical field in Nigeria. The second part will deal with interreligious relationships, especially between Islam and Christianity. Finally, in the third part I will offer some suggestions for a way forward in our efforts to live together in peace and harmony, not only within our different countries, but in the increasingly globalized world that is emerging before our very eyes.

I: Ecumenism in Nigeria

1. Ecumenical Babel

I would like to describe the ecumenical situation in Nigeria as a sort of Babel—a confusion of many voices and different churches. Nigeria is a place where, even as we speak, people are founding new churches and getting membership. The Christian faith therefore, has a variegated color with all the consequences of this. The diversity of the church in Nigeria is also a form of disunity to the extent that it makes working together very difficult.

We have some inherited disunity, which derives from the history of the planting and growth of the Christian faith in our country. The foreign missionaries who evangelized our nation, mainly in the last 150 years, not only came from different countries but also belonged to different Christian denominations. Thus, the major division and disunity of Christians in Europe in the middle of the nineteenth century was transferred to Nigeria. As missionaries were inviting Nigerians to accept the Christian faith, they also tried to recruit them to join their own type of Christianity. Thus, it was not enough merely to be a Christian—one must be a Christian in the right denomination.

In many parts of Nigeria, the Catholic Church, then called the Roman Catholic Mission (RCM), and the Anglican Church, through the Church Missionary Society (CMS), spread the Christian message over much of our nation. At the same time, there were missionaries of Baptist stock who were mainly from America, and also Methodists from England. In the southeastern part of Nigeria there were Presbyterians from Scotland and other Evangelical groups.

The northern part of Nigeria did not receive consistent evangelization until much later. This was through both the Catholic Church and the other mainstream churches that we have just mentioned. It is noteworthy too that northeastern Nigeria received missionaries who planted the Lutheran Church and the Church of the Brethren. We must mention also the various Evangelical groups that came mainly from Northern Ireland and the United States. These groups founded little churches here and there, especially around the Middle-Belt. They went by names like the Sudan United Mission (SUM) or the Sudan Interior Mission (SIM). These have left behind very strong roots among our people in what later became known as the Evangelical Churches of West Africa (ECWA). Thus, our Christianity in Nigeria today very much retains the color of disunity with which it was brought to us.

Then, there is our own self-inflicted disunity. The first case of this is the classic so-called African Independent Churches (also called the "White Garment Churches" since they attended worship in white garments). These left the mainstream Protestant churches around the 1920s to found their own churches, with the intention of having a Christian congregation that would take on some of the concerns of African culture. This was the beginning of the *Aladura* Churches, mainly among the Yorubas of South Western Nigeria. This project soon took on different forms. Thus, we have not only the Christ Apostolic Church but also the Cherubim and Seraphim Churches in their various denominations.

Then, rather recently (largely in the last twenty years), there has been a major growth of the so-called Pentecostal Churches, which started off as prayer groups or Charismatic movements within the main Protestant churches. In the last twenty years, however, they have managed to gather a large following. It is noteworthy, however, that the Pentecostal following came largely from the existing churches, even including the Catholic Church. Few of their members have, in fact, been results of conversion either from Islam or from African traditional (indigenous) religions. The result, therefore, is that there are literally hundreds of churches that have been registered with the Nigerian government, each operating on its own with its own autonomy, with little or no control by anyone other than their founders and general overseers.

2. Little Concern for Christian Unity

In this circumstance, it has become rather sad that there is little concern for Christian unity. There have been efforts in the past to bring Christians together under an umbrella organization. The most well known is the Christian Association of Nigeria (CAN). This was an attempt to rally Christians together in an effort to pursue commonly felt challenges and needs. The weakness of the Christian Association of Nigeria is precisely that the emphasis was not on Christian unity, but rather a kind of a ganging up against what were considered to be common challenges or enemies. The result is that where there are no such challenges, there is little or nothing to bring churches together.

The history of the Christian Association of Nigeria, when it is written, will show how much the lack of true ecumenism has been the cause of much of its crisis. As we are talking now, CAN is still struggling to find its feet. I believe that it will make progress only when we begin to look at ourselves as fellow Christians, seeking ways to link hands, break down our barriers, and reduce our sense of rivalries.

Unfortunately, there is a feeling in many quarters that to found a new church is a great thing. We hear, "The more churches there are, the better." But as we have noted above, most of the new churches are not really attracting new converts. Rather, it is the existing churches that are splitting into groups, each one gathered around a new pastor or overseer. Thus, Nigerians now move freely from one church to another, making up their minds as to what kind of Christianity they will follow.

This situation obviously has a negative impact. For one thing, it introduces a great deal of harmful rivalry. Different churches seek to mobilize as many members as possible, and, in the process, it becomes difficult for many of them to avoid criticizing other churches in order to demonstrate their own superiority. It is unfortunate, therefore, that very often we have to deal with narratives of demonizing other churches—"Don't go there," "Don't follow them, follow us." This kind of rivalry is obviously very little of Christianity.

Another fallout resulting from this proliferation of churches is that the depth of faith often suffers—after all, church leaders may not necessarily be people of deep theological base. Therefore, there is the danger that many church leaders simply try their best to make a success of their financial enterprise. In this way, charlatans abound. Unfortunately, too, many of the churches focus very much on the prosperity of their members. Indeed, they draw many of their members in with the promise of prosperity and miracles. There is often a feeling that churches have become business ventures, with the founder or general overseer as the chief executive officer. We often hear that many of our Nigerian Pentecostal leaders are among the richest pastors in the world. We sincerely need to ask ourselves whether this is a record for which we should be proud or a matter that should give us cause for concern.

3. The Need for Ecumenism

The Catholic Church continues to insist that it is not the will of the Lord Jesus that we end up with confusion in our churches. Indeed, we are reminded that Jesus actually prayed that His members should be united (Jn 17:21). They should be united not so that they will be powerful but so that the world may believe that the Father has sent His Son Jesus Christ into the world. This means, therefore, that our dividedness certainly obstructs the clarity of the Christian message. I have heard some of my Muslim friends saying: "Even if I wanted to become a Christian, I don't know which church to go to." We see this very clearly before our eyes.

It is interesting that those who do not want to take ecumenism seriously want to downplay the negative impact of our divisions. People often say: "We don't have to be in the same church, all that is necessary is that we believe in Jesus Christ." Well, that is easier said than done, because we know that there are many ways of professing faith in the Lord Jesus Christ. After all, Jesus said, "Not everyone who says to me 'Lord, Lord' shall enter the kingdom of heaven" (Mt 7:21 RSV). We cannot forget also the observation of Jesus Himself, who said on the last day He will reject certain people who claim to have preached in His name, even including those who have worked miracles in His name. This should give us cause for serious observation and concern.

There is need for greater ecumenism—otherwise, the Christian church in Nigeria will continue in institutional disorder. We all see how difficult it is for us to take any common position as Christians. At the end of the day, each church is on its own. It is like in ancient Israel when "there was no king [and] every man did what was right in his own eyes" (Jg 17:6 RSV).

Of course, this is the price we pay for the freedom of religion that we enjoy in Nigeria. From the point of view of government, every religion is free to operate according to its own doctrines and according to its own rules and regulations, provided that these do not go against the law of the land. We must appreciate that freedom and be ready to pay the price, which is the disorder and the disunity that we have on our hands. But I believe that it is possible to work within the ambit of the law, to make proper use of the freedom that we enjoy and still work together towards a Christian faith that seeks the profession of a common truth and work together in closer unity to give a credible witness to the society in which we live.

II: Interreligious Dialogue in Nigeria

Theoretically, we often say that in Nigeria, there are three main religions: African traditional religion, Islam, and Christianity. In fact, this is precisely the order of their arrival in Nigeria.

1. African Traditional Religion

There was a time when, in Nigeria, there was neither Christianity nor Islam. In other words, Nigerian Christianity and Islam both grew out of a people that already had an existing traditional religion (or religions, if we consider this in the light of plurality of tribes and cultures). We have already pointed out that the present population of Nigeria is divided almost equally between Christians and Muslims. But that is where we are now. Only a hundred years ago, it was not so. There were a good number of Nigerians who were considered followers of African traditional religion. The early missionaries called them pagans, and targets for conversion.

The history of our conversion from our traditional religions to Christianity and Islam is very fascinating. It is enough to mention here that, if Nigerians and Africans were, broadly speaking, so easily moved to embrace these two religions, it is largely because the two new religions had elements that were congenial to the existing spiritual basis of the people. Both Christianity and Islam built upon the existing deep faith in God, the Almighty, the creator of all. It was not difficult for our people to welcome such religious values from both Christianity and Islam. The differences between Christianity and Islam, then, formed the basis of our present division and distinction.

Christianity, in particular, brought with it the idea that in Jesus, God has come into this world to save us, and to redeem us. Islam brought a faith in the prophet Muhammad, who had his own teachings both in terms of beliefs and of practices. From this point of view, every Nigerian is either directly or indirectly a convert from the traditional religions. Whether we are Christians or Muslims, our shared spiritual roots in the traditional religion are still present in each and every one of us. I am a Cardinal in the Catholic Church, but I am also a Yoruba. And I see no contradiction in my being both a Yoruba and a Bishop in the Catholic Church. Others have the same kind of experience.

There are of course some things that our traditional religion did, especially in terms of practice and worship, which had to be put aside when we embraced the Christian faith. That, however, has been the history of evangelization all over the world—not only in our lands. In that sense, therefore, most of us are spiritually bilingual. That is, we are Christians or Muslims, and at the same time, to some extent, also members of our traditional religion.

2. Muslim-Christian Relations

Today, however, in concrete fact, interreligious dialogue in Nigeria hardly takes notice of African traditional religion. Since most Nigerians are either Christians or Muslims, it is Christian-Muslim relations that is our concern.

The mass media has all kinds of narratives about Christian-Muslim relations in Nigeria. In this way, we have received very poor press. For most people, once they hear about Nigeria, they immediately imagine a place where Muslims and Christians are always killing one another. In reality, this is not so.

Traditionally, Christians and Muslims have always lived together in relative understanding. In fact, in many cases, especially in the South West and the Middle-Belt, Christians and Muslims emerge from the same families, and also from the same African traditional religions. And so, most people are used to having neighbors who belong to the other religions.

However, this traditionally good relationship has, in recent years, undergone negative reversals. There are many reasons for this change. Our rivalries have become more acute as the pool of prospective converts from African traditional religions has practically dried up. For a long time, Christians and Muslims were able to undertake their conversion programs by converting the remaining unattached members of the traditional religions. Now, with very few or hardly any left, whom are we to convert, if not one another? And in a situation where Christians and Muslims are facing the other's proselytic claim that their own faith is the best, if not the only true one, the atmosphere therefore becomes very charged.

We should also add onto this the fact that we are now witnessing several waves of fanaticism on both sides, but in different forms. There are many Christian sects that have highly fanatical views of Christianity that are entirely inward-looking and exclusive of everyone else. And very often, they openly condemn Islam as a false religion. Of course, this does not endear them to their Muslim neighbors, who often react violently against what they consider to be an insult to their faith. We see the same phenomenon on the other side, especially from Muslims who have imbibed fanatical ideas from certain Middle-Eastern schools of thought. And they too believe that only in Islam is there true religion, and they do not hesitate to insist that everybody must follow their own way of thinking.

Even though such groups on each side are relatively few, their impact can nonetheless have a very serious bearing on Christian-Muslim relations. When the fanatics clash, they ignite a fire that can easily become a conflagration consuming everybody. And then we have to do a lot of fire brigade work to cool things down.

Right now, there is really no serious law in Nigeria to deal with those holding unhelpful exclusive positions in religion. Efforts have been made to curb what is seen as hate speech. But it has not been properly outlined nor have we seen any efficient way of dealing with this situation. The result, therefore, is that the struggle continues.

3. Intra-Religious Dimensions

In our effort to seek good relations between our two religions, we now realize that we need to pay attention to our intra-faith divisions as well. We can no longer ignore the fact that there are diversities within each of our two faiths. When Muslims reach out to Christians to work together, they often meet different kinds of Christians with different opinions about the Muslim faith. The same thing happens when as Christians, we try to reach out to Muslims—we often find different kinds of Muslims, and it becomes difficult to know whom to deal with or how to deal with them.

In Nigeria, there was an effort to set up the Nigeria Interreligious Council (NIREC). For some years it worked very well. The idea behind it was very good—namely, that both Christianity and Islam should find a way of meeting. We actually did arrive at a clear organization of twenty-five representatives from each tradition. We met and cleared the ground for initial dialogue. We were even close to dealing with some more serious issues.

However, the intra-religious squabbles soon ended up grounding the organization. And so today, NIREC remains in a coma, if not dead. There was no way for the two groups to meet when, among Christians, there were those who believed that such meeting was useless; you do not dialogue with the devil. That also provoked a strong reaction from Muslims, many of whom did not support the idea of their leaders talking with Christians.[1]

The situation, therefore, is that religious leaders in Nigeria have remained divided. And in their division, they have remained practically incompetent and unable to join hands in dealing with any of our national problems as religious leaders.

Nevertheless, it is not all so gloomy—some Christians have been able to reach out to some Muslims and so many interreligious groups are emerging here and there. It has therefore largely become a matter of the "coalition of the willing." Still, while this enterprise admittedly has its own advantages, there is no doubt that it is

---

1. Since this was first written, there has been an appreciable revival of interest in NIREC, mainly due to a new leadership of CAN more open to dialogue with Muslims. Regular national meetings have resumed—and efforts are once again being made to tackle some national common issues.

not nearly as effective as if there had been national meetings: a mutual reaching-out of Christian and Muslim leaders alike, despite all of our internal difficulties. Again, in this regard, the struggle continues. We cannot give up hope.

III: Seeking the Way Forward

This third section will also act somewhat like a conclusion. In it, we begin to seek a way forward. This search is rooted in the belief that if, as religious leaders, we are not able to find a way to work together, then there can be no real peace in the society—still less can religious leaders play any effective role in solving the many problems that ravage our nation. This is why, therefore, we must continue to seek ways and means of making such Christian-Muslim relations possible.

We have come to the conclusion that, of course, not every Christian is prepared to dialogue with Muslims. And not every Muslim is ready to dialogue with Christians. Therefore, we must rely more and more on those who are prepared to reach out to one another. This reticence is a result of the differences we have already mentioned within our different faiths. While this has its negative impact, there are nonetheless always Muslims who are prepared to work with some Christians, if not with all of them. How do we recognize the groups that are ready to work together? That is a matter that requires proper handling. Here, we are not talking of those for whom their religion is not so important and therefore do not allow their religion to disturb working together. This is not what we are talking about. Sometimes people ask me: "Can't you find some moderate Muslims with whom you can dialogue?" My reply is that first I am not a moderate Christian; I am a very deeply committed Christian. And I don't want to be described as a moderate Christian. So also my good Muslim companion doesn't want to be described as a moderate Muslim. And I am not looking for a moderate Muslim or a Muslim who does not care too much about his faith. I am looking for a convinced Muslim, who, however, still has room to listen to others and reach out to others.

For this to happen, there are many observations that I would like to raise. Each of them can be a subject of further discussion. I mention five of them here.

1. One God, Many Faiths

We cannot go further in interreligious and intra-religious relationships if we do not have a clear idea of One God and many faiths. That is, if we are not able to believe that our different faiths can be in the same God, then there is hardly any room for serious dialogue. We ought to be able to admit that the One God whom we worship is worshipped in many ways, and has given rise to many faiths. We have seen this all through human history, and we continue to see it all around us today. It is for me a fact that we cannot deny. Thanks be to God, Vatican II has made this very clear in *Lumen Gentium*, which speaks about different grades of the people of God.[2] This is clear too in the declaration on the relationship between the Church and the people of other religions, *Nostra Aetate*.[3]

2. One Faith, Many Theologies

We must also take seriously the fact that even within the same faith, we can have many theologies. Of course, this is well known now in Christianity. And we know that each theology is an intellectual packaging of the faith. This packaging can be done in different ways, while the truth of the dogma remains. If we can acknowledge this with regard to the same one faith, then how much more when we go outside our own circle of belief? It means that we

---

2. See http://www.vatican.va/archive/hist_councils/ii_vatican_council/documents/vat-ii_const_19641121_lumen-gentium_en.html.

3. See http://www.vatican.va/archive/hist_councils/ii_vatican_council/documents/vat-ii_decl_19651028_nostra-aetate_en.html.

need to be broad-minded in our disposition, so that we can relate to others with whom we do not totally agree.

3. Distinguishing Essentials and Non-Essentials of Faith

Related is the ability to distinguish between the essentials of the faith and those things that are not essential. Our Catholic Magisterium sometimes speaks of faith at different levels. What it means is that we must be able to draw a distinction between a dogma itself and the expression of that dogma. And if we take this distinction seriously, then we will not continue to fight over those things that are not essential. Instead, we might spend our time working to preserve the essential.

4. Humility before God

All of this means that we must be humble and respect others in the way we project our own religion. This humility means that we admit that God is much greater than us, much greater than our religion, which is, after all, a mere human construct. Even as Christians, we cannot claim that we have totally comprehended God's being in a way that is complete. In other words, we must make room for God to reveal Himself in other ways than He has revealed Himself to us. We cannot limit how far God can go. If this is true, then there is room to respect other religions as different but not necessarily wrong expressions of God Himself. This recognition will also make us respect people of other faiths not simply out of mere politeness, but out of sincere respect for them.

5. Seeking Common Ground

Finally, dear friends, we need to seek the common ground that unites us. Unfortunately, in the context of religious pluralism, we tend to emphasize the things that separate us and the things that are different. It is as though we were defined in terms of where we differ from each other. If only we were to change our attitude and focus instead on the things that we share in common, we would discover that this common ground is far more important than our differences, even if our differences are by no means insignificant.

We see a prime example of this in our common faith in God as the Father, Creator of Heaven and Earth; the One who is in charge of all creation; the provident Father who will judge the living and the dead. We share this with a great number of people, but we often don't take it seriously. We argue and fight over points of doctrine, on which we differ. However, we must notice that the more we seek out common ground, the more we will discover. And when we find common ground (not only in terms of doctrine but also in terms of moral principles), we are able to work together on the basis of these shared points. This, of course, does not mean that our differences are unimportant. It merely means that there is a diversity, which can also be a richness. One of the great advantages in pursuing interreligious dialogue is the profound spiritual enrichment that participants draw from the ideas and the spiritual values of others. This happens without in any way putting aside our own faith.

In light of the ever-growing religious diversity of our globalizing world, we must recognize that the future of humanity will require more and more effort in pursuing this type of dialogue. So, we had better get used to having neighbors who approach God differently than us. Once this is accepted, we can start to devise strategies for working together in order to face the challenges that all of us are facing, irrespective of our different faiths.

Chapter Two

WHOLES AND PARTS: ECUMENISM AND INTER-RELIGIOUS ENCOUNTERS IN POPE FRANCIS'S *TEOLOGÍA DEL PUEBLO*

Peter Casarella

Pope Francis likes to talk about wholes and parts. One of his most recurrent metaphors about wholes and parts is that of the polyhedron, for the polyhedron is a unity in which the parts are organized in a different relationship to the center. Unity born of a polyhedron *preserves difference*, and unity born of the sphere *reinforces homogeneity*. As Pope, Francis has utilized this metaphor to make two distinct but related points. First, the epoch of globalization commends us to think about the cultural and economic exchanges in the world today in such way that difference is never abandoned for the sake of wanton hegemony and, thus, radical inequality is never left unchallenged. Second, the unity of charisms in the Church can also be understood polyhedrically, for the Church in its essence is a differentiated unity greater than the sum of its homogenized parts.

This introductory paper consists of two parts. In the first part, I will offer a systematic presentation of how Pope Francis, especially in his Apostolic Exhortation *Evangelii Gaudium*, has applied this polyhedric notion of encounter to the questions of ecumenism and interreligious dialogue. In the second part, I will demonstrate that the roots of this type of thinking extend back to his time in Argentina. The Argentine *teología del pueblo* is also a mode of reflection about wholes and parts. From this vantage point, it will be much easier to surmise the theological roots of this way of thinking and draw some consequences for the theological paradigm that the Argentine Pope is offering to us.

At a non-overlapping point of intersection between interreligious and ecumenical dialogue lies the relationship between Christianity and Judaism. In the Christian order of salvation history, Judaism is not just one non-Christian religion among many others. Likewise, dialogue with faithful Jews is not predicated upon a Christian confession of faith. Judaism thus plays a crucial role in understanding the difference and relationship between these two forms of dialogue. I thus conclude with a reflection based upon a Biblical metaphor about the mystery of divine election closely related to the Bergoglian polyhedron, namely, the Pauline thinking in his Letter to the Romans about the roots and branches of Israel.

1. Wholes and Parts in the Pontificate of Pope Francis

The image of the polyhedron emerged early in the pontificate of Pope Francis. Even though it is presented as nothing more than a geometrical likeness, it contains rich theological content. God establishes the polyhedron out of God's own love, and this mystery of God's love is present even as we are perplexed about how to relate wholes and parts in everyday life. As it says in 1 John 4:10: "In this is love: not that we have loved God, but that he loved us and sent his Son as expiation for our sins." This is the same verse that Pope Francis cited when discussing *primereando* in *Evangelii Gaudium*.[1] This neologism drawn from the *argot* of Buenos Aires

---

1. The full impact of this paragraph is only evident if one consults that Spanish text. *Evangelii Gaudium*, para. 24: "'Primerear': sepan disculpar este

signifies the grace of God that goes before us. At least as subtle and mysterious as *gratia preveniens* ("prevenient grace") in its classical articulation, this is the love of God that seeps into our lives before we are even aware of its presence. In his address to the College of Cardinals on March 15, 2013, just two days after his election to the see of Peter, he speaks to those who elected him to this office with an image that recalls the Johannine image of the Paraclete.

> He, the Paraclete, is the ultimate source of every initiative and manifestation of faith. It is a curious thing: it makes me think of this. The Paraclete creates all the differences among the Churches, almost as if he were an Apostle of Babel. But on the other hand, it is he who creates unity from these differences, not in "equality," but in harmony. I remember the Father of the Church who described him thus: "*Ipse harmonia est.*" The Paraclete, who gives different charisms to each of us, unites us in this community of the Church, that worships the Father, the Son, and Him, the Holy Spirit.[2]

The Paraclete represents unity in diversity. The true harmony that is *not* equality is the same image as the polyhedral unity that is not spherical. The community of Cardinals and the community of the Church that worships the Holy Trinity will be united by this Spirit of witnessing to a unity that is both identifiably Christian and reverberating beyond the confines of the Church. In any case,

---

neologismo. La comunidad evangelizadora experimenta que el Señor tomó la iniciativa, la ha primereado en el amor (cf. *1 Jn* 4,10); y, por eso, ella sabe adelantarse, tomar la iniciativa sin miedo, salir al encuentro, buscar a los lejanos y llegar a los cruces de los caminos para invitar a los excluidos. Vive un deseo inagotable de brindar misericordia, fruto de haber experimentado la infinita misericordia del Padre y su fuerza difusiva. ¡Atrevámonos un poco más a primerear!"

2. See https://w2.vatican.va/content/francesco/en/speeches/2013/march/documents/papa-francesco_20130315_cardinali.html.

a new Babel is the situation in which we find ourselves, and the Spirit is the apostle sent by Christ who makes a new Pentecost out of this Babel.[3]

The polyhedron appears in the section of *Evangelii Gaudium* dedicated to the common good and undergirds the principle of unity as greater than the sum of its parts. The principle of unity accompanies three other key Bergoglian insights: 1.) time is greater than space, 2.) unity prevails over conflict, and 3.) reality is more important than ideas.[4] The polyhedron preserves unity and identity in a deracinated world that tends toward every greater homogeneity: "The global need not stifle, nor the particular prove barren."[5] It is a mode of intercultural fruitfulness and fundamentally about how one's roots are not only preserved but actually enhance the unity of the human family in this new situation in which we find ourselves today. Instead of merely "tolerating" different cultures and identities, the present remaining task is to highlight difference *for the sake of* unity. In the specific case of polyhedric unity, Pope Francis accentuates the convergence of the pastoral and the political, the inclusion of the poor and their culture, and the search for a contributory element from those "people whose conduct may seem questionable on account of their errors."[6] Accordingly,

---

3. On the new Babel, see George Steiner, *After Babel*, 3rd ed. (Oxford: Oxford University Press, 1998). The ecumenical and interreligious significance of a new Pentecost is explored in a fruitful manner by the Bulgarian Pentecostal theologian Daniela C. Augustine in *Pentecost, Hospitality, and Transfiguration: Towards a Spirit-Inspired Vision of Social Transformation* (Cleveland, TN: CPT Press, 2012).

4. According to Francesca Ambrogetti and Sergio Rubin, *Pope Francis: The Authorized Biography* (London: Hodder and Stoughton, 2013), Bergoglio speaks openly about the fact that this section of EG is taken verbatim from his unfinished thesis on Guardini. I turn to this topic below.

5. *Evangelii Gaudium*, paras. 217–37.

6. *Evangelii Gaudium*, para. 235. The English translation in the Vatican website leaves the false impression that those who commit errors are dubious characters. In fact, those who commit errors include the clergy and other persons of high standing in the institutional Church. I am translating here

the polyhedron is not derived from a worldly politics or from a merely supernatural realm. The polyhedron arises from a faith-filled vision of reality and history that seeks greater inclusion of those at the margins and the promotion of the common good in the midst of real strife and individualizing fragmentation.

What, specifically, does polyhedric unity contribute to ecumenical and interreligious encounters? Let us consider four elements of this teaching in the Apostolic Exhortation itself: 1.) the power of Christian witness and counter-witness, 2.) Christianity's primordial rootedness in God's covenant with Israel, 3.) the founding religious insight, shared in an exemplary way with Muslims, that all of life comes from God, and 4.) the practical and still unrealized synodal wisdom of the Spirit.

Pope Francis begins his discussion of Christian unity with the recognition that this is the unity that the Lord himself sought and that the credibility of the Christian message would be much greater if Christians could overcome their divisions.[7] He links this insight to the teaching of Vatican II that the fullness of Catholicity requires the members of the Catholic Church to seek unity with their separated brethren. This witness to Christian unity is then presented as a form of pilgrimaging alongside other pilgrims on a common journey.[8] The witness to unity is also a witness to global peace and thereby contributes to the unity of the human family. The presence of both the Patriarch of Constantinople and the Archbishop of Canterbury at the 2012 Synod of Bishops on "The

---

    from the Spanish: "Aun las personas que puedan ser cuestionadas por sus errores, tienen algo que aportar que no debe perderse."

7. *Evangelii Gaudium*, para. 244.
8. Ibid., citing *Unitatis Redintegratio*, para. 4: "The credibility of the Christian message would be much greater if Christians could overcome their divisions and the Church could realize 'the fullness of catholicity proper to her in those of her children who, though joined to her by baptism, are yet separated from full communion with her.'"

New Evangelization for the Transmission of the Christian Faith" is seen as a sign of this unity.[9]

Counter-witness is taken just as seriously and for a variety of reasons.[10] Missionaries report that the scandal of a divided Christianity impairs the task of evangelization. A commitment to Christian unity is thus seen as an indispensable path to a new evangelization. Finally, "signs of division between Christians in countries ravaged by violence add further causes of conflict on the part of those who should instead be a leaven of peace."[11] Indifference to division, indifference to the power of faith, and blindness to tribal violence are all impediments to a robust Christian unity that not only assents to propositions but offers testimony to a wider ecumenism and sense of unity on the globe. Christian unity is not thereby turned into an instrument of social betterment, but its scope is still significantly widened beyond the realm of doctrinal agreement.

"Rootedness" is a key word in the Bergoglian vocabulary. As the Pope who was taken to Rome by his brother bishops "from the ends of the earth," this is no surprise. In 2007 he once even referred to his native Buenos Aires as *mi esposa*.[12] The affinity between Judaism

---

9. *Evangelii Gaudium*, para. 245. On these encounters, see John Allen, "At Synod of Bishops, 'Ecumenism Lives!'" *National Catholic Reporter*, Oct. 13, 2012, available on-line at https://www.ncronline.org/blogs/ncr-today/synod-bishops-ecumenism-lives.

10. On counter-witnessing, see Michael Budde, "Giving Witness, Receiving Testimony," in *Witnessing: Prophecy, Politics, and Wisdom*, ed. Maria Clara Bingemer and Peter Casarella (Maryknoll, NY: Orbis, 2014), 13–29.

11. *Evangelii Gaudium*, para. 246. On this topic, see Emmanuel Katongole and Jonathan Wilson-Hartgrove, *Mirror to the Church: Reconciling Faith after Genocide in Rwanda* (Grand Rapids, MI: Zondervan, 2012).

12. "Lo que hubiera dicho en el consistorio," Interview with Cardinal Bergoglio, *Trenti Giorni*, Nov. 2007, available on-line at http://www.30giorni.it/articoli_id_16503_l2.htm. Notably, he uses the same image of the Holy Spirit as symphony here that he would later use on March 15, 2013.

and Christianity thus plays a key role in discovering the full implications of the polyhedron.[13]

> We hold the Jewish people in special regard because their covenant with God has never been revoked, for "the gifts and the call of God are irrevocable" (*Rom* 11:29). The Church, which shares with Jews an important part of the sacred Scriptures, looks upon the people of the covenant and their faith as one of the sacred roots of her own Christian identity (cf. *Rom* 11:16–18). As Christians, we cannot consider Judaism as a foreign religion; nor do we include the Jews among those called to turn from idols and to serve the true God (cf. *1 Thes* 1:9). With them, we believe in the one God who acts in history, and with them we accept his revealed word.[14]

If Judaism is no foreign religion to the new dispensation of the Christian covenant, then foreignness in general can be re-examined in the light of the irrevocable covenant that God has made with the Jewish people. This is the sense in which the role of Judaism within the polyhedric unity deserves a special mention—for their covenant with God is not only more ancient than Christian unity but also both irreducibly particular and a goad in its counter-witness to idolatry to a wider unity based upon God's action in word and deed in human history. Jews in their faithfulness to this special bond between God and his people disclose a way for all peoples to be more inclusive of the stranger.[15] Jews can be seen as an

---

13. Jorge Mario Bergoglio has considerable experience in this regard. Below I address his encounters with Rabbi Skorka and the other Jews of Buenos Aires.
14. *Evangelii Gaudium*, para. 247.
15. The Talmudic writings of Emmanuel Levinas develop this theme, which stands radically at odds with interpretations of the notion of being a people of God that are overtly nationalistic or xenophobic. This article includes

inherently (but not necessarily in all cases) polyhedric people. The terrible persecution of Jews by Christians, in all ages, thus destroys the very novelty of a polyhedron since it smacks of a totalizing, spherical understanding of the Christian task of evangelization.

In turning to the question of interreligious encounters, Pope Francis highlights that these encounters are, in the first instance, an openness to the other, a sharing of the joys and sorrows of everyday life.[16] Such openness never involves letting go of one's most basic convictions: "True openness involves remaining steadfast in one's deepest convictions, clear and joyful in one's own identity, while at the same time being 'open to understanding those of the other party' and 'knowing that dialogue can enrich each side.'"[17] The love for the truth is met in discovering how the other deals with basic questions of human existence. There is no path to interreligious encounter without this love for the truth, and there is no path to the love for the truth that bypasses these fundamental experiences of everyday life. Beauty, truth, and goodness are refracted in these ordinary circumstances as well as in the ethical understanding based therein that generates a new and more just social situation.

In this spirit, it is noteworthy what Pope Francis says about the religion of Islam. In addition to noting the Christian truths found embedded in the Qur'an, he states regarding Muslims: "Many of them also have a deep conviction that their life, *in its entirety*, is from God and for God. They also acknowledge the need to respond to God with an ethical commitment and with mercy towards those most in need."[18] Many believers of different faiths will affirm that their life is from God. Yet it is still important that Pope Francis accords as much

---

a report from a private meeting with French Catholics of Pope Francis's admiration for Levinas: https://onepeterfive.com/pope-francis-reveals-his-mind-to-private-audience/.

16. *Evangelii Gaudium*, para. 250.
17. Ibid., para. 251, citing John Paul II, Encyclical Letter, *Redemptoris Missio* 56.
18. *Evangelii Gaudium*, para. 252. Italics added.

importance to this affirmation as he does to the Qur'an's endorsement of the miracle of the Virgin birth. What appears to be "polyhedric" here is the accentuation of the whole of life in its relationship to God. Neither faith nor ethics issues from a compartment in human existence. The insight here regarding Catholic-Muslim accord deals with the notion that the faith covers an entirety of existence that is greater than its individual parts. As with Judaism, a counter-witness to ignorance or needless generalization of the faith of the other runs contrary to every principle of openness to encounter. The need for Christians to engage in a careful study of Islam and in particular its commitment to those most in need thus becomes paramount to all inter-religious encounter and to the overcoming of many of the most violent conflicts that divide our world today.

Finally, we come to the practical wisdom of the Spirit, the very point at which Pope Francis in his first public address to the College of Cardinals enjoined the Church to consider a new approach to unity in diversity. In speaking of fraternal relations with the Orthodox, he mentions the positive value of their experience of synodality.[19] Non-Christians, including atheists, "can be channels which the Holy Spirit raises up" in order that they be freed from immanentism or "purely individual religious experiences."[20] The same Spirit allows Christians to see a common journey towards God in the signs and symbols of religious expressions of other faiths and also moves non-Christians to be "justified by the grace of God and thus be associated to the paschal mystery of Jesus Christ."[21] He continues the same pneumatological theme in his encounter with the Pentecostals in Caserta on July 28, 2014. Here the polyhedric unity in diversity is called "the path that we Christians do what we call by the theological name of

---

19. Ibid., para. 246.
20. Ibid., para. 254.
21. Ibid., para. 254, citing International Theological Commission, *Christianity and the World Religions* (1996), 72: *Enchiridion Vaticanum* 15, no. 1061.

ecumenism."[22] In sum, the polyhedron of *Evangelii Gaudium* has become enshrined as a pneumatological principle that applies *mutatis mutandis* to ecumenical and interreligious encounters.

In the Apostolic Exhortation, there is a fluid relationship between the polyhedric unity of ecumenism and interreligious dialogue and the polyhedron that guides both ecclesial life and social concerns. Another example of the former took place on July 3, 2015, when Pope Francis met with the Renewal in the Holy Spirit Movement. Here he invokes the differentiation between the sphere and the polyhedron in *Evangelii Gaudium*, saying that the latter

> reflects the confluence of all the parts which maintain their originality in it and these are the charisms, in unity but in their own diversity—unity in diversity. The distinction is important because we are speaking of the work of the Holy Spirit, not our own. Unity in the diversity of expressions of reality, as many as the Holy Spirit wills to arouse. It is also necessary to remember that the whole, namely, this unity, is greater than the part, and the part cannot attribute the whole to itself. For instance, one cannot say: "We are the current called the Catholic Charismatic Renewal and you are not." This cannot be said. Please, brothers, this is how it is;

---

22. Translation altered. See also his Address to Catholic Fraternity of Oct. 31, 2014: "Uniformity is not Catholic, it is not Christian. Rather, unity in diversity. Catholic unity is different but it is one: this is curious! The cause of diversity is also the cause of unity: the Holy Spirit. The Holy Spirit does two things: he creates unity in diversity. Unity does not imply uniformity; it does not necessarily mean doing everything together or thinking in the same way. Nor does it signify a loss of identity. Unity in diversity is actually the opposite: it involves the joyful recognition and acceptance of the various gifts which the Holy Spirit gives to each one and the placing of these gifts at the service of all members of the Church. It means knowing how to listen, to accept differences, and having the freedom to think differently and express oneself with complete respect towards the other who is my brother or sister. Do not be afraid of differences!"

it does not come from the Spirit; the Holy Spirit blows where he wills, when he wills and as he wills. Unity in diversity and in truth that is Jesus himself. What is the common sign of those who are reborn of this current of grace? To become new men and women, this is Baptism in the Spirit. I ask you to read John 3, verses 7–8: Jesus to Nicodemus, rebirth in the Spirit.

Here the pneumatological metaphor is turned on its head. Being "charismatic" is not by itself a sufficient principle for maintaining unity in diversity. Since "the Holy Spirit blows where he wills, when he wills and as he wills," no one group or faction in the Church can take comfort in maintaining polyhedric unity as opposed to spherical homogeneity. Polyhedrism, like the Pauline pneumatology of the body of Christ, is not a way of being a part but is rather a way of relating the members to one another organically. Nicodemus's misunderstanding of the Spirit, which is mentioned at the end of this counsel, is a caution to every group that holds a legitimate ecclesial charism. The Spirit who comes from above in the third chapter of John is the same Spirit who proceeds *primereando*. To say that the whole is greater than the sum of its parts is to also to recall that *Lumen Gentium*'s first model of the Church, even before the image of being a people of God, is that of a mystery.[23]

So much for the pneumatological polyhedron. Regarding intercultural encounters, however, the polyhedron has been invoked in many diverse contexts by Pope Francis since 2013. Here we will consider four, mutually reinforcing encounters: 1.) the Council of Europe, 2.) the address given in front of Independence Hall in Philadelphia, 3.) his remarks on inculturation to the Jesuits in their General Congregation, and 4.) his speech at l'Università degli Studi Roma Tre (La Sapienza). In each case, Pope Francis deployed the polyhedron to promote a culture of encounter in the face of fears that

---

23. *Lumen Gentium*, para. 5: "The mystery of the holy Church is manifest in its very foundation."

have spread around the world in the wake of economic globalization. In each of these cases, the metaphor of the polyhedron is not just about unity, but about the need for a renewal of a culture of encounter.[24]

On November 25, 2014, he spoke about tensions in Europe before the Council of Europe in Strasbourg, France, in this way:

> *Creatively globalizing multipolarity* calls for striving to create a constructive harmony, one free of those pretensions to power which, while appearing from a pragmatic standpoint to make things easier, end up destroying the cultural and religious distinctiveness of peoples. To speak of European multipolarity is to speak of peoples which are born, grow and look to the future. The task of globalizing Europe's multipolarity cannot be conceived by appealing to the image of a sphere—in which all is equal and ordered, but proves reductive inasmuch as every point is equidistant from the center—but rather, by the image of a polyhedron, in which the harmonic unity of the whole preserves the particularity of each of the parts. Today Europe is multipolar in its relationships and its intentions; it is impossible to imagine or to build Europe without fully taking into account this multipolar reality.[25]

Europe cannot be controlled by two powers or even three (e.g., Rome, Moscow, Byzantium). Here polyhedric unity points to the intercultural mixing that can take place both between and within nations. Multipolarity is the cultural equivalent of the polyhedron in the European context, a point that he basically reiterates at La Sapienza.

---

24. A good resource on this topic is Diego Fares, *The Heart of Pope Francis: How a New Culture of Encounter Is Changing the Church and the World* (New York: Crossroad, 2015).

25. Address of Pope Francis to the Council of Europe, Nov. 25, 2014, available online at https://w2.vatican.va/content/francesco/en/speeches/2014/november/documents/papa-francesco_20141125_strasburgo-consiglio-europa.html.

Intercultural encounters are also the theme of his impromptu remarks in front of Independence Hall in Philadelphia, words that are not to be found in the official transcript.[26] There he frames his speech in Spanish about religious liberty and the integration of Hispanics and their culture into the mix of culture and politics in the United States with another reference to how the polyhedron helps us to cope with globalization:

> Globalization is not evil. On the contrary, the tendency to become globalized is good; it brings us together. What can be evil is how it happens. If a certain kind of globalization claims to make everyone uniform, to level everyone out, that globalization destroys the rich gifts and uniqueness of each person and each people. But a globalization which attempts to bring everyone together while respecting the uniqueness and gifts of each person or people is a good globalization; it helps all of us to grow, and it brings peace. I like to use a geometrical image for this. If globalization is a sphere, where every point is equidistant from the center, it cancels everything out; it is not good. But if globalization is like a polyhedron, where everything is united but each element keeps its own identity, then it is good; it causes a people to grow, it bestows dignity and it grants rights to all.

Here the message is to maintain the wisdom of inherited cultural traditions as part of a national heritage and as a goad to maintaining an identity that is still novel for that culture. In this sense, the message of polyhedric unity applies to both the European community and the United States of America, not because he is proposing a secular ethics of global citizenship that bridges these two worlds,

---

26. Speech at Independence Hall in Philadelphia from Sept. 6, 2015, available online at http://www.vatican.va/content/francesco/en/speeches/2015/september/documents/papa-francesco_20150926_usa-liberta-religiosa.html

but because the metaphor reinforces the need for both a particular identity and a robust sense of social belonging that involves a larger whole that is applicable in both contexts.[27]

This admonition is essentially repeated in his dialogue with the Jesuits at their Thirty-Sixth General Congregation on October 24, 2016. Here he responds to an interlocutor who asks about the serious problem of the way in which colonizers have treated indigenous peoples. The Pope tells his fellow Jesuit,

> it must be said that today we are more aware of the significance of the richness of the indigenous peoples, especially when, both politically and culturally, other forces tend to suppress them even more through globalization conceived as a "sphere," a globalization where everything becomes standardized. Today, our prophetic audacity, our consciousness, must be on the side of inculturation. And our image of globalization should not be the sphere, but the polyhedron. I like the geometric figure of the polyhedron, because it is one but has different faces. It expresses how unity is created while preserving the identities of the peoples, of the persons, of the cultures. That is the richness that today we have

---

27. In the United States, there is a strong resistance to Pope Francis's progressive views on migrants among certain Catholic conservatives precisely because his rhetoric of globalization *sounds* like the new cosmopolitanism of Kwame Anthony Appiah, Martha Nussbaum, or Lawrence Summers. These trumpeters of globalism do not grasp the transcendent horizon of polyhedric unity nor the radical sense of both popular and national particularity that Francis invests in his vision of the common good in an age of globalization. In his address at La Sapienza, for example, he will speak about *communis patria* (see below), which signifies a way of being at home in the land of one's residence without losing any essential part of one's historical, personal, ethnic, racial, or cultural identity.

to give to the process of globalization, because otherwise it is homogenizing and destructive.[28]

In 2015, he had spoken about indigenous cultures extensively during his trip to Paraguay, Ecuador, and Bolivia.[29] Here he reiterates that same point with the image of the polyhedron. It is significant that he praises the indigenous as a people, as persons, and as bearers of a culture. In this sense, the mission of the Society to go the peripheries is also polyhedric. Pope Francis, a great admirer of the method of encounter practiced by Peter Faber (1506–46) and enshrined in the political philosophy of Francisco Suárez (1548–1617), allows the distinct faces of the indigenous to be reflected on the multiple faces of the polyhedric unity of a Church that goes forth.[30] This remark is not so much a reconciliation of historic misdeeds as a call to avoid homogenizing in the name of the Gospel in the future.

The sprawling speech at La Sapienza is probably Pope Francis's most bold and creative use of the polyhedron to date. Once again, the words about the polyhedron were recorded by the press in print and on video but not included in the official transcript that was

---

28. Address of Pope Francis to the General Curia of the Thirty-Sixth General Congregation of the Society of Jesus, Oct. 24, 2016, available on-line at https://w2.vatican.va/content/francesco/en/speeches/2016/october/documents/papa-francesco_20161024_visita-compagnia-gesu.html.

29. See Luis Herrera Rodríguez, S.J., "Whisper to those in Despair: 'The Best Wine is yet to Come': Memory, Hope, and Resistance," in *Search for God in América: The Early Visits of Pope Francis to the Americas*, ed., María Clara Bingemer and Peter Casarella (Washington, D.C.: The Catholic University of America Press, forthcoming).

30. Francis has initiated the canonization of Faber and frequently speaks of him as a model of the culture of encounter. See Antonio Spadaro's interview, "A Big Heart Open to God," *America*, September 30, 2013, available on-line at http://www.vatican.va/content/francesco/en/speeches/2013/september/documents/papa-francesco_20130921_intervista-spadaro.html.. On Suarez, one may consult Thomas Rourke, *The Roots of Pope Francis's Social and Political Thought* (Lanham, MD: Rowman & Littlefield, 2016).

handed to the Rector of the University.³¹ Large crowds and intercultural gatherings seem to elicit the metaphor involuntarily from the Pope's lips even when it is not present in his prepared text. Here polyhedric unity is again counterposed to globalization.³² He also refers to Baumann's notion of an increasingly liquid culture in which transcendence has been lost. What is distinctive about his use of the polyhedron here is twofold. First, he is responding to a question from a Syrian student who is worried about the fears of the other in Europe. Second, he is presenting the polyhedron as a task for the entire university community. He concludes by asking in a typically Jesuitical fashion:

> As you continue along your path of teaching and learning in the university, try asking yourself: is my *forma mentis* becoming more individualistic or more solidary? If it is more solidary, it is a good sign because you will be going against the current, but going in the only direction that has a future and that offers a future. Solidarity, which is not proclaimed in words but rather experienced concretely, creates peace and hope for all countries and for the whole world. And you, because of the fact that you

---

31. Address of His Holiness Pope Francis to Roma Tre University, Feb. 17, 2017. The official transcript is available on-line at https://w2.vatican.va/content/francesco/en/speeches/2017/february/documents/papa-francesco_20170217_universita-romatre.html. The full video is available on-line at https://www.cercoiltuovolto.it/vaticano/discorso-papa-francesco-la-visita-alluniversita-degli-studi-roma-tre/. See also Anna Maria Brogli, "La visita a Roma Tre. Il Papa agli universitari: dialogo, concretezza, integrazione," *Avvenire.it*, Feb. 17, 2017, available on-line at https://www.avvenire.it/papa/pagine/visita-all-universita-degli-studi-roma-tre.

32. In the report cited above, he said: "Mi piace parlare di un'altra figura geometrica: il poliedro che è unità nella diversità. Quando si va per quella strada il livello culturale cresce perché è un dialogo continuo fra i diversi lati del poliedro. Credo che il pericolo di oggi sia concepire una unità, una globalizzazione, nella uniformità. Questo distrugge."

work and study at university, have a responsibility to leave a positive mark on history.

The task of the university is therefore to create a culture of encounter in which solidarity is not just "proclaimed in words but rather experienced concretely." This task is not to be imposed by administration or ventured by the students acting on their own. It is a matter of forming new relationships between all the participants in the university that foster concrete bonds within and outside of the walls of the institution. This is indeed a tall order, but one that lies at the heart of the entire educational and catechetical reform of Pope Francis. We turn now to examine the Argentine roots for this broad and ambitious program.

2. *The Latin American Sources for Polyhedric Unity*

The four Bergoglian principles in *Evangelii Gaudium* (time is greater than space, unity prevails over conflict, reality is more important than ideas, and the whole is greater than its parts) were present in an almost complete form as early as Bergoglio's 1974 Meeting with Province of Jesuits in Argentina.[33] The complete list is already evident in a talk published by Bergoglio in 1980.[34] The polyhedron was also discussed prior to the pontificate in a prologue to a book that Cardinal Bergoglio sent in 2005 to Guzmán Carriquiry.[35] For a Pope so well known for his surprise moves, there is therefore an astonishing consistency to his thought on this particular issue.

---

33. Jorge Mario Bergoglio, "Una institución que vive de su carisma," in idem, *Meditaciones para Religiosos* (San Miguel, Buenos Aires: Diego de Torres, 1982), 48.
34. "Formación permanente y reconciliación," in *Meditaciones para Religiosos*, 92.
35. The text is dated April 4, 2005, and appears in Guzmán Carriquiry, *Una Apuesta por América Latina* (Buenos Aires: Sudamericana, 2005). See *The Great Reformer*, 95, n. 44, location 5767.

There is likewise no doubt that the idea of polyhedric unity was engendered within the Argentine context and alongside the development of a uniquely Argentine *teología del pueblo*. This is not to say that he borrowed the idea from other Argentines. In fact, the very notion bears a distinctively Bergoglian watermark. Nonetheless, the genesis and meaning cannot be extracted from its legitimate birthplace. Its significance as an exercise of Petrine ministry for the Church universal thus becomes *more* enhanced if we now consider its situatedness in Bergoglio's beloved *patria*, in his exercise of episcopal ministry in the city of Buenos Aires, and in his own experiences of belonging to both wholes and parts in Latin America. In considering the context of this development, three of the most important factors are 1.) the idea that was developed by Lucio Gera, Rafael Tello, Methol Ferré, and others of being a unique *pueblo* situated on the Southern Cone of the Latin American continent, 2.) Bergoglio's intellectual formation in the Argentine Province of the Society of Jesus (which included a decisive sojourn in Germany), and 3.) the actual interreligious and ecumenical encounters that Bergoglio undertook as the Archbishop of Buenos Aires. These three points hardly cover all the dimensions of the pre-papal thought of Jorge Mario Bergoglio, but they will suffice in order to uncover the main theological lines of reflection on wholes and parts that he inherited from his intellectual and pastoral engagement in his native land.

1. *The Argentine People and the Integration from the Southern Cone of a* Patria Grande

Spiritually, culturally, and politically, Jorge Mario Bergoglio was very conscious of being an Argentine. At the same time, there is no innocence to his patriotism. Nor has this identity ever wavered as a source for hope and sustenance, even with his election as the Bishop of Rome. Although he has written directly on the question of the nation, his position on the polyhedric nature of being

Argentine is best seen indirectly, i.e., through the lens of non-Argentine reference points.[36] For example, he was very taken by the notion promoted by the Uruguayan Methol Ferré, *el genial pensador rioplatense*, that Latin America could be united in a *Patria Grande*. Second, one can examine his devotion to Argentine letters, e.g., the epic Martín Fierro or the poetry of his friend Borges as a source of spiritual reflection. I will consider here a different and less well-known reference point, namely, Bergoglio's preface to a new Argentine commentary on the introduction to Hegel's *Phenomenology of Spirit*.

A people is itself an aggregate made up of wholes and parts, and the whole people is greater than its individual parts. There is a sense of being a people that is not reducible to any of its particular elements. The family of Bergoglio came to Argentina as immigrants from the Piedmontese region of Italy. They participated in a process of integration into Argentine peoplehood that coincided in part with the rise of a Catholic version of Peronism, a multivalent political movement whose origins in Bergoglio's youth were unmistakably allied to the well-being of working-class, immigrant Catholics and especially their unions. The notion of feeling a sense of *belonging* to a particular people is also mentioned in *Evangelii Gaudium* and plays a very large role in Bergoglio's understanding of wholes and parts.[37]

---

36. Cardenal Jorge Mario Bergoglio, S.J., *Ponerse la patria al hombro. Memoria y camino de esperanza* (Buenos Aires: Claretiana, 2013).

37. See, for example, *Evangelii Gaudium*, par. 268: "When we stand before Jesus crucified, we see the depth of his love which exalts and sustains us, but at the same time, unless we are blind, we begin to realize that Jesus' gaze, burning with love, expands to embrace all his people. We realize once more that he wants to make use of us to draw closer to his beloved people. He takes us from the midst of his people and he sends us to his people; *without this sense of belonging we cannot understand our deepest identity*." Italics added. Some have criticized Pope Francis for attending more to peoplehood than to citizenship, a more juridical concept more familiar to North Americans. Archbishop Víctor Manuel Fernández notes that Francis cites the U.S. bishops on faithful citizenship in *Evangelii Gaudium*.

How does Bergoglio/Pope Francis use the word "people"? It cannot simply refer to a passive aggregate of inhabitants of a certain territory. That definition belies the dynamic and ethical sense of the word as used by Bergoglio. In Europe words like *das Volk* and *il popolo* have become linked to totalitarian regimes of the past. This language seldom meets with acclaim except for those who seek to pursue a dubious populism. Bergoglio has been accused of populism, but he is not using the word "people" in the European sense. Likewise, the word *pueblo* has a rich set of connotations in Spanish that are not evident with the English word. Some political analysts in Latin America use the word *pueblo* to refer to the masses or even to a specific rung of the social ladder, e.g., the proletariat or working class. Bergoglio is very aware of this connotation and takes great pains not to limit his usage to this particular meaning. One astute commentator distinguishes between the term *people* and the term *masses* in the Bergoglian vocabulary. The very idea of a theology of the people is not intended to imbue a static group with privileges that they do not already have in their possession. *People*, on the contrary, "assumes a collective capable of generating its own historical processes."[38] The poor in the theology of the people are protagonists with their own unique wisdom, culture, and social agenda.[39] They are also called upon to be self-critical of

---

Víctor Manuel Fernández, *The Francis Project: Where He Wants to Take the Church* (New York/Mahwah, NJ: Paulist, 2016), 72.

38. Fernández, *The Francis Project*, 75.
39. Austen Ivereigh writes: "Who were *el pueblo*? The word was used at the time by demagogues and ideologues—not least Marxists—as an abstract absolute. But for the La Plata school it had a much richer, deeper, and more specific connotation, drawn from the people-of-God ecclesiology of *Lumen Gentium*. For the COEPAL theologians, *el pueblo* meant the distinctive hybrid culture of Latin America born of the twin experiences of racial and cultural *mestizaje* on the one hand, and the evangelization of America on the other. Through baptism, the ancient Indian peoples and the mestizos became a new people (*Pueblo Nuevo*) with an awareness of their common dignity, and their equal participation in the common good." "The Pope

their shortcomings, open to the insights of others, and forgers of a destiny that serves the common good of all classes as well as bearers of wisdom and culture in a society.

The larger story of how Lucio Gera, Rafael Tello, and Methol Ferré galvanized Bergoglio's commitment to an Argentine theology of the people, particularly in the run-up to the CELAM General Conference at Puebla, has been told elsewhere. This story, as we shall see below, synthesizes a political tradition of thinking about the people with a love for popular piety. This fusion has no real equivalent in North American civil religion and alienates many of my fellow Catholics in my country because its religious roots stand at odds with both the Puritan and the Jeffersonian strand in U.S. religious history. As a secular language of independence, its initial defenders were José de San Martín and Simón Bolivar. Later figures like the Dominican preacher Bartolomé de las Casas found a religious and truly popular idiom for forging a language of independence. For our purposes, the specific contribution of Bergoglio's contemporary, Methol Ferré, on the idea of being and defending *un pueblo fiel* cannot go unmentioned.[40] In Ferré, Bergoglio found a fellow traveler who shared his deep trust in the sense of faith and common wisdom among the faithful people of God of the Southern Cone and in their instantiation of the Vatican's new vision of *mestizo* catholicity. In a certain sense, this is true of all Popes and what they bring to the see of Peter, but here you have the additional element of a theology of the people with universal ramifications. Austen Ivereigh writes:

> Just as St. John Paul II saw his pontificate as a providential means of facilitating the liberation of Eastern Europe

---

and the *Patria Grande*,": How Francis is promoting Latin-America's Continental Destiny," in: *Search for God in América*, forthcoming.

40. On the general influence of Ferré, one should consult Alver Metalli's introduction to Alver Metalli and Methol Ferré, *El Papa y El Filósofo* (Buenos Aires: Biblios, 2013), 19–34, and the other literature cited by Ivereigh.

from the Soviet yoke, Francis sees his as a God-given opportunity to further the emancipation of Latin America from the various colonialisms that have held the continent back from realizing its God-given potential. The Miami Strait [between the Cuba of exiles in Miami and the island nation of Cuba] and the Mexican-American border are to this pontificate what the Berlin Wall was to John Paul II's.[41]

In fact, the universality of this vision taken from the Southern Cone for all of Latin America and beyond cannot be ignored. In the 1970s and 1980s Ferré and Bergoglio both seemed to think that there was a confluence of a "Catholic resurgence" with the call of Paul VI and John Paul II for a new evangelization.[42] The theologians from the Southern Cone (Gera, Tello, Ferré, and the Chilean Schönstatt priest, Joaquín Alliende) appeared too nationalist to the other liberation theologians in Latin America, and the other liberation theologians appeared too abstract ("reality prevails over the idea") to the theologians of the people from the Southern Cone. In this reading of the "signs of the times," the countries of the Southern Cone had a very special role to play and, in fact, their sometimes despised "theology of the people" began at

---

41. Ivereigh, "The Pope and the *Patria Grande*," forthcoming.

42. Ibid.: "Noting how the experience of the US and postwar Europe showed that the future lay in 'continent-states,' Methol argued that the *Patria Grande* could be reborn from Perón's frustrated 'ABC' idea of a tariff-free zone between Argentina, Brazil and Chile outlined in a speech the Argentine leader gave in November 1953. In the same essay, Methol gave strong support to the formation of Mercosur following the Asunción Treaty of 1991, seeing it as similar to the Franco-German coal and steel agreement that paved the way to the European Union. For Methol, the Argentine-Brazilian nexus was key, for it allowed the *Patria Grande* to move beyond the exclusively Spanish-American vision of San Martín and Bolívar (Brazil was an empire until 1898). For Methol, this represented the recovery of an historical precedent, the 60 years (1580–1640) in which the Iberian Peninsula was united under one king, Philip II."

this time to have an impact on the agenda of CELAM. Bergoglio once offered a simple and direct synthesis of this vision in what was originally an impromptu remark made to an Argentine rabbi:

> One issue that typifies our history is the capacity for *mestizaje* that we witnessed in Argentina. This shows a certain degree of universality and a respect for the identity of the other. I believe that in Latin America—[especially in Argentina] along with Uruguay, the south of Brazil, and part of Chile—*mestizaje* in the good and rich sense of the term became recognizable. I like to see where the encounter of cultures, as opposed to a fusion, prevailed. I like it when diverse collectivities appear in the celebrations (*en las fiestas*). For this reason, the government agreed to the organization of a Bicentennial, making room for all the collectivities and showing off our multi-facetedness.[43]

What is most particular to a regional grasp of identity therefore becomes a hermeneutical key for the vision of the pontificate as a whole. By including Brazil and the new consciousness of the indigenous peoples in present-day Latin America in their synthesis, the new sense of identity was a new whole that overcame the narrow binomial between Spain and New Spain in the periods of colonialism and independence. The "whole" of the *Patria Grande* in the revisionist La Plata school of thought guided by Ferré reflected an unprecedented and to this day largely unfinished "new *mestizaje*."

What about the relationship between the sense of popular unity in the Argentine theology of the people and cultural integration?[44] One distinctive feature of the Argentine theology of the people was to seek an integration of popular piety and the theology of culture

---

43. Jorge Mario Bergoglio and Abraham Skorka, *Sobre el Cielo y la Tierra* (Buenos Aires / New York: Vintage Español, 2010), 150–1.
44. Fernández, *The Francis Project*, 79–81.

such that the pastoral orientations of theology truly reflected a new *mestizaje* of culture.[45] This too is a topic that was addressed in many contexts by the Provincial, the Churchman, and the Archbishop. One important element has been overlooked in most of the English-speaking literature. On February 20, 2006, the Archbishop of Buenos Aires wrote a brief prologue to Amelia Podetti's posthumously published commentary on the introduction to Hegel's groundbreaking work, *The Phenomenology of Spirit*. The words reflect a deep devotion to the philosophical career and intellectual witness of Podetti, a fellow traveler in Peronist politics, and her assiduous preparation for her influential seminars.[46] These words reveal surprisingly little by way of evaluation of Hegel's speculative thought. Cardinal Bergoglio notes that a renaissance of German philosophy was underway in Argentina and that Podetti held both Hegel and Augustine in high regard as two necessary poles in the history of philosophy. He also notes that Podetti herself engaged the Hegelian notion of "universal history" in a fairly critical manner, claiming that the heritage of Argentine sources still needed to be plumbed and that the "planetarization" (her word) of philosophy was still in process. He wanted to take the Hegelian idea of universal history to the peripheries in the same way that the Church needed to go to the peripheries. He concludes, however,

---

45. On this point, there are unmistakable similarities between the theology of Pope Francis and the theology of Virgilio Elizondo, a comparison I have pursued elsewhere.

46. Borghesi captured this testimony: "Influyó en mí el pensamiento de Amelia Podetti, decana de Filosofía de la Universidad, especialista en Hegel, que falleció joven. De ella tomé la intuición de las 'periferias.' Ella trabajaba mucho en eso. Uno de sus hermanos sigue publicando sus escritos y apuntes. Leyendo a Methol Ferré y a Podetti tomé algunas cosas de la dialéctica, en una forma antihegeliana, porque ella era especialista en Hegel pero no era hegeliana." Cf. Massimo Borghesi, "Amelia Podetti: La mujer que inspire a Bergoglio," *Aleteia*, Nov. 24, 2017, available on-line at https://es.aleteia.org/2017/11/24/amelia-podetti-la-mujer-que-inspiro-a-bergoglio/.

with a fascinating word about the philosophical setting and aspirations of Argentina in the Latin American context:

> I hope that the re-reading and dialogue with a classic of the history of philosophy, brought about from a distant shore of the West, continues to bear fruit in our universities and in all those places in which we have to re-affirm our passionate vocation for the mastery of philosophy. We are after all inheritors of a magnificent tradition in this regard, starting with the prophetic moment in which Alonso de Veracruz and Vasco de Quiroga in Mexico, or José de Acosta in Peru were moved to think for America, from America and as Americans (*a América, desde América, y como americanos*).[47]

Podetti's still nascent but prematurely ended project is lauded on its own terms and for its own worth. At the same time the Archbishop and future protagonist at the fifth General Conference of CELAM in Aparecida thinks about what the Argentine reception of a speculative genius who prematurely envisioned what a totalizing history from Germany might mean for a new trajectory of Latin American thought. This "Americanizing" of the flawed Hegelian project of a universal history thus spurs a culture of encounter in which Latin Americans can reclaim their own view of universal history. In a typically Argentine manner, the parochialism of the local will be called into question through this global expansion of thought. Yet the starting point in Argentina is suddenly a starting point for a new reflection, an insight Hegel did not imagine. Just as Methol Ferré advocated the transformation of Latin American culture from being a recipient to a source, the Archbishop advocates the completion of an already underway project of generating a universal form of encounter for "multipolar cultures" in Latin America derived from

---

47. Amelia Podetti, *Comentario a la Introducción a la Fenomenología del Espíritu* (Buenos Aires: Editorial Biblos, 2006), 13.

the philosophically fertile ground in and near the La Plata river basin. In other words, from Podetti's and Bergoglio's own unique location in time and space, an indigenous, post-colonial, and polyhedric history of philosophy might be possible that questions the fragmentation of Euroamerican postmodernism as well as the false hegemony of Hegel's myopic vision of modernity.

2. Jesuit Obedience as the Untier of Knots

Obedience for a Jesuit is a function of *obedire*, of listening to the Lord through colloquies and in dialogue with one's superior and one's fraternity of companions. The capacity to learn from the Lord through an act of *obedire* is particularly true of the Jesuit Jorge Mario Bergoglio and his thinking about wholes and parts.[48] Because he was named Provincial at an uncommonly young age and in a period of great political strife, he was not only tested in his obedience to the Society of Jesus but he was charged with forming Jesuits and other religious in their *obedire* at a particularly tender and formative stage of his life. One key to polyhedric unity is not only its unfolding within the context of his being formed and forming of others in an Ignatian way, but also his early insights into the universality of the particular Ignatian charism for the sake of the enhancement and nurturing of other charisms within the Church. In a very real sense, Jesuit obedience—and all the intellectual and spiritual gifts associated with it—is, to use a favorite phrase of Bergoglio, "the untier of knots" in the life and thought of the current Pope.

Jorge Mario Bergoglio was sent to Germany to work on a doctoral dissertation between May and December of 1986. He had already served a tumultuous time as a young and controversial Provincial General of the Jesuits in Argentina and had just turned fifty.

---

48. Cf. Jorge Mario Bergoglio, "Formación en la vida comunitaria," in *Meditaciones para religiosos*, 77–81, on the relationship between feeling part of a community and Jesuit obedience.

According to Austen Ivereigh, his time in the Jesuit Hochschule of Sankt Georgen in Frankfurt am Main was meant to be a kind of cooling off period for the ex-Provincial. A new Provincial had been appointed, and it would be easier for him to develop his own agenda in the absence of his predecessor. The title of the never finished and still unavailable thesis has now been revealed by Massimo Borghesi: *Polar Opposition as Structure of Daily Thought and Christian Proclamation*. The origins of the polyhedron seem to be hidden inside this conundrum. In any case, it is worthwhile to consider the similarities between the Bergoglian polyhedron and Romano Guardini's *Der Gegensatz*, an affinity already suggested by Austen Ivereigh and confirmed by Borghesi.[49]

Guardini's book was published in 1925 and reprinted in an unchanged edition in 1955, but the thoughts were the fruits of an early, unpublished study from 1914 ("Opposition and opposites") as well as his Berlin lectures that had begun in 1923 and continued until the Nazis came to power in 1933. It is worth noting that Niels Bohr first published his theory about the complementarity of wave and particle physics in 1928. In other words, the European discussion of a science of opposites or enantialogy was certainly in the air in the 1920s.

Two determinative historical factors are salient to grasping the genesis of *Der Gegensatz*. The first concerns the strong emphasis in *Der Gegensatz* on the concept of life, a connection already suggested in the Bergoglian thesis. Opposites are not first logical and

---

49. Juan Carlos Scannone has also said that this work of Guardini is a source for the polyhedron. See "Pope Francis and the Theology of the People," *Theological Studies* 77, no. 1 (2016): 118–35. *Der Gegensatz* had been available in Spanish translation since at least 1985, and it appears that Bergoglio was already familiar with some works of Guardini before he arrived at Sankt Georgen, perhaps even this one, from Spanish translations available in Buenos Aires. Ivereigh emphasizes the influence of Johann Adam Möhler and Yves Congar's *True and False Reform in the Church* on Guardini's enantiology or science of opposition. These influences are not inconspicuous, but it seems that there were also more proximate sources on Guardini's work, as I shall demonstrate below.

then later conceived in the realm of everyday life. Guardini's presence at the Prussian university had a pastoral dimension even if that was expressed in the form of seeking a new basis in intellectual life for a Catholic worldview. The entire project of *Der Gegensatz* is the attempt to think about opposites as they are experienced in real life by individuals and groups. This concept (*eine Lebesphilosophie*) had been made famous in the nineteenth century by the philosopher Wilhelm Dilthey. In 1920s in German-speaking lands, it was being reinterpreted by Edmund Husserl, his disciple Martin Heidegger, and especially by thinkers working out a biological understanding of organic form like Hans Driesch as well as by the father of modern sociology, Georg Simmel.[50] The second contrast that flows through *Der Gegensazt* is the opposition between the fusion of opposites in German Idealism (especially in the trajectory that leads from Goethe's Romantic *Gegensatz* to Hegel's Absolute philosophy) and the sharp dialectical opposition found in Hegel's disaffected student, Søren Kierkegaard. Guardini's lectures on Kierkegaard from 1925 to 1927 show that he was completely immersed in the great Dane's "vitalism" and was intent on discovering a Catholic and ecclesial response to his rejection of a Hegelian completion of the system of opposites.[51] In rejecting this opposition, Guardini's metaphysical thought lies close to that of his contemporary Erich Przywara.[52] Guardini follows Kierkegaard

---

50. Heidegger published his *Sein und Zeit* in 1927, and para. 77 of this work was dedicated to the reinterpretation of Dilthey's and his interlocutor Count von Yorck's conception of historicity as it relates to the new philosophy of life. Driesch published *Philosophie des Organischen*, 2nd ed., 1921, in Leipzig (cf. *Der Gegensatz*, 52, n.17). Guardini explicitly refers (35, n.7) to Simmel's *Lebensanschauung* (Berlin, 1918) and *Philosophischen Kulturen* (Potsdam, 1923) on the question of *das Leben als Strom* [life as a current].

51. The young Hans Urs von Balthasar, Josef Pieper, and Hannah Arendt visited Guardini's lectures in Berlin in this period.

52. Bergoglio is very devoted to Erich Przywara and often cites him, but Przywara is not named in the book by Guardini, most likely because of the dispute that would later emerge between them. Guardini preferred think-

in rejecting the Hegelian resolution of the problem of opposites in a fusion that transcends daily life in a transempirical realm of absolute philosophy. There must be a point of reference to the individual existence of the believer without a reduction of this foundational standpoint to that of Kierkegaardian individualism. In this regard, Guardini favors the mediation of a lived tension (*Spannung*) over the insuperability of dialectic as the proper mode for grasping a living system of opposites.[53]

Bergoglio is devoted to Guardini's synthesis but, but by his own account in an interview with Borghesi, was also heavily influenced by the interpretation of *The Spiritual Exercises* by the Hegelianizing French Jesuit Gaston Fessard.[54] The underlying polarities for Bergoglio as an avid reader of Fessard in the 1970s are still those of Ignatius of Loyola: from above and from below, the search for a

---

ing about contrasts from "above and within" to Przywara's approach from "above and below." The concept of personal interiority accordingly is central to *Der Gegensatz* and not fully developed by Przywara. Both thinkers are very indebted to the conception of being as a polarity, as would become clear in 1928 when Przywara published his magnum opus, *Analogia Entis*.

53. *Der Gegensatz*, 23. Ivereigh writes: "At the core of this kind of "in-the-tension" thinking—Francis uses the untranslateable Spanish word *tensionante*—the value of each pole is recognized and held together, rather than being resolved in contradiction. The synthesis that results is always an encounter between grace and nature, and is essentially the work of the Holy Spirit.": "Austen Ivereigh, "New book looks at intellectual history of Francis, and why he is 'pope of polarity'," Crux, November 18, 2017," available on-line at https://cruxnow.com/book-review/2017/11/18/new-book-looks-intellectual-history-francis-pope-polarity/.

54. Borghesi writes in *Osservatore Romano* (2017): "In quattro documenti audio, tra gennaio e marzo, il Papa, con somma cortesia, ha offerto delucidazioni fondamentali sul suo pensiero e sulla sua formazione intellettuale. La prima e fondamentale è la confessione dell'importanza della lettura degli anni sessanta, più volte ripetuta, del libro *La dialectique des 'Exercices spirituels' de saint Ignace de Loyola* di Gaston Fessard. Il nome di Fessard, uno dei più grandi intellettuali gesuiti della seconda metà del Novecento, amico di Henri de Lubac e protagonista con lui della Scuola di Lione, mi ha aperto lo sguardo sull'intera riflessione di Bergoglio. Era come trovare il filo rosso, l'unità di un pensiero poliedrico."

form of contemplation that arises from and is generative of action, being in the world but not of the world, etc. Fessard taught the young Bergoglio to approach these spiritual axioms of everyday life knowing that the total reconciliation was the work of God at the end of time but "as if" their fulfillment depended upon what we do in the here and now. Guardini confirmed the Jesuit's deeply felt need to address the crisis of history that he had faced in Argentina, a study in political, social, and economic contrasts, contrasts that were not going to be resolved theoretically. Fessard saw the dialectics of history quite differently than Hegel, basically in terms of three fundamental polarities: man and woman, master and slave, and pagan and believer. The crucial category, and on this point the convergence between Fessard and Guardini is critical for Bergoglio, is the encounter of two persons who meet face-to-face. Fessard took these three essential polarities to lie deep within each of us. But the master-slave was particularly evident in the political struggle between nations. The complementarity of male and female lies at the heart of the nuptial mystery. And the struggle of converting the unbeliever determines finally the role that belief in God will play in the resolution of all conflicts—spiritual, personal, and political—that envelop our world today. Bergoglio's polyhedric thinking is mutually determined by Guardini's open-ended polar tension in the struggle of daily life and Fessard's dialectical process of discerning God's place in our exercise of all human liberty.

Bergoglio returned to Argentina at the end of 1986 very eager to be back in his homeland and with a stack of prayer cards in hand.[55] These contained the image of *Maria, Knotenlöserin* that he had picked up in a trip to a Marian chapel in Augsburg. The image depicted a Virgin with a belt that contained both tied and untied knots, symbolizing the unresolved and resolved issues that we confront in daily life. Bergoglio not only promoted the devotion to the Virgin as the

---

55. When he was in Frankfurt, he reported that he watched the airplanes depart from the airport because he was so homesick for his native land. His early return needs to be viewed in this light.

"untier of knots" in Buenos Aires but had the image installed in parishes so that an Argentine devotion could take root.[56] In other words, the "knots" represent a kind of enantiology of its own sort on the level of the popular understanding of everyday life.

When Bergoglio became Archbishop of Buenos Aires in the late 1990s, he set out to foster a culture of encounter in many domains, including in the service of the Church to those at the margins. The most exemplary of these encounters were with non-Catholics. Between 1998 and 2013, Jorge Bergoglio participated with great frequency in numerous ecumenical and interreligious encounters as Archbishop of Buenos Aires. His "shocking" decision on June 19, 2006, to request a blessing from Pentecostal brethren in Luna Park Stadium is perhaps the most frequently remembered of these events, but there are many others of equal and even more lasting value.[57] During 2012–13, the Archdiocese of Buenos Aires published four slim volumes for popular dissemination that were the fruit of a trialogue between Archbishop Bergoglio, Rabbi Abraham Skorka, and the Presbyterian Bible scholar and pastor Marcelo Figueroa. These catechetical-style books treated: 1.) Solidarity, 2.) Prayer, 3.) Dignity, and 4.) Faith and Reason.[58] The common cause that united these three men all equally dedicated to reasoning about sacred and profane matters from the standpoint of Sacred Scripture

---

56. Mariano de Vedia, *Francisco: El Papa del Pueblo* (Santiago: Planeta, 2013), 81–2. The Facebook page for the parish San José del Talar confirms that this devotion is still strong today in Argentina: https://www.facebook.com/notes/parroquia-san-jose-del-talar-y-santuario-de-la-virgen-que-desata-los-nudos/historia-del-cuadro-de-nuestra-señora-que-desata-los-nudos/431014946921425.

57. Austen Ivereigh, *The Great Reformer: Francis and the Making of a Radical Pope* (New York: Henry Holt and Company, 2014), 293–6. Cf. Bergoglio and Skorka, *Sobre el Cielo y la Tierra*, 204, and this press report: https://gloria.tv/article/yRKWFU4eppdB61aQZjCpVrYgG.

58. *Solidaridad* (Buenos Aires: Editorial Santa María, 2012), *Oración* (Buenos Aires: Editorial Santa María, 2012), *Razón y Fe* (Buenos Aires: Editorial Santa María, 2013), and *Dignidad* (Buenos Aires: Editorial Santa María, 2013). All four of these were edited by Prof. Gustavo Escobar and include study texts that supplement the conversations.

was the paganism of the Argentine people.⁵⁹ They are each involved in a common spiritual project to reconcile the Argentine people to one another and to God. The particular insight of Archbishop Bergoglio in these and other similar encounters is the discernment of a reconciled diversity already present in the midst of the dialogue.⁶⁰ Reconciled diversity is a corollary of the fourth principle whereby the whole is greater than the sum of its parts. This is the very reality that he signaled in Luna Park in the meeting in 2006 with the Pentecostals and Evangelicals.⁶¹ Reconciled diversity is an achievement but also part of a larger process, one that requires us to see wholes as greater than their fragmented and disjointedly temporal parts:

> [We have] to dialogue with culture, with people, with science, with the human person in its very origins (*el hombre en toda su concepción*). But you must also understand that we are part of a dialogue that must continue, that begins from afar, that perdures in the future, that we *are* a space, a place, a mile-marker in a path of dialogue and encounter.⁶²

In his early reflections on Jesuit piety, Bergoglio maintained that this standpoint not only possesses but is *un espacio, un ámbito, un*

---

59. The links between the Bergoglian practice of seeking a whole greater than its parts through dialogue and encounter and the Scripture reasoning project initiated by Peter Ochs and David Ford in the Anglo-Saxon world still needs further reflection.

60. He derives this insight from Oscar Cullman. See Bergoglio and Skorka, *Sobre el Cielo y la Tierra*, 201.

61. See Martin Brauer, "Pope Francis and Ecumenism," *Ecumenical Review* 69, no. 1 (2017): 4–14, and the remarks on ecumenism in his interview with Fr. Antonio Spadaro, S.J., "A Big Heart Open to God," *America*, September 30, 2013, see N. 30.

62. See *Razón y Fe*, 46. Italics added.

tiempo ["a space, a milieu, a time"].[63] Here he reclaims that innovative formulation. The situatedness, locatedness, and temporalizing of a renewed and not merely Catholic popular piety are applied to the fruits of an ecumenical and interreligious dialogue. In the dialogue and encounter between Catholics and non-Catholics, we do not just occupy time and space, we participate in an ongoing process whereby our time with God is infinitely greater than the space allotted to it by the world. Space itself thereby becomes the space in which God and humanity can become personally and corporately reconciled to one another.

The dialogue between Christianity and Judaism is itself a process in which spiritual and temporal concerns become intertwined. With Rabbi Skorka, Archbishop Bergoglio published a book entitled *On Heaven and Earth*. The written text did not originate as a written work. It came as a result of a long-standing mutual respect, a profound friendship, and a deep conviction that the spontaneous and intimate baring of one's soul to a trusted interlocutor reveals noteworthy thoughts.[64] These conversations preceded the Pope's election but have become a widely disseminated window into the interior life and spiritual motivations of the Holy Father. For our purposes, four themes are noteworthy. First, for both interlocutors and especially for Cardinal Bergoglio, true dialogue about our deepest human concerns is focused on the question of God and is always itinerant, *un camino*.[65] Second, both stake a claim against proselytism and ultra-right neo-traditionalism while also seeking to be a counter-current in

---

63. Jorge Mario Bergoglio, *Meditaciones para Religiosos*, 57–60, drawing upon a speech from 1978 to the Province.
64. Bergoglio and Skorka, *Sobre el Cielo y la Tierra*, 10.
65. Ibid., 13–15, 17–21. Bergoglio highlights a remark by Skorka that recognizes an image on the façade of the Metropolitan Cathedral of Buenos Aires of the elder figure of Joseph meeting and embracing his brothers for the first time. He sees his interreligious dialogue with Rabbi Skorka through the mirror of the Israelites offering hospitality to one another while sojourning in a foreign land. Discovering oneself as having roots and being a foreigner in one's own land could be a watchword for the Bergoglian culture of encounter.

the overtly "pagan" city of Buenos Aires.[66] Skorka mentions the New Testament verse, "Blessed are the poor, for the kingdom of God shall be theirs," and this commitment to maintaining solidarity with the poor even through political structures while avoiding anti-Biblical and secularizing ideologies binds them together in a firm resolve.[67] Finally, the Bergoglian polyhedron is explicitly mentioned in the context of an exchange about globalization. His sharp language here about the imperialism that smooths out the rich virtues of distinct cultures (like a billiard ball) is as strong as in any place that he has used this signature metaphor.[68]

Equally noteworthy were his public conversations with the Imam of Buenos Aires, Omar Abboud.[69] Abboud was a prominent Muslim scholar whose father created the first modern Spanish translation of the Qur'an. Abboud maintained that Bergoglio taught the Muslims about dialogue and that the Archbishop created a civic space among and with Muslims by bringing minorities to the table.[70] Abboud was impressed that Bergoglio invited Muslims for the first time to the annual *Te Deum* homily that he gave in the Metropolitan Cathedral of Buenos Aires, a patriotic event in which the Cardinal spoke about national unity and current politics. Most remarkably for our present purposes, Bergoglio taught Abboud about his four founding principles for dialogue (time is

---

66. Ibid., 205, 216. Bergoglio names their beloved city "pagan" but does not consider this to be a pejorative usage. He insists that he is using it in a factual way to identify the many forms of consumerism and idolatry that infect believers and unbelievers alike. They are both repulsed by naïve attempts to label Argentina as a "cradle of races" (*un crisol de razas*), much like the notion in the United States of the "melting pot."

67. Ibid., 143–7, 212–14. Bergoglio's remarks about Jewish radicalism and the Catholic roots of the Peronist party are illuminating (190–3). It is in this context that he says that the witness of the saints, and especially Saint Francis on poverty, is the only truly revolutionary path open to people today.

68. Ibid., 149–51.

69. Ivereigh, *The Great Reformer*, 321–4.

70. Ibid., 321.

greater than space, unity is greater than conflict, reality prevails over the idea, and the whole is greater than its parts), and Abboud had them translated into Arabic and disseminated among Muslims.[71] In other words, among the Arabic-speaking people of Argentina, the Bergoglian idea of unity that prevails over conflict therefore has its own translation into Muslim theology.

3. Conclusion: Divine Love Inclines towards the Good of the Other

The true mystery of wholes and parts is that there is no *one* empirical whole that we can clearly indicate of which the different parts of either ecumenical or inter-religious encounters are the distinct parts. There is no "Esperanto creed" or universalist ethic that we can disseminate as the fulfillment of the search for parts in wholes apart from the whole that is infinitely surpassed by the Gospel of Jesus Christ.[72] The difference between the parts and the greater whole is both approachable and infinite. That is, finally, the analogical truth behind Bergoglio's insight into wholes and parts. We have in view some whole that goads us to think creatively about a new configuration of the parts even as we are aware that the true whole will be revealed in the fullness of time when we can see the whole of the Gospel without distortion. For the time being, we are left with a piecemeal vision and a deep desire to integrate.

God's love nonetheless approaches us from this widening chasm and makes it possible to enter into ecumenical and inter-religious dialogue with genuine commitment to one's own identity and a firm resolve that one will deepen one's understanding of the truth. In this regard, the reflections about roots and branches in Romans

---

71. Ibid., 322.
72. Cf. *Evangelii Gaudium*, para. 237.

are worth citing. Here, Paul begins by looking to the Jewish roots as the source of the goodness of the Christian branches:

> If the first fruits are holy, so is the whole batch of dough; and if the root is holy, so are the branches. But if some of the branches were broken off, and you, a wild olive shoot, were grafted in their place and have come to share in the rich root of the olive tree, do not boast against the branches. If you do boast, consider that you do not support the root; the root supports you. Indeed, you will say, "Branches were broken off so that I might be grafted in." That is so. They were broken off because of unbelief, but you are there because of faith. So do not become haughty, but stand in awe. (Rom 11:16–20).

Up to this point, Paul is mainly interested in impressing upon his fellow Christians their debt, his debt, to the Jewish inheritance. But he also turns the tables on this one-sided view of roots and branches. By itself, it is too human, too much of a project of human ways of viewing our rootedness. In fact, he continues, God is the one who establishes the relationships between roots and branches:

> For if God did not spare the natural branches, [perhaps] he will not spare you either. See, then, the kindness and severity of God: severity toward those who fell, but God's kindness to you, provided you remain in his kindness; otherwise you too will be cut off. And they also, if they do not remain in unbelief, will be grafted in, for God is able to graft them in again. For if you were cut from what is by nature a wild olive tree, and grafted, contrary to nature, into a cultivated one, how much more will they who belong to it by nature be grafted back into their own olive tree? (Rom 11:21–24)

As we have already seen, Pope Francis too is a thinker of rootedness. His lifelong project of reclaiming the Ignatian exercises (also for those outside of the Society of Jesus) is about rediscovering the fact that true selfhood is rooted in God.

Pope Francis also extends the Pauline metaphor into the domain of human activity and creativity in order to deal with the new Areopagus of a de-christianized culture. In the already cited address to the Council of Europe, he offers this reflection drawn from an Italian poet who converted to Catholicism in the first half of the twentieth century, Clemente Rebora (1885–1957):

> In one of his poems, Rebora describes a poplar tree, its branches reaching up to the sky, buffeted by the wind, while its trunk remains firmly planted on deep roots sinking into the earth. In a certain sense, we can consider Europe in the light of this image.... Rebora notes, on the one hand, that "the trunk sinks its roots where it is most true." The roots are nourished by truth, which is the sustenance, the vital lymph, of any society which would be truly free, human and fraternal. On the other hand, truth appeals to conscience, which cannot be reduced to a form of conditioning. Conscience is capable of recognizing its own dignity and being open to the absolute; it thus gives rise to fundamental decisions guided by the pursuit of the good, for others and for one's self; it is itself the locus of responsible freedom.[73]

Being rooted in God is thus being rooted in a mystery of truth that can guide human action regardless of one's confession of faith. We

---

73. Address of Pope Francis to the Council of Europe, Nov. 25, 2014, available online at https://w2.vatican.va/content/francesco/en/speeches/2014/november/documents/papa-francesco_20141125_strasburgo-consiglio-europa.html. This same image of Rebora is also discussed in Luigi Giussani, *The Religious Sense* (San Francisco: Ignatius Press, 1990), 117, a favorite text of Bergoglio.

usually refer to this root source of morality as conscience. For Pope Francis, the exercise of responsible freedom is also the fruit of a process of discernment of spirits.

The difference between the modern secular and the ancient Pauline notion of being rooted in conscience lies in the idea of a divine election, of being chosen for a mission to be exercised in public and on the stage of history. God chooses the Jews as his people, but he is also responsible for choosing Paul and the disciples of Christ as the new grafts onto the Jewish root of salvation history. This is the mystery of election and not just the switching of an old part for a newer, more modern one. St. Thomas Aquinas says that there is a divine "pre-dilection" involved in God's will towards the other. This is quite different from a human predilection. It is not a matter of favoritism. In fact, the divine *pre*-dilection, in its orientation to a divinely willed good that is by definition prior to and distinct from any human *diligere* ["loving"], serves as a salutary caution against arbitrary or self-serving favoritism.[74] It also cautions against a secular indifference to the call of a God who chooses a holy, faithful people. Aquinas writes:

> I answer that, since to love a thing is to will it good, in a twofold way anything may be loved more, or less. In one way on the part of the act of the will itself, which is more or less intense. In this way God does not love some things more than others, because He loves all things by an act of the will that is one, simple, and always the same. In another way, [he loves all things] on the account of the good itself that a person wills for the beloved. In

---

74. This way of speaking about the Thomistic doctrine of divine election is typical of Garrigou-Lagrange and his followers. It does not seem to be a phrase used explicitly by the Angelic Doctor. For detailed study of Aquinas's reading of Romans 9–11, one can consult Stephen Boguslawski, O.P., *Thomas Aquinas on the Jews* (New York: Paulist Press, 2008) and idem., "Thomas Aquinas," in *Reading Romans through the Centuries*, ed. Jeffrey P. Greenman and Timothy Larson (Grand Rapids, MI: Brazos, 2005), 81–99.

this way, we are said to love that one more than another, for whom we will a greater good, though our will is not more intense. In this way, we have to say that God loves some things more than others. For since God's love is the cause of goodness in things, as has been said, no one thing would be better than another, if God did not will greater good for one than for another.[75]

God's love is the cause of the good in the other and the impetus for dialogue with the other. This formulation is basically a restatement of the Bergoglian dialogical idea that the whole is greater than the sum of its parts. God can elect Jews *and* Gentiles not out of a human kind of partiality but only out of a truly divine love. Out of this impartial and essentially in-different (and Ignatian) love of God for his creatures, Christians can be goaded not only to seek greater unity amongst themselves but also to witness to their faith in a dialogical and polyhedric way with non-Christians.[76] In this sense, the teaching that the whole is greater than its parts is eminently practical and worthwhile in the context of both ecumenical and inter-religious dialogue. Such a vantage point on these encounters might also inspire Christians to be better witnesses to the form of unity that the globalized but fragmented world in which we live desperately seeks and needs.

---

75. St. Thomas Aquinas, *Summa Theologiae*, Ia, q. 20, a. 3, *Utrum Deus aequaliter diligat omnia, responsio*: "Respondeo dicendum quod, cum amare sit velle bonum alicui, duplici ratione potest aliquid magis vel minus amari. Uno modo, ex parte ipsius actus voluntatis, qui est magis vel minus intensus. Et sic Deus non magis quaedam aliis amat, quia omnia amat uno et simplici actu voluntatis, et semper eodem modo se habente. Alio modo, ex parte ipsius boni quod aliquis vult amato. Et sic dicimur aliquem magis alio amare, cui volumus maius bonum; quamvis non magis intensa voluntate. Et hoc modo necesse est dicere quod Deus quaedam aliis magis amat. Cum enim amor Dei sit causa bonitatis rerum, ut dictum est, non esset aliquid alio melius, si Deus non vellet uni maius bonum quam alteri."

76. On Ignatian indifference, see Fessard, *La dialectique des "Exercices Spirituels" de Saint Ignace de Loyola*, II (Paris: Aubier, 1966), 26–35.

Bibliography

Bergoglio, Jorge Mario. *Meditaciones para Religiosos*. San Miguel, Buenos Aires: Diego de Torres, 1982.

———. *Ponerse la patria al hombro. Memoria y camino de esperanza*. Buenos Aires: Claretiana, 2013.

———, and Skorka, Abraham. *Sobre el Cielo y la Tierra*. Buenos Aires/New York: Vintage Español, 2010.

Borelli, John. "The Dialogue of Fraternity." In *Pope Francis and the Future of Catholicism*, edited by Gerard Mannion. London: Cambridge University Press, 2017. 221–44.

Fares, Diego. *The Heart of Pope Francis: How a New Culture of Encounter Is Changing the Church and the World*. New York: Crossroad, 2015.

Fernández, Víctor Manuel. *The Francis Project: Where He Wants to Take the Church*. New York/Mahwah, NJ: Paulist, 2016.

Ivereigh, Austen. "The Pope and the *Patria Grande*: How Francis Is Promoting Latin-America's Continental Destiny." In *The Search for God in America*, edited by Maria Clara Bingemer and Peter Casarella. Washington, D.C.: The Catholic University of America Press, forthcoming.

Kasper, Walter, and Madges, William. *Pope Francis' Revolution of Tenderness and Love: Theological and Pastoral Perspectives*. New York: Paulist Press, 2015.

Rourke, Thomas. *The Roots of Pope Francis's Social and Political Thought*. Lanham, MD: Rowman & Littlefield, 2016.

Scannone, Juan Carlos. "Pope Francis and the Theology of the People." *Theological Studies* 77, no. 1 (2016): 118–35.

Chapter Three

HINDU, CHRISTIAN, CATHOLIC: FOUR WESTERN JESUITS IN INDIA AND THE BALANCE THEY ACHIEVED

Francis X. Clooney, S.J.

St. Francis Xavier (1506–52) reached India in 1542, just two years after the founding of the Society of Jesus. His famed 1544 letter to Ignatius Loyola describes his missionary practices and his detestation of idolatry and of the brahmin class, which he considered greedy and dishonest. But near the end of the letter, he admits his fascination with one educated brahmin who revealed to him details about Hindu practice that he found amazingly parallel to his own Catholic practice:

> The language used for teaching in their schools is like the Latin used in ours. [One brahmin] recited their commandments for me very well, giving a good explanation to each one of them. Those who are wise observe Sundays, something that is quite incredible. On Sundays they say no other prayer than the following, which they repeatedly recite, *"Om Śrī Nārāyaṇāya namaḥ,"* which means, "I adore thee, God, with your grace and assistance for ever"; and they recite this prayer very gently and softly in order to keep the oath they have taken. He told me that the natural law keeps them from

having many wives; and that in their writings it is stated that a time will come when all are to live under one law.¹

Xavier is happy to find resemblances to familiar Catholic practices. But perhaps too he was disturbed by parallels too close to Protestant Christianity. Karl Barth famously reports that Xavier feared he had found in Japan inklings of Luther:

> As distinct from the other Japanese sects Yodo-Shin-Shu has never let itself be supported legally or financially by the government. From the outset it has been completely free from the state, its main activity being in the large cities. We are not really surprised that St. Francis Xavier, who was the first Christian missionary to live in Japan (1549–1551), thought that he recognized in Yodo-Shin-Shu the "Lutheran heresy."²

Barth probably got this undocumented story from Rudolf Otto's *India's Religion of Grace and Christianity Compared and Contrasted*, though Otto too does not document the report.³ In the opening chapter, "India's Religion of Grace and Christianity," we find the Xavier anecdote in the section, "A Competitor to Christianity?" As Otto puts it, "The first news of this [parallel regarding grace] reached the Occident when the great Catholic missionary Xavier and his followers arrived in Japan and wrote home that they had

---

1. Francis Xavier, S.J., *The Letters and Instructions of Francis Xavier*, trans. M. Joseph Costelloe (St. Louis: Institute of Jesuit Sources, 1992), 72.
2. Karl Barth, *Church Dogmatics*, trans. G.T. Thomson (Edinburgh: T & T Clark, 1936), 341.
3. Rudolf Otto, *India's Religion of Grace and Christianity Compared and Contrasted*, trans. F.H. Foster (New York; London, 1930). See also S.P. Dubey, *Rudolf Otto and Hinduism*, Bharatiya Vidya Prakashan (Varanasi: Bharatiya Vidya Prakashan,1969), 77.

met with the 'Lutheran heresy' among the Japanese Buddhists."[4] Otto goes on to relate how a young Japanese scholar he met had learned German in order to read Martin Luther, "a Shinran in Germany."[5] Xavier was not intrigued by the parallel, whereas Otto's young scholar seems pleased by the unexpected parallel.

It is not surprising that correlations would be made between truth and error in Europe, and their parallels in Asia; we see the "far other" in light of our experiences with the "near other." The early Jesuits brought Europe with them when they went to India and encountered religions there, and that India in various ways came home to Europe in their reports and letters.

The larger principle is easy to grasp: Christians relate in many different ways to people of other faith traditions. How those encounters proceed and are signified sheds light on how Christians think of themselves and their place in the world. Attitudes vary according the religion encountered, the Christian community involved, and the era and location of the encounter. Interreligious encounters are mirrors in which Christians can and must take a deeper look at their choices, because not all Christians act alike.[6]

A magisterial overview of world Christianity could show in depth the interplay of Catholic identity, attitudes toward other Christians, and interreligious dispositions, and such would require many examples. This essay ambitions a more modest contribution, by looking to four examples of Western Jesuit missionaries in India (three in Tamil Nadu, the fourth in Bengal), to see how interreligious and ecumenical attitudes are interconnected in interesting and different ways, express and implicit: Robert de Nobili, S.J. (1579–1656), believed that the Church in India could replicate in India the fundamental inculturation of Catholicism—entering

---

4. Otto, *India's Religion of Grace*, 18.
5. Ibid., 20.
6. A third mirror would be the intra-Catholic, as believers come to note differences among themselves based on how they, all Catholics, react differently to other faiths.

and fulfilling, not undercutting, a culture— that happened in the Roman Empire; Jean Venance Bouchet, S.J. (1655–1732), found that his experience in India would help the Church to resist skeptical Enlightenment views of oracles and demons; Constantine Beschi S.J. (1680–1742) wrote gracious and beautiful Tamil poetic compositions that he thought worked more effectively in communicating the Christian message than the Gospels themselves; and William Wallace, S.J. (1863–1922), discovered in Bengal's Hinduism spiritual depths that he found lacking in his own Evangelical Anglicanism, and so became a Catholic and a Jesuit.

Robert de Nobili, S.J. (1579–1656): Catholic Culture, India's Catholic Culture

De Nobili is remembered as a pioneer in the work of inculturation, determined to make the Gospel at home in the Indian context. He improvised a way of engaging Indian culture and religion that was distinctively Catholic (even if not accepted by all Catholics) in its ambition to infuse Indian culture with Christian values, without destroying the culture. On the precedent of the classical cultures of the Roman Church, he stressed respect for classical cultures, confident in the enduring Catholic capacity to respect and take to heart whole cultures. His writings demonstrate a robust defense of adaptation on the one hand, alongside sharp polemic against whatever in Indian culture he identified as pagan and contrary to the Gospel; the former category marks perhaps 99 percent of what he encountered in Hinduism. De Nobili argued with other Catholics, not with Protestants, but throughout his controversies he holds to a Catholic view of culture, religion, and the Gospel: the Church can set down cultural roots again and again, re-rooting the faith in new contexts.

De Nobili was no liberal. What seemed explicitly and stubbornly religious had necessarily to be labeled superstitious, condemned, and forbidden to converts. Hindu deities had to be labeled false insofar as they indicated anything more than reasonable inklings of the true God as known in Christian philosophy and theology. The error of idolatry can be traced in theory (e.g., in the *Inquiry into the Meaning of "God"*) and in worship (e.g., in the *Refutation of Calumnies*), to particular epistemological origins (in the *Dialogue on Eternal Life*), and shown to be a harmful overlay, spoiling generally sound social structures (in the *Report on Indian Customs*).[7] But the larger point of such condemnations was that, while evils needed to be ruled out, as much of the culture as possible ought to be left intact, beyond the need for purification.

De Nobili saw his work as "reclothing" Christianity in Indian garb; others saw it as an attractive but deceptive way of misleading Indians curious about Christianity. It is not surprising that the Protestant missionary Elijah Hoole, writing in the early nineteenth century, looks back without much sympathy on de Nobili's era, accusing the Jesuits of pretense and of concealing their European and Christian identities:

> Their whole life was a practical falsehood. They professed that they were not Europeans; that they were Brahmans, and San-yasis; their assumed character was frequently challenged by the natives, and had frequently to be met by direct denial, or by evasions unworthy of the Christian character. Nor is it probable that they succeeded to any great extent, or for any considerable time, in keeping up the delusion, either amongst their converts, or the Heathen…. The continual practice of deceit, on their part, furnished the most powerful sanction to their converts to indulge in deception, a crime to

---

7. For a translation of the *Report* and the *Inquiry*, see Roberto de Nobili, *Preaching Wisdom to the Wise: Three Treatises by Roberto de Nobili in Dialogue with the Learned Hindus of South India*, introduced, annotated, and translated by Anand Amaladass, S.J., and Francis X. Clooney, S.J. (St. Louis: Institute of Jesuit Sources, 2000).

which the Hindoos are proverbially prone. How shocking to reflect, that, in inducing the heathen to take upon themselves the profession of Christianity, they should use such means as must necessarily result in rendering them more the children of hell than they were in the heathen state![8]

De Nobili saw continuity as a virtue; Protestants would come to see it as a failure to live up to the robust and prophetic transformative power of the Gospel.

Jean Venance Bouchet, S.J. (1655–1732): India's Confirmation of Catholic Truths

Jean Venance Bouchet, S.J. (1655–1732), lived in Tamil Nadu, Andhra Pradesh, and Karnataka for over forty years, most of the first half of the eighteenth century. In 1687 he had gone to Siam as part of a new Jesuit mission, but after a 1688 revolution, the fourteen Jesuits were ejected from the kingdom, and Bouchet was one of just three who, upon reaching Pondicherry in 1689, stayed on to join the French mission. He was a vigorous missionary; he tells us that by 1702 he had baptized 20,000 adults and heard 100,000 confessions. He built a large church at Avur, which remained the center of the Madurai Mission until 1773. He also worked for some time in Takkolam (Tarcolam) in northern Tamil Nadu. Bouchet was a friend and spiritual advisor to St. John de Britto, and was the last Jesuit to see de Britto before his martyrdom. In 1702 he

---

8. Elijah Hoole, *Madras, Mysore, and the South of India: or, Personal Narrative of a Mission to Those Countries from 1820–1827*, 2nd ed. (London: Longman, Brown, Green and Longmans, 1844), 88. See also Ines Zupanov, *Disputed Mission: Jesuit Experiments and Brahmanical Knowledge in Seventeenth-Century India* (New York: Oxford University Press, 1999), whose book works with the thesis of the cleverness, sometimes to the extreme, of de Nobili and those following his way.

became the first superior of the new Carnatic (French) mission in south India.[9]

In Bouchet's letters, we learn that he led a spartan existence, his eating and drinking marked by an austerity owing both to a paucity of resources and to a determination to live as an ascetic. He was a prominent member of the group of Jesuits known as "pandarasamis," who, in Savarimuthu Rajamanickam's words, "were sufficiently respected and at the same time could deal with all the castes, even with the Brahmins, though they could not be their teachers. They did not need to be Sanskrit scholars nor strict vegetarians nor were they obliged to fast every day. They could look after the low castes more easily."[10] What had been de Nobili's personal adaptive practice had become a standard form of missionary acculturation, adjusted so as to match the complexities of caste and the realities of the growing Christian community.

Bouchet wrote a series of long letters back to Europe: on the austerity and needs of the mission: to Cochet de Saint-Valtier, a vivid account of his trials and tribulations, a kind of Biblical recasting of the persecution of the early Church; to Pierre-Daniel Huet, Bishop of Avranches, on parallels between the religions of the Bible and India; to Jean François Baltus, S.J., on the presence of demons, their speech by way of human oracles, and their defeat by the Gospel and Christian witness; to Melchior Cochet de Saint-Valtier, on the legal system; to Huet, on reincarnation; to an unnamed Jesuit, on Bouchet's own map of south India; to an unnamed young Jesuit, on the austerity of the mission, the challenges and sufferings of missionary work, but also their consolations as well.

---

9. See Léon Besse, *Fr Beschi of the Society of Jesus: His Times and His Writings* (Trichinopoly: St. Joseph's Industrial School Press, 1918), 95. See also Augustin Saulière, *Red Sand: A Life of St. John de Britto, SJ* (Madura: De Nobili Press, 1947), 403, 418.

10. Savarimuthu Rajamanickam, *The First Oriental Scholar* (Tirunelveli: De Nobili Research Institute, 1972), 49.

Bouchet studied Indian culture and religion in a depth impressive for his era, the work of the missionary standing side by side with the work of the scholar. He showed interest in historical explanations, even in tracing Indian religion back to the biblical roots. His letter on reincarnation shows not only his missionary distaste for the idea, but also his growing interest simply in the details of Indian religion. He placidly points to the errors of the Indians and the errors of the Greeks, and then ponders which version might have been derived from the other. He aimed, then, to use his Greek and Indian knowledge of reincarnation for the sake of the refutation of Hindu beliefs, relying on a rigorous logic surely unsuited to a matter as mysterious as life after death.

Bouchet's 1712 letter to Jean François Baltus, S.J., on the topic of the reality of demons and oracles in India is pertinent for this essay. It draws on his observations of religion in India in order that he might add his voice to a debate occurring back in Europe. Baltus (1667–1743) was a Christian apologist whose most notable work was the wonderfully entitled *Response to the History of Oracles by Mr. de Fontenelle in Which He Refutes the System of Mr. Van-Dale Regarding the Authors of Pagan Oracles, the Reason for and Time of Their Silencing, and in Which There Is Established the View of the Fathers of the Church on This Topic* (Strasburg, 1707). Baltus was challenging a thesis of Bernard Le Bovier de Fontenelle's (1657–1757) in his *History of Oracles* regarding oracles and demons, and in turn critiquing the thesis of the Dutch Mennonite Anthony van Dale (1638– 1708) regarding the notion of oracles and of the reality of demons (1700). The skeptical view favored by both van Dale and Fontenelle held that oracles were human institutions, not empowered by demons. They were fraudulent businesses, merely traffic in superstition, eventually pushed aside by the religious and political Christian movement. The demise of oracles was due to the social and political rise of the Christian empire, and not to the innate power of the Resurrection; the demons who ceased to have power had never existed in the first place.

Though as real as in the ancient Mediterranean, demons in India too were defeated and stripped of power by the arrival of the Gospel. Experience in India thus supports this truth of the early Christian tradition. We can see, he says, the lively and malicious presence of demons here in India, and likewise the way that the sheer fact of Christian presence leads to the muting and demise of the demons and their oracles.[11] Bouchet thus agrees with Baltus in arguing that the oracles were real, genuinely inspired by demons. This new knowledge traveling from India to Europe was used not only to support and strengthen the work of the missions, but also to dispute European views that, in Bouchet's view, detracted from the power of the Gospel.[12] News from the missions thus helped to buttress a besieged Catholic Europe.

Constantine Beschi, S.J. (1680–1747): The Flourishing of a Catholic Imagination

Constantine Beschi was in south India from 1710 until his death in 1747. He was a parish priest and a builder of mission churches, and supervisor of other pastoral activities in the growing mission. He was notable most of all for his expertise in the Tamil language, and for his diverse writings: the first grammars and dictionaries of Tamil for foreigners, and the first translation (into Latin) of a large part of the *Tirukkuraḷ*, a famed set of ethical aphorisms beloved by all Tamils. He also wrote the *Paramārta Guru* (a collection of

---

11. Jean Vanance Bouchet, S.J., *Fr. Bouchet's India: An 18th-Century Jesuit's Encounter with Hinduism* (Chennai: Satya Nilayam Publications, 2006), 43–44.
12. The use of Hinduism obliquely to criticize European ideas may be seen in other cases too. For example, Leo Meurin, S.J. (1825– 1895), a famed Bombay missionary and later a bishop, wrote a polemical essay, "God and Brahm." Though it is dedicated to a refutation of Hindu ideas of divinity, the essay seems as much a diatribe against what he considered to be the lazy interreligious openness of the British in nineteenth-century India.

ironic tales about a brahmin and his disciples) and hymns for use in church services. Notable too is his *Vētiyar Olukkam* (On the Right Behavior of Catechists), a book of instructions and advice for catechists that was admired even by his Protestant rivals in nearby Tranquebar.

In the nearly 4,000 verses of *Tempāvaṇi* (*The Unfading Garland*) he offered an eloquent and grand re-telling of the story of the Nativity and early life of Jesus, from the perspective of Joseph. It is characterized by complex versification and the ambition of a most beautiful presentation of the Gospel, including cultural and literary adaptation and embrace as the way to make known the Gospel. The beauty of poetry might be seen as a balance to the sharp polemic elsewhere in his writings, and even ameliorates the occasionally fierce argumentation of *Tempāvaṇi* itself. Beschi's Joseph, the hero of the story, is a man of natural virtue, embodying the values of patience, humility, generosity, etc. Beschi hardly mentions Joseph's Jewish identity, and though Joseph is centrally placed as a husband to Mary and father to Jesus, he is presented as a man of natural virtue and humane prudence. Since Jesus's public teaching had not yet begun in Egypt, Joseph was missioned by Jesus to present the true and good insofar as these were available to natural reason.[13]

Beschi also wrote several apologetic treatises, in debate with the Lutherans in Tranquebar. The most important is the *Vētaviḷakkam*, which covers a variety of topics debated in the Reformation period and thus also among missionaries in south India, including the worship of saints, the status of the Virgin Mary, the Catholic veneration of images, the identity of the true church, the proper way to read scripture in the context of tradition, and the status and

---

13. See Chapter 27 of *Tempāvaṇi*. For a chapter-by-chapter summary of the work, see Louis Dupuis, *Notice sur La Poésie Tamoule, Le Rév. P. Beschi et Le Tempāvaṇi* (Pondichérry, 1851).

value of miracles.¹⁴ On my reading, chapter 16 shows a theological justification of the Catholic view of scripture and tradition. He notes, among other points, that the Bible did not appear suddenly as a fully written book. Revelations, such as God's dealings with Abraham, occurred long before the books about revelation were written, only to be recorded later by Moses. Even the words of Jesus were *spoken* and had force *orally*, only later to be recorded in the Gospels. Thus, the word needs to be interpreted, as the New Testament amply testifies; nor does the Bible say that only the Bible is to be respected. Furthermore, he argues that the whole Bible need not be taught all at once—the story can be told in various ways and in many stages. A Catholic view of scripture thus opens the way for Catholic imaginative works such as *Tēmpāvaṇi*.

Like de Nobili, Beschi too provoked strong reactions from Protestants against his imaginative and selective refashioning of the Gospel story. After praising the style of *Tēmpāvaṇi*, Hoole observes,

> It was intended to supply the place of a translation of the holy Scriptures; but every doctrine, fact, and super-added legend is so accommodated to the notions of the Hindoos that the whole might be supposed to have been the composition of a native, who had never set his foot beyond the boundaries of his own country; and whilst it recognizes many important and sublime truths, it has

---

14. The full list of chapter themes is given in Besse, *Fr Beschi of the Society of Jesus*, 193. Will Sweetman describes the tone: "[In the] *Vētaviḷakkam*, Beschi describes the Tranquebar Bible as 'like a gem thrown in the mud, like poison mixed with ambrosia, like black ink spilt on a beautifully drawn picture.'... In another work, *Luttēriṉattiyalpu* (*The Essence of Lutheranism*), Beschi described the effect of reading the Lutherans' Tamil: 'Already in reading the first line the reader's eyes burn, his tongue dries up and his ears must burst; one looks around and bursts into loud laughter.'" In "The Prehistory of Orientalism: Colonialism and the Textual Basis for Bartholomäus Ziegenbalg's Account of Hinduism," *New Zealand Journal of Asian Studies* 6.2 (2004): 29

a tendency, at the same time, to confirm and establish innumerable errors. The hero of the poem is Joseph, the reputed father of our Lord. The particulars of his life, and those of the life of the blessed Virgin, are recounted with pretended accuracy; and innumerable miracles are feigned, to heighten the interest. The colouring given to the facts of the extraordinary birth and infancy of the divine Redeemer must shock anyone who has tasted the simplicity of the Gospel-history; and is calculated to reduce it, in the estimation of the Hindoos, to the rank of one of their own mythological fables.[15]

And,

Amazing ingenuity, indefatigable industry, and the zeal of a mind worthy of a better cause may be traced in every page of this work.... As a literary composition, and as an amusing book, it is invaluable; but when regarded as the masterpiece of the most celebrated Romish writer that has appeared among the Hindoos, and as the best information, as to Scripture history and doctrine, supplied to them by the talented men sent from Rome for their evangelization, it conveys a revolting but correct idea of the regard to expediency, rather than to truth, and to the inclinations of their converts, rather than to their best interests, shown by that body, whose exertions and successes were for a time the astonishment of Europe.[16]

Despite the generally caustic edge, it seems that for Hoole and other Protestants, the real fear was that Beschi was all too successful in harmonizing Christian faith with Indian culture, such that Hindus

---

15. Hoole, *Madras, Mysore, and the South of India*, 202.
16. Ibid., 205.

would hardly feel the difference entailed by conversion.¹⁷ The basic question recurs: Is the arrival of Christianity in a new culture to be considered an incarnational harmony, or a prophetic disruption?

William Wallace, S.J. (1863–1922): Trust in Hindu Culture and the Healing of Christianity

Our final example is complicated, since it involves an Irish convert to Catholicism from Anglicanism, who was alienated from his Anglican roots, learned about Hinduism, ultimately became a Jesuit, and discovered a better "Catholic way" to think about Hinduism.¹⁸ Wallace came to India as an Evangelical Anglican missionary, worked in the Calcutta region from 1889 to 1896, and quickly became disillusioned with the missionary approach and the fruits of missionary activity. After his initial stay of seven years in India, he returned to England, and then moved back to Ireland where he had been born. After much discernment, he converted to Roman Catholicism and became a Jesuit. He returned to India as a Jesuit missionary in 1901.¹⁹ In his remarkable, though neglected,

---

17. On the Protestant critique of Beschi, see also Hephzibah Israel, *Religious Transactions in Colonial South India: Language, Translation, and the Making of Protestant Identity* (New York: Palgrave Macmillan, 2011), chapter 4, "Prose Truth versus Poetic Fiction: Sacred Translations in Competing Genres."
18. Parts of this section are indebted to Francis X. Clooney, "Alienation, Xenophilia, and Coming Home: William Wallace, S.J.'s *From Evangelical to Catholic by Way of the East*," *Common Knowledge* 24.2 (2018), 208–290.
19. Wallace was not the only Anglican of his era with a strikingly hopeful attitude toward the new grounding of Christian faith in India. Bishop Brooke Foss Westcott, who had been an Oxford don and was one of the founders of the Anglican mission in Delhi (and also of St. Stephen's College, still one of the best colleges in India), was of the view that the mission would generate a new and vital form of Christian culture that would then come to the United Kingdom and revivify the Church of England. See Francis

autobiography, *From Evangelical to Catholic by Way of the East*,[20] he recounts his journey to Catholicism, showing how it was driven by an ever-deeper appreciation for Hinduism. There is, I propose, a complicated xenophilia at work here: Wallace loves the religion of the other (Hinduism) in proportion to his disillusionment with his own religion (Anglicanism), leading not to a (for him impossible) conversion to Hinduism, but rather to a different form of Christianity (Roman Catholicism). Hinduism, to put it briefly, led him into the Catholic Church.

Wallace explains the constructive work of acquiring a proper conception of Indian religion in Chapter 6, "Indian Work." He recounts his intense and inventive efforts to understand the religion or religions called "Hinduism," now viewed apart from the distortions imposed by Western missionaries and scholars invested in finding the religion to be defective and justly supplanted by Protestant Christianity. He learned the Bengali language, in the ordinary mode rather than the refined classroom and literary style, even as he was in the process of learning Sanskrit. He engaged in conversations with both educated and ordinary Hindus, simply in order to be educated about the culture and religion around him. He set up his own residence in the bazaar—a *dharma-śikṣālaya* (house of religious instruction).[21] His new and more intimate relationship with Indians was satisfying. He admired their hard work, frugality, and simplicity; their temperance; and their respect for authority and honesty: "their natural thoughtfulness and spirituality surprised me."[22] As a result, he notes: "the familiar conversation I now enjoyed with natives showed me that there was more in

---

X. Clooney, *The Future of Hindu-Christian Studies* (London: Routledge, 2017), 2–3.

20. References are to William Wallace, S.J., *From Evangelical to Catholic by Way of the East* (The Light of the East Series, no. 35. Calcutta: Catholic Orphan Press, 1923).
21. Ibid., 87.
22. Ibid., 89.

them in every way than we missionaries were giving them credit for."[23] Even idolatry, which he had been taught to despise, began to make sense to Wallace as an elaborate spirituality of symbol and sacrament. He soon learned to understand the symbolic nature of idols, imbued for a time with divine presence; such objects were not, of themselves, salvific. While this insight was hardly unique to Wallace, it was for him a great step forward. Engaging Indians in a fair and open manner helped him to think differently about Hinduism.

Wallace's new respect for Hinduism was marked by a growing negativity toward Anglicanism and a growing nearness to Catholicism. He found that if Indian ideas were allowed to stand on their own, they would not infrequently turn out to be superior to ideas that he had learned in the West. Familiar Anglican teachings seemed, his Indian friends told him, baked on the outside but still raw and indigestible on the inside, and hardly persuasive to a Hindu audience. Over time, he decided that the missionaries "were making a very great mistake in thinking that the Hindus were interiorly convinced of the falsity of their religion and the truth of ours (Anglicanism)," as if "secretly they admired Protestantism and were only kept back from embracing it by fear of the temporal consequences."[24]

By knowing Hindus and beginning the study of Hindu texts, Wallace fathomed much that was new to him about religion, himself, and God: "And I learned much from them, not merely by the new way of thinking which they suggested to me, nor only by the fresh view of the universe and of my own person which they opened up to me, but also by seeing something of how great and how fervent must be the devotion in God and self-annihilation at His feet, if my salvation was to be won." In the end, it was through this hard-won insight into the religious fervor of the Hindus that he was to

---

23. Ibid., 88.
24. Ibid., 94.

find his own way spiritually: "Though I knew it not, everything I was learning and every progress I was making, was a step to my true home as a believer in Jesus Christ—the Catholic Church."[25]

He rather sharply condemns the counterproductive means of missionary efforts that fabricated a hapless or evil religious other, in order to attack it and show the advantages of Christianity; such means missed the true contribution of Christianity in India. Wallace sought instead a form of Christianity more able to engage Hinduism in a way that would enrich the Christian rather than water it down: "India did not show me the falsity of my own religion. India never ceased to illumine my faith, and to confirm it from reason and observation. What India did was to show me that anti-religious character of Protestantism and of its principle, Private Judgment."[26] Udayan Namboodiry notes that the extreme negativism of Wallace's views made more difficult the publication of his book:

> His first book, *From Evangelist to Jesuit*, created a storm in Anglo-India. At first no publisher would touch it because of its high anti-Anglicism content, but Father Wallace managed to get it printed by a Calcutta publisher. His second book, *Hindoo Clairvoyance*, never saw the light of day and is still preserved in manuscript form in the Goethals library, where the author found it. In this book Father Wallace wanted to point out how grossly generations of missionaries had failed in translating Christian tenets into Indian form, principally because of their narrow view of Hinduism, their deliberate steering away from the doctrine of Jesus Christ.[27]

---

25. Ibid., 94–95.
26. Udayan Namboodiry, *St. Xavier's: The Making of a Calcutta Institution* (New Delhi: Viking/Penguin Books India, 1995), 133.
27. Ibid., 115.

I have not yet found Anglican reactions to Wallace's fierce critique, but it is easier to discover, by an indirect route, Protestant critiques of the new learning of Hinduism that he promoted. Wallace was inspired by Brahmabandhab Upadhyay, himself a convert to Catholicism from Hinduism, and a pioneer in the work of establishing a more Indian Catholicism, and Wallace cleared the way for later Jesuits who found Vedānta to be fulfilled in Christ.

Upadhyay thought, and Wallace agreed, that there could be a harmonious and positive transition to Christianity from Hinduism, enhancing but not breaking the former. In turn, in the midst of this ecumenical crisis, an extraordinary opening occurred, in the context of which we can see more clearly a different kind of ecumenical difference. Wallace persuaded the Belgian Jesuits in Calcutta to facilitate the Indological education of bright young Jesuits, who could lead the way in a new, positive approach to Hinduism and its fulfillment in Christ. As a result, in the early twentieth century, an informal school of Jesuit Indology flourished in Calcutta, under the notable leadership of Pierre Johanns (1882–1955) and Georges Dandoy (1882–1962). Johanns and Dandoy cooperated in the famous "To Christ through the Vedānta" essays, published serially in the magazine *The Light of the East*.[28] Johanns himself puts it this way in his introduction:

> From this dispensation the East has not been excluded: rather it received it abundantly. The East has lights already: religious, philosophical, moral. We have no intention to put out these lights. Rather we shall use them to guide both ourselves and our readers on the path that leads to the fulness of the Light. We shall try to show

---

28. See Sean Doyle, *Synthesizing the Vedānta: The Theology of Pierre Johanns, S.J.* (New York: Peter Lang A.G., 2006).

that the best thought of the East is a bud that, fully expanded, blossoms into Christian thought.[29]

M.M. Thomas's critique of Upadhyay in his *The Acknowledged Christ of the Hindu Renaissance* can be taken to represent a Protestant critique of this whole Jesuit movement.[30] Thomas has doubts about the *kind* of Christian intellectual system Upadhyay uses in correlation with Vedānta and with the Vedāntic triad of attributes, *sac-cid-ananda* (being-consciousness-bliss), marking Brahman, the absolute reality. However uncertain one might be about the depth or permanency of Upadhyay's Christian identity, insofar as he was a Christian, he was quite definitely Roman Catholic and even Thomist in his Indian Christian theology. Thomas criticizes Upadhyay's Christology—"Possibly it does not distinguish clearly between the eternal Logos and the incarnate Logos, and therefore lacks the basis of concrete human individuality of Jesus Christ"[31]—but more notably Upadhyay's vision of a smooth completion of Hinduism in Thomism. According to Thomas, Upadhyay treated revelation as if it were a supernatural "extra layer" on top of an intact natural realm that includes already settled cultural and social patterns. Thomas is uncomfortable with this naturalist and non-activist vision of Christianity as perfection- and fulfillment-making[32] since this prevents Upadhyay from critiquing Hinduism sufficiently, and from fully recognizing the potency of grace.

---

29. Pierre Johanns, *To Christ through the Vedānta*, ed. Theo de Greeff (Bangalore: United Theological College, 1996), 3.
30. On Thomas on Upadhyay and the critique in terms of Catholic-Protestant differences, see Francis X. Clooney, "Protestant, Catholic, Hindu: Some Reflections on M.M. Thomas' Assessment of Brahmobandhav Upadhyaya," in *The Life, Legacy and Theology of M.M. Thomas: "Only Participants Earn the Right to Be Prophets,"* eds. Jesudas Athyal, George Zachariah, and Monica Melanchthon (London: Routledge, 2016).
31. M.M. Thomas, *The Acknowledged Christ of the Indian Renaissance* (London: S.C.M. Press, 1969), 109–10.
32. Ibid., 110–11.

None of this is to be taken for granted, since the nature-supernature distinction can and should be much more nuanced in Christian theology. Lipner has defended Upadhyay's Thomism. But for now it suffices to note Thomas's understanding of the matter: a Catholic fulfillment model, whether or not couched in the language of Aquinas, will, from his Protestant perspective, turn out to be woefully lacking.

Like de Nobili and Beschi before him, Upadhyay, the Hindu convert to Catholicism, and Wallace, the Anglican convert who became a Jesuit, ended up holding to a very Catholic view of what the Church was to do in India. Fulfillment and completion were the desired goals for the missionary's work, while an intact Indian society, enriched by faith, was the goal, visibly, in terms of societal outcomes. All of this, of course, might be pushed back against by Hindus, but more immediately by Protestants who could not accept this form of Christianity.

Constructing Global Catholicism

It is a commonplace to observe that Catholic identity is now global, and necessarily open to interreligious engagement. In various cultural settings, the drama of the Incarnation is, as it were, enacted anew, the Word taking flesh in new circumstances. Catholics work with sacramental instincts, proposing that the Bible be imagined and enacted according to a Catholic view of the harmony of nature and grace; arts and literature are given due respect; tradition and traditions are taken seriously; and elite cultures are honored as potentially the best curators and transmitters of truth. The practice of the (Jesuit) missions aimed at the maximalization of cultural adaptation and minimalization of interreligious difference. And yet, as we have seen, the choices of these Jesuits turn out, over and again, to be very Catholic choices, even when doctrine is not at issue.

De Nobili was inventive and innovative, even as he was adhering to a very Catholic paradigm of adaptation in the Roman

Empire, now applied in India. Deep adaptation did, in fact, put aside the Roman model, but still evidenced trust in the model of the Roman Church, such as had worked and would continue to work. Beschi ambitioned a Christian high culture in Asia, and believed that the full resources of revelation, including a Catholic way of expressing the revelation, as well as indigenous religious imagination, could all be employed to tell the Christian story seamlessly and persuasively in India. His was a Catholic way of imagining the liberties that could be taken in the telling of that story. Wallace was rejecting what he condemned as an evangelical debasement of Hinduism, proposed in order to justify the Christian presence in India. Impressed by Hinduism, Wallace found in Catholicism a superior form of Christianity, better suited for engagement with Hinduism. Bouchet's contribution differed in that he saw the value of a more explicit Catholic pushback against the Enlightenment's historicizing and secularizing tendencies—a pushback in part energized by what the missionaries found in India, which supported the plausibility of Catholicism in Europe.

None of these Jesuits was without some or great opposition, though the story of this opposition cannot be told here. Gonçalo Fernandez complained to Goa about de Nobili's methods and his distancing himself from Fernandez's already-established mission.[33] In the early twentieth century, Ernest Hull, S.J., obliquely critiqued the hopes of Johanns and the Calcutta Jesuits for accommodation with Vedānta.[34] Many a Jesuit, Western or Indian, had little time for the learned reading and writing of our four Jesuits. Even if interreligious differences seem most important in India, debates about mission methods will divide as well as unite Christians—and intra-Catholic and intra-Jesuit debates will not be far behind.

---

33. See Fernandez's letter of complaint against de Nobili, in de Nobili, *Adaptation*, 114–20.
34. See Ernest R. Hull, *The Great Antithesis: Hinduism vs. Christianity* (The Examiner, 1923).

While interreligious tensions are on the rise today in India, and while Catholic-Protestant differences have not entirely dissipated, it is perhaps the nature of Catholicism itself that is contested. Charismatic Catholics envision a pure Church that is entirely oriented to Christ and has no time for Hindus or Muslims or others, except to bring them to Christ. Theologians and others dedicated to questions of justice are opting for Dalit theological reflection and critique. While the Church still stands solidly in the midst of Indian society with a confidence in inculturation enhanced particularly by education, this mainstream Catholicism is somewhat marginalized by charismatics and liberationists. The alternative now seems to be the localization of Catholic inculturation, with pride in local culture: Catholicism on the ground. Here Ignatius Hirudayam, S.J. (1910–95), stands as a good example of the effort to allow Catholicism once again to grow in a new (old!) culture, with commitment to ideas and rites, the arts and music, etc.—and without divisive rhetoric about brahmins or others in Indian society.

What Jesuits did and what happened to their experiments is not only a matter of concern for the Society of Jesus. There is no firm wall between competing Christian views regarding how to engage other religions and competing Christian views regarding what is necessary or sufficient to Christian identity. Nor is "what happens in India" reserved for Indians or those interested in India, since every issue raised there is, as we have seen, potentially of wider influence. Every community is, after all, but an example of how the Church might flourish in a different civilization. It is imperative, then, to keep open our eyes, attentive to the changing face of Christianity—in its various forms—in its many encounters with other faith traditions.

Bibliography

Beschi, Constantine. *Vētaviḷakkam. Putuvai: Caṉmavirākkiṇimātākōvilaic cērnta accukkūṭam, 1868.*

Besse. Léon. *Fr. Beschi of the Society of Jesus: His Times and His Writings.* Trichinopoly: St. Joseph's Industrial School Press, 1918.

Clooney, Francis X. "Alienation, Xenophilia, and Coming Home: William Wallace, SJ's *From Evangelical to Catholic by Way of the East.*" *Common Knowledge* 24.2 (2018): 280–90

———. *The Future of Hindu-Christian Studies.* London: Routledge, 2017.

———. "Protestant, Catholic, Hindu: Some Reflections on M. M. Thomas' Assessment of Brahmobandhav Upadhyaya." *The Life, Legacy and Theology of M. M. Thomas: "Only Participants Earn the Right to Be Prophets."* Edited by Jesudas Athyal, George Zachariah, and Monica Melanchthon. New York: Routledge, 2016. 253–68

de Nobili, Roberto. *Adaptation.* Original Latin text with translation by John Pujo. Palayamkottai, India: de Nobili Research Institute, 1972.

———. *Preaching Wisdom to the Wise: Three Treatises by Roberto de Nobili in Dialogue with the Learned Hindus of South India.* Introduced, annotated, and translated by Anand Amaladass, S.J., and Francis X. Clooney, S.J. St. Louis: Institute of Jesuit Sources, 2000. Indian edition, Chennai: Satya Nilayam Publication, 2005.

———. "Some Reflections on Caste according to Fr. J. Bertrand, SJ, 19th-Century French Jesuit." *Indian Church History Review* (December 2009): 148–157.

Doyle, Sean. *Synthesizing the Vedānta: The Theology of Pierre Johanns, S.J.* New York: Peter Lang A.G., 2006.

Dupuis, Louis. *Notice sur La Poésie Tamoule, Le Rév. P. Beschi et Le Tempāvaṇi.* Pondichérry, 1851.

Fr. Bouchet's India: An 18th-Century Jesuit's Encounter with Hinduism (Chennai: Satya Nilayam Publications, 2006), 43–44.

Hoole. Elijah. *Madras, Mysore, and the South of India: or, Personal Narrative of a Mission to Those Countries from 1820–1827.* 2nd ed. London: Longman, Brown, Green and Longmans, 1844.

Johanns, Pierre. *To Christ through the Vedānta*, two volumes. Edited by Theo de Greeff. Bangalore: United Theological College, 1996.

Martin, Fr. Peter. *Letters of Fr. Peter Martin, Madurai Mission, 1699–1713*, typescript in the de Nobili Research Centre, Loyola College, Chennai, India.

Thomas, M.M. *The Acknowledged Christ of the Indian Renaissance*. London: S.C.M. Press, 1969.

Otto, Rudolf. *India's Religion of Grace and Christianity Compared and Contrasted*. Student Christian Movement Press, 1930.

Saulière, Augustin. *Red Sand: A Life of St. John de Britto, SJ*. Madura: De Nobili Press, 1947.

Soares-Prabhu, George, S.J. "From Alienation to Inculturation: Some Reflections on Doing Theology in India Today." In *Bread and Breath: Essays in Honor of Samuel Rayan, SJ*. Edited by T. K. John. Gujarat Sahitya Prakash, 1991: 55–99.

Sweetman, Will. "The Prehistory of Orientalism: Colonialism and the Textual Basis for Bartholomäus Ziegenbalg's Account of Hinduism." *New Zealand Journal of Asian Studies* 6.2 (2004): 12–38.

Wallace, William, S.J. *From Evangelical to Catholic by Way of the East*. The Light of the East Series, no. 35. Calcutta: Catholic Orphan Press, 1923

Xavier, Francis, S.J. *The Letters and Instructions of Francis Xavier*. Translated by M. Joseph Costelloe. St. Louis: Institute of Jesuit Sources, 1992.

Zupanov, Ines. *Disputed Mission: Jesuit Experiments and Brahmanical Knowledge in Seventeenth-Century India*. New York: Oxford University Press, 1999.

Chapter Four

THE RELATIONSHIP BETWEEN ECUMENISM AND INTERRELIGIOUS DIALOGUE: INSIGHTS FROM THE CATHOLIC MISSIONARY EVANGELIZATION OF EASTERN AFRICA

Paul Kollman, CSC

Interreligious dialogue and ecumenism raise many pressing theological issues facing the Catholic Church.[1] When addressing such issues abstractly, however, one can easily forget that interreligious dialogue and ecumenism also embody practices

---

1. See Terrence Merrigan, "Ecumenism and Interreligious Dialogue: The Foremost Challenge for the Churches at the Dawn of the Twenty-First Century," *Louvain Studies* 33 (2008): 159–78. More recent discussions can be found in these two volumes: Vladimir Latinovic, Gerard Mannion, and Jason Welle, O.F.M., eds., *Catholicism Opening to the World and Other Confessions: Vatican II and Its Impact* (Cham, Switzerland: Palgrave Macmillan, 2018); and Vladimir Latinovic, Gerard Mannion, and Jason Welle, O.F.M., eds., *Catholicism Engaging Other Faiths: Vatican II and Its Impact* (Cham, Switzerland: Palgrave Macmillan, 2018).

As Merrigan suggests, these challenges engage all Christians—and I would say, all those desirous of the common good. Mindful of the focus of this volume, however, this paper will examine the Catholic Church in particular, under no illusions that it has all the answers to these vexed issues, nor that Catholics should consider such questions in isolation.

shaped by distinct circumstances and carried out by particular people. Questions like the relationships between Christianity and other religions, the place of the Catholic Church among other Christian bodies, and the role of Christ in salvation—questions that preoccupy theologians addressing ecumenism and interreligious dialogue—arise amid historical encounters of Catholics with other Christians and other believers. Though such encounters raise formal theological questions that are subject to appropriate abstraction and theoretical elaboration, addressing such questions substantially requires inevitably attending to individual and collective human agents acting in complex circumstances shaped by historical and social factors.

Among Christian practices that most directly engage other Christians and other believers, traditional missionary activity has a certain pride of place, since it presumes contact with religious others. This is true though missionary evangelization in practice has also thwarted productive ecumenical relations and a proper approach to other religions. Yet even when missionaries attacked other Christians as dishonest or heretical, and denounced other religions as savagery or foolishness, they nonetheless usually encountered these religious others in person, and not in the abstract or only through texts. Thus, practical considerations invariably affected interactions. In addition, other Christians and non-Christians often occupied a single frame in the missionary imagination: as regular opponents or targets of missionary efforts. The record of historical contacts and missionary predispositions to place other Christians and other religious believers in one frame are reasons that, despite its considerably checkered history, the history of mission has lessons for those interested in engagement with religious others.

The heritage of Christian missionary activity furnishes many pertinent examples for contemporary ecumenism and interreligious dialogue. Important precursors to what we today see as interreligious dialogue, for example, occurred among early modern Catholic missionaries in the Americas and in Asia.² Today, centuries later, interreligious dialogue has become integral to most missiological thought, with early modern Catholics representing important landmark figures in this history.³

Catholics played almost no part in the formal origins of the ecumenical movement, yet a strong link between mission and ecumenism also exists. This is because the modern ecumenical movement arose alongside the late-nineteenth-century upsurge of European Christian missionary activity, especially in Africa and Asia.⁴

Mindful of these missionary precursors, this paper will argue that missionary practice, despite its uneven role, can nonetheless generate historical and practical insight into ecumenism and interreligious dialogue. Guided by that belief, this paper considers the Catholic missionary evangelization of eastern Africa and its approach to other Christians and non-Christians. After a brief historical overview of Catholic mission in the region, it will

---

2. These include Bernardino de Sahagún (1499–1590), a sixteenth-century Franciscan who described the peoples and religions of central Mexico. His near-contemporaries, the Jesuits Matteo Ricci (1552–1610) in China and Roberto de Nobili (1577–1656) in India, also depicted and interacted quite consequentially with non-Christians in Asia. Describing the practices of these figures as interreligious dialogue would be anachronistic, yet certain habits and impulses guiding and motivating some early-modern missionaries to the Americas and Asia resemble instincts sought by many proponents of interreligious dialogue today.

3. Stephen B. Bevans and Roger P. Schroeder, *Constants in Context: A Theology of Mission for Today* (Maryknoll, NY: Orbis, 2004), 174–95; Henning Wrogemann, *Intercultural Hermeneutics* (Downers Grove, IL: InterVarsity Press, 2016), 245–48.

4. Today's World Council of Churches (WCC) was preceded by a number of events organized to coordinate missionary work among Protestants in many parts of the world that were, or were soon to be, subjected to European colonialism. The most notable was the 1910 Edinburgh Missionary Conference, which helped give rise to the International Missionary Council, which in turn helped to form the WCC. See Brian Stanley, *Christianity in the Twentieth Century: A World History* (Princeton: Princeton University Press, 2018), 127–49, 193–215.

proceed to consider how that process engaged the religious others encountered, three types of which merit particular attention. Missionaries considered and represented each as an obstacle to Catholic mission. First, Islam was present in eastern Africa before the Catholic Church appeared and represented the dominant religion at the coast of the Indian Ocean, as well as various points inland. Second, other Christian bodies operated and Catholics often competed with them. Third, African traditional religions pre-existed the arrival of Christian missionaries and persist to this day, sometimes formally and nearly always informally and implicitly.

As will be seen, the Catholic missionary legacy in engaging Islam and cooperating ecumenically in eastern Africa is poor, and not only because interreligious dialogue and ecumenism were rarely self-conscious Catholic missionary priorities. Other factors linked to global and regional conflicts, national rivalries in Europe, and the imposition of colonial governmentality rendered inter-confessional and inter-religious understanding unlikely. Today, historical legacies of negative regard and hostility are less, yet these tendencies persist. With regard to African traditional religions, a theology and set of practices for dialogue and engagement are still under construction, remain urgent, and face significant obstacles that theologians need to address.

The paper will conclude by drawing several lessons from this history. First, it will urge awareness of the ways that historical and social forces realities that shape interactions between Catholics and other religious believers, whether missionaries or not, past and present. In eastern Africa, such encounters with Islam, Protestantism, and African traditional religions all unfolded amid colonialism and its attendant social dynamics, which rendered difficult any serious theological engagement with them by missionaries, at least until national independence. Second, theological assumptions, though easily occluded by practical concerns, become particularly important when constraining structures are lifted, and theological perspectives (indeed, missiological perspectives) must guide future efforts to integrate ecumenism and interreligious dialogue. Recent missiology provides a number of promising developments in this regard, even though missionaries per se recede in practical importance since African Catholics themselves assume prominent roles. Third, eastern African Christian history suggests that inter-Christian competition—sometimes very anti-ecumenical—can create significant growth in churches that take their rivalry seriously. Fourth, African religions represent ongoing challenges for theologies and practices of engagement with religious others as currently conceived, something already seen in early missionary work.

Catholic Missionary Foundations in Eastern Africa

The current Catholic presence in eastern Africa derives from a mid-nineteenth-century reengagement after a century and a half of absence, subsequent to the withdrawal of the Portuguese in the early eighteenth century.[5] Unsurprisingly, European missionaries who arrived in eastern Africa brought habits of representation that, in retrospect, look to be unfortunate postures toward non-Christians and non-Catholic Christians.

For example, one of the earliest public reports on Catholic missionary activity in the modern period in eastern Africa—understood here as the area covered by the nation-states of Kenya, Tanzania, and Uganda[6]—described Islam and Protestantism quite negatively. It appeared in the 1863 *Annals of the Propagation of the Faith,* a journal sponsored by the Society for the Propagation of the Faith, an official Catholic body founded in 1822 in Lyons, France, which collected funds from Catholics to support missionary work around the world. The report, dated August 1862, came from Father

---

5. There had been sporadic missionary work in an earlier period by the Portuguese, but it ended in the early eighteenth century. See Paul V. Kollman and Cynthia Toms Smedley, *Understanding World Christianity: Eastern Africa* (Minneapolis: Fortress Press, 2018), 27–28, 216–17.
6. Ibid., xxvi–xxvii.

Armand Fava, a French priest from Réunion who had overseen the 1860 return of a Catholic presence to the region at Zanzibar after nearly a century and a half's absence. "Mahometanism [sic]," Fava wrote, is "not purely a speculative error," for it was also "a denial of Christian doctrine at every turn." It is, he added, heaping insult onto misrepresentation, "Protestantism in its full development." The "Koran [sic]," he claimed, relishes and emphasizes a "life of sense" while Christianity—Catholic Christianity, that is—holds up the life of faith, drawing on the intellect as well.[7]

Fava's was only the first of many Catholic missionary writings from eastern Africa that denigrated Islam and Protestantism, and later reports regularly justified missionary evangelization by the need to counter Islam and non-Catholic Christian missionary efforts. Fava's successor at the Zanzibar mission, Antoine Horner, in 1870 asked for support from Europe in his expansion into the interior of the continent, lest "the marabout" and "heretics" (shorthand for Muslims and Protestants, respectively) get there first.[8] Attacks on Protestants and Muslims figured prominently in Catholic missionary fund-raising efforts in the half-century that followed, often with dire warnings of non-Catholic advances if support for Catholic work was insufficient.[9]

However we might today lament Fava's and others' denigrations and mischaracterizations of Islam and Protestantism, eastern Africa represents one of the missionary successes of Christian[10]— and Catholic—evangelization in the modern period. In a space of 150 years or so, through the labors of many later missionaries and especially African converts, about 75 percent of its population has

---

7. "Zanzibar," *Annals of the Propagation of the Faith* 24 (1863): 107.
8. *Annals of the Propagation of the Faith* 31 (1870): 41.
9. Paul V. Kollman, *The Evangelization of Slaves and Catholic Origins in Eastern Africa* (Maryknoll, NY: Orbis, 2005), 24–26, 51.
10. Protestant missionaries had arrived several decades earlier and over time achieved similar success. See Kollman and Toms Smedley, *Eastern Africa*, 29–67.

become Christian. Most global Christian bodies have a significant presence in the region, and Catholics constitute the largest Christian group in each country.[11]

Beginning in the 1860s, several Catholic men's missionary societies received Vatican-conferred responsibility for parts of eastern Africa. The Zanzibar mission soon passed to the Holy Ghost missionaries, or Spiritans, and, by the late 1860s, the Spiritans had founded a large mission on the mainland at Bagamoyo. From Bagamoyo, the Spiritans inaugurated other missions farther inland, in what would become Tanzania and Kenya. Then in the late 1870s, the Missionaries of Africa, or White Fathers, arrived, intent on missionary work farther into what they deemed "inner Africa"— namely western Tanzania and Uganda, thus inland from Spiritan areas and, promisingly, far from Muslim interference. Like the earliest Spiritans predominantly French at first, the Missionaries of Africa achieved remarkable success building a large Catholic presence within several decades, especially in Uganda.

Catholic missionary bodies centered outside France also joined. In the 1890s, a conflict with Anglican missionaries and their converts in Uganda—degenerating into a notorious inter-denominational armed battle in 1892—prompted the Missionaries of Africa and the Vatican to ask for English-speaking missionaries for their territory, soon becoming a British colony. Consequently, in the mid-1890s, the Mill Hill missionaries, founded as Catholic missionaries from the United Kingdom though eventually mostly Dutch in membership, arrived to assume Catholic control over eastern Uganda and western Kenya. Meanwhile, ten years earlier, in the mid-1880s, German Benedictines came to what is today mainland Tanzania at the invitation of the Vatican, mindful of the German colonialism then making itself felt. They founded large missions in the southern part of German East Africa—later called Tanganyika, after British control following World War I. In 1902, Consolata

---

11. Ibid., 83–118.

missionaries from Turin, Italy, arrived in central Kenya and soon took over the region around Mount Kenya. The Spiritans, already present, retained responsibility over much of central and eastern Kenya. Meanwhile, in northern Uganda, Comboni missionaries, also Italians and sometimes called the Verona Fathers, who had been at work in Egypt and Sudan since the 1870s, arrived and took over in 1910.

These six male Catholic missionary groups effectively managed the church's life in eastern Africa by the early twentieth century. Sisters usually served with them, also shaping developing Catholic communities in each region, yet the men's groups remained in charge. Each male group had a considerable autonomy where it operated. Though all took direction from the Vatican's missionary office, Propaganda Fide, and received funding from Europe— from the Propagation of the Faith, to whom Fava had written, and other groups—they had different priorities linked to the distinctive nature of their societies, as well as the national and other backgrounds from which they came. Yet all subscribed to Catholic missionary ideals of converting non-Catholics to the one true faith, founding the Catholic Church especially by quickly forming a native clergy, and steering clear of political conflicts when possible. They all faced similar challenges of converting the Africans whom they met, supporting their efforts financially, and adapting to the changing political circumstances on the ground. All acted amid the turmoil of the coming of European colonial overrule, which by the early twentieth century saw the British in charge in what would become Kenya and Uganda, as well as Zanzibar, and the Germans in charge of Tanganyika, or mainland Tanzania. Finally, all faced religious others during their efforts—occasionally as supportive but usually as competitors in their missionary efforts, and, in the case of African traditional religiosity, as the default religious profile of most of those targeted for evangelization.

As Fava's early letter suggests, Catholic missionaries wrote little that models the ideals of ecumenism or interreligious dialogue. In fact, competition, denigration, contempt, ridicule, and undermining of each other featured in missionary discourse—in relation to other Christians and non-Christians. The expressed purpose of Catholic missionary evangelization in eastern Africa was often to combat heresy, paganism, and Islam, each seen more as threat or obstacle than potential partner. This pattern of viewing religious others as foes to be vanquished and errors to be corrected, exemplified by Fava's early letter, persisted well into the twentieth century. Yet the settings in which Catholic missionaries operated placed different religious others in proximity to them, shaping actual historical interactions and evolving perceptions.

To think through the issue without resorting to historical anachronism, therefore, the wrong question is, "How have interreligious dialogue and ecumenism *occurred* in eastern Africa?" They have not much occurred until recently, and even now remain sporadic. A better question is, "How have Catholics in eastern Africa engaged religious others of various sorts? And why?" Catholic missionaries in eastern Africa encountered, first, Muslims; second, Protestants; and third, African traditional religions. What circumstances shaped such encounters? And does this history provide lessons for ecumenism and interreligious dialogue today?

Encountering Islam in Eastern Africa

The Catholic missionaries arriving in Zanzibar in 1860 entered a place under formal Islamic rule by the Sultan of Zanzibar. A strong Muslim presence had existed at the Indian Ocean coast for perhaps a millennium, with sporadic influence as well onto the mainland. Zanzibar's political reach inland, already significant, advanced in 1840 when it became the headquarters of the Sultanate of Oman, the Islamic polity on the Persian Gulf engaged with the island since the late seventeenth century. Though the Sultanate was split between two sons in 1856, with one ruling Oman proper from Muscat, the other son remained in Zanzibar. Zanzibar's consolidation under Omani rule extended its influence, and the Sultan at times claimed power deep onto the mainland, sending caravans from the coast for ivory and slaves.

The Sultan's authority inland was uneven, yet in Zanzibar it was nearly absolute. Consequently, the French Catholic missionaries who arrived there in 1860 did so only with his permission and blessing. The long-term Catholic missionary desire to evangelize the region, beginning from Zanzibar, coincided with the Sultan's hope for a French presence in Zanzibar to counter the vigilantly anti-slavery British. The Sultan also expressed appreciation for the technical prowess and medical care that the missionaries brought. Public preaching, however, was never even requested, so the early Catholic missionaries—like the Anglicans soon to follow them to Zanzibar in 1864—worked with slaves. Each anticipated better opportunities inland, where non-Islamized peoples promised better missionary prospects.

The Spiritans who took over at Zanzibar in 1863, and who oversaw the Catholic presence in eastern Africa for fifteen years before any other Catholic male group arrived, inherited a long history of European depictions of Islam. The Muslims they met similarly drew upon existing views of Christianity. For Muslims, Christianity was a respected but superseded religion. Christians saw Islam variously as a heresy, sometimes as a different religion—in either case denying central Christian truths. Muslims also notoriously resisted Christian evangelization. Both groups also knew that global Muslim power, once formidable, had waned, while European power, with its accompanying normative Christianity, was ascendant.[12]

Catholic missionaries observed that Zanzibar had various types of Muslims in its diverse population—Omanis and Muslims from India, and others from the Middle East and Persian Gulf, not to

---

12. J.D.Y. Peel, *Religious Encounter and the Making of the Yoruba* (Bloomington: Indiana University Press, 2000), 188; Hugh Goddard, *A History of Muslim-Christian Relations* (Chicago: New Amsterdam Books, 2000).

mention local African Muslims.[13] Aside from brief descriptions of that diversity, however, they show little interest in Islam. Instead, they paid attention to the Sultan, since his permission and support allowed them to carry out their work, as well as gain title to land for building residences, schools, clinics, and churches. Moreover, they did not disparage him or Islam in general at great length, wary that their superiors and potential European benefactors deem their missionary enterprise unworthy of support. They usually kept public denigrations of Islam muted and praised the Sultan's generosity and warm welcome. Though they depicted cruelties toward slaves and other vulnerable peoples that, they claimed, typified an Islamic society, they also lauded the social order that allowed them to educate, heal, and worship safely without interference. At times their internal communications mentioned longing for a fuller European—and at times, overtly French—presence, sometimes even hinting at the desirability of colonial overrule. They rarely went so far as to call for intervention, however, before the 1880s.

The experiences of the earliest Catholic missionaries at Zanzibar established a pattern that governed the initial Catholic depictions of, and engagement with, Islam in eastern Africa. Though unfortunate, Muslim rule created a workable social order for organizing a small Catholic presence at the coast while hatching fuller plans for mission on the mainland. There, away from the coast of the Indian Ocean, the absence of Islam—or at least its mitigated presence—promised more evangelical latitude. Missionary engagement with Islam was thus initially pragmatic, and missionaries occasionally even adduced its advantages. Little evidence appears of any serious engagement with Islamic theology or jurisprudence. The overarching concerns remained practical. This was the case even though two of the major Catholic missionary groups, the Missionaries of Africa and the Comboni missionaries, saw encountering and evangelizing Muslims as central to their

---

13. Kollman, *Evangelization of Slaves*, 51–58.

mission, both groups beginning in northern Africa before heading to eastern Africa.

Circumstances on the ground led to important changes in Catholic approaches to Islam in eastern Africa, beginning in the early 1880s. Already the Missionaries of Africa, who ventured farther than the Spiritans into what is now western Tanzania beginning in the late 1870s, had met Muslim authorities in various places inland. Such encounters took place at caravan stopping points where Islam had a notable presence, and where representatives of the Sultan jockeyed with other local political leaders, sometimes violently, for control over trade routes and other issues of local sovereignty. Since the slave trade often figured as a factor in these conflicts, the Missionaries of Africa sometimes depicted local Muslims and indigenous African leaders in relation to their perceived cruelty toward slaves.

Two other historical changes (besides missionary expansion into new areas) raised tensions with Muslims even more than the intermittent conflicts between Zanzibari-linked agents of the Sultan and other African political interests. First, Mahdism arose in the area just north of eastern Africa, in today's Sudan. Beginning first as militant and prophetically inspired Islamic resistance to Egyptian attempts, also Islamic, to control Sudan, Mahdists later attacked the British who supported the Egyptians.[14]

A second, more enduring source of tension came with heightened European engagement with eastern Africa that culminated in colonialism. German adventurer Carl Peters became a catalyst for eventual European overrule when in 1884–85, without Berlin's

---

14. When Lord Gordon died after the siege of Khartoum in January 1885, then allegedly was beheaded by the Mahdi's forces, a new lurid image of Islamic terror entered European consciousness. Forces linked to the Mahdi had also kidnapped several Catholic missionaries in 1882, holding for several years some priests and sisters, with several dying in captivity before their release in 1887. See Mario Cisternino, *Passion for Africa: Missionary and Imperial Papers on the Evangelisation of Uganda and Sudan, 1848–1923* (Kampala, Uganda: Fountain Publishers, 2004), 198–238.

permission, he pursued dubious formal treaties with local African leaders in Tanganyika.¹⁵ As both European colonial pressure and African resistance intensified, Islam served at least partly to unite those opposed first to German and later British colonial claims. Inland, expanded slave-raiding by Zanzibar-linked Arabs led to attacks on missions in the late 1880s.¹⁶ Nearer the coast, as Germans sought to control today's mainland Tanzania, a prominent local Arab Muslim, Bushiri, led a resistance campaign in which a few German settlers and colonial officials, as well as some German Benedictine missionaries, were killed.¹⁷ Many saw Islam as uniting those in the uprising, though Bushiri evinced little of the religious motivation of the Mahdists.

Over the next decades as formal colonial rule advanced—the British over Kenya and Uganda, as well as Zanzibar, and Germans over Tanganyika—Islam remained a dominant coastal presence in Kenya and Tanzania. Certain towns and settlements inland also remained strongholds where Muslim traders settled and local people joined. Missionaries could express satisfaction that Europeans had chastened "insolent Arabs," yet they also protested the ways colonizers, they believed, favored Islam in comparison to Christianity.¹⁸

---

15. Soon the British and Germans especially jockeyed for territory, overtly defending their rights to trade. With the growing pressure, previous cooperation between missionaries and Muslims inland—over the latter's willingness to hand over sick slaves to the missionaries, for example—lessened. See Roland Oliver, *The Missionary Factor in East Africa* (London: Longman, Green & Co., 1952), 98–101.

16. Ibid., 110–11.

17. Frumentius Renner, ed., *Sheltered by God in His Service: Brother Michael Hofer's Memoirs* (St. Ottilien, Germany: EOS, 2008), 60–67.

18. Those active near areas where Islam grew—for example, in southern Tanganyika after World War I—especially lamented its insurgence. On the dynamism of Islam after World War I in the region, see Felicitas Becker, *Becoming Muslim in Mainland Tanzania, 1890–2000* (Oxford: Oxford University Press, 2008), as well as Oliver, *Missionary Factor*, 202–5. On missionary complaints about German favoritism toward Muslims, see Henry Aloysius Gogarty, *Kilima-njaro: An East-African Vicariate* (New York: So-

Missionary complaints were not groundless. German colonial officials in particular relied upon Muslim interlocutors to govern inland regions, and the Benedictines in German East Africa's south decried what they saw as a German preference for Muslims to serve as *akidas* (local officials who represented the colonial government) and *askaris* (soldiers) in the local colonial armed force.[19] In addition, local Muslim authorities at times protested missionary practices, and colonial officials could side with them in defense of traditional customs like initiation rites, countering missionary efforts to reform or end such practices.[20] Though one Spiritan argued that Muslims were not the enemies of missionaries and admitted his admiration of their piety,[21] his confreres lamented when their earliest catechist, Hilarion, became a Muslim after appointment by the Germans as an *akida*.[22] In all of this, there is no evidence of a serious engagement with Islamic thought or Islamic communities in eastern Africa prior to Vatican II. Some of the major Catholic missionary groups—the Consolata missionaries in central Kenya and the Mill Hill missionaries in eastern Uganda and western Kenya—had little need to engage Islam, even if Muslims were many, as in eastern Uganda. Others, like the Spiritans, Benedictines, and Missionaries of Africa, faced conflicts with Muslims—near the coast of the Indian Ocean, in southern Tanzania—and thus could

---

ciety for the Propagation of the Faith, 1927), 30; and Siegfried Hertlein, *Ndanda Abbey,* Part II: *The Church Takes Root in Difficult Times, 1932–1952* (St. Ottilien, Germany: EOS, 2011), 1, 55.

19. Siegfried Hertlein, *Ndanda Abbey,* Part I: *Beginning and Development until 1932* (St. Ottilien, Germany: EOS, 2008), 247–48; Michael Moyd, *Violent Intermediaries: African Soldiers, Conquest, and Everyday Collaboration in German East Africa* (Athens: Ohio University Press, 2008), 170–77; John Iliffe, *Tanganyika under German Rule: 1905–1912* (Cambridge: Cambridge University Press, 1969), 180–99; Hertlein, *Ndanda Abbey,* Part II, 54–55, 84.
20. Hertlein, *Ndanda Abbey,* Part I, 317ff.; Hertlein, *Ndanda Abbey,* Part II, 194ff.; Becker, *Becoming Muslim,* 127–29.
21. Alexandre LeRoy, *Annals of the Propagation of the Faith* 66 (1904): 262–67.
22. Kollman, *Evangelization of Slaves,* 256–60.

not ignore Islam. Yet interreligious dialogue with Muslims was far from Catholic missionary consciousness.

Starting in the years prior to independence, formal dialogue between Catholic missionaries and Muslim groups in eastern Africa began in a tentative way. In 1959, a group of concerned Christian and Muslim leaders founded the Programme for Christian-Muslim Relations in Africa (PROCMURA).[23] Catholics have been prominent among the mixed group of Christians who participate, and in Kenya, Uganda, and Tanzania there are chapters of PROCMURA. In Uganda, the regime of Idi Amin in the 1970s at times used Islam to cement his control, but to little effect. Still, eastern Africa remains a place where interreligious dialogue with Muslims continues to be underdeveloped compared to other places in the world. The colonial legacy continues to animate some Muslims, who see in contemporary nation-states continuations of colonial policies that favored Christians.[24]

The one semi-exception to missionary inattention to Islamic theology was temporary and somewhat inconsequential. In the late 1870s and early 1880s, at the beginning of one of the most celebrated Christian missionary successes in history, the initial evangelization of Uganda brought about the first missionary encounters with Islam in that country. These encounters occurred mostly at the court of the kabaka, or ruler of Buganda, the largest kingdom comprising the soon-to-be-colonized territory. The kabaka in the late 1870s, when both Anglicans and the Catholic Missionaries of Africa arrived, was Mutesa. He had in previous decades received trade delegations and political pressure from Muslims coming from two different directions—from the north, in Sudan, site of the later Mahdi uprising, and from the east, in Zanzibar. Some of his chiefs and sub-chiefs had adopted Islam while most remained traditional believers.

---

23. See the website: http://www.procmura-prica.org/. Accessed March 10, 2019.
24. Kollman and Toms Smedley, *Eastern Africa*, 291–93.

Desiring to keep the Muslims at arm's length, Mutesa, who died in 1884, assuredly saw both groups of missionaries, British Anglicans and French Catholics, as potential support. His court thus at times resembled a debating chamber, with Catholics and Anglicans attacking each other fiercely. Both also parried Muslims—about whose arguments they write very little—all the while mindful of the religious traditions of the Baganda people linked to their *lubaale*, or gods. According to Catholic accounts a few months after their arrival, the Anglican mission leader Alexander Mackay jousted effectively with Muslims, ridiculing alleged Muslim fatalism and defending the divinity of Christ, and a few months later the Catholics say that they attacked the Qur'an and the prophet Muhammad.[25] Yet Anglicans' and Catholics' chief targets in their debates were each other, while Mutesa repeatedly asked for ammunition and firearms.[26]

Meeting Protestant Missionaries

Mutesa's court in Uganda was not the first place that Catholic missionaries had met their Protestant counterparts in eastern Africa, for Protestant missionaries arrived in eastern Africa nearly two decades before the Catholics came to Zanzibar.[27] In the early 1840s, Anglicans of the Church Mission Society, or CMS—so-called

---

25. Archives, Missionaries of Africa, Rubaga Journal, 27 July 1879, 16 September 1879, 20 September 1879.
26. Alexina Mackay Harrison, *A.M. Mackay: Pioneer Missionary of the Church Missionary Society of Uganda* (London: Cass, 1890), 116–33; Kollman and Toms Smedley, *Eastern Africa*, 37–44.
27. The presence of Orthodox Christians in eastern Africa historically has been negligible (Kollman and Toms Smedley, *Eastern Africa*, 70–71, 181–82, 259–60). Some of the early Catholic missionaries who attempted to enter the region from Ethiopia, however, did relate to non-Catholic Christians in that country. See Donald Crummey, *Priests and Politicians: Protestant and Catholic Missions in Orthodox Ethiopia, 1830–1868* (Oxford: Clarendon Press, 1972), especially chapter 4.

"low-church" Anglicans due to their informal liturgical practices and wariness toward Anglo-Catholicism, among other things—arrived in Kenya. None ventured much farther south, so that when Catholics first settled in Zanzibar they were quite far from any Protestants. Thus, Catholic and Protestant missionaries in the early 1860s had almost no contact with each other, the only Protestants in Zanzibar being among the European residents and visitors to the island trading center. This changed in 1864, when Anglicans of the Universities' Mission to Central Africa (UMCA)—so-called "high Anglicans" due to their Anglo-Catholic prayer styles, their predilection for episcopal prominence, and other features of their religious practice—came to Zanzibar itself after a failed mission on the Zambezi River to the south.

The initial descriptions by Catholic and Anglican missionaries of each other in Zanzibar reflected longstanding prejudices. As was the case with Islam, the Catholic missionaries who came to eastern Africa arrived predisposed to distrusting Protestants, in this case shaped by tensions between Catholics and non-Catholics in Europe.[28] The mostly French missionaries among the Spiritans and Missionaries of Africa knew the history of French anti-clericalism, which waxed and waned through the nineteenth century and into the twentieth, and Catholic polemics could link Protestantism and anti-Catholicism in France. German Catholic missionaries arrived in the mid-1880s just as the *Kulturkampf*, in which the newly formed German state curbed Catholic institutional life quite dramatically, was dying down, yet Catholic fears lingered. English Catholic missionaries, too, came from a place where the Catholic Church had only a half-century before achieved public recognition after several centuries of opprobrium and intermittent persecution. Even Italian Catholic missionaries came as citizens of a nation-state whose recent historical emergence reflected anti-Vatican—at times,

---

28. Jean-Paul Wiest, "Roman Catholic Perceptions and Critiques of British and American Missions, 1807–1915" (Position paper 73, North Atlantic Missiology Project, Cambridge University, 1998).

anti-Catholic—sentiments. Catholic missionaries derisively linked European Protestantism to "rationalism" that was drying up faith everywhere, or the "pretended rights of man" that undermined proper Catholic control of the state, and missionary publications recounted Protestant efforts to undermine Catholics around the globe.[29]

Yet in practice, cordiality was common. At Zanzibar, relations between the mostly French Spiritans and the Anglican UMCA, both of whom arrived in the 1860s, were typically warm. In many practical ways the two groups assisted each other—sharing insights into language and culture, providing hospitality and medical care when need arose. Later Catholic missionaries who used Zanzibar as a supply post for their eastern Africa efforts also got along with the Anglicans. Still, the long history of mutual antagonism in Europe did not remain hidden. The diaries, letters to mission superiors, and public reports of both groups are replete with abuse of the other, detailing grievances recent and longstanding. Bitter descriptions of the Anglicans fill Catholic reports to their superiors in Europe and broader publications, with the Spiritans quick to repeat local opinions that diminished their rivals' efforts and exalted their own.[30]

The antagonisms at Zanzibar remained both muted in public and ultimately rather unimportant in light of later history. Neither mission grew there, nor extensively near the mainland coast. Even as they moved inland, where both Catholic and Protestant missions expanded away from the Muslim environment, new territory stretched in every direction so that physical contact during evangelization itself was infrequent. Caravans inland led by each group sought and received assistance from the other on their stops, but their work brought them together only rarely. When proximity put them in contact, competition for converts and territory could prompt mutual recriminations. Still, such language within reports had little impact on actual evangelization, whether by Catholics or

---

29. *Annals of the Propagation of the Faith* 33 (1872): 218; *Annals of the Propagation of the Faith* 50 (1889): 344.

30. *Annals of the Propagation of the Faith* 28 (1867): 34.

other Christians, in what is today Tanzania, at least into the early twentieth century.

As the nineteenth century moved into the twentieth, many other Protestant groups sought to evangelize in eastern Africa: Methodists, Baptists, Presbyterians, Lutherans, and other German groups spurred by German colonialism in Tanganyika, as well as so-called faith missions in the late nineteenth century, then later Pentecostals. Due to their respective geographic dispersal and the timing of their arrivals, different Catholic missionary bodies met different Protestant counterparts. Spiritans and Missionaries of Africa encountered different kinds of Anglicans in Zanzibar, Uganda, some of Kenya, and parts of Tanganyika. Benedictines met Anglicans and numerous German groups in southern Tanganyika. Consolata missionaries met Presbyterians and numerous smaller groups in central Kenya, while Mill Hill missionaries met Anglicans in Uganda and many Protestant groups in western Kenya. Combonis encountered Anglicans in northern Uganda.

The advance of colonialism created new antagonisms as Catholics and Protestants found themselves linked to different colonizers, and both sought to advance their evangelical, educational, and territorial ambitions in changing political circumstances.[31] Throughout the region a "schools race" emerged in the first half of the twentieth century,[32] with resources expended in rivalries that especially sought to bring the sons of influential chiefs into their respective Christian-sponsored settings for education, all the while satisfying expectations of colonial officials to educate a populace for colonial governance.

In Uganda, 1,500 kilometers inland, inter-Christian tensions peaked. Whatever harm might have been caused by lack of ecumenical amity at the coast or elsewhere in eastern Africa pales in comparison to the damage and mutual sabotaging that occurred, beginning at the

---

31. Renner, *Sheltered*, 133–34; Hertlein, *Ndanda Abbey*, Part I, 59ff: Hertlein, *Ndanda Abbey*, Part II, 98–103, 345; *Annals of the Propagation of the Faith* 61 (1889): 47ff.
32. Kollman and Toms Smedley, *Eastern Africa*, 144–49.

kabaka Mutesa's court in Buganda and continuing into the colonial period. There the poisonous relations established between leading Anglican and Catholic missionaries in the first years had disastrous consequences, even well into the post-independence period.

The highly charged atmosphere in Uganda in the late 1870s and 1880s, though formative of Anglican-Catholic tensions for a long time there, was unusual in that Protestant and Catholic missionaries operated at close quarters in the king's court, sometimes on a daily basis. Yet proximity was not the only cause of the heightened rivalry, for other reasons raised the stakes in the eyes of both groups of missionaries to Uganda. Already in the mid-1870s, Anglicans and Catholics had read reports from Henry Morton Stanley about the kingdom of Buganda, describing a centralized and comparatively civilized political order led by an enlightened, if violent, king. Stanley's reports excited Protestant missionary societies and the Vatican, not to mention the Missionaries of Africa. Unlike the Islamized coast of eastern Africa, as well as the territory of Kenya and most of German East Africa that were allegedly inhabited by de-centralized peoples who were difficult to evangelize, here was a place that resembled the European kingdoms of old. These predecessors of contemporary nation-states, many national origin stories in Europe told, underwent Christianization following the conversion of their kings in late Antiquity and the early medieval period. Mutesa could be a new Clovis, eager missionaries—Anglican and Catholic—imagined, bringing an entire people to faith, something much more momentous than the creating of small mission outposts and the evangelization of slaves.

Seeing this gleaming possibility, the European Christians attacked each other vociferously in Uganda, hoping to bring the kabaka to their side with the boilerplate accusations of the day.[33] Amid all this, the important aspect of the interreligious conversations and contestations at Mutesa's court from a historical perspective

---

33. Ibid., 37–44.

is not their content. Nor was it in fact that Mutesa himself was present. Mutesa certainly skillfully played the groups of visitors against each other—Anglicans, Catholics, and also Muslims—all the while also soothing the feelings of his own traditional priests. Yet he would soon die, replaced by his son, having successfully maintained Buganda's detachment from any single religious identity, especially a foreign one.

Instead, more important than the rulers or the recriminations were the young palace apprentices whom the missionaries called "pages" listening attentively to the debates between the European groups. Often sons of prominent chiefs from among the Baganda or neighboring groups, their curiosity already piqued by Islam and literacy, these ambitious youths soon gravitated toward the European missionaries. Both missionary factions expressed astonishment at the earnest zeal of the young (mostly) men who came to them, baptizing them more rapidly than the guidelines they had received allowed. Such pages comprised the majority of the Uganda Martyrs of the mid- to late 1880s, sentenced to death by Mutesa's son Mwanga. Other early converts among the pages became the leaders among the huge groups of Anglican and Catholic converts starting in the late 1880s and continuing over the next decades.

In fact, many have argued that the competition between the Anglicans and Catholics, though deplorable from an ecumenical perspective to be sure, helped expand both groups, first among the Baganda, then elsewhere in Uganda.[34] Rivalry between Christians advanced growth among Christians, something that can also be observed in the heavily Christian area around Mount Kilimanjaro in northern Tanzania, where both Catholics and Lutherans were numerous.

In Uganda, the coming of colonial overrule, in which Anglicans enjoyed favorite status, cemented the Catholic-Anglican rivalry, which persisted through most of the twentieth century and still

---

34. Kollman and Toms Smedley, *Eastern Africa*, 37–44, 55–57.

can be felt at times.³⁵ The restriction of Catholics first to the region around Masaka, then to other chieftaincies in a series of attempted accommodations of their complaints, reinforced the differences between the two groups. The coming of the Mill Hill missionaries, who were non-French, arose from attempts to mitigate the tensions by presenting Catholics as less stridently anti-British, yet even in Mill Hill territories similar tensions arose.³⁶

Uganda was especially volatile, but nineteenth-century antagonisms between Catholics and Protestants in eastern Africa persisted well into the twentieth century and continue in some places. Both sides claimed that the other had more resources—the Catholics complaining about Protestant money, connections to colonial authorities, and skilled teachers; Protestants lamenting the more numerous Catholic missionary priests and the appeal of supposed Catholic superstition to credulous African converts. Each claimed that its evangelizing strategy created better converts than the other, accusing their opponents of watering down the faith to ease conversion.³⁷

In the twentieth century, Protestants advanced ecumenically among themselves, especially in Kenya and Tanzania, where there were numerous non-Catholic Christian groups—unlike Uganda, where Anglicans dominated.³⁸ Catholics never formally engaged as participants in those processes until the late twentieth century, but ecumenical relations among Lutherans, Anglicans, Presbyterians, and others—usually beginning around so-called comity arrangements that respected each other's missionary territory without encroachment—advanced significant inter-Christian cooperation by the 1920s.³⁹ Catholics at times informally abided by comity arrangements, but the Vatican forbade them, so Catholic

---

35. Oliver, *Missionary Factor*, 139–46; Kollman and Toms Smedley, *Eastern Africa*, 112–18.
36. Kollman and Toms Smedley, Eastern Africa, , 41–42.
37. Ibid., 83–118.
38. Oliver, *Missionary Factor*, 222–27.
39. Kollman and Toms Smedley, *Eastern Africa*, 52–55, 63–64.

participation was unofficial. Meanwhile, Catholics could mock Protestant ecumenism, arguing that all groups in these agreements abandoned their hitherto central principles.[40]

Ever-Present African (Traditional) Religion(s)

The first modern Catholic converts in eastern Africa tended to be slaves whom missionaries brought to their missions through various means. Protestants near the Indian Ocean followed the same strategy. Both defended this approach, which self-restricted public evangelization, in light of the Islamic milieu. The evangelization of slaves, who came from diverse places and cultures, predisposed missionaries to downplay cultural and related religious differences of local peoples, at least in the beginnings and at the coast, where converts were few. Consequently, missionary appreciation for pre-existing ways of being religious remained muted.[41]

Inland, as missionaries met other people groups in less Islamized settings, such inattention to African cultures and the religious sensibilities that went with them quickly became impossible to maintain. Already in the late 1860s, Catholic Spiritan missionaries noted the variety of people-groups in mainland Tanzania and the diversity of their religious practices.[42] The Missionaries of Africa, as they moved toward Uganda in the late 1870s, described the alleged religion of peoples they encountered, following the stern commands of their founder to depict local customs.[43] Yet missionaries understandably focused their energies on negotiating sites for new

---

40. Robert Hugh Benson, *Annals of the Propagation of the Faith* 77 (1914): 2–4.
41. Kollman, *Evangelization of Slaves*, 272–73.
42. Antoine Horner, *Annals of the Propagation of the Faith* 31 (1870): 39–41.
43. For Lavigerie's *Instructions*, see the *Cardinal Lavigerie Anthology*, collected and ed. Jean Claude-Ceillier (Rome: Society of Missionaries of Africa History Series), volume II (2017), 140–57, at 156, and volume III (2018), 5–47, at 44. In the archives of the Missionaries of Africa, the journal of Fr. De-

missions in politically unsettled circumstances, and on forming in faith the vulnerable people who usually came to their missions: refugees and former slaves, for example.

Until the early twentieth century, therefore, few Catholic missionaries were inclined to view the customary beliefs and practices of African peoples as "religion." Instead, they called such beliefs and practices "customs," and those objectionable found their way into missionary strategies of eradication. Examples of customs fought included polygamy, infanticide, and initiation rites that featured what the missionaries deemed obscene words and deeds.[44]

Missionaries usually ignored African religions well into the twentieth century, blaming resistance to their message on superstition's grip on potential converts, often highlighting the deleterious power of local healers, or "witchdoctors," who assumed the role in much missionary discourse as archenemies of Christianity and civilization.[45] African catechists were among those most critical of traditional religious practices that persisted. Witch-finding movements, often leading to stigmatization or harm to those deemed to have caused local misfortune, also faced predictable missionary opprobrium.[46]

---

niaud, dated 22 August 1878, describes the religious beliefs and practices of the Wagogo, where the missionaries stopped on their trek inland.

44. Among many examples, see Kollman, *Evangelization of Slaves*, 200–201. For a fuller discussion of the difficulty for outside observers to appreciate African religions, see Paul Landau, "'Religion' and Christian Conversion in African History: A New Model," *The Journal of Religious History* 23:1 (1999): 8–30. There were occasional exceptions, for example in the Missionaries of Africa archives, Rubaga mission journal, dated 14 August 1879, the writer describes the three main "idols" of the *lubaale* religion of the Baganda. Less than a month later, however, the same writer on 14 September 1879 claims that the Baganda have "no religion."

45. For example, see F. F. Bugeau, "Sorcerers of Kikouyou," *Annals of the Propagation of the Faith* 72/73 (1909–1910): 16–22; Gerard Rathe, *Mud and Mosaics: An African Missionary Journey from the Niger to the Copper Belt* (Westminster, MD: Newman Press, 1960), 141–42, 177–78.

46. Lambert Doerr, ed., *Peramiho 1898–1998: In the Service of the Missionary Church*, Vol. 1 (Ndanda-Peramiho, Tanzania: Benedictine Publications, 1998), 140–41.

Over time, reflexive missionary dismissal of such customs waned. Like other European observers, missionaries presented fuller descriptions of ritual practices observed and local beliefs as gleaned from conversations with Africans. Missionaries described the religious lives of African people-groups among whom they worked, and larger and more centralized groups drew missionary appreciation more naturally. Thus the Missionaries of Africa described the religious beliefs of the Baganda, while Consolata missionaries did the same for the Kikuyu in Kenya,[47] and Spiritans for the Chagga around Mount Kilimanjaro.[48] Missionaries working among diverse peoples recognized that cultural-linguistic variations also meant religious differences. German Benedictines in southern Tanzania, for example, evangelized both patrilineal and matrilineal people-groups. They struggled to develop coherent and consistent pastoral practices across their territory due to these differences, especially linked to practices of bride-wealth and initiation. These operated differently, reflecting how descent was determined and shaping respective cultural-religious practices.[49] By the 1920s, the Missionaries of Africa could describe the diverse religious lives of people-groups among whom they worked in Uganda and Tanzania.[50] Mill Hill missionaries, whose territory spanned eastern Uganda and western Kenya, also worked among very diverse people-groups with associated cultural and religious practices.

A variety of overlapping Catholic missionary approaches and opinions emerged. Some observers, for example, Catholic and

---

47. See the discussion of the Consolata missionaries in Samuel G. Kibicho, "The Continuity of the African Conception of God into and through Christianity: A Kikuyu Case-Study," in *Christianity in Independent Africa*, eds. Edward Fasholé-Luke, Richard Gray, Adrian Hastings, and Godwin Tasie (Bloomington: Indiana University Press, 1978), 370–88.

48. Gogarty. *Kilima-njaro*, 45–47.

49. Hertlein, *Ndanda Abbey*, Part I, 317–20, 346; idem, *Ndanda Abbey*, Part II, 158–74, 179–81.

50. J. Bouniol, *The White Fathers and Their Missions* (London: Sands & Co., 1929), 212–84.

Protestant, saw the religious beliefs of eastern African peoples as evidence of a prior Christian identity erased over time.[51] Missionaries thus thought of themselves as restoring a latent religious sensibility.

Others tried to use existing religious beliefs to advance Christianity. As missionary awareness grew about the coherence that these beliefs provided local peoples, and their resilience in the face of criticism, certain missionaries sought to leverage local assumptions about sources of power to undermine people's attachment to them and demonstrate the new vitality of Christianity. For example, during a period of tension between the throne and the missionaries, the kabaka of Buganda in 1885 sent the Missionaries of Africa in Kampala emaciated animals, which they recognized as an attempt to curse them in line with traditional beliefs. Instead of immediately discarding the animals and engaging in practices to reverse the curse—the expected practice following local logics—the missionaries instead ate the animals, seeking, the missionary reported, "to swallow all the evils that threaten the Baganda."[52]

Beginning in the late nineteenth century, certain missionaries began to gain an appreciation for the sophistication of African religions and subject them to academic study. These included Alexandre LeRoy, a Holy Ghost missionary in Tanzania and Kenya who later became the first professor of the history of religions at L'Institut Catholique in Paris as well as Archbishop and Superior General of his congregation. The Protestant missionaries Edwin Smith and John V. Taylor of Great Britain, and the German missionary Bruno Gutmann, also showed keen appreciation for African religions, shaped by eastern African experiences. Beginning in the 1950s, scholars of African religions, some of them African Christian clergy, argued that the normative African traditional cosmology

---

51. Frederick Tusingire, *The Evangelization of Uganda: Challenges and Strategies* (Kisubi, Uganda: Marianum Publishing Company, 2003), 19–22.
52. Rubaga diary, *Chronique Trimestrielle* 32 (1886), citing entry of 25 November, 1885. Thanks to Alison Fitchett Climenhaga for this reference.

was compatible with Christianity. Many discerned in African religions a generally distant high god with numerous lesser spirits, sometimes ancestral. According to most of the earliest African theologians, that high God was in continuity with God as revealed in Christianity, identical with the God of Jesus Christ, a position commonly assumed among contemporary African theologians.[53]

Even today, however, challenges exist in attempting to engage African religions with theological approaches deriving from contemporary interreligious dialogue. One such challenge lies in determining the number of African religions, or in older terminology, African traditional religions. Are they many, linked to the variety of ethno-cultural-linguistic identities and corresponding people-groups in Africa? Or are they uniform, or nearly so, in important emphases, all united at a deep level despite considerable variations? Contemporary African theologians tend to emphasize the unity of African religion—in the singular—over their predecessors in the colonial or immediate post-independence periods, who sought to respect the cultural integrity of particular groups, and crafted African theology in relation to cultural specificity.[54]

A second challenge lies in assessing the status of African religion vis-à-vis Christianity and, by extension, Islam. Is it best seen as in competition with Christianity and Islam, or as preparation for—and often ongoing vitality with—identities linked to Christianity and Islam?[55] Different groups of Christians and Muslims evince varying degrees of comfort with ongoing features of traditional religiosity in their adherents.

A third concerns the nature of religious authority in African religions. Who speaks for these religions in any dialogical

---

53. Kollman and Toms Smedley, *Eastern Africa*, 172–90.
54. Ibid., 172, 187.
55. Laurenti Magesa, "On Speaking Terms: African Religion and Christianity in Dialogue," in *Reconciliation, Justice, and Peace: The Second African Synod*, ed. A.E. Orobator (Maryknoll, NY: Orbis Books, 2011).

undertaking?[56] Very often engagement between and among religions takes place among clearly authorized leaders of such groups, yet African religion(s) often has less formal leadership roles, which creates obstacles to productive dialogue.

Conclusion

The foregoing historical overview of Catholic evangelization in eastern Africa and accompanying missionary approaches to religious others encountered suggests a dubious legacy. Yet these events from the past can teach us much. Here I conclude with four possible lessons.

First, the Catholic missionary focus until the latter twentieth century, at least in eastern Africa, preoccupied as it was with saving souls and founding the church, did little to conduce toward serious ecumenical and interreligious engagement. The operative Catholic missionary imagination prior to Vatican II—often cartographic and historical as well as theological in its lineaments—initially put other Christians and believers in other religions into the same category: that is, as targets of missionary evangelization. Yet missionary instincts also operate within time and space, thus facing practical issues. These often join instinctive predilections, as in this case, to undermine any possibility of ecumenism and interreligious dialogue. In eastern Africa, such practical issues included European denominational prejudices that generated polemics and antagonism, collective distortions about Islam that shaped missionary prejudices,

---

56. Missiologists are beginning to address this issue. See Jim Harries, "Intercultural Dialogue—An Overrated Means of Acquiring Understanding Examined in the Context of Christian Mission to Africa," *Exchange* 37 (2008): 174–89. For a more recent reflection by an African sociologist, see Ludovic Lado, "Experiments of Inculturation in a Catholic Charismatic Movement in Cameroon," in *The Anthropology of Catholicism: A Reader*, eds. Kristin Norget, Valentina Napolitano, and Maya Mayblin (Berkeley: University of California Press, 2017), 227–42.

racism, and colonialism. Colonial interference could favor one Christian group at the expense of another, as it did when the British intervened on behalf of Anglicans in Uganda, thus hampering Catholic evangelization. Colonial interference could favor Islam, something that German colonizers in eastern Africa stood accused of by Christian missionaries. In light of this, it is unsurprising that both ecumenism and interreligious dialogue remained undeveloped in eastern Africa until the 1960s. Even in the post-colonial period, the most notable examples of productive interreligious and ecumenical relationships have been prompted by practical concerns, with little engagement around theological matters. Examples include cooperation among Christians in Uganda during the regime of Idi Amin, when Catholics and Anglicans worked together since both faced oppression. More recently, all three countries have seen episodic violence linked to Islamic extremism. Since it has been usually traceable to outside agents instead of Muslims in eastern Africa, this has led to new forms of Christian-Muslim cooperation.[57]

Second, regardless of such practical realities, the theology of mission matters, and contemporary theologies of mission need to learn from limitations within theological motivations in the past. Fortunately, there have been commendable efforts to advance Catholic missiological thought, embodied in Vatican II's *Ad Gentes*, Paul VI's *Evangelii Nuntiandi*, John Paul II's *Redemptoris Missio*, and subsequent teachings such as the document *Dialogue and Proclamation*, not to mention reflection by many eminent theologians. Catholic missionary thought today embraces ecumenism and the best practices and ideals of interreligious dialogue. Such thought has had little practical impact in eastern Africa, but there are signs that it advances in some circles.[58]

---

57. Kollman and Toms Smedley, *Eastern Africa*, 291–93.
58. Frans Wijsen, *Seeds of Conflict in a Haven of Peace: From Religious Studies to Interreligious Studies in Africa* (Amsterdam: Rodopi, 2007). See also Benjamin Durheim and David Farina Turnbloom, "Tactical Ecumenism," *Theological Studies* 76 (2015): 311–29.

Third, African traditional religions—or African religion, as some would prefer—remain a religious other of a different sort, with no clear way to engage them/it. On the one hand, many missiologists and other theologians acknowledge its persistence in the lives of many African believers; yet, at the same time, becoming conscious of its role in shaping faith is very difficult. Thus dialogue with it—as in the case of religions like Islam or other Christian bodies—becomes nearly impossible. The dialogue of necessity become implicit, interior, in some ways personal for each African believer, as he or she considers how Christian faith calls them from certain aspects of their cultural-religious inheritance and more deeply into others.

Fourth and finally, it is somewhat disturbing that Christianity in eastern Africa—Catholic and non-Catholic—grew most quickly and has grown most strikingly in places where inter-Christian rivalries were acute and often bitter. A polarized evangelical reality can inspire missionary resolve. It seems that denominational forms of Christianity grow when more than one denomination is at work in a given area, and where both are strong.

God's mission in the world is one, and it is our privilege and task to participate in it. Learning from missionary practices of the past remains an ongoing way to advance our participation in that mission in the present.

Bibliography

Bevans, Stephen B., and Roger P. Schroeder. *Constants in Context: A Theology of Mission for Today*. Maryknoll, NY: Orbis, 2004.

Cisternino, Mario. *Passion for Africa: Missionary and Imperial Papers on the Evangelisation of Uganda and Sudan, 1848–1923*. Kampala, Uganda: Fountain Publishers, 2004.

Gogarty. Henry Aloysius. *Kilima-njaro: An East-African Vicariate*. New York: Society for the Propagation of the Faith, 1927.

Hertlein, Siegfried. *Ndanda Abbey, Part I: Beginning and Development until 1932*. St. Ottilien, Germany: EOS, 2008.

———. *Ndanda Abbey, Part II: The Church Takes Root in Difficult Times, 1932–1952*. St. Ottilien, Germany: EOS, 2011.

Iliffe, John. *Tanganyika under German Rule: 1905–1912*. Cambridge: Cambridge University Press, 1969.

Kollman, Paul V. *The Evangelization of Slaves and Catholic Origins in Eastern Africa*. Maryknoll, NY: Orbis, 2005.

———, and Cynthia Toms Smedley. *Understanding World Christianity: Eastern Africa*. Minneapolis: Fortress Press, 2018.

Latinovic, Vladimir, Gerard Mannion, and Jason Welle O.F.M., eds. *Catholicism Engaging Other Faiths: Vatican II and Its Impact*. Cham, Switzerland: Palgrave Macmillan, 2018.

———. *Catholicism Opening to the World and Other Confessions: Vatican II and Its Impact*. Cham, Switzerland: Palgrave Macmillan, 2018.

Magesa, Laurenti. "On Speaking Terms: African Religion and Christianity in Dialogue." In *Reconciliation, Justice, and Peace: The Second African Synod*, edited by A.E. Orobator, 25–36. Maryknoll, NY: Orbis Books, 2011.

Oliver, Roland. *The Missionary Factor in East Africa*. London: Longman, Green & Co. 1952.

Renner, Frumentius, ed. *Sheltered by God in His Service: Brother Michael Hofer's Memoirs*. St. Ottilien, Germany: EOS, 2008.

Wrogemann, Henning. *Intercultural Hermeneutics*. Downers Grove, IL: InterVarsity Press, 2016.

CHRISTIAN UNITY IN THE AGE OF GLOBAL ENCOUNTERS

Chapter One

ECUMENISM FROM THE VIEWPOINT OF THE PONTIFICAL COUNCIL FOR PROMOTING CHRISTIAN UNITY

Bishop Brian Farrell

Let me start with Pope Francis's most recent reference to ecumenism (December 21, 2017). His words offer a good framework for the points that I would like to make.

In his Christmas speech to the Roman Curia he mentions ecumenical relations as "an essential requirement of our faith, a requirement that flows from the depth of our being believers in Jesus Christ." It is one of the Church's "irreversible commitments."

Then he makes an interesting point. Without using the terminology of "dialogue of truth" and "dialogue of life," he makes a clear distinction between them and, in a sense, makes a preferential option for the dialogue of life. The theological and ecclesiological differences that still divide Christians will only be overcome along the path of a shared "journey." Catholics "walking together with other Christians, meeting as brothers and sisters, praying together, working together in the proclamation of the Gospel and in service to the least. Doing this we are already united."[1]

---

1. See https://w2.vatican.va/content/francesco/en/speeches/2017/december/documents/papa-francesco_20171221_curia-romana.html.

The second point that he makes is that this journeying together demands "untying the knots of misunderstanding and hostility, counteracting prejudices and the fear of the other: all of which prevent us from seeing the richness in diversity and the depth of the mystery of Christ and the Church. For that mystery is always greater than any human words can express." The whole is greater than the parts.

The journey that Francis is proposing is about Catholics, Orthodox, Anglicans, and Protestants "walking together." Without forgetting the ultimate ecumenical goal of the visible communion of all the baptized, but realizing that that goal, which will be a gift of God, needs an appropriate climate—a fertile ground—Pope Francis wants to concentrate on the journey itself, not on the final goal.

Based on his understanding of the search for Christian unity, Francis calls for a shift from the traditional mode of ecumenism— the search for progressive notional agreement—to a methodology of "life together": a real sharing in and of what Christians hold in common, with respect for the differences that remain complementary and do not reach the level of contradiction. Differences are, in fact, not all of the same weight! The churches would move towards one another, giving priority to the essentials that already unite them, without using their differences as a reason to continue living and acting separately. The first step, then, would be for the various Christian communities no longer to "compete with one another," but to work together for one fundamental goal: the preaching of the Gospel to every creature.

Francis had already presented this vision of ecumenism in *Evangelii Gaudium*: "If we concentrate on the convictions we share, and if we keep in mind the principle of the hierarchy of truths, we will be able to progress decidedly towards common actions of proclamation, service and witness."[2] Ecumenism for the sake of mission—this, briefly, is the outline of the ecumenism that Pope

---

2. Para. 246.

Francis is introducing through his style, his words, and his exhortations. Notably, Francis introduced his talk to the Curia by saying that his reflections were based not only on fundamental principles, but also "on the personal vision that I have sought to share with you in my addresses of recent years, within the context of the reform currently underway." Reform of the Church and ecumenism go hand in hand.

In practice, divided Christians would, in fact, really begin to practise the "Lund principle"—formulated by the World Council of Churches in 1952—which Pope Francis explicitly recommended to the Plenary Assembly of the Pontifical Council for Promoting Christian Unity shortly after his return from Lund in November 2016,[3] where he took part in the joint ecumenical commemoration of the fifth centenary of the Reformation: to "act together in all matters except those in which deep differences of conviction compel them to act separately."

I. The Whole Is Greater Than the Parts....

There are many ways in which such an idea applies to the quest for Christian unity.

Not much over sixty years ago, our Catholic part thought it was the whole, with enormous consequences for Catholic relations with other Christians and their churches. Still today, a marginal part of the Catholic world refuses to see that the catholicity of the Catholic Church itself is defective, as long as there is division among the baptized. Certain Orthodox circles are closed to admitting spiritual bonds with the non-Orthodox; and of course "restorationist" Protestants hold that they alone are the one true Church. The idea that the part is the whole is still present.

---

3. See https://w2.vatican.va/content/francesco/en/speeches/2016/november/documents/papa-francesco_20161110_plenaria-unita-cristiani.html.

Most of the bishops who arrived in Rome for the Second Vatican Council in 1962 held very definite views on Catholic exclusivism. The miracle is that in three short years the whole body of the bishops moved to a clear recognition that not only are other Christians our brothers and sisters in Christ because of our common baptism and other shared elements of grace and faith; but that God uses their communities for salvation. With this change of perspective, a door that had been closed for centuries was opened, and the Catholic Church launched itself vigorously into the ecumenical movement.

There is an interesting entry in Yves Congar's *Diary of the Council,* for Friday, November 30, 1962, a time of an open clash of ideas in the Council hall. That morning he had a testy meeting with Cardinal Ottaviani. He writes: "I realize that I am still, as always, under suspicion.... They don't like my work because, and they know it, it aims are recirculating certain ideas that for four hundred years, but especially in the last hundred, they have tried in every way to eliminate."[4]

What "certain ideas" does he have in mind? Exactly what the Council eventually proposed: namely, that the Church is not a "perfect society" modeled on Roman legal structures, but a mystery of communion—the communion of the Father, Son, and Holy Spirit that flows from the resurrection of Christ and is endlessly communicated to the baptized by the Spirit, especially through the liturgy.[5] In other words, a return to a more traditional, patristic, sacramentally grounded ecclesiology! So the Second Vatican Council did not invent a new vision of the Church or a new ecclesiology, but merely returned to something more traditional. A longer, broader, more profound continuity thus came into play.

And Pope Francis's efforts to reform Church life and governance are not introducing a revolution, but merely trying to apply *Lumen*

---

4. Yves Congar, *Diario del Concilio (1960–1963)* (Edizioni San Paolo: 2005), 278. My own translation.

5. See *Acta Synodalia Sacrosancti Concilii Oecumenici Vaticani II*, II/5, 543.

Gentium, Unitatis Redintegratio, and all the other parts of Vatican II that speak of what the Church is and how she should organize and fulfill her mission. Again, I hope to return to Pope Francis and his reform later.

The point that I am trying to make is simply that this change of perspective is still a work in progress and that, while recognizing the enormous ecumenical achievements in the intervening years, Pope Francis offers the opportunity to advance a change in perspective, and therefore to accelerate the pace of ecumenical progress.

II. *The Pontifical Council for Promoting Christian Unity*

The Pontifical Council for Promoting Christian Unity (PCPCU), in addition to developing and organizing inter-Church relationships, visits, celebrations, etc., organizes and is involved in at least seventeen formal dialogues, as well as takes part in many multilateral relationships and activities. Whole libraries are needed to tell the story of the PCPCU's ecumenical engagement since its establishment in 1960 by John XXIII.

Allow me to mention just two areas of our work: one from the Eastern section and one from the Western, as two of the most significant and promising parts of the journey towards full communion.

1) The Eastern Orthodox

An important phase of this dialogue concluded in 2007 with the "Ravenna Document," entitled *"Ecclesiological and Canonical Consequences of the Sacramental Nature of the Church: Ecclesial Communion, Conciliarity and Authority."* For the first time, Catholics and Orthodox together agreed that at every level of the ontological structure of the church—the local church, the regional communion of churches, and the universal Church—there must be primacy and synodality: no primacy without synodality, no synod without its primate. At the universal level, according to the ancient order (*taxis*) of the Churches, the *protos* is the Bishop of Rome. Still, the question looms: What are the prerogatives of that Roman primacy?

The Commission's work is conditioned by centuries of controversy and polemic regarding the role of Rome, and must make its way forward with great sensitivity towards profoundly held attitudes. It took nine years of exhaustive study and mostly inconclusive discussion to finally reach an agreed position. In September 2016, at a Plenary Session held in Chieti, Italy (after three failed Plenary sessions in Paphos 2009, Vienna 2010, and Amman 2014), the Joint International Commission agreed on a document entitled: "Synodality and Primacy in the First Millennium: Towards a Common Understanding at the Service of the Unity of the Church."[6] It is a short document, but solidly rooted in theological and sacramental principles already agreed upon in previous documents of the Commission. It recognizes that the relationship between primacy and synodality (collegial relations between bishops rooted in the communion of all the faithful in the Church) at the various levels of the Church is analogous and is concretely realized in very different ways. The document is careful to formulate matters as they were experienced in the life of the Church in the first millennium, avoiding any intrusion of elements that resulted from developments in the second millennium.

Developments in the first millennium regarding papal primacy are presented as a locus of divine guidance in the life of the Church, without indulging in theological interpretations of those developments, about which Orthodox and Catholics sometimes have divergent views.

To give an example: the Chieti document affirms that, from the fourth century, in the West the primacy of the Bishop of Rome was

---

6. See http://www.vatican.va/roman_curia/pontifical_councils/chrstuni/ch_orthodox_docs/rc_pc_chrstuni_doc_20160921_sinodality-primacyen.html.

increasingly understood as a prerogative tied to the fact of his being the successor of the Apostle Peter.[7] It recognizes that this view never prevailed in the Churches of the East. But the fact that Catholics and Orthodox acknowledge that in the first millennium there existed two distinct theological traditions that diversely justified the primacy of the See of Rome and its Bishop, without, consequently, effecting a break in communion between the Churches of East and West, is a significant step forward.

The Chieti document, then, synthetically presents the practical patterns of the exercise of Roman primacy in the first millennium. It examines the liturgical order of the patriarchs, the role of the Bishop of Rome in the reception of councils as ecumenical, and his role in receiving appeals even from the Churches of the East. It is important to point out that the Chieti document underlines the fact that the Bishop of Rome exercised these prerogatives in a synodical way, either in association with the bishops of other important sees or in the context of the Roman synod itself.

Some of this may seem a bit minimalistic and might even come as a kind of shock to some Catholics. The language of universal jurisdiction, for example, which Catholics immediately associate with the Pope, is very much a concept and terminology of the second millennium and is therefore absent from the Chieti study.

There is a guiding principle here: the restoration of unity is not a matter of uniformity or of the absorption of one Church by another, but of spiritual and sacramental communion in the legitimate and enriching diversity of the many ways the Gospel of Jesus Christ has been assimilated and experienced by peoples and cultures. At the moment of the restoration of communion between East and West, nothing can be demanded that did not belong to the experience of the Church in the time when East and West were in communion. In this sense, the first millennium is not meant to become the perfect model of a future united Church, but to

---

7. Para. 16.

mark the sufficient and irrenouncible structures and dynamics that would have to be recognized in that reunited Church.

The Commission's study of the interdependence between synodality and primacy is timely and especially relevant. The recent celebration of the Pan-Orthodox Council, with all its limits, can only be understood as a genuine exercise of synodality and primacy as the Orthodox world sees them—while Pope Francis's efforts to give new weight to the concept of synodality within the Catholic Church is a fundamental part of the reform he is leading, and is extremely important for the restoration of the unity of Christians.

When Pope Benedict could say, at a public Angelus Prayer (June 29, 2007[8]), that with the Orthodox Churches we Catholics are already in almost complete communion, he was not ignoring the difficult journey ahead, but was stating a fact: with God's help, the remaining obstacles will be overcome through the Churches helping each other to correct within themselves any unilateral developments that have occurred down the centuries. When they see that the whole is much greater than the separate parts, they will embrace each other in fully restored love.

2) Relations with the Protestant World

In 1521 Pope Leo X excommunicated Luther as a notorious heretic; 495 years later Leo's successor traveled to Lund, solemnly to commemorate with the Lutheran World Federation the 500th anniversary of the Reformation.

The idea that perhaps best describes how a common commemoration of the Reformation became possible can be found in the Joint Statement[9] signed by Pope Francis and Bishop Younan during the common prayer at Lund: "While the past cannot be

---

8. See http://w2.vatican.va/content/benedict-xvi/en/speeches/2007/june/documents/hf_ben-xvi_spe_20070629_costantinopoli.html.

9. See https://w2.vatican.va/content/francesco/en/homilies/2016/documents/papa-francesco_20161031_omelia-svezia-lund.html.

changed, what is remembered and how it is remembered can be transformed." This is the principle that, in ecumenical dialogue, guides the process called "purification of memory": the search for a more truthful way of understanding and judging the deep disagreements that have given rise to separation.

Social memory works by stereotyping the adversary and by selecting those parts of history that support our particular view of ourselves as the good ones, the ones who were unjustly treated and hurt. Listening carefully to the other leads to correcting our unilateral perceptions and to recognizing that, behind the confrontation, there remains a substantial unity in diversity. This is not about being nice or naive. Purification of memory can only be realized on the basis of a deeper understanding of the truth of things, overcoming the deformed truths transmitted from generation to generation in service of each confession's identity and self-affirmation.

On the basis of solid scholarship, Catholics recognize that Luther had a genuine right to be scandalized at the idea that the eternal salvation of souls, and first of all his own, was subordinated to a "system," including indulgences, almost a trade-off, run by Churchmen who were not always examples of good conduct and theological competence. It was to be expected that his criticism, which went straight to the heart of that system, would draw a strong reaction. At the same time, Lutherans recognize that Luther's temperamental excesses and the religious, social, and political upheaval he sparked led not to the reform of the Church, but to its division.

Five centuries of conflict, rivalry, and prejudice between Catholics and Protestants can only be overcome through a profound conversion—a journey in the opposite direction—that allows the churches together to discern and take up the much that is positive in the Reformation, and to distance themselves from the mistakes and exaggerations that led to division. Ecumenical dialogue is an effort to see things as the other part sees them, and to harvest what is good in each tradition, learning and receiving from one another. Here too the whole is much more than the separate parts.

III. Ecumenism in the Time of Pope Francis

It is easy to point to the splinters in the eyes of my Orthodox and Protestant brothers and sisters. But what about the ecumenical splinters in Catholic eyes? In other words, what is happening in the Catholic Church that gives us solid hope for movement towards the restoration of unity?

Let me offer a context. Around the year 2000, the World Council of Churches organized a consultation to reflect on the progress of the ecumenical movement in the twenty-first century. Many communions took part, including Catholic participants. The consultation pointed out that "the churches have entered the twenty-first century aware that their differences have emerged in new ways...[,] that the goal of full and visible unity has been eclipsed by a return to institutional concerns, the defense of their sectarian identity and a return to fundamentalism...[, and that] ecumenism seems to have passed from the prophetic edge to a comfortable centre."[10]

So, as a Catholic I ask: Where in the Catholic Church can we see that "prophetic edge" capable of promoting growth in communion with our ecumenical partners? Vatican II's Decree on Ecumenism told us where to look: "renewal of the Church is...the basis of the movement toward unity.... Church renewal has therefore notable ecumenical importance."[11] So, according to the Council, ecumenism and Church reform go hand in hand. Many Catholics and many of our ecumenical partners perceive a "newness" in Pope Francis's ministry—in attitudes, gestures, and intentions, which has profound implications for the ecumenical movement. At bottom, all ecumenical reflection ultimately faces

---

10. World Council of Churches, "Ecumenism in the 21st Century," Report of the second meeting of the Continuation Committee, Belem, Brazil, 10–17 January 2009.
11. *Unitatis Redintegratio*, para. 6. See http://www.vatican.va/archive/hist_councils/ii_vatican_council/documents/vat-ii_decree_19641121_unitatis-redintegratio_en.html.

this question: How might the churches reform in order to be more faithful to God, to Christ, and to the Gospel? And how they can help one another in this process, and learn from one another? This is where walking together becomes more than mere rhetoric. We are actually helping each other to address the serious questions that all Churches are wrestling with today.

Every Pope since Saint John XXIII has recognized that a different, broader sharing of authority and responsibility and accountability—a genuine practice of the collegial and synodical nature of the Church—is needed if the Church's dialogue with its own members, with the rest of the Christian world, and with the vast world outside Christianity is to succeed. The choice is either to lock ourselves up in a fortress and refuse to accept any responsibility for what happens in the rest of the human family, or to be strong in faith and grace in order to be convincing witnesses to the saving power of the Cross of Jesus Christ in every human context. This is precisely what Pope Francis means when he talks about a church that is outgoing, a church that is a field hospital.

So, among other things, he is asking how we can re-imagine the ministry of the Bishop of Rome, of bishops and bishops' conferences, in search of a "genuine practice of the collegial and synodical nature of the episcopate." To this end, he writes, "I too must think about a conversion of the papacy. It is my duty, as the Bishop of Rome, to be open to suggestions which can help make the exercise of my ministry more faithful to the meaning which Jesus Christ wished to give it and to the present needs of evangelization."[12] As he said at the commemoration of the fiftieth anniversary of the Synod of Bishops, on October 17, 2015: "The Pope is not, by himself, above the Church; but within it as one of the baptized, and within the College of Bishops as a Bishop among Bishops, called at the same time—as Successor of Peter—to lead the Church of Rome which

---

12. *Evangelii Gaudium*, para. 32.

presides in charity over all the churches."[13] Likewise, he proposes a profound renewal of Bishops' Conferences: "since a juridical status of episcopal conferences which would see them as subjects of specific attributions, including genuine doctrinal authority, has not yet been sufficiently elaborated."[14] In short, fifty years after the Second Vatican Council, some core aspects of the Council's vision of the Church are being re-presented as a reform that can no longer be postponed.

Many see this kind of reform as a major source of hope for ecumenism in the twenty-first century. It will indeed be such if the Church finds the courage to re-assimilate an ecclesiological vision valid in the first millennium, detaching itself from elements too closely linked to the juridical and political notions that strongly influenced Catholic ecclesiology in the second millennium. This decisive challenge cannot be seriously met by a Church that prefers the "comfortable centre" to the "prophetic edge."

Bibliography

Congar, Yves. *Diario del Concilio (1960–1963)*. Cinisello Balsamo: Edizioni San Paolo, 2005.
Original edition: *Mon journal du concile*, I et II. Paris: Les Editions du Cerf: 2002.

---

13. See http://w2.vatican.va/content/francesco/en/speeches/2015/october/documents/papa-francesco_20151017_50-anniversario-sinodo.html.
14. *Evangelii Gaudium*, para. 32.

Chapter Two

REVITALIZING THE FADING ECUMENICAL MEMORY AND REENERGIZING THE PROMISE OF OUR ECUMENICAL FUTURE: CAN ECUMENISM BE TAUGHT?

J. Jayakiran Sebastian

Introduction: A "Fooled Ya'" Moment?

The translator extraordinaire, Sarah Ruden, whose recent rendition of Augustine's *Confessions* has opened evocative vistas into this venerable work, in reflecting on the translators' task takes us back to the time where she was learning Hebrew:

> Don't be like me, sitting in beginning Hebrew class during the fourth week of the term and becoming convinced that this was all a practical joke, and that any moment the teacher would whip out the real, logical rules, exclaiming "Fooled ya!" As it is elements as simple (you'd think) as prepositional phrases may be quite different from verse to verse, depending on such variables as their

placement in a clause, and sometimes for no apparent reason.[1]

Having recently completed a semester-long course on "Ecumenism in the Twenty-First Century: Challenges and Opportunities" at the United Lutheran Seminary, I could be forgiven if, following our intense journey through the history of the ecumenical movement, our students were disappointed that there was not a "Fooled Ya" moment in the class where I could say, "It's far easier than that. Let's all just get along, shall we?" and this, after innumerable visits to https://www.oikoumene.org/en; patiently enduring lots of examples drawn from the Indian context; detailed readings of ecumenical documents ranging from *Baptism, Eucharist, and Ministry* (1982)[2] to *The Church: Towards a Common Vision* (2013);[3] after trying to get them excited as we marked the 500th year of the Protestant Reformation[4] on the convergence between

---

1. Sarah Ruden, *The Face of Water: A Translator on Beauty and Meaning in the Bible* (New York: Pantheon Books, 2017), 163. As an already accomplished scholar of ancient Greek and Greek classical writings, she goes on to exclaim, "Luckily, ancient Greek, in contrast to Hebrew, inhabits the Stoic empyrean of rationality and consistency. Yeah." Her translation of Augustine is *Confessions: A New Translation by Sarah Ruden* (New York: The Modern Library, 2017).

2. *Baptism, Eucharist and Ministry*, Faith and Order Paper No. 111 (Geneva: World Council of Churches, 1982).

3. *The Church: Towards a Common Vision*, Faith and Order Paper No. 214 (Geneva: World Council of Churches Publications, 2013).

4. A sober, frank, and pointed look back at 500 years of Protestantism and what this movement has meant and continues to mean today is found in Alec Ryrie, *Protestants: The Faith That Made the Modern World* (New York: Viking, 2017). One such assessment states: "Protestantism's formal and informal divisions are not about to heal. Protestants will not run out of things to argue about, and while some arguments will simmer down, others will flare up. Formal denominational structures will continue to weaken. There will be more independent, self-governing congregations, and where denominations hold together, they will do so by becoming loose

many Protestant families and the Roman Catholic Church on the doctrine justification;[5] attempting to get them involved in ongoing work of reconciliation after the tragic violence inflicted by the Protestants on the Anabaptists[6]—all in a class in which I had students from the Lutheran, Presbyterian, Episcopalian, Baptist, African Methodist Episcopal, United Methodist, and Pentecostal persuasions, not to say anything about, in some cases, those who had made very convoluted journeys through other denominations and faith-traditions to get where they were at that point.

---

confederations. The reality of a democratic age is that churches are answerable to the footloose believers who fund them" (456).

See my "Celebrating the Dynamic Legacy of the Reformation—An Indian Perspective," in *Reformation Observances: 1517–2017*, ed. Philip D. W. Krey (Eugene, OR: Cascade Books, 2017), 43–68.

5. My syllabus instructions read: "Come prepared and ready to discuss the *Joint Declaration on the Doctrine of Justification: The Lutheran World Federation and the Roman Catholic Church* (Grand Rapids, MI: Eerdmans, 2000), which exemplifies one of the best bilateral dialogue outcomes. Please read it through, paying attention especially to section 4 (4.1–4.7) and its structure. You can browse through the following link to get some ideas on the bilateral dialogue between the Roman Catholics and the Lutheran Churches: http://www.vatican.va/roman_curia/pontifical_councils/chrstuni/sub-index/index_lutheran-fed.htm.

"The 'Pontifical Council for Promoting Christian Unity' gives you a good idea about how the Roman Catholic church is involved in and contributes to the ecumenical movement: http://www.vatican.va/roman_curia/pontifical_councils/chrstuni/."

6. Again, my syllabus states: "Related to this, check out sections of one more example of how the bitter legacy of the Reformation is being addressed, this time between the Lutheran World Federation and the Mennonite World Conference through the process reported in *Healing Memories: Reconciling in Christ—Report of the Lutheran-Mennonite International Study Commission* (Geneva, Switzerland: The Lutheran World Federation / Strasbourg, France: The Mennonite World Conference, 2010).

"This document is also interesting in that it addresses the issues of baptism in relation to how the church understands civil authority."

A Personal Note

Permit me to step back for a minute and indulge in reminiscence about the fortuitous family connection that has convinced me that our future on this our inhabited earth has to be an ecumenical and interfaith one—a recollection that I never tire of. The question of ecumenical and interreligious dialogue has been part of my faith journey from my middle school days. From 1968, when I was in Grade 4 and ten years old, material from the World Council of Churches (WCC), along with postcards from different parts of the world, arrived at my house in Bangalore from my uncle who had just joined the staff of the WCC, after having taught at the United Theological College, in Bangalore, for a number of years. In 1971, he became the first director of the program then called "Dialogue with Men of Living Faiths" at the WCC, and went on to reshape this program as "Dialogue with People of Living Faiths and Ideologies" and organize a number of path-breaking conferences and edit numerous publications, details of all of which continued to come home regularly and were avidly devoured by me, even though several of the concepts were rather fuzzy. My uncle, Dr Stanley J. Samartha's, annual visits, complete with slide projector, served to humanize his work and to open up for me the promise, potential, and indeed the vital necessity of dialogue. It took some time for me to understand that dialogue could not be manufactured in Geneva, but that my neighborhood, the place where we lived, the school where I studied, the church where I worshipped, the compound in which I played, the city of Bangalore itself, were all fertile fields to practice and perceive the meaning of dialogue in community at multiple levels, the cheek-by-jowl presence of worshipping communities and worshippers, all going about the business and busy-ness of everyday life.

This initial enthusiasm has never left me and played a strong role in my subsequent decision to go to seminary and become a pastor and later professor, and throughout my career as a parish priest, first full-time, and then as an honorary associate minister, I have been fascinated by the promise and peril of dialogue across the spectrum. The opportunity to serve for many years at the United Theological College in Bangalore, and now, for the last thirteen years, at the Lutheran Theological Seminary at Philadelphia, which in July 2017 consolidated with its sister seminary at Gettysburg to form the United Lutheran Seminary,[7] have only broadened my appreciation of the vital necessity of keeping the flame of dialogue alive, even as all kinds of forces threaten to extinguish and pull back on the many gains that have been made down the years.

The Fading of Ecumenical Memory

As a teacher, I could spend a lot of time in this section lamenting the loss of ecumenical memory and trying to analyze the reasons for this and to offer ways and means of restoring this in the present context. However, given my teaching experiences, I would like to list the following observations, not in judgmental terms, but as a sober reality:

- The word "ecumenical" was an alien concept to a vast majority of my students.
- Very few of them had heard about the World Council of Churches or even the National Council of Churches in the USA.
- None of them seemed to be aware that at the national level, many of the so-called Mainline Protestant denominations were engaged in ecumenical activity all over the world.
- Hardly anyone had browsed the websites of their local, national, or international church bodies with the intent to find out if there were wider connections and interconnections

---

7. See Maria Erling, "How We Were Joined," *Seminary Ridge Review* 20, no. 1 (2017): 15–24.

between and among church bodies. The only thing that seemed to "click" was the mention of mission trips.

Among the books that we used, two by the veteran ecumenical thinker Michael Kinnamon seemed to resonate immediately with the class. The more recent one, which was required reading, posed the question as to how a renewal movement itself could best be renewed, and proceeded in fifteen chapters to interrogate and respond to sharp questions, like Chapter 14: "What Will It Take to Revitalize the Ecumenical Movement?"[8] It is in concluding this section that Kinnamon writes:

> Ecumenical Christians today may be less optimistic than our earlier colleagues, but surely we have no less reason to hope for the day when one part of Christ's body will not say of another, "We have no need of you." Perhaps our role in such a time as this is to keep alive such hope—and to call ourselves to demonstrate the credibility of our hope by acting together, in response to God, to help make it so.[9]

While acknowledging the major gap in their ecumenical awareness, and while pointing out that several of them had engaged in service activities across various divides without necessarily recognizing this kind of engagement as "ecumenical," I must say that my students—once they got over the "Why didn't we know about this?" response and recognized quickly that "reception" had indeed happened in various ways in their communities of faith without a label being put on it—hope indeed surfaced and there was a shift to positive celebration about what had been and what could be. Obviously a sobering note was injected by Kinnamon who, in

---

8. Michael Kinnamon, *Can a Renewal Movement Be Renewed? Questions for the Future of Ecumenism* (Grand Rapids, MI: Eerdmans, 2014).

9. Ibid., 159.

his earlier book (which was a "recommended" textbook for our course), poignantly and pointedly asked as to whether the "insiders" or ecumenical bureaucrats had in some way contributed to the emaciation of ecumenical memory and vitality.[10]

Reenergizing the Promise

One of the pleasures of being a teacher is recognizing the growing awareness and appreciation of something that has meant so much to you with yet another cohort of students. I have seen this happen through the word-for-word reading and interactive "annotating" of the three sections of the BEM document in three of my courses: Baptism in the course "Baptism and the Unity of the Church," Eucharist in "The Lord's Supper and the Fellowship of the Church," and Ministry in the course that I just finished teaching this last semester (the very course that I mentioned earlier). Each time, I was energized by my students' gradual recognition of the significance of this incredibly rich ecumenical document produced by the Faith and Order Commission as Study Paper No. 111, now more than thirty-five years ago. However, I also alerted them to the growing cottage-industry of publications ranging from congregational Study Guides to major journal articles, from collections of essays to a compendium of responses from the churches, not to say anything about the rapid translation of this into a variety of vernacular languages.

I still remember taking copies of the BEM document that had been translated into my mother tongue, Kannada, to the rural village congregations where I began my ministerial journey and

---

10. Michael Kinnamon, *The Vision of the Ecumenical Movement and How It Has Been Impoverished by Its Friends* (St. Louis, MO: Chalice Press, 2003). There is an unambiguous call to repentance in the conclusion of this book, and Kinnamon writes: "If renewal of the church is our *ultimate* goal, then we have missed the ecumenical (the *oikoumene*-centered) vision set forth in scripture" (119).

using it in the first confirmation classes that I taught. To see the document come alive in young members coming from the so-called untouchable Dalit backgrounds, a few of whom were illiterate, and all trying to equip themselves for life in a rapidly globalizing India, despite limited access to modes of formal education, was gratifying and deeply satisfying.[11] I have experienced this time and again in class settings in Bangalore and Philadelphia.

At the same time, I am aware of the admonition of my teacher in his reflections commemorating the twenty-fifth anniversary of the publication of the document, in which he remarks:

> Even if the churches agree on the basic theological understandings concerning baptism, eucharist, and ministry as presented by the BEM document, in order to accept and recognize each other's baptisms, eucharistic celebrations, and ministries, there are yet more things which have to take place. As important as BEM was and is, it by no means convers all the areas of division among the churches. In addition to this, it seems that new areas of possible division are developing since the response process for BEM.[12]

---

11. I have written about my experiences in this pastoral setting in several places, including "On Walking through the Cemetery: Continuity and Transformation in Reading Death in an Indian-Christian Community," in *Postcolonial Interventions: Essays in Honor of R. S. Sugirtharajah*, ed. Tat-siong Benny Liew (Sheffield: Sheffield Phoenix Press, 2009), 178–89, and "Evoking the Bible at a Funeral in an Indian-Christian Community," in *Colonialism and the Bible: Contemporary Reflections from the Global South*, eds. Tat-siong Benny Liew and Fernando F. Segovia (Lanham, MD: Lexington Books, 2018), 187–97.

12. Jacob Kurien, "From '*anamnesis*' to '*metanoia*'—Beyond Convergence Texts, towards Attitudinal Conversions," in *BEM at 25: Critical Insights into a Continuing Legacy*, eds. Thomas F. Best and Tamara Grdzelidze (Geneva: WCC Publications, 2007), 272.

While facing the uncomfortable reality that "new areas of possible division are developing" we should at the same time recognize, along with a veteran ecumenist reflecting on BEM after thirty years, that "we need today, urgently, many small groups of ecumenical interest as well as many small areas of ecumenical progress in order to create a climate of listening and enriching each other."[13]

In class, along with the many resources that were made available and accessed, the textbook that accompanied us was a comprehensive and carefully chosen collection of ecumenical documents.[14] In their preface, the editors express the hope that the "volume will serve the training and education of young ecumenical leaders all over the world. Through reading these texts, may they be inspired by the ecumenical work that has been done in the generation before them. Through learning about the ecumenical past and present, may they empower themselves to shape the future of ecumenism in the years to come."[15] Except for quibbling with the use of "young" (given the age range in my class and my conviction that the fostering of ecumenical sensitivity cuts across age distinctions), I have found that attention to ecumenical texts, statements, thinking, and processes does have the power to inspire. As examples, let me offer some passages from documents that we examined:

- From the rich surprises that a reading of the BEM document always stimulates, a comment in the "Commentary" section on the Eucharist argues that, "in the light of the biblical conception of memorial, all churches might want to review the old controversies about 'sacrifice' and deepen their understanding of the reasons why other traditions

---

13. Hans-Georg Link, "The Lima Process: *After Thirty Years*," *The Ecumenical Review* 65, no. 3 (2013): 367.
14. Mélisande Lorke and Dietrich Werner, eds., *Ecumenical Visions for the 21st Century: A Reader for Theological Education* (Geneva: WCC Publications, 2013).
15. Lorke and Werner, "Editors' Preface," in *Ecumenical Visions*, xvii.

than their own have either used or rejected this term."[16] Hence, for those who have taken their own denominational traditions for granted, or, even more strikingly, have not interacted with or thought about their own denominational traditions in a serious and sustained manner, the invitation to understand another's point of view and its Biblical, theological, and pastoral background and implications is a welcome call to move beyond the superficial slogans to the possibility of an in-depth interaction—especially in a world that, on the surface, appears increasingly connected, but in reality seems to encourage even more isolation.

- From the evident sincerity of the more recent "The Church: Towards a Common Vision," which valiantly tries to move away from a "least common denominator" approach to a theologically nuanced attempt to talk about the church, we read that "[o]ne blessing of the ecumenical movement has been the discovery of the many aspects of discipleship that the churches share, even though they do not yet live in full communion."[17] There is no doubt that there is a high level of frustration about the many things that continue to divide us, including questions about the appropriate way to read and understand the Bible, teaching on sexuality and hierarchy, the popularity of prosperity- and success-oriented megachurches, divisions at the table of the Lord, experiences of not being made to feel welcome during visits to local faith communities, and the sometimes startling

---

16. *BEM*, part of the Commentary on section 8 of "Eucharist."
17. "The Church: Towards a Common Vision," part of section 68. A crisp response from the Indian theologian Peniel Jesudason Rufus Rajkumar, now the World Council of Churches' Program Executive in the area of inter-religious dialogue and cooperation, is found in his article "A Prophetic, Polysemic and Proleptic Prompt," *The Ecumenical Review* 65, no. 3 (2013): 338–41, where he writes: "In the Indian context the question of unity cannot be discussed without denouncing the sin of casteism, which cuts through and across church denominations" (339).

recognition that even within what seemed like comfort zones of shared theological values, political opinions could vary wildly. The struggle to understand the consequences of faithful discipleship, which includes partnering across the many divides in moving beyond the simplistic slogan of "doctrine divides but service unites," has been seen as an important aspect of our shared commitment to reconciliation and transformation.

- In the 2005 WCC document "Christian Perspectives on Theological Anthropology," we read about the "visible manifestations of a broken world, such as acute forms of poverty, increased violence and suffering, but also…new challenges to humanity, posed, for example, by pandemics such as HIV/AIDS. The conflicts arising all over the world through ethnic, cultural and religious differences now affect us immediately."[18] Given the ongoing commitment of individuals, local communities, and denominations to addressing persistent health challenges and the eradication of diseases like leprosy and dracunculiasis (Guinea worm disease), the ongoing commitment to provide and subsidize the therapy related to antiretroviral drugs to treat those afflicted by HIV/AIDS, and the use of local materials including treated mosquito nets to contain the spread of malaria, not to say anything about gun violence on the streets of Philadelphia, it is encouraging to recognize the investments of individuals in the private-public-NGO-faith-based partnerships—partnerships that the ecumenical movement has done so much to foster and nurture.

---

18. Reprinted as "Christian Perspectives on Theological Anthropology, Faith and Order Study Document, Geneva, 2005," in *Ecumenical Visions for the 21st Century*, 147–65. Here part of paragraph 18 on 149.

Conclusion: Can Ecumenism Be Taught?

The influential cultural critic Gayatri Chakravorty Spivak in many of her writings has raised the question of teaching and being taught. There is a difference between talking at and "teaching to change mental habits." She talks about "a long-term education which is a kind of non-coercive rearrangement of desires."[19] The huge number of documents, insights, reports, and analysis generated by ecumenical and interfaith programs worldwide, ranging from the great international conferences organized down the years by the World Council of Churches and the Pontifical Council for Christian Unity, the reception by the churches of documents like *Ecumenical Considerations for Dialogue and Relations with People of Other Religions* (2004),[20] which built on the famous *Guidelines on Dialogue with People of Living Faiths and Ideologies* (1979), the undoubted and persistent trickle-down of this at the level of National Councils of Churches, Bilateral Dialogues, interfaith groups, local congregations, and "mission" statements cannot be lost down the ecumenical memory hole or relegated to the vagaries of "It's all available on the Internet" or "You can find it stored here in our library." Instead, they must receive a fresh lease on life so that these brittle pages will flutter again and that the black words on white paper or the pixels arranged on the screens of electronic devices will continue to inspire, instruct, challenge, and critique the situation in which we are today. We cannot be those who regret the loss of ecumenical memory, but the group that nourishes and enlivens this, since I am convinced that ecumenism and this way of life can be taught and learned.

Given the reality in places like India—the laboratory of dialogue—where all kinds of exciting things happen, but also the place where horrible and destructive eruptions of violence (often under a

---

19. See Swapan Chakravorty, Suzana Milevska, and Tani E. Barlow, *Conversations with Gayatri Chakravorty Spivak* (London/New York/Calcutta: Seagull Books, 2006), 24, and the earlier quote on 41.

20. Found in *Ecumenical Visions for the 21st Century*, 332–36.

misguided sense of nationalism[21]) have led to the tragic loss of life throughout her history, we need to understand that while attempts to look for certain commonalities and a shared vocabulary are all welcome and worthy pursuits, the honest interrogation of difference, perceptions of history, understandings of identity, limits of "toleration," and the majority-minority questions, along with the reality of believing and belonging, are all issues and themes that need renewed and concentrated attention today.[22] The search for the lowest common denominator or the "essentials," while well meaning, seems to me to be misguided. Indeed, an honest recounting and interrogation of difference is an unrelenting and pressing task.

Recognizing that we meet to address "The Whole Is Greater Than Its Parts: Christian Unity and Interreligious Encounter Today," and that we are attempting to draw interconnections between ecumenical dialogue and interreligious or interfaith interaction, I would like to say that I have noticed easy slippages but also substantial overlap in terms of approaches and outcomes. Slippages include the supposition that there is something the "same" about the two undertakings, which leads to hasty generalizations and quick assumptions. Unless there is a substantial amount of "tidying up" that is done when handling the mass of data that we have on ecumenical questions, we risk carrying disentangled luggage into the broader work of interfaith interaction. Samartha subtitled one of his books,

---

21. See my "Neither Fellowship or Patience, nor Toleration or Acceptance: Believing, Belonging, Luther, the Jews, and Questions on Contemporary Nationalism," *Seminary Ridge Review* 20, no. 1 (2017): 3–14.

22. One attempt to recover the work of an ecumenical pioneer is my "'Only Christ and No Formulation of Christ Can Determine the Frontier': J. Russell Chandran's Ongoing Challenges to Christian Ecumenism," in *A Light to the Nations: The Indian Presence in the Ecumenical Movement in the Twentieth Century*, ed. Jesudas M. Athyal (Geneva: World Council of Churches, 2016), 143–52, notes 238–40. The entire book offers much to think about and re-appropriate in today's context, not just in India but in the worldwide ecumenical task.

"Ecumenical Issues in Inter-Religious Relationships,"[23] thereby pointing to the mutuality as well as the distinctiveness of ecumenical and inter-faith dialogue. In addition, in subsequent writings he raises many questions regarding being and doing, believing and practicing, all located within his unflinching testimony to the centrality of one's commitment to Christ,[24] a commitment not diluted by the affirmation of pluralism, since, as he writes: "Where absoluteness of the absolute is acknowledged, and the relativity of relatives accepted, Truth is cherished because, then, it does not become the possession of any one particular community. Plurality does not relativise Truth; it relativises different responses to Truth."[25] This is not to say that in ecumenical endeavors there is some special way in which certain things must be done, sorted out, packaged neatly, and then used as a stepping-stone to interreligious work, but to recognize that there is much to be done in terms of calmly, soberly, sincerely, and humbly recognizing where we have reached in our ecumenical dialogues and the undoubted gains all over the world where people of goodwill from all kinds of religious and ideological commitments are willing to interact with one another, without shirking difficult conversations and hard questions. A re-appreciation of these gains, as well as an honest and sober recognition of the roadblocks in the last 100 years will be of salutary benefit to the broader dialogical enterprise.

Coming to terms with the rich complexity and glorious simplicity of the message of the man from Galilee should not be an embarrassment, but a necessity for those of us whose ecumenical

---

23. S. J. Samartha, *Courage for Dialogue* (Geneva: World Council of Churches, 1981).
24. Explored in depth in his *One Christ—Many Religions: Toward a Revised Christology* (Maryknoll, NY: Orbis Books, 1991). He writes, "Ethical insights and activities are dependent on theological insights. Doing does not exhaust being.... This is why Christology, to which so much importance is given in this volume, becomes thrustingly relevant to the church's life and witness in the world today" (152–53).
25. In his "In Search of a Revised Christology: A Response to Paul Knitter," in *Current Dialogue* 21 (1991): 30–37, here on 32.

imagination and interfaith commitment have been forged in the fires of 2,000 years of fragmentation and frustration. Christianity without dialogue is like a road without a map, a quest without a destination, a journey without a goal. Dialogue helps us to draw that map, define our destination, and alert us to the goal, something that our commitment to, and openness towards, the person and work of Christ demands of our life, work, and witness, which can lead us to pray, along with Augustine: "Among all these different true interpretations, let Truth itself beget agreement between our hearts, and may our God in his mercy let us use the law lawfully, for the purpose for which it was made, which is unsullied love."[26]

Bibliography

Augustine. *Confessions: A New Translation by Sarah Ruden*. New York: The Modern Library, 2017.

Erling, Maria. "How We Were Joined." *Seminary Ridge Review* 20, no. 1 (2017): 15–24.

Kinnamon, Michael. *Can a Renewal Movement Be Renewed? Questions for the Future of Ecumenism*. Grand Rapids, MI: Eerdmans, 2014.

——— *The Vision of the Ecumenical Movement and How It Has Been Impoverished by Its Friends*. St. Louis, MO: Chalice Press, 2003.

Kurien, Jacob. "From '*anamnesis*' to '*metanoia*'—Beyond Convergence Texts, Towards Attitudinal Conversions. In *BEM at 25: Critical Insights into a Continuing Legacy*, eds. Thomas F. Best and Tamara Grdzeldize, 267–75. Geneva: WCC Publications, 2007.

Link, Hans-Georg. "The Lima Process: After Thirty Years." *The Ecumenical Review* 65, no. 3 (2013): 352–67.

Lorke, Mélisande and Werner, Dietrich, eds., *Ecumenical Visions for the 21st Century: A Reader for Theological Education*. Geneva: WCC Publications, 2013.

---

26. Augustine of Hippo, *Confessions: A New Translation by Sarah Ruden* (New York: The Modern Library, 2017), 424.

Rajkumar, Peniel Jesudason Rufus. "A Prophetic, Polysemic and Proleptic Prompt." *The Ecumenical Review* 65, no. 3 (2013): 338–41.

Ruden, Sarah. *The Face of Water: A Translator on Beauty and Meaning in the Bible.* New York: Pantheon Books, 2017.

Ryrie, Alec. *Protestants: The Faith That Made the Modern World.* New York: Viking, 2017.

Samartha, S. J. *Courage for Dialogue.* Geneva: World Council of Churches, 1981.

Sebastian, J. Jayakiran. "Celebrating the Dynamic Legacy of the Reformation—An Indian Perspective." In *Reformation Observances: 1517–2017,* edited by Philip D. W. Krey, 43–68. Eugene, OR: Cascade Books, 2017.

———. "Evoking the Bible at a Funeral in an Indian-Christian Community." In *Colonialism and the Bible: Contemporary Reflections from the Global South,* edited by Tat-siong Benny Liew and Fernando F. Segovia, 187–97. Lanham, MD: Lexington Books, 2018.

———. "Neither Fellowship or Patience, nor Toleration or Acceptance: Believing, Belonging, Luther, the Jews, and Questions on Contemporary Nationalism." *Seminary Ridge Review* 20, no. 1 (2017): 3–14.

———. "On Walking through the Cemetery: Continuity and Transformation in Reading Death in an Indian-Christian Community." In *Postcolonial Interventions: Essays in Honor of R. S. Sugirtharajah,* edited by Tat-siong Benny Liew, 178–89. Sheffield: Sheffield Phoenix Press, 2009.

———. "'Only Christ and No Formulation of Christ Can Determine the Frontier': J. Russell Chandran's Ongoing Challenges to Christian Ecumenism." In *A Light to the Nations: The Indian Presence in the Ecumenical Movement in the Twentieth Century,* edited by Jesudas M. Athyal, 143–52. Geneva: World Council of Churches, 2016.

Chapter Three

AN INITIAL SCHISM BETWEEN THE SYNAGOGUE AND THE CHURCH? SOME IMPLICATIONS OF AN ANCIENT DEBATE FOR ECUMENISM TODAY

Marie-Hélène Robert, Professor of Missiology, UR CONFLUENCE, Sciences et Humanités, Université Catholique de Lyon and Sister of the Missionary Institute of Our Lady of the Apostle

Introduction

In the middle of the twentieth century, Dom Nicholas Oehmen courageously opined:[1]

> All scissions that sever the body of the Church are in the end simply manifestations and consequences of the interior scission of the Christian as an individual person, this scission being itself a consequence of the fate of a separated Israel.... And if, up to that point, as long as the time of the nations persists, and the reunion of the Christian

---

1. This chapter appears for the first time in English translation with permission of the publisher from: *Histoire et théologie des relations judéo-chrétiennes; un éclairage croisé*, ed. Olivier Rota (Paris: Parole et Silence, 2014), 127–47.

Churches is not accomplished or is not attained in its perfection, that reunion will not be realized, at least in a perfect way, because of the fundamental schism that has up to now divided Israel.... The reunion [of the body of the Church] belongs to the eschatological domain.[2]

Certain people speak about a primitive fissure that does not of itself imply an ecumenical vision.[3] Others, for their part, chime in with this reflection and claim that the universality and unity of the Church are not brought to completion until the initial schism between the Church and synagogue is healed.[4] We are, however, in the midst of a theological re-reading of history that unfolds by analyzing the socio-historical factors behind the division of Jews and Christians.

The term "schism" in the Church is not neutral. It designates a serious rupture of communion and not, in the first place, a doctrinal heresy. In order to account for the development of the Church after the death and resurrection of Christ, a large number of terms have been employed, as much in exegesis and Church History as in theology: fissure, tear (*déchirure*), rift (*fêlure*), break (*déchirement*), separation, rupture, divorce, scission, division, and schism. These terms seek to express that the Jews are not recognized in the preaching of the Gospel and that Christians have become progressively aware of their identity as distinct from Jewish identity and that Christians discover the realization of their identity in the communion of the mystical body of Christ and in the relationship to the Scriptures of Israel. On the other hand, the attachment to the Synagogue and to that which it implies is no longer in effect for

---

2. Nicholas Oehmen, "Le schisme dans le cadre de l'économie divine," *Irenikon*, t. 21, 1er trimester (1948), 6–31, here at 25, 29, and 30.
3. See, for example, George H. Tavard, "Christianity and Israel: Is the Church Schismatic?" *Downside Review* 73 (1954–1955): 347–358.
4. For example, one may refer here to Catholics like Paul Démann, Erich Przywara, Yves Congar, Louis Bouyer, Carlo-Maria Martini, and Hans Urs von Balthasar and Protestants like Karl Barth and Jürgen Moltmann.

Christians. The relationship between the Jewish disciples and the Jewish non-disciples, which had become increasingly hostile, are largely abrogated after the epoch of the New Testament.

For my part, I will speak about an "initial schism" rather than an "original schism" in order to liberate the separation between Jews and Christians from its exclusively theological dimension. It will behoove us nonetheless to remain aware of the reservation of Clemens Thoma for whom "the expression 'schism' ought to be avoided when one describes the current state of affairs between Christianity and Judaism. Christianity does not find itself in the same sense in a situation of rupture with respect to Judaism as is the case between the Church of the West and the Church of the East."[5] The separation between Christians cannot in effect be confused with the separation between Jews and Christian—the Christological element being here decisive—, but the division between Christians would come from the initial schism and would not be capable of being resolved except through the reunification of Israel and the Church.[6]

In order to determine, for the sake of ecumenical reflection, that which the thesis of Oehmen and its developments imply with respect to the relations between Jews and Christians,[7] we will examine the theological presuppositions of the initial schism. Positively, it comes from the recognition of a common origin before the initial schism, but also from the one sole people of God in spite of the schism, and therefore of even one eschatological hope whereby the schism will be reabsorbed at the time of the

---

5. Clemens Thoma, *Théologie chrétienne du judaïsme. Pour une histoire reconcilié des juifs et des chrétiens* (Paris: Parole et Silence, 2005; Essai de l'École cathédrale, original German: 1978), 199.

6. Paul Démann, "Israël et l'unité de l'Église," *Cahiers sioniens* 1: (March 1953), 1–24.

7. Without, however, developing the evolution of the question in the history of the twentieth century, we will take note below of some of the theologians named above (see note 4).

reintegration foreseen by Paul in Romans 11:11–32. Certainly, the initial schism has had dramatic consequences not only for the internal unity of the Church (according to Oehmen's thesis) but also in the history of the Jewish people. Nonetheless, if it belongs to the plan of God himself, it opens up a certain number of positive consequences for the dialogue between Jews and Christians. The mission of the Church is thereby explained in a different manner since the Church needs Israel in order to re-discover its lost unity.

1. *The Theological Presuppositions of the Schism: Which Unity?*

To speak about an initial schism presupposes that Judaism and Christianity are originally one, in the sense that the Church is born from Israel and later becomes differentiated from it. But the Church can also be understood as pre-existing Israel. The way in which one understands the Church in a certain way determines the way in which one understands Israel.

Original Unity

If the Church is seen as having an existence from the beginning of the world, and even pre-existing the world (in the sense of Origen[8] or of

---

8. Origen, *Commentary on the Song of Songs*, I, 12. See Origen, *The Song of Songs: Commentary and Homilies*, tr. R.P. Lawson (New York: Newman Press, 1956), Commentary: Book Two, p. 149: "She is so called from the beginning of the human race and from the very foundation of the word—indeed, if I may look for the origin of this high mystery under Paul's guidance, even *before* the foundation of the world. For this is what he says: 'as He chose us in Christ before the foundation of the world, that we should be holy and unspotted in his sight, predestinating us in charity unto the adoption of sons (Ephesians 1:4–5).'....And indeed the first foundations of the congregation of the Church were laid at the very beginning; and for this reason the Apostle says that the Church is built on the foundation not of the apostles only, but also of the prophets. And among the prophets,

Augustine[9]), the Church and Israel are originally one in the sense that "the church of Old Testament is transcended by the Church of the New Testament."[10] Israel in this case is a figure of the church.

Karl Barth sees this unity as a relationship of reciprocal inclusion. The Church is integrated into Judaism. The Church receives itself from Israel, in a process of continuity and differentiation, for Judaism is for its part also integrated into the Church, in the sense that the Church, as pre-existent, is its internal realization and its implementation.

In the decree *Nostra Aetate*, the Second Vatican Council re-established the fundamental continuity between the Church and Israel,[11] drawing from the initial and final unity of the whole human race.[12] But this unity was broken by sin. For Paul Démann, "the history of redemption paradoxically begins with a new division,"[13] that which separates the people of God from being with the nations: "The Catholic unity of redemption will express itself before all else by the suppression of this primordial division. Christ came to 're-establish' peace, 'to make one people out of two' (Ephesians 2:15, 14:17)."[14] The history of redemption of a humanity that was originally one thus continues through the Incarnation, which for its part gives rise to a schism between Israel and the Church, with a view to the final reintegration

---

when he said: 'For this cause a man shall leave his father and his mother, and shall cleave to his wife, and they shall be two in one flesh (Psalm 73:2).' It is clearly with reference to these words of his that the Apostles say that this is a great mystery, but I speak in Christ and in the Church. Adam too is reckoned, who prophesied the great mystery in Christ and in the Church."

9. St. Augustine, *De catechizandis rudibus*, III, 6 (*Patrologia Latina* 40, 314).
10. Oehmen, "Le schisme dans le cadre de l'économie divine," 10.
11. *Nostra Aetate* 4.
12. *Nostra Aetate* 1.
13. Démann, "Israël et l'Unité de l'Église," 1.
14. Démann, "Israël et l'Unité de l'Église," 3.

of humanity. God actually acts in this way from his own unity and from the unity of his design, with an eschatological purpose.

God no longer tends to the division of his people Israel so much as to his Church and to the fratricidal battles in the world. The plan of salvation, from the beginning, aims for the reconciliation of a humanity that is one, created, and loved by God, from which neither Israel nor the nations would be excluded. The initial unity (before the schism) between the Church and Israel is thereby incorporated into this original unity placed in the Jewish scriptures, which is broken but on the way to reintegration. The Church pursues the work of redemption that began with the primordial but paradoxical separation between Israel and the nations. How do we define this initial unity?

Initial Unity

To be sure, Christology allows the following word of Christ to resound in the Gospel of John: "Before Abraham came to be, I am" (8:58). This Christian view, the view of faith, whereby, following Origen and Augustine, the Church pre-exists in Israel—does this view do justice to the novelty of the Church? The Catholic Church does not dispute the fact of the original unity between the Church and the synagogue in the sense that the Church considers itself the prolongation of Israel, as if it were its realization. But the Church is also God's means in history to render his offer of salvation to humanity, admittedly in the prolongation of the covenant, in continuity with the proper vocation of Israel, but also for the sake of a new beginning, a new childbirth. This novelty presumes a rupture, however provisional, of the continuity in order to permit the coming into being of alterity, but without for that matter disavowing the original unity and the necessary unity between the Israel and the Church.

In this case, the separation is less that of a schism than a new birth, one that takes place at the very interiority of the unique covenant. At the moment of the historical foundation of the Church, the original unity is thus realized in an initial unity, in the sense of initiating a unified novelty. The Church still regards Israel as its own entity that faithfully pursues its covenantal history with God. The Church does not replace Israel, as that claim could be sustained by the Church in the past. The Church encounters Israel in its own mission. John Oesterreicher, for example, falls right in line with the initial unity thus understood. Oesterreicher later will become part of the sub-commission organized by Cardinal Bea for Jewish questions at the Second Vatican Council and in their 1955 project expressed himself in these terms:

> To show the unity of God's design as it leads from the Law to the Gospels—the unbroken economy of salvation [remains]. Never can the Church forget that the Rock on which it stands is embedded in the revealed wisdom of patriarchs and prophets and in the mighty events which dominate the history of the children of Israel.[15]

Similarly, according to Jürgen Moltmann, an initial unity is to be posited between Israel and the Church because:

> At root, there are not two peoples of God, one old and one new. Just as God is one, so too is God's people also one. Both the ecumenical movement and its reflection collide in the end and always anew at the first schism whence comes the departure of paganism: the separation of the Church and Israel. That is the point from which schismatic thought is born in Christianity, and that's the point where it should disappear. Not only is the true God and the true man which is made manifest to us as pagan-Christians in the Jew Jesus Christ. It's also Israel.

---

15. John M. Oesterreicher, "A Statement of Purpose," in *The Bridge: A Yearbook of Judaeo-Christian Studies*, ed. John M. Oesterreicher, vol. 1 (New York: Pantheon Books, 1955), 9.

Through him, we know Israel, and we are bound to Israel, for it's by him that the promises that God made to Abraham, Isaac, and Jacob have come to us.¹⁶

Does the Church as such bear responsibility for the separation? Different arguments can be put forward by theology in order to respond in the negative:

1) According to Folker Siegert, the rupture between the Church and Judaism would repeat the ruptures internal to Judaism.¹⁷ The separation between Israel as a community of believers and non-believing Israel is linked to the schism between the house of Judah and the house of Israel; even their destiny remains in common.¹⁸ It's because Israel had been divided that Israel did not know how to welcome the Messiah. Nor could Israel recognize that the Church was intrinsic to it. The initial schism can thus be traced back upstream of the rupture between the synagogue and the Church.

2) Reading the Gospels can lead one to think that the schism must be attributed to Israel, on account of Israel's false understanding of fidelity to the covenant. The Gospel of John starts by saying that "his own are not accepted" (John 1) and bears witness to the expulsion of the Christians from the synagogue (John 9). The Gospel was first preached to the Jews, and the door was never

---

16. Jürgen Moltmann, "Quelle unité? Le dialogue entre les traditions de l'Orient et de l'Occident," lecture delivered to the World Council of Churches, 1977. This talk was published in *Ökumenische Rundschau* 26 (1977): 287–296, here at 294. (The French text lies in the archives of the WCC.)
17. Folker Siegert, "Le judaïsme au premier siècle et ses ruptures intérieures," in *Le Déchirement. Juifs et chrétiens au 1er siècle*, ed. Daniel Marguerat (Geneva: Labor et Fides, Le monde de la Bible, 32, 1996), 25–65.
18. See Oehmen, "Le schisme dans le cadre de l'économie divine," 12.

closed.[19] But for Barth Israel, were it to desist, puts at peril the existence of the unique community of God which cannot do without her. Israel "thus created the schism, the abyss at the bosom of the community of God."[20]

These two arguments attribute the cause of the separation to Israel and accentuate the rupture between the Church and Israel. But for Paul, the disciples of Christ are the branches grafted on to the true olive tree, Israel. The image of grafting in the Letter to the Romans shows the necessity of understanding Christianity in its initial linkage to Judaism.

Nostra Aetate 4 states: "As the sacred synod searches into the mystery of the Church, it remembers the bond that spiritually ties the people of the New Covenant to Abraham's stock."[21] In the mystery of the Church itself, one can discover that which unites the Church and Israel. Through the notion of mystery in which the bond with Israel begins to be eliminated we discover the entire will and the very possibility of the initial schism with Israel that can be imputed to the Church.

---

19. Daniel Marguerat, "Juifs et chrétiens selon Luc-Actes," in *Le Déchirement. Juifs et chrétiens au 1er siècle*, ed. Daniel Marguerat, 151–78, here at 163–164: "À la crise déclenchée par sa mission aux non-Juifs, Paul réagit d'une part en revendiquant pour son action l'appui des Écritures, d'autre part en refusant de s'accommoder d'une rupture dont il n'assume pas la responsabilité. La rupture voulue par la Synagogue conduit Luc à renforcer les indicateurs de continuité théologique : l'octroi du salut aux païens n'opère pas contre Israël; il ne remplace pas les promesses faites à Israël. L'universalité du salut naît de l'histoire même d'Israël où il trouve sa source et sa légitimité (Ac 13,32–39), mais cette ouverture est paradoxalement mise en oeuvre dans l'histoire par le refus juif de la mission chrétienne."
20. Karl Barth, *Dogmatique* II, 2 (Geneva: Labor et Fides, 1958 [original German, 1942]), 216. Translated from the French.
21. *Nostra Aetate* 4, accessed on-line at: http://www.vatican.va/archive/hist_councils/ii_vatican_council/documents/vat-ii_decl_19651028_nostra-aetate_en.html.

These two arguments seek in this instance to valorize the bond of continuity between the Church and Israel. But in the four positions that we have evoked, the responsibility for the rupture is not attributed to the Church because it would disown itself if it cut itself off from its roots. On the other hand, can the Church be exonerated of all responsibility in the breaking of the initial unity? A more historicized reading, more attentive to the course of history, seems to invite the reader to reconsider the question of responsibility.

In fact, Israel cannot be held to be the only responsible party in the separation, receiving the provocation head-on. What was the point of the decisive rupture? The confession of Jesus as the Messiah, the Son of God? The interpretation of the Torah and of the Scriptures? The freedoms taken in the face of the purity laws? Faith in the resurrection? The overture to the pagans of the privileges of Israel? Daniel Marguerat informs us, "The proper response is not self-evident inasmuch as a bundle of factors were at play in the historical circumstances."[22] Accordingly, recent historical studies invite us to re-read the chronology of the Jewish-Christian distinction in a different way.[23]

Depending upon which historical factor we take into account, we encounter the elaboration of a particular theology. Hans Urs von Balthasar opines that the "primitive scission" is internal to the Jewish people in which some followed Christ and others did not. But only the Church, in the words of von Balthasar, "fulfils and at the same time shatters Israel from within, incorporating into itself the 'nations' as equals in rights (that which Israel itself could not absolutely realize on its own, even though Israel was oriented to this

---

22. Marguerat, "Introduction," in *Le Déchirement. Juifs et chrétiens*, 19.
23. See, for example, the contributions of Marc Rastoin and Philippe Loiseau to *Histoire et théologie des relations judéo-chrétiennes; un éclairage croisé*, ed. Olivier Rota (Paris: Parole et Silence, 2014).

aspiration by its own nature)."²⁴ For Erich Przywara²⁵ and Louis Bouyer,²⁶ certainly the majority of Israel is responsible for the initial schism by refusing to believe in Jesus Christ, a fact that repeats itself on manifold occasions in history inasmuch as the wound is not healed. But the responsibility of Israel in the division of the Church is not separable from the failure of Jesus's mission to the Jewish people, the mission of the Apostles, and thus of the Church, even if Jesus and the initial core of the Church were Jewish.

The initial schism is not brought to completion in the epoch of the New Testament. This will take place later in the history of the relations between Jews and Christians. "Judaism shut itself off from Christianity, and the Church turned its back on the people which rejected it," states Hans Urs von Balthasar.²⁷ In the wake of the Patristic period, the final completion of the schism can be imputed to the Church (in the construction and development of its identity, especially in adopting a new relation to the Law), and to Israel (in its survival strategy in the face of a Christianity that was

---

24. Hans Urs von Balthasar, *La dramatique divine* II. *Les personnes du drame*, 2. *Les personnes dans le Christ* (Paris et Namur: Lethielleux, Culture et vérité, 1988), 337. The translation is based upon the French.

25. Erich Przywara (1889–1972) is of the opinion that "the fissure [*Riss*, 'fissure, *fossé*'] between the Church of the East and the West, [as well as] the fissure between the Roman Church and the '*pluriversum*' of the Reformation (countless Churches and sects) participate in the primitive fissure between Judaism (non-Christian Jews) and Christianity (the 'Gentiles' in the language of the Pauline letters), in the sense that the primitive fissure is the archetype of the separations that take place afterwards. This fissure is of an eschatological character, "theological" in the strong sense of the term, because the only response possible lies in the "fathomlessness of unfathomable realities" of God, i.e., in God's own unfathomable being." Erich Przywara, "Römische Katholizität—All-christliche ökumenizität," in *Gott in Welt: Festschrift für Karl Rahner*, eds. Johannes Baptist Metz et al. (Freiburg im Breisgau, 1964), 524–28, here at 526.

26. Louis Bouyer, *L'Église de Dieu. Corps du Christ et Temple de l'Esprit* (Paris: Le Cerf, Antiquariat, 1970), 643.

27. Hans Urs von Balthasar, *Martin Buber and Christianity: A Dialogue between Israel and the Church* (New York: Macmillan, 1961), 12.

increasingly intent on integration). The Church has consequently been able to rely upon the harsh comments of the New Testament against the Jews who did not listen in order to take one's proper distance from Judaism, as will be testified to by the Councils of Nicea and Constantinople I. This development was not without prejudice for either the Church or for the Jewish people.[28] Judaism, for its part, was not able to recognize itself in the writings that were in part hostile to the Jews and therefore separated itself from the Church in order to form a notably Rabbinic Judaism.

To be sure, there never was a complete rupture with the covenant borne by the Scriptures of Israel on the part of the Church. Marcionism, the movement that rejected the God of Israel in the Old Testament, is a veritable schism that doubled as a heresy. It is true that Marcionite tendencies regularly resurface in the history of the Church and that they are not without injury for the Jewish people. But it is not the case that these tendencies constitute Christian thought in its essence.

The original unity of humanity thereby includes the pre-existent Church as well as the initial unity between the Church and Israel, the unity that existed at the historical origin of Christianity. This nuance permits us to understand the schism in multiple ways. The fracture of the original unity comes from the totality of historical relations between God and God's people, and this history is marked by sin and the restoration of the covenant. The final reconciliation will overcome this fracture, just as it will overcome all the schisms in Israel and in the Church. The fissure between the historical Church and Israel is very much in keeping with the general history of the covenant, but it also opens a new page in history and more and more puts into relief the discontinuity between the Church and Israel, i.e., the specificity of each one, without having breached the original unity. Under this banner, one can advance an ecumenical position that respects otherness.

---

28. Marcel Simon, *Verus Israel. Étude sur les relations entre Chrétiens et Juifs dans l'Empire romain (135–425)* (Paris: Boccard, 1964; original ed., 1948), 518.

Universal Unity and Ecumenism

Ecumenism can take as its starting point that, if Christians are divided, the Church itself, no more than Christ himself, should not be so. The tunic of Christ is seamless. The process and the project of ecumenism are grounded, therefore, on the reclaiming of the universal unity that is at once a reality, an original gift of God (Ephesians 2:14ff.), and an aim, a responsibility (Ephesians 2:22). This is true for Israel, born within the covenant and promised at their gathering. This is true for the Church. Unity is for the church a reality because it is one, holy, catholic, and apostolic, a gift of the One God, the indivisible body of Christ. Unity is an aim and an agenda because the recapitulation in Christ does not absolve the Church of the re-discovery of the communion awaited by the disciples of Christ. It cannot be simply relegated to the last times. Under this banner, the epistles of the New Testament should caution us against every threat to unity, either through doctrinal or practical plans. We will come back to that point.

The fact that unity is a real gift and a task to be accomplished permits us to grasp the complementarity of the two approaches. The former recalls for us that the initial unity existed from the very beginnings of the Church and that the divisions arose at a later point. It is therefore necessary to return to the time of the foundation, in order to re-absorb the schisms. This approach is that of the traditional position that one often encounters among Catholics and the Orthodox. The other approach, in accordance with a more Protestant position, thinks that the original unity was to be realized in the Church since the beginning. Jesus prays that his own will be one (John 17:11) because they are not one and because he knows that unity will not come about without harm.

Holding these two approaches together permit us to understand the meaning of unity between Israel and the Church. The Church proceeds originally and initially from the root of the Jewish people and thus participates in the unique covenant, reiterated and without repentance, that God established with his people. This is why the divisions of the initial period and the traumas within history should not triumph. They can be transcended in the present as a result of the unity that is universal, original, adamic, transcendent, and even present at the beginning, equally so in the name of an eschatological reconciliation that is anchored in the covenant. Moreover, it is possible, even necessary, to work for the reunification of the unique people of God, a reunification concerning which God alone knows the terms. Even if the origin and endpoint are both grounded in unity, the gift of unity is also a task for the future, in the sense that the responsibility of the partners in the one covenant becomes engaged in this history. The history of this engagement ought not to be a parenthesis. Rather grace arises and unfolds at the very site of this engagement. But this unity is still not self-evident.

2. *The Question of Unity Reconsidered*

First Reflection. One of the major difficulties, once the accent is placed upon unity (original, initial, and universal), pertains to the fact that the Jews, who do not recognize themselves in the Church (pre-existent or otherwise), cannot subscribe to such a vision. Throughout the historical manifestation of the Church, a majority of the people of Israel did not join it. In the eyes of the Church, they did not separate themselves from the Church. They refused to be assimilated.

But Karl Barth responds that Israel cannot recognize itself in the Church because only Christ gives this knowledge and awareness of the unicity of the assembly of God, which is formed from Israel and the Church of Jews and pagans.[29] Barth considers that

---

29. Barth, *Dogmatique* II, 2, "La doctrine de Dieu," chap. 7: "L'élection gratuite de Dieu," §34 "L'élection de la communauté," pp. 205–304, here at 208, 210, and 221.

Israel, "the Jewish people who take exception to their divine election are also secretly the font of the Church."[30] On that basis,

> It is wrong to call the Jews the "reprobate" people and the Church "the elect." ... Behind the divine call that gives shape to the ecclesial form of the community, there is in fact the act of election. But there is also the reprobation He assumed himself (on the Cross). One must take note of the irreducible distinction between these two aspects of the people of God. But we must also consider the indissoluble unity that this brings to light. This distinction and this unity cannot be discerned without Jesus Christ and his election, in other words, by the faith of the Church.[31]

We return below to Barth's way of thinking. Let us recognize here the interesting differentiation that Barth offers with the reductive vision of the radical novelty of the Gospel with respect to a now obsolete law. This vision was not rare in Protestantism, certainly among Lutherans.

Second Reflection. To envisage the Gospel in its historical manifestation, which provokes the separation of Israel while proclaiming the Gospel, must still take into account that Judaism of the time of the New Testament is less unified than it seems and must also acknowledge the diverse strands, of which the Pharisees and the Sadducees are only the most well known. Even if Christianity is placed into the lineage of Judaism, from precisely which strand does it emerge?

John T. Pawlikowski, for his part, calls into question the [...] principle of a unique covenant, which rests upon an overly uniform and linear interpretation of the Jewish tradition. One

---

30. Barth, *Dogmatique* II, 2, 208. Translation from the French.
31. Barth, *Dogmatique* II, 2, 209. Translation from the French.

must concede that the theory of a unique covenant often masks the attachment to a Christianity conceived as an accomplishment of Judaism, following the classical Christian view of the matter. Even if they have a positive conception of the Biblical tradition of Judaism and are favorable to the idea of the continuity of the Jewish covenant after the event of Christ, these theologies of accomplishment have difficulties in answering the question of knowing to which form of Judaism that Christianity had been allied and which form it is supposed to have fulfilled. Most adherents to this theory of the unique covenant have not faced this new and more complex description of the Jewish tradition.[32]

But these diverse strands of Judaism are all bound together in the unique covenant in Abraham and then later in Moses, just as the different Christian traditions are brought back to the same Gospel, which itself is rooted in the plurality of Judaism, even if it favors the Pharisaic strand.[33] The plurality of the strands does not therefore change the original and initial unity that includes a certain form of diversity.

Third Reflection. The foundations in the Gospel of the unity in the Church are not shared by the largest part of Israel.[34] Rather, they are the inheritance of all of Christ's disciples. It is thus difficult to make Israel responsible for the later schisms of the Church. That which unites Christians with other Christians derives from the original unity but also from the initial unity. If the Church is not responsible for the initial schism and if its responsibility is nonetheless

---

32. John T. Pawlikowski, "Repenser la relation entre Chrétiens et Juifs: Examen des perspectives contemporaines," *Sens*, n° 277 (April 2003): 148–58, here at 154–55. Translated from the French.

33. Christopher Tuckett, "Les Pharisiens avant 70 et le Nouveau Testament," in *Le Déchirement. Juifs et chrétiens au 1ᵉʳ siècle*, ed., Daniel Marguerat, 67–95.

34. See Pontifical Council for the Promotion of Christian Unity, "The Ecumenical Dimension of Those Engaged in Pastoral Work," March 1998, available online at http://www.vatican.va/roman_curia/pontifical_councils/chrstuni/general-docs/rc_pc_chrstuni_doc_19950316_ecumenical-dimension_en.html.

taken seriously, it is difficult to draw the conclusion for that matter that the Church is innocent of the internal divisions and to reject all fault on its part for the first separation between the Church and Israel.

As a matter of fact, the Church, one and holy in its foundation, is still divided by the fact of sin (envy, jealousy, rivalries). The Church is already responsible for the internal divisions at the time of Paul. The apostle in his Letter to the Romans put forward a paradoxical relationship to the Law in order that neither the Jews nor the Gentiles make an excuse of the Law in order to remain deaf to the promise.[35] And even if he does not surrender to the separation that emerges between the synagogue and the community of Christ, by praying for his fellow Jews, by recalling their privileges and the irrevocability of the covenant (Romans 9–11), Paul makes neither himself nor the community responsible for the division. In fact, all who have heard the Word are susceptible to respond to it affirmatively (Romans 10). One part of Israel has surely answered in the negative, through blindness, and thus remains responsible for the separation, but this is not definitive.

For Paul the divisions internal to the community do not come from these Jews who are temporarily "blind," they come from a lack of faith or from a lack of the deepening of the faith of the disciples themselves, who have not understood in all its depth God's own plan of salvation, whether they be Jews or Greeks. To be baptized and to have decided for Christ did not suffice to make the community fully united. Paul then proposes to the Christians the theological foundations of unity (Romans 1–11) that you have to live (Romans 12–15) in the community formed out of both Jews and Gentiles. The disciples are exhorted to strengthen their faith in Christ in order to live the imperative of unity and love.

As a result, "The debate of the apostle Paul with Jewish piety between 50–60 CE is still absolutely internal and has nothing to

---

35. On this question, one may consult the following monograph: Marie-Hélène Robert, *Israël dans la mission chrétienne. Lectures de Rm 9–11* (Paris: Le Cerf, Lectio Divina, 2010).

do with interreligious dialogue," Daniel Marguerat underscores.[36] Hans Urs von Balthasar followed another position. According to him, to make the initial schism responsible for the divisions in the Church, even to dress it up as a divine intentionality, makes it "insurmountable." For this theologian, the Church may not be culpable for the initial schism, but it is culpable for the ones that follow.[37] Under these conditions,

> it would be difficult to maintain that the Israel that refused Christ was responsible for disputes within the Christian Church; according to Paul, the unity of Christians is based upon an entirely different principle (Ephesians 4:3ff.) from that of the Jewish "sects" (and Paul had been a member of one of them). Precisely this principle of unity, however—the Eucharist of the pneumatic Lord—is a wholly new and incomparable principle, and this makes the initial split, which becomes aggravated into full-blown schism, to be practically irreversible.[38]

This principle of unity should therefore stimulate ecumenical search for unity and above all the battle against any sin that leads to intra-ecclesial divisions and from there to schisms.

The separation between Jews and Christians is not only a lamentable encounter devoid of history. The separation was not willed by the Church, and it occurred to the vast majority of the Jewish people for diverse reasons. If the initial schism results paradoxically from the original unity, in view of the realization of the final unity,

---

36. Daniel Marguerat, "Introduction," in *Le Déchirement. Juifs et chrétiens au 1ᵉʳ siècle*, ed. Daniel Marguerat, 7–22, here at 12.

37. Hans Urs von Balthasar, "L'absoluité du christianisme et la catholicité de l'Église," in *Chemins de dialogue* 37 "L'espérance pour mémoire" (June 2011): 109–38 (original text, 1977).

38. Hans Urs von Balthasar, *Theo-Drama III: The Dramatis Personae, The Person in Christ* (San Francisco: Ignatius Press, 1992), 445.

it is because the separation falls within the divine plan, at the junction of revelation and a mystery that has not yet been fully unveiled. The Church, therefore, must rethink its approach to Judaism.

3. Eschatological Unity and the Mission of the Church

Is God responsible for the schism?

To speak about the schism makes it possible to replace Israel in the mystery of the plan of salvation: Israel's "No" has meaning, even if this meaning is still not yet fully revealed. For Karl Barth, the hardening of Israel and its unbelief are not by chance, nor due to capriciousness or God's arbitrariness. "It's a matter of facts explained and not motivated by the guilt and sin of Israel."[39] The nuance is important. God makes the decision and not Israel, and God does so in order to extend his mercy, and not for the sake of punishing Israel for any particular sin. Everything remains in the hands of God. The attitude of the Church must be that of solidarity, of prayer, and of waiting with an attitude of hope.

According to Franz Mussner:

> God himself has "hardened" Israel, as this fact was mysteriously proclaimed in the Scripture.[40] God has placed in Jesus Christ and before the feet of Israel "the stone that causes stumbling" (Rm 9:33); on this stone Israel has stumbled. That is why the "unbelief" of Israel is and remains the absolute mystery of God.[41]

---

39. Barth, *Dogmatique* II, 2, 299.
40. Cf. Rm 9:18; 10:8ff. with reference to Dt 29:3; Is 6:9ff.; and Ps 69:23ff.
41. Franz Mussner, *Traité sur les Juifs* (Paris: Le Cerf, 1981; original German, 1979), 64.

In a footnote, Mussner indicates that "the Church should now reflect on this matter. That's why it's a little less pointless to speculate about the question 'What would happen if... (e.g., if Israel had accepted Jesus and the Gospel)?"[42] If God himself had hardened Israel, then God alone can bring healing to the matter. Since the Church does not have the primary responsibility for the healing, it must rethink its missionary attitude towards the Jews and specifically to not seek their conversion.

It is true that chapters 9–11 of Romans can be read as saying that one part of Israel is separated from the Church by God, thanks to a "remnant," in order to allow for the entrance of all the Gentiles in the history of salvation and for the sake of their salvation. Israel will rediscover then its unity between its unbelieving part and the remnant that remained faithful. But for von Balthasar, God is in no way responsible for the hardening of Israel as such because Israel would have been able to hear and ought to have listened to God (Romans 10).[43] But one can respond that at least one part listened.

The schism can be seen as a theological statement, in the sense of God having willed it, but that statement does not mean that the Church has only to endorse the rupture without working for unity. Certainly, this unity will not be accomplished except by God, but will it take place in history (Barth) or in eschatology (Erik Peterson, D. N. Oehmen)? The eschatological horizon of Erik Peterson, for whom Israel and the Church belong to two different eons and who will not be joined together again except in the last times, calls the Church and Israel to coexist in the best way possible. But this approach risks that we lose sight of the necessity of a rapprochement,

---

42. Mussner, *Traité sur les Juifs*, 64.

43. Von Balthasar, *Dramatique divine*, 311. Besides, von Balthasar maintains, following Barth: "Israel's obduracy enters incontestably into God's plan of salvation in its historical working characterized by election and reprobation." Von Balthasar, "The Church and Israel," *Explorations in Theology II, Spouse of the Word* (San Francisco: Ignatius Press, 1991), 323–34 [translated from: "Die Wurzel Jesse," in: *Skizzen zur Theologie*, II, *Sponsa verbi* (Einsiedeln: Johannes Verlag, 1971), 306–16.

of a relationship, that constitutes the ground of the mission of the Church.[44] The Church has not abandoned completely its mission towards Judaism, but it has certainly abandoned a certain idea of mission that would obliterate otherness.

The Church Needs Israel in Order to Rebuild Unity

If one postulates, on the one hand, an original and initial unity between the Israel and the Church and, on the other hand, the attribution of an initial schism with regard to God's will for universal salvation, the unity of the Church will not be complete without Israel. The Church is called to work for the unity of humanity in accordance with the imperative and modalities of the Gospel, in particular as expressed in the Letter to the Ephesians. The attitude of fraternity is neither optional nor partial in Christianity. Father Théomir Devaux adds:

> How does a Catholic not realize that very often anti-Semitism is equally a form of anti-Christian hatred? The Church professes only one humanity and that all women and men are and will remain, by virtue of their common origin, sisters and brothers by nature.[45]

This exigency is not the prerogative of a church or a particular confession. It is the common evangelical bedrock upon which unity is built.

According to Jürgen Moltmann:

> The ecumenical movement will not find rest and will not be fulfilled without Israel. That's why we recognize

---

44. Erik Peterson, *Le mystère des juifs et des Gentils dans l'Église* (Paris: Desclée de Brouwer, Courrier des Iles, 1936).
45. Théomir Devaux (NDS), "Préface," in Oscar de Férenzy, *Les Juifs, et nous Chrétiens* (Paris: Flammarion, 1935), xi.

that "the Church in its entirety" remains imperfect and unfinished without Israel. We hope together in this great Kingdom of God in which Israel and the Church will be one. To be in ecumenical community with Israel means to learn to recognize the witnesses to the faith and life of Israel as witnesses of the sole people of God. To be in ecumenical community with Israel means waiting for the perfect kingdom while living in the imperfect kingdom.[46]

Fr. Paul Démann, a precursor in joining the question of Israel to ecumenical reflection,[47] understood the manifold dimensions of this imbrication, and his contribution can be summarized as follows:

1) It is necessary that the Church re-appropriates the Biblical tradition without subjugating itself to foreign cultures.
2) The respective memories must be healed.
3) A certain complementarity has to be honored whereby one is enriched by the other. This complementarity bears witness to the fact that God has not "preserved the Jewish people so long and so miraculously in order to then have them slowly disband and disappear from history without saying goodbye."[48]
4) The Jews are thus no longer the objects of Christian mission. This schism from the origins introduces Israel into a theology of ecumenism and, by underscoring the parentage of faith, replaces efforts for conversion with a willingness to seek rapprochement.
5) It is thus a matter of:

---

46. Moltmann, "Quelle unité?," 294.
47. "The Relationship with the Jews" will henceforth be under ecumenism rather interreligious dialogue.
48. Démann, "Israël et l'Unité de l'Église," 21. See also Olivier Rota, "Dépasser les cadres du philosémitisme. La vision oecuménique de Paul Démann," *Archives Juives* 40/1 (1er semestre 2007): 117–30.

Defining with regard to Israel an attitude that is fully Christian and ecclesial, which, without either enervating in any way the universal mission of Christ and Christ's Church nor veiling the difference between the Jewish and the Christian conception of unity, invites the Church and Israel—as Christians divided amongst themselves—to share in the communion of one and the same prayer and one and the same hope towards Unity, in the same submission to the mysterious ways whereby God will realize this final manifestation and absolute victory of his one and unifying love.[49]

These five points are common to both the dialogue between Jews and Christians and ecumenical dialogue. They necessitate a long patience and "reciprocal efforts that call upon one another and inspire one another." However, as we mentioned above, these five issues do not completely overlap with one other. The Church needs the faith of Israel and its witness and cannot realize its mission except in terms of a model of complementarity. For the Church, it is not a matter of announcing to Israel the God who was made known first to Israel. But as for knowing whether it is necessary to announce to Israel the revelation in Jesus Christ of the Trinitarian God, the response of the Church is to maintain that witnessing is necessary, but according to modalities that are other than those of either interreligious dialogue or the wholly new proclamation of the Gospel to a people for the very first time.

Conclusion

After fifty years, the Jewish roots of the Church have been restored to their rightful place, Christians gather on the common basis of

---

49. Démann, "Israël et l'Unité de l'Église," 24.

the Scriptures, and the Church does not call the Jews to conversion (with the exception of certain evangelical Protestants). In different words, the wishes of Paul Démann seemed to have been granted. However, even if the unity among Christians and the rapprochement between Christians and Jews have progressed, unity is still not realized. Is it because the time of eschatological reunification has not arrived? Is it because the separation bears witness to our condition as sinners?

But if the common source of our division is in fact sin—which touches every community and every individual—is it right to place on the same level the divisions of Israel (in Biblical terms and also today), the separation between Jews at the time of Jesus as a result of his preaching, the later separation between Jews and Christians, and the separation that exists today among Christians?

All of these divisions impart the same lesson for today: unity is precious and fragile. Unity demands our total commitment even though it is, before all else, a gift of God.

Bibliography

Bouyer, Louis. *L'Église de Dieu. Corps du Christ et Temple de l'Esprit*. Paris: Le Cerf, Antiquariat, 1970.

Démann, Paul. "Israël et l'unité de l'Église." *Cahiers sioniens* 1 (March 1953): 1–24.

Marguerat, Daniel, ed. *Le Déchirement. Juifs et chrétiens au Ier siècle*. Geneva: Labor et Fides, Le monde de la Bible 32, 1996.

Mussner, Franz. *Traité sur les Juifs*. Paris: Le Cerf, Cogitatio Fidei, 1981. (Original edition: *Traktat über die Juden*. Munich, 1979.

Oehmen, Dom Nicholas. "Le schisme dans le cadre de l'économie divine." *Irenikon* 21 (1er trimestre 1948): 6–31.

Oesterreicher, John M. "A Statement of Purpose." In *The Bridge: A Yearbook of Judaeo-Christian Studies*, vol. 1, ed. John M. Oesterreicher. New York: Pantheon Books, 1955.

Peterson, Erik. *Le mystère des juifs et des Gentils dans l'Église*. Paris: Desclée de Brouwer, Courrier des Iles, 1936.

Robert, Marie-Hélène. *Israël dans la mission chrétienne. Lectures de Rm 9–11*. Paris: Le Cerf, Lectio Divina, 2010.

Simon, Marcel. *Verus Israel. Étude sur les relations entre Chrétiens et Juifs dans l'Empire romain* (135–425). Paris: Boccard, 1964.

Tavard, George H. "Christianity and Israel: Is the Church Schismatic?" *Downside Review* 73 (1954–55): 347–58.

Thoma, Clemens. *Théologie chrétienne du judaïsme*. Paris: Parole et Silence, Essai de l'École cathédrale, 2005. (Original edition: *Christliche Theologie des Judentums*. Aschaffenburg: P. Pattloch, 1978.)

Von Balthasar, Hans Urs. "The Church and Israel." In *Explorations in Theology II, Spouse of the Word*, 323–34. San Francisco: Ignatius Press, 1991. (Original edition: "Die Wurzel Jesse." In *Skizzen zur Theologie, II, Sponsa verbi*, 306–16. Einsiedeln: Johannes Verlag, 1971, 306–16.)

Von Balthasar, Hans Urs. *Martin Buber and Christianity: A Dialogue between Israel and the Church*. New York: Macmillan, 1961.

THEOLOGY OF RELIGIONS AND
INTERRELIGIOUS LEARNING

Chapter One

ROMAN CATHOLICS AND JEWS: TOWARDS A MINIMALIST CATHOLIC ZIONISM

Gavin D'Costa

Introduction

After Vatican II (1962–65), the status of the Jewish people shifted in Catholic theology.[1] Previously, there were venerable traditions (though not formal magisterial teachings) that viewed the Jewish people as deicidal, and thus cursed to wander the earth. Sometimes the sole positive role of the Jews was to testify to the promises made that were now inherited by the "new Israel," the Catholic Church. This view came to be called *theological supersessionism*, whereby the Catholic Church superseded the Jews as God's chosen people. The Jews were forsaken, doomed to be a negative testimony, and deserved this because of their rejection of their messiah and the promises made to them. The complex but clear relation between theological anti-Judaism (theological supersessionism) and political anti-Semitism has negatively affected Catholic cultures. The Council was unequivocal

---

1. This paper is developed and defended at length in my book: *Catholic Doctrines about the Jewish People after Vatican II* (New York: Oxford University Press, 2019). I am very grateful to Gabriel Said Reynolds for the invite to present this paper in Rome at the Notre Dame Gateway conference.

in condemning anti-Semitism from whatever source. Thus began a slow chain of criticism directed against theological supersessionism.

After the deicide charge against the Jewish people was formally pronounced invalid at the Council (*Nostra Aetate* 4), the links in the chain that I have described above slowly became clearer. The Jews, as a people, could not be deemed guilty of deicide and, thus, cannot deserve its attendant punishments. This led to a reimagining of the reality of the Jewish people and their theological meaning. Fifty years on from *Nostra Aetate*, a reflection on this journey and its new horizons was published by the Commission for Religious Relations with the Jews (CRRJ). Their document took St. Paul's letter to the Romans as its title: "'The Gifts and the Calling of God Are Irrevocable' (Rom 11:29): A Reflection on Theological Questions Pertaining to Catholic-Jewish Relations on the Occasion of the 50th Anniversary of *Nostra Aetate* (no. 4)" (G&C).[2] G&C stressed that the "Church does not replace the people of God of Israel" (23). The document resolutely condemns "supersessionism," "replacement," and "annulment" theology,[3] because they invalidate post-biblical Judaism as a covenantal religion. "The New Covenant for Christians is...neither the annulment nor the replacement, but the fulfillment of the promises of the Old Covenant" (32). The document contains two critical teachings that are held together in tension (and which form the title of my paper):[4] (a) The irrevocability

---

2. Found at (September 2017, as with all websites cited): http://www.vatican.va/roman_curia/pontifical_councils/chrstuni/relations-jews-docs/rc_pc_chrstuni_doc_20151210_ebraismo-nostra-aetate_en.html.

3. "Supersede" is used thrice (17, 17, 28), "replacement" five time—and synonymously with "supersede" (17, 17, 18, 30, 32), and "annulment" once (32). In every instance, these three positions are strongly rejected.

4. The "tension" is considerable. See Gavin D'Costa, "Supersessionism: Harsh, Mild or Gone for Good?," *European Judaism* 50.1 (2017): 99–107, https://doi.org/10.3167/ej.2017.500113; Elena Procario-Foley, "Fulfillment and Complementarity: Reflections on Relationship in 'Gifts and Calling,'" *Studies in Christian-Jewish Relations* 12.1 (2017), https://doi.org/10.6017/scjr.v12i1.9800; William Madges, "Covenant, Universal Mission, and

of Judaism's covenantal life,⁵ and (b) the covenant's fulfillment in Jesus Christ.⁶ While this document does not have formal doctrinal teaching status, let us, for the sake of argument, grant that these two teachings are true. Where do they lead us in relation to the question of the meaning of the contemporary Jewish state, Israel?

If the magisterium continues repeating that the covenants and promises made by God to the Jews are irrevocable, without putting flesh on this claim, the refrain will eventually sound hollow. The one aspect of this covenant that has been constantly raised by Jews in dialogue with the Vatican is that the covenant entails the promise of the Land, which, for the majority of Jews, is minimally embodied in the State of Israel. Rabbi David Rosen pointed this matter out in the official Vatican launch of G&C: "Perhaps then I may be permitted in the spirit of our mutual respect and friendship to point out that to fully respect Jewish self-understanding, it is also necessary to appreciate the centrality that the Land of Israel plays in the historic and contemporary religious life of the Jewish People, and that appears to be missing."⁷ Jews have raised this

---

Fulfillment," *Studies in Christian-Jewish Relations* 12.1 (2017) https://doi.org/10.6017/scjr.v12i1.9798.

5. See G&C, 8. Saint Pope John Paul II in 1980 begins this tradition (address to the Jewish community in Mainz, West Germany) when he spoke of two dimensions of "the meeting between the people of God of the Old Covenant, never revoked by God" and "the meeting between present-day Christian Churches and the present-day people of the Covenant concluded with Moses." Pope Francis continues: "We hold the Jewish people in special regard because their covenant with God has never been revoked, for 'the gifts and the call of God are irrevocable' (Rom 11:29)," in *Evangelii Gaudium*, 2013, 247.

6. "Fulfillment" occurs ten times (14, 22, 23, 23, 27, 30, 32, 33, 35, 36) and is seen as a post-supersessionist position.

7. 2015, at: http://www.ccjr.us/dialogika-resources/documents-and-statements/analysis/crrj-2015dec10/1365-rosen-2015dec10). Irving Greenberg captures the situation well: "In this generation ... have occurred ... [two] major normative events in Jewish history.... They are the event of the Holocaust—unparalleled tragedy and destruction, towering over the other great tragic

issue, as they want clarification on the matter. Given the importance of Jewish voices in dialogue, a minimal respect for their questions is required. Even rejecting their claim or giving grounds for not being able to decide on the claim is respectful. Ignoring it is not an option. Ignoring it for political and diplomatic reasons is another matter, and a matter I set aside for now.

For sake of clarity in what follows I shall use the word "Israel" to designate the Jewish state, "Judaism" to designate the religion of the Jewish people, and "Catholicism" to designate the "new Israel" of G&C, the Catholic Church.

Here is a snapshot of my argument: I want to argue that the first teaching, the irrevocability of the gifts and promises made to the Jewish people, requires Catholics to attend to the majority religious Jewish (and Christian) claim that (a) the Land of Israel (*Eretz Yisrael*) is part of God's covenant with the Jewish people and (b) the founding of a Jewish country, modern Israel (*Medinat Yisrael*), is somehow part of God's plan.[8] It is possible to hold (a)

---

watershed of 1,900 years ago, the destruction of the Second Temple—and the event of the rebirth of Israel—the experience of redemption as has not been experienced by Jews on this scale since the Exodus," in *For the Sake of Heaven and Earth: The New Encounter between Judaism and Christianity* (Philadelphia: Jewish Publication Society, 2004), 129. I have been particularly influenced by the positions of Michael Wyschogrod and David Novak in their writings on the Land. See Michael Wyschogrod, "A King in Israel," *First Things* 203 (2010): 48–50; David Novak, *Zionism and Judaism: A New Theory* (New York: Cambridge University Press, 2015). In contrast, Hartman's attractive position refuses to see a triumphal messianic moment: "It is important to understand the significance of Israel without having to make it the precursor of messianic redemption." In David Hartman, "The Theological Significance of Israel," in *A Legacy of Catholic-Jewish Dialogue: The Cardinal Joseph Bernardin Jerusalem Lectures,* ed. Thomas A. Baima (Chicago, IL: Liturgy Training Publications, 2012), 55–73.

8. There is a wide range of claims made regarding (b). See some of the range of Jewish views in Aviezer Ravitzky, *Messianism, Zionism, and Jewish Religious Radicalism* (Chicago: University of Chicago Press: translated by Michael Swirsky and Jonathan Chipman [1993], 1996); and Ruth Langer, "Theologies of the Land and State of Israel: The Role of the Secular in Christian

and not (b), and this is true of Jews and Christians, but if both these claims are true, this would amount to minimal "Catholic Zionism." This acknowledges that *Medinat Yisrael* is somehow part of God's plan and has a positive theological significance. This is the position I shall propose and defend.

Eventually, minimal Catholic Zionism must face a range of further questions, all of which remain in the background of this paper: If part of God's plan, does this position (a) require the rebuilding of the temple? (b) require a theocracy of sorts so that the Torah might become central to the life of the nation? (c) imply the impending return of the messiah and the end times? If all three questions were answered positively, we might see a maximal Zionism, but I am not arguing for that.[9] Please note, neither minimal nor maximal Catholic Zionism would necessitate theologically underwriting any political party in power or defending any Israeli government policies, but simply recognizes that the land requires governance. More importantly, neither minimal nor maximal Zionism would require betraying the legitimate claims made by Palestinians to their own state. For the rest of the essay "Catholic Zionism" only refers to minimal Catholic Zionism as I have defined it.[10]

---

and Jewish Understandings," *Studies in Christian-Jewish Relations* 3 (2008): 1–17.

9. For forms of Christian Zionism, see Donald M. Lewis, *The Origins of Christian Zionism: Lord Shaftesbury and Evangelical Support for a Jewish Homeland* (Cambridge; New York: Cambridge University Press, 2010). This literal understanding of the Bible has not been present amongst Catholic exegetes. For recent shifts in the traditional dispensationalist Zionism see Craig A. Blaising and Darrell L. Bock, *Progressive Dispensationalism* (Wheaton, IL: BridgePoint, 1993). See below for "the New Christian Zionism." For a wide-ranging denomination view, see Paul Charles Merkley, *Christian Attitudes towards the State of Israel* (Montreal: McGill-Queen's University Press, 2001).

10. Catholics who might be classed as minimal Zionists are Edward Flannery ("Christian Zionist Ethos Should Be Revived," *Providence Journal Bulletin*, April 26, 1966, 22–26); Richard Lux (*The Jewish People, the Holy Land, and the State of Israel: A Catholic View* [New York: Paulist Press, 2010]);

I also want to argue that the second teaching—that Jesus is the fulfillment of the covenant—means that Catholic Zionism presents a challenging ecclesiology and complicates Catholic-Jewish dialogue. G&C 43 prophetically recalls: "It is and remains a qualitative definition of the Church of the New Covenant that it consists of Jews and Gentiles, even if the quantitative proportions of Jewish and Gentile Christians may initially give a different impression." If the church is genuinely interested in recovering its Jewish roots, rather than effacing them as in the past, then Catholic Zionism not only entails tentative theological support for Israel and for the Jewish people, but it also entails support for Hebrew Catholics, their continued Jewish identity within the church, and their participation in Israel, the land promised to them and through them as Jews. Since many Jews view Hebrew Catholics as non-Jews this position presents serious problems—for Jews and, of course, Catholics committed to good relations and dialogue with Jews.

The Tentative Trail Emerging from Vatican Documents

First, let me briefly sketch the steps that have been taken by the Holy See so far.[11] These steps are a kind of dance taken by two

---

and Anthony J. Kenny (*Catholics, Jews, and the State of Israel*, Studies in Judaism and Christianity [New York; Mahwah: Paulist Press, 1993]). All three differ from my position in not pursuing the implications of the argument in relation to Hebrew Catholics and Messianic Jews. See also various Catholic ecclesiastics who support this position in the unpublished paper by Raymond Cohen, "The Document That Never Was: People, Land, and State after *Nostra Aetate*," shared by the author and presented to a conference in Heidelberg in 2014.

11. See the excellent coverage of relevant Vatican documents in Lux, *The Jewish People*; Kenny, *Catholics, Jews, and the State of Israel*; and more recently, Philip A. Cunningham, *Seeking Shalom: The Journey to Right Relationship between Catholics and Jews* (Grand Rapids, MI: William B. Eerdmans Publishing Company, 2015), 220–34; and Adam Gregerman, "Is the Biblical

arms, or legs, of the Vatican; the Secretary of State dealing with political and diplomatic areas, and the Secretariat / later Council for Religious Relations with the Jews dealing with "religious" areas. I start here because, I contend, the Vatican's teachings and actions all point towards a tentative Catholic Zionism. This argument from Vatican documents and actions will be further supplemented later by my presentation of biblical arguments.

Which set of arguments should be presented first depends on many factors. If I were presenting this in an ecumenical forum, I would start with the Bible. If presenting in a Catholic forum, I would start with the magisterium. If presenting to Jews, I might have started with the state of the discussion amongst Jews on the religious significance of the state of Israel.

Political and diplomatic recognition of Israel was established by the Vatican Secretary of State in 1993, when a Fundamental Agreement was signed by the two countries, immediately after Yasser Arafat and Yitzhak Rabin had signed a Peace Agreement that same year. This led to full diplomatic relations in 1994.[12] A parallel Fundamental Agreement with the Palestinian Liberation Organization was signed in 2000. In 2015, recognition of a Palestinian state was given treaty status.[13] This balancing act, undertaken by the Secretary of State, shows that the Vatican was

---

Land Promise Irrevocable?: Post-Nostra Aetate Catholic Theologies of the Jewish Covenant and the Land of Israel," *Modern Theology* 34,2 (2018): 137–58.

12. See Raymond Cohen, "Israel and the Holy See Negotiate," *The Hague Journal of Diplomacy* 5.3 (2010): 213–34. See also Eugene Fisher and Leon Klenicki, *A Challenge Long Delayed: The Diplomatic Exchange between the Holy See and Israel* (New York: Anti-Defamation League of B'nai B'rith, 1996)—slightly dated; and Lux, *The Jewish People*.

13. Andrej Kreutz, *Vatican Policy on the Palestinian-Israeli Conflict: The Struggle for the Holy Land* (New York; London: Greenwood, 1990), while earlier than the formal Agreements contains an invaluable background. For the Fundamental Agreement: http://www.vatican.va/roman_curia/secretariat_state/2000/documents/rc_seg-st_20000215_santa-sede-olp_en.html.

not taking sides in the dispute over Israel and its borders, other than to indicate, drawing on international law and the 1947 UN resolution, that both states had a legitimate right to exist and both were important to the Vatican.

While none of these agreements are theological in their rationale, there are discreet theological underpinnings in the 1993 Agreement with Israel. The preamble acknowledges both communities' religious dimensions. It reads: "Mindful of the singular character and universal significance of the Holy Land; Aware of the unique nature of the relationship between the Catholic Church and the Jewish people, and of the historic process of reconciliation and growth in mutual understanding and friendship between Catholics and Jews." It then launches into the legal Agreement. The "unique nature" can only refer to the *sui generis* religious relationship that the Church has with the Jewish people, which the Council established by citing Saint Paul in Romans 11:9. The "reconciliation and growth" must refer to the steps taken by the Council for Religious Relations, although it can obviously also refer to the diplomatic steps that led to this agreement. But "reconciliation" has serious theological overtones.

This is further underwritten at the public signatory speech given by Msgr. Claudio Maria Celli, Undersecretary for Foreign Affairs. He claims that the Agreement must be "acknowledged to have a fundamental religious and spiritual significance—not only for the Holy See and the State of Israel, but for millions of people throughout the world."[14] Lux is surely right to suggest that we see here the Vatican's recognition that the State of Israel cannot be divorced from religious Jews and their covenantal aspirations.[15]

The only existent Vatican document explicitly to broach the theological status of Israel was the CRRJ "Notes on the Correct Way to Present Jews and Judaism in Preaching and Catechesis in

---

14. *Christians and Israel*, 3:1 (1993/1994): 4.
15. Lux, *The Jewish People*, 77.

the Roman Catholic Church" (1985).¹⁶ It too continued a very careful balancing act:

> VI, 1. The history of Israel did not end in 70 A.D. (cf. *Guidelines* II). It continued, especially in a numerous Diaspora which allowed Israel to carry to the whole world a witness—often heroic—of its fidelity to the one God and to "exalt him in the presence of all the living" (Tobit 13:4), while preserving the memory of the land of their forefathers at the hearts of their hope (Passover *Seder*).
>
> Christians are invited to understand this religious attachment which finds its roots in Biblical tradition, without however making their own any particular religious interpretation of this relationship (cf. *Declaration* of the US Conference of Catholic Bishops, November 20, 1975).
>
> The existence of the State of Israel and its political options should be envisaged not in a perspective which is in itself religious, but in their reference to the common principles of international law.
>
> The permanence of Israel (while so many ancient peoples have disappeared without trace) is a historic fact and a sign to be interpreted within God's design. We must in any case rid ourselves of the traditional idea of a people *punished*, preserved as a *living argument* for Christian apologetic. It remains a chosen people.¹⁷

It delicately affirms the continued presence of the Jewish people and accords this a theological status: part of "God's design." It acknowledges the central liturgically preserved hope of the land

---

16. There are important national bishops' conference documents, especially the French and the American, that form a backdrop to this statement. The US Bishops Conference statement is cited.
17. See http://www.vatican.va/roman_curia/pontifical_councils/chrstuni/relations-jews-docs/rc_pc_chrstuni_doc_19820306_jews-judaism_en.html.

(*Eretz*) and the state (*Medinat*), but indicates that Catholics need not hold any particular theological interpretation regarding these two matters. It acknowledges and affirms an international legal status to Israel (*Medinat/Eretz*). While some have read from this text that no theological interpretation and affirmation should be given by Catholics,[18] there are reasons to suggest that the sentences just cited leave the matter open, because unresolved, rather than closed, because tacitly decided.

The first reason is the unpublished proposed CRRJ document of 1969. It resolved the matter tentatively in the direction of Catholic Zionism. The leaked document theologically affirms both the land (*Eretz*) and state (*Medinat*). It says, in describing the Jewish people: "The same God has revealed himself to his people Israel and made to it the gift of the Torah.... Fidelity to the covenant was linked to the gift of a land, which in the Jewish soul has endured as the object of an aspiration that Christians should strive to understand." This is what we find in the 1985 document, but note the following related sentence: "It would seem that Christians, whatever the difficulties that they may experience, must attempt to understand and respect the religious significance of this link between the people and the land. The existence of the State of Israel should not be separated from this perspective; which does not itself imply any judgement on

---

18. Gregerman, "Is the Biblical Land Promise Irrevocable?," reads it as "a *general* statement against Christians as Christians giving the land promise to the Jews any religious significance. While Jews, they admit, do view the promise of the land in theological terms, Christians should not look upon the same promise from a 'religious' perspective." Alain Marchadour and David Neuhaus, *The Land, the Bible, and History: Toward the Land That I Will Show You*, 1st ed. (New York: Fordham University Press, 2007), concur based on their biblical exegesis. In contrast, Fisher suggests that this is simply against fundamentalist readings, both Jewish and Protestant, in "Reflections on 'the Common Bond,'" *Christian Jewish Relations* 18 (1985): 54–57. The Eckardts are very critical of Fisher's caution: Alice L. Eckardt and A. Roy Eckardt, "The Place of the Jewish State in Christian-Jewish Relations," *European Judaism: A Journal for the New Europe* 25.1 (1992): 3–14, 10.

historical occurrences of decisions or of a purely political order."[19] This is moving in the direction of minimal "Catholic Zionism." It explicitly distances itself from any form of political support for the State of Israel's political actions, but implies a required "respect" for the "religious significance" of the event. Respect could be read as what is required due to the principle of religious liberty, but the context suggests something stronger.

This non-existent, or rather unpublished, document disappeared after a leak prior to its proposed publication. The clear reason for its disappearance is not to be found in the public arena, but likely reasons cluster around diplomatic and theological issues. The diplomatic issues probably included a tension between the Secretariat for State and the Secretariat for the Jews, working at different paces but with overlapping concerns; and the visceral reactions of Arab countries prompted by the leak.[20] I shall leave these concerns aside. The theological opposition would have come from some Arab and Eastern Christians, some of whom held and still hold supersessionist forms of theology, along with the unresolved biblical questions on the matter.

For such Arab Christians, it is impossible to see the State of Israel as being part of God's plan as this "plan" entails the oppression of their people, who are God's people (with or without a superses-

---

19. "Excerpts from the Vatican-Approved Document on the Improvement of Roman Catholic-Jewish Relations," *New York Times*, December 11, 1969. See timesmachine.nytimes.com/timesmachine/1969/12/11/88869828.html?pageNumber=14. See also Cohen, "The Document That Never Was." I am grateful to Gregerman for drawing my attention to this document and Cohen's unpublished paper. An account of it is tersely given on p. 4 and the document printed on p. 19 of "The Secretariat for Promoting Christian Unity Information Service," 9 February 1970, *Information Service* (published by the Secretariat, Vatican city, Rome), found at: http://www.vatican.va/roman_curia/pontifical_councils/chrstuni/information_service/pdf/information_service_9_en.pdf.

20. Cohen, "The Document That Never Was," provides strong evidence for all four factors named here.

sionist extra added).[21] A non-supersessionist version is persuasive. However, and I can only state this too briefly here, Catholic Zionism of the sort that I am defending can argue that God's plan requires that justice must be exercised within *Eretz/Medinat* Israel as part of the covenantal tradition (accepted by most Jews and Old Testament Catholic exegetes). In this respect, Catholic Zionism must be indivisible from the Catholic support of a Palestinian state, such as is already expressed by the Vatican. I do not expect Arab Catholics to cheer my proposal, but I argue that their objections, as stated, can in principle be met by Catholic Zionism. After all, the Kingdom is about justice and the Church cannot leave that justice "aside." However, there are genuinely unresolved biblical interpretative questions to which I return below.

The second reason for reading the 1985 published CRRJ statement as open and unresolved is that, in 1985, the Fundamental Agreements with Israel and with Palestine did not exist. Hence, any theological underwriting of Israel would have been premature and inflammatory as it could easily have been perceived as supporting Israel during a very turbulent period between two groups, both of which the Vatican sought after good relations. This is also

---

21. See, for example, the powerful and eloquent argument advanced by Naim Stifan Ateek, *Justice, and Only Justice: A Palestinian Theology of Liberation* (Maryknoll, NY: Orbis Books, 1989), and further, eds. Naim Stifan Ateek, Cedar Duaybis, and Maurine Tobin, *Challenging Christian Zionism: Theology, Politics and the Israel-Palestine Conflict* (London: Melisende, 2005). Rowan Williams's essay and responses to it in this collection are instructive for seeing that any unguarded support for Israel is a potentially dark cloud for Arab Christians. There are Eastern Christians, like Fr. George Makhlour of Ramallah, who argue the full traditional supersessionist view: "The church has inherited the promises of Israel. The church is actually the new Israel. What Abraham was promised, Christians now possess.... [T]he land itself belongs to the Christians. This is not a manner of speaking or a metaphor. The land literally belongs to the People of God, the Christians. And the Christians on the land are Palestinians." Cited in Merkley, *Christian Attitudes towards the State of Israel*, 187. There is a wide variety of Christian Arab views. See Lux, *The Jewish People*, 61–69.

why the 1969 document was probably withdrawn—it would have been premature given the state of political tensions. But to assert in 1985 a divine "sign" related to the enduring permanence of the Jewish people after the 1967 War is quite remarkable. One might argue that the precondition of the enduring existence of the Jewish people is the state established by that people. We see a building block towards an explicit future affirmation of the flourishing of that people: a state of their own.

The third reason for reading this statement as open and unresolved is that in 1985, as now, there is no consensus by Catholic biblical scholars on the question of Israel (*Eretz*) in the New Testament. There is strong consensus that the Old Testament does contain this promise of *Eretz Yisrael* as part of the Jewish covenant. But there is no consensus that the New Testament underwrites this promise. Herein lies the theological heart of the matter, for Catholics cannot commend Catholic theological positions based on another religious community's holding them, let alone the fact of the multiple and diverse views held within that "other" religious community on this matter. An answer to our Catholic question will only be possible through reading both Testaments in the light of current realities.

Tentative Biblical Arguments

First, let me turn to the Old Testament. The Old Testament is read nearly unanimously by Catholic and Jewish exegetes to assert three things about the Land. Jewish exegetes cannot of course determine Catholic teaching, but when both groups concur, as in this case, this is an important moment.[22] The three teachings are this: First,

---

22. The two most comprehensive Christian examinations of the Old Testament biblical texts concur. See Walter Brueggemann, *The Land: Place as Gift, Promise and Challenge in Biblical Faith*, 2nd ed. (Philadelphia: Fortress Press, 2002); W. D. Davies, *The Gospel and the Land: Early Christianity and*

the Land (*Eretz*) is promised to Abraham as part of God's covenant to his people. Second, the promise is unconditional and relies on God's love and initiative; it is not merited by the Jewish people. Third, the Jewish people's behavior within the Land is subject to punishment by God, and even expulsion from the land if they fail to live by God's law and do not respect and honor the "alien" within the land.[23]

Some Catholics who argue for a "dual covenant" position—meaning that there are two separate ontological pathways to salvation, one with the Jews and one with the Christians—can at this stage use the authority of the Old Testament to clinch their argument that Catholic Zionism is legitimate. If for most Jews, their sacred scripture, shared by Catholics, tells them that this is the nature of God's covenant, then the matter is concluded. If the Church teaches that their covenant is irrevocable, then one must accept the two different ways in which God deals with his two peoples.[24]

This position is not feasible for several reasons. First, G&C criticizes the "theory that there may be two different paths to salvation,

---

Jewish Territorial Doctrine, 2nd ed. (Sheffield: JSOT Press, 1994). See also Langer, "Theologies of the Land and State of Israel."

23. Genesis 12.7: "I give this land to your descendants"; Deut 28.11: "The Lord will make you prosper greatly in the fruit of your body and of your cattle, and in the fruit of the ground in the land which he swore to your forefathers to give you"; Deut 28:64: If Israel fails to remain faithful, "The Lord will scatter you among the peoples from one end of the earth to the other, and there you will worship other gods whom neither you have known nor your forefathers, gods of wood and stone."

24. The liberal orientation of two covenant theologians can sometimes work against Zionism, in their aversion to particularity. This is true of Rosemary Radford Ruether, *Faith and Fratricide: Theological Roots of Anti-Semitism* (New York: Seabury Press, 1974); and her stringent criticism of Zionism: Rosemary Radford Ruether and Herman J. Ruether, *The Wrath of Jonah: The Crisis of Religious Nationalism in the Israeli-Palestinian Conflict* (New York: Harper & Row, 1989). The classical two-covenant position is found in the Jewish work of Franz Rosenzweig (translated William W. Hallo), *The Star of Redemption* (Notre Dame, IN: Notre Dame Press, 1985 [1930]).

the Jewish path without Christ and the path with the Christ, whom Christians believe is Jesus of Nazareth," for this "would in fact endanger the foundations of Christian faith" (35). It cites the 1985 document and Acts 4:12 (and it could have cited a number of formal magisterial teaching texts[25]) to show, "The Christian faith confesses that God wants to lead all people to salvation, that Jesus Christ is the universal mediator of salvation, and that there is no 'other name under heaven given to the human race by which we are to be saved' (Acts 4:12)." This means that while there may be different historical ways in which God reaches out to people, none can bypass Christ as the "universal mediator of salvation." G&C does not back away from the awkward position that it advances: "That the Jews are participants in God's salvation is theologically unquestionable, but how that can be possible without confessing Christ explicitly is and remains an unfathomable divine mystery" (36). I have nothing against unfathomable divine mysteries, especially in the right place—but I am not sure that all routes to understanding this mystery are in fact exhausted.[26] The point is that this type of dual covenant position endangers the foundations of Christian faith.

Second, such a solution fails to resolve the way in which the New and Old Testaments must be read together in harmony. It allows for a strange autonomy in the reading of the Old, as if the Christologically centered New was not the final arbiter in reading the Old. This is not just a matter of saying historical-critical readings of the Bible cannot be dogmatically normative. Nor am I supporting a purely allegorical reading of the Old in the light of the New, as is the way of the traditional supersessionist hermeneutic. Rather, I

---

25. The notion of two independent paths to salvation was rejected at Vatican II. Some would argue this is a *de fide* teaching. See Gavin D'Costa, *Vatican II: Catholic Doctrines on Jews and Muslims* (Oxford: Oxford University Press, 2014), 59–112.
26. See Gavin D'Costa, *Christianity and World Religions: Disputed Questions in the Theology of Religions* (Oxford: Wiley-Blackwell, 2009), particularly the last two chapters, wherein I suggest a resolution.

want to argue that, from a Catholic viewpoint, the affirmation of Israel's enduring covenant must finally find legitimation in the New Testament and the Old Testament, read together, or not at all. The very positioning of Romans 11:29 at the head of the CRRJ document indicates this recovery of rereading the scriptures, both Old and New, as the only way to rethink doctrine and relations with the Jews. So while listening carefully to Jewish exegesis, the Pontifical Biblical Commission has indicated that each community's reading begins with differing presuppositions and starting points and thus are "irreducible."[27]

Let me now turn to the New Testament. This is key to my thesis, but given the context, must be only a gesture for the moment. It has normally been assumed, in the light of a long tradition of supersessionist readings, that the risen Christ forms the new Israel with his people, the Christian church. The new Israel, including gentiles, marks the evaporation of the boundaries of territorial Israel that is the gift to the Jews. They have lost the gift and promises. But is this the only reading of the texts, especially given that supersessionism has been declared problematic? Is it coherent to affirm territorial *Eretz/Medinat* and see it as a factor for rejoicing for both Jew and Christian? I think so, although a lot of biblical discussion will be required—and it has only recently begun in Catholic circles.

Let me indicate a trajectory for an alternative biblical reading that harmonizes the Old and New Testaments, without denying the discontinuity between Judaism and Christianity. Jesus and Paul (and the earliest disciples) were Jews and continued their practices as Jews. They were circumcised, went to the temple, followed the Law/Torah, and more importantly, Paul can be seen to argue that after the resurrection, *this should continue*. The crisis in Acts 15,

---

27. Pontifical Biblical Commission, *The Jewish People and Their Sacred Scriptures in the Christian Bible* (Città del Vaticano: Catholic Truth Society, 2002), 22. This is akin to Lindbeck's notion of intra-textual communitarian authority, developed in George A. Lindbeck, *The Nature of Doctrine: Religion and Theology in a Postliberal Age* (London: SPCK, 1984).

the first Council of Jerusalem, has often been read as the defeat of the Jewish Christians who wanted to enforce Jewish practice upon all. It marks the beginning of gentile Christianity, which shook free from this Jewish particularizing. But G&C counters this in acknowledging a quantitative ecclesiological dimension that constitutes the church of the circumcision and is very explicit about the continued Jewish practices.

Some exegetes argue that Paul is resisting the imposition of Jewish practices upon gentiles such as circumcision and dietary laws, but takes for granted that Jews will continue their practices—which would of course also include the hope of the restoration of Israel (*Medinat*) as part of the covenant promise. The lengthy discussions in the Jerusalem church in Acts 15 indicate precisely that the question was to whom the Torah/Law should apply. The decision is that no further burden other than the Noahide Laws should be placed upon gentiles. This was continuous with Rabbinic Judaism. The rabbis, it is argued, discouraged circumcision of gentiles and encouraged the following of the Noahide Laws.[28] In fact, of the debate in Acts 15, Michael Wyschogrod writes:

> It is not difficult to infer from this episode that for Jews the Torah obviously was thought of as remaining obligatory in the view of the Jerusalem church. Had the thought that with the coming of Christ the Law had been abolished entered anyone's mind in Jerusalem, there could clearly not have ensued a long discussion, settled with some difficulty, as to whether circumcision and the Law ought to be made obligatory for gentiles. If it was no longer obligatory for Jews, how could it possibly become so for others?[29]

---

28. Michael Wyschogrod, *Abraham's Promise: Judaism and Jewish-Christian Relations*, ed. R. Kendall Soulen (London: SCM Press, 2006), 193.
29. Ibid., 94.

Furthermore, the crucial verse in Romans 11:29 that forms the title of G&C can be illuminatingly explicated against supersessionist readings both intra-textually (biblically) and through the use of a broader range of early extra-biblical texts that illuminate the phrases Paul employs in his phraseology.[30] R. Kendall Soulen has argued for the importance of the present-tense frames for Romans 9–11 regarding the two book-end references to Israel.[31] Paul initially wishes himself "accursed" if it would help his people accept Jesus. His people are the "Israelites, and to them belongs the adoption, the glory, the covenants, the giving of the law, the worship, and the promises; to them belong the patriarchs, and from them, according to the flesh, comes the Messiah." (9:3–5). The "gifts" (χαρίσματα) mentioned in 11:9 (for the gifts and the calling of God [to Israel] are irrevocable) points back to the list of 9:3–5. In the light of extensive Second Temple Jewish literature that uses the term "gifts," Philo, Josephus, and Ezekiel the Tragedian all include "Lan" as part of this "gift." Likewise "calling" (κλῆσις) is the same phrase used in 1 Corinthians 7:12–20, where Paul enjoins circumcised Jews to remain faithful to their Jewish state. First Corinthians 7:18 literally

---

30. See David Rudolf, "Zionism in Pauline Literature: Does Paul Eliminate Particularity for Israel and the Land in His Portrayal of Salvation Available for All the World?," in *The New Christian Zionism: Fresh Perspectives on Israel and the Land*, ed. Gerald R. McDermott. (Downers Grove, IL: IVP Books, 2016), 167–97. See the very important studies: *Between Gospel and Election: Explorations in the Interpretation of Romans 9–11*, eds. Florian Wilk and J. Ross Wagner (Tübingen: Mohr Siebeck, 2010), and Joseph Sievers, "A History of the Interpretation of Romans 11:29," *Annali di storia dell'esegesi* 14.2 (1997): 381–442, which shows the multiple interpretations and translations that this passage has been given. Sievers identifies Barth's reading as an important turning point. For the influence of this text in Catholic theology, again through Protestant influences, leading to Vatican II, see John Connelly, *From Enemy to Brother: The Revolution in Catholic Teaching on the Jews, 1933–1965* (Cambridge, MA: Harvard University Press, 2012). For one of the best biblical studies on the Gospels and Acts see McDermott, ed., *The New Christian Zionism*.

31. See R. Kendall Soulen, "The Priority of the Present Tense for Jewish-Christian Relations," in *Between Gospel and Election*, 498–99.

rendered would be "do not put on foreskin," meaning, do not assimilate to the gentiles. This is entirely compatible with Paul's argument that in Christ there is neither Jew nor Greek, just as he says that there is neither male nor female, but enjoins different practices related to each. The differences are transformed within Christ in the eschaton and indicate a common "slavery"/service of each to the other.

Romans 9–11 concludes with a strong sense that the final redemption, when "all Israel will be saved," is located in *Eretz Yisrael:* such that the deliverer comes "out of Zion" (citing Isaiah 59:20; see also Galatians 4:26–30). William Horbury concludes that "Paul envisaged a coming messianic reign in the divinely prepared Jerusalem" which is constant with "the eschatological importance of Zion or the land in Romans 9:25–26."[32] The Pontifical Biblical Commission recognizes this messianic bond between Jews and Catholics when it says (5.21.d): "Jewish messianic expectation is not in vain. It can become for us Christians a powerful stimulant to keep alive the eschatological dimension of our faith. Like them, we too live in expectation. The difference is that for us the One who is to come will have the traits of the Jesus who has already come and is already present and active among us."

This all just scratches at the surface and certainly does not achieve a clear victory for my argument. One would also have to show that Jesus, Paul, and the early witness did not exclude the hope for *Eretz/Medinat* and also show why the New Testament pays so little attention to this issue (again, scholars have attended to these issues quite plausibly). And most importantly, one would have to show why this expectation for the restoration of the land is important not only for Jews, but is thus also important for Christians, both Jewish and gentile Christians. I turn to this issue to complete my tentative proposal, fully acknowledging that my argument is now even more tentative than at the outset.

---

32. See William Horbury, *Messianism among Jews and Christians: Biblical and Historical Studies*, 2nd ed. (London; New York: T&T Clark, 2016), 218.

Why Catholic Zionism Is Not Merely Jewish Religious Zionism

G&C 43, already cited, recalls the qualitative definition of the New Testament church: it "consists of Jews and Gentiles," even if quantitatively today one gives a different impression. G&C 15 grounds this ecclesiology: "The first Christians were Jews; as a matter of course they gathered as part of the community in the Synagogue, they observed the dietary laws, the Sabbath and the requirement of circumcision, while at the same time confessing Jesus as the Christ, the Messiah sent by God for the salvation of Israel and the entire human race." It continues: "In the early years of the Church, therefore, there were the so-called Jewish Christians and the Gentile Christians, the *ecclesia ex circumcisione* and the *ecclesia ex gentibus*, one Church originating from Judaism, the other from the Gentiles, who however together constituted the one and only Church of Jesus Christ."

This raises two important issues regarding my question. The first is whether the Catholic Church is actively reversing its supersessionist eradication of Jewish rites when Jews become Catholics. Is it actively fostering and cultivating the *ecclesia ex circumcisione*? I am not suggesting an idealized return to the first century, ignoring changes in both Judaism and Christianity over time, but rather a recovery of an ecclesia that enacts the reality that the Jewish covenant is still valid. The Fourth Lateran Council represents one height (or low moment) of Catholic anti-Jewish sentiments. It contained clear canons to ensure the eradication of Jewish practices within Catholicism.[33] It may even be important

---

33. Canon 70: "Some [Jews], we understand, who voluntarily approached the waters of holy baptism, do not entirely cast off the old man that they may more perfectly put on the new one, because, retaining remnants of the former rite, they obscure by such a mixture the beauty of the Christian religion. But since it is written: 'Accursed is the man that goeth on the two ways' (Ecclus. 2:14), and 'a garment that is woven together of woolen and linen' (Deut. 22:11) ought not to be put on, we decree that such persons be

to revoke those canons, more as an aid in forming Catholic culture than as a goodwill token in interfaith dialogue (although it would helpfully be that as well). Revoking a canon is not the same as revoking formal doctrinal teaching from an authoritative Council. Some Jewish converts have become distanced from their Jewish heritage, and it may be artificial to enjoin upon them the practice of Jewish prayers and rites (in so much as these do not contradict Christian doctrine). However, most religious Jews, after their conversion, have never encountered statutes that encourage the practice of their Jewish heritage. The opposite has always been the case. The logic of this position in the light of G&C requires a kind of "ordinariate" granted to Hebrew/Jewish Catholics, as was granted to Anglicans, who wished to be in full communion with Rome, while retaining much of their own spiritual patrimony.

Currently, the Catholic Church has accepted and encourages "Hebrew Catholics" in the United States and Israel—homes of the two largest Jewish populations in the world—to retain their Jewish heritage while being Catholics.[34] This is deeply encouraging. The challenge of the Jewish philosopher Michael Wyschogrod to the Jewish Cardinal convert, Jean-Marie Lustiger, is worth recalling. Lustiger wrote to his Jewish parents upon his conversion: "I'm not leaving you. I'm not going over to the enemy. I am becoming what I am. I am not ceasing to be a Jew; on the contrary, I am discovering another way of being a Jew."[35] Wyschogrod accepts Lustiger's act of conversion as compelled by conscience, even if this means Lustiger is viewed as accepting idolatry. But Wyschogrod challenges

---

in every way restrained by the prelates from the observance of the former rite, that, having given themselves of their own free will to the Christian religion, salutary coercive action may preserve them in its observance, since not to know the way of the Lord is a lesser evil than to retrace one's steps after it is known" (https://sourcebooks.fordham.edu/basis/lateran4.asp).

34. For the USA, see the Association of Hebrew Catholics: http://www.hebrewcatholic.net/. For Israel, see: http://www.catholic.co.il/index.php?lang=en.
35. Michael Wyschogrod, "Letter to a Friend," *Modern Theology* 11.2 (1995): 165–71, 168; Lustiger quotation cited on 165.

Lustiger: "Because you are a Jew, you are obligated, like all Jews, to obey the *mitzvoth* (e.g., tefillin [phylacteries] in the morning, kashrut, sabbath, etc). Like all other Jews, you are not perfect. You have violated some of the commandments of the Torah and you (and I) should repent of these violations.... From the Jewish point of view you are obligated to live in accordance with the mitzvoth just like any other Jew."[36] Jewish identity requires such practices. Wyschogrod cites the apostle Paul to buttress his argument. I think his challenge has hardly been taken seriously.[37] But it is a challenge that can no longer be ignored.[38]

The second ecclesiological question that this raises now comes into view: dialogue with Messianic Jews. For some years the Vatican has been informally engaged in dialogue with Messianic

---

36. Ibid., 168.
37. Lindbeck begins to take his challenge seriously: George Lindbeck, "Response to Michael Wyschogrod's Letter to a Friend," *Modern Theology* 11.2 (1995): 205–10, https://doi.org/10.1111/j.1468-0025.1995.tb00062.x. Wyschogrod's final response notes: "my letter is ultimately most relevant for Jewish Christians. It is their reply that I await most" (241). Such a response is to be found in Mark S. Kinzer, *Postmissionary Messianic Judaism: Redefining Christian Engagement with the Jewish People* (Grand Rapids, MI: Brazos Press, 2005), 182–83. See below for more on Kinzer.
38. The challenge does not just face Catholics. It also faces Jews. For example, since the restoration of Israel is intrinsic to the Jewish covenant and can now be affirmed by Catholics (if my suggestions are plausible), then Jewish/Hebrew Catholics may wish to return to Israel under the Law of Return. However, the Israeli Supreme Court has regularly and consistently ruled against Jewish Catholics and Messianic Jews as having no Jewish status and, thus, having no right of return. See Dan Cohn-Sherbok, *Messianic Judaism* (London; New York: Continuum, 2000), 191–202. Atheist Jews, agnostic Jews, and even Jewish Buddhists can be Israeli citizens. And of course, early Jewish Zionism was atheistic. It is finally a matter for the High Court, not theologians, although the Vatican diplomatic mission to Israel might express views in private on this matter.

Jews.[39] While Mark Kinzer is not representative of the wide spectrum that operates under this umbrella term,[40] he is particularly interested in seeking communion with institutional Christians, including Catholics, in fidelity to Jesus Christ. Kinzer represents a position that I have been envisaging: a Jew who takes seriously their religious Jewish identity; their recognition that this was not eradicated in the New Testament, but rather, that the Land was part of the hope of Jesus and many first-generation Jewish Christians; and their obligation to seek visible unity with gentile followers of Jesus, as this was also Paul's vision. One cannot keep Romans 11:29 in view and such messianic Jews out of view.

I am aware that this section of my argument will leave many Jewish friends deeply unsettled. Talk of Jews who are Christians understandably invokes a deep trauma, so well expressed by Rabbi Abraham Heschel. Heschel said, "I am ready to go to Auschwitz any time, if faced with the alternative of conversion or death."[41] The latter allowed him to remain a Jew; while the prospect of being a Christian shamefully eradicated that reality. It is a tragic irony that in seeking good relations with the Jewish people, Catholics may now support what jeopardizes good Jewish-Catholic relations. But it is important and necessary to explore all paths with trust and sensitivity.

---

39. See the preface by Cardinal Christoph Schönborn in Mark S. Kinzer, *Searching Her Own Mystery: Nostra Aetate, the Jewish People, and the Identity of the Church* (Eugene, OR: Cascade Books, 2015), xi–xii, and Kinzer's own account: 35–37. Fr Peter Hocken also belonged to this group. See his *Azusa, Rome, and Zion: Pentecostal Faith, Catholic Reform, and Jewish Roots* (Eugene, OR: Pickwick Publications, 2016). I am personally indebted to both for many illuminating exchanges and advice.
40. See Patricia A. Power, "Blurring the Boundaries: American Messianic Jews and Gentiles," *Nova Religio: The Journal of Alternative and Emergent Religions* 15.1 (2011): 69–91.
41. Cited in Thomas Merton, *Merton & Judaism: Recognition, Repentence and Renewal: Holiness in Words*, ed. Beatrice Bruteau (Louisville, KY: Fons Vitae, 2003), 223–24.

Conclusion

Catholic relations with the Jewish people have overcome many obstacles and since Vatican II have begun a new lease on life. The journey ahead looks complex, but amidst the complexity, I hope that I have at least shown very tentatively that there is a case for Catholic Zionism and that it is possibly required both by the internal logic of strands of magisterial teaching that are emerging and by a non-supersessionist rereading of the New Testament. It is difficult to imagine the cluster of difficulties facing this proposal being pushed aside rapidly. The Catholic Church is well known for taking hundreds of years to make important decisions. That is often a good thing. This is a decision that I propose it must seriously consider making.

Bibliography

D'Costa, Gavin. *Catholic Doctrines about the Jewish People after Vatican II* (New York: Oxford University Press, 2019).

D'Costa, Gavin. "Supersessionism: Harsh, Mild or Gone for Good?" *European Judaism* 50.1 (2017): 99–107. https://doi.org/10.3167/ej.2017.500113.

———. *Vatican II: Catholic Doctrines on Jews and Muslims.* Oxford: Oxford University Press, 2014.

Greenberg, Irving, *For the Sake of Heaven and Earth: The New Encounter between Judaism and Christianity.* Philadelphia: Jewish Publication Society, 2004.

Gregerman, Adam. "Is the Biblical Land Promise Irrevocable?: Post-*Nostra Aetate* Catholic Theologies of the Jewish Covenant and the Land of Israel." *Modern Theology* 34.2 (2018): 137–58.

Kenny, Anthony J. *Catholics, Jews, and the State of Israel.* Studies in Judaism and Christianity. New York; Mahwah: Paulist Press, 1993.

Kinzer, Mark S. *Searching Her Own Mystery: Nostra Aetate, the Jewish People, and the Identity of the Church.* Eugene, OR: Cascade Books, 2015.

Langer, Ruth. "Theologies of the Land and State of Israel: The Role of the Secular in Christian and Jewish Understandings." *Studies in Christian-Jewish Relations* 3 (2008): 1–17.

Lux, Richard C. *The Jewish People, the Holy Land, and the State of Israel: A Catholic View*. New York: Paulist Press, 2010.

Merkley, Paul Charles. *Christian Attitudes towards the State of Israel*. Montreal: McGill-Queen's University Press, 2001.

Wyschogrod, Michael. *Abraham's Promise: Judaism and Jewish-Christian Relations*, edited by R. Kendall Soulen. London: SCM Press, 2006.

———. "Letter to a Friend." *Modern Theology* 11.2 (1995): 165–71.

Chapter Two

THE WAY FORWARD

Abraham Skorka,
Institute for Jewish-Catholic Relations,
Saint Joseph's University, Philadelphia

In order to chart the way forward with any venture or project, it is first necessary to take a look back on the journey already made for clues and suggestions about how to continue. I recall that when I began becoming involved with interreligious dialogue in general—and the Jewish-Catholic relationship in particular—my first goal was to do something to eliminate antisemitism or any other kind of hatred for any human being. In retrospect, I now realize that this attitude was my reaction to the images of piles and piles of corpses and skeletons as numerous as dust molecules that were scattered throughout the Nazi camps of death and extermination. In the Jewish school that I attended in my childhood, as well as in my home, the things that occurred during the Second World War were named explicitly—not indirectly or delicately mentioned using euphemisms. My family came from Poland, but not a single one of its members are still there. Out of two big families on both my mother's and father's sides, there only remain those who abandoned Poland between the wars, and a few survivors. The cruelty of the Nazis, the humiliation and torture suffered by the victims until they died, the image of my father trying to understand the incomprehensible, haunted me throughout my life. There are different ways to react after such a trauma. One option is to learn how to respond to physical aggressions. A second is to try the change the aggressiveness of people.

During my rabbinic studies I had a course in Jewish philosophy that studied the thought of Martin Buber. I discovered then the power and the deep meaning of the concept of dialogue. Afterwards, my teacher introduced me to the works of Abraham Joshua Heschel, whom Buber had met in Germany. Although they did not agree on many points, their attitude toward life, both deeply rooted in the Jewish tradition, was very similar.

From both of them I learned that violence is not the ultimate solution to conflict. Conflict can only be prevented by the transformation of the human being. Violence generates violence, and meanwhile, the conflict persists and attitudes continue unchanged. Thus, violence goes on and on. This idea has been expressed in the Talmud through a very significant story. In Berachot 10a we read:

> There were once some thugs in the neighborhood of Rabbi Meir who caused him a great deal of trouble. Rabbi Meir accordingly prayed that in God's mercy they should die. Rabbi Meir's wife Beruria said to him: What are you thinking? Is such a prayer permissible? Are you thinking of the verse, "Let sinners cease in the land" (Psalm 104:35)? But what really is written is "let *sins* cease!" … Therefore, you should pray that they stop sinning, not for their demise.[1]

When I thought about the Shoah, I asked myself why so many of the good and spiritual ancestors of my people were pursued like savage animals, stripped of their human dignity, and killed in industrial factories of death. Why were one-and-a-half million children and adolescents massacred? I thought to myself: Maybe because the societies in which they lived did not deserve their presence. In a world full of hate, it is very difficult for human beings with great values and spiritual courage to arise. Even if they are virtuous, their societies will cause them to lose heart. Their societies were antithetical to

---

1. English text adapted from www.sefaria.org.

their religious and spiritual values. The virtuous had to be eliminated. Judaism cannot coexist with a Nazi society.

After the war, the Jewish answer to the Shoah had to be better than simply learning how to take up arms to physically defeat threatening enemies, as David said after Saul's defeat and his and his sons' deaths in the war against the Philistines (2 Sam 1:18). This might be an understandable initial reaction to the terrible and brutal things that had occurred and to the Jews' overwhelming abandonment by the great majority of people and nations both before and during the war. But our tradition teaches that, in addition to learning from the cruel lessons of history, we Jews must strive to change the status quo, to create a turning point. Antisemitism—the hatred toward Jews only because they are Jews—as with hatred toward other peoples, is the result of a poisoned culture. That culture must be transformed, an antidote administered. I learned that the way to promote such conversion is through dialogue. And because the world's religions affirm the sanctity of each human being and champion the values of mercy and justice, it is the religions that must be the most effective promoters of dialogue.

Heschel addressed this theme in a very deep and extraordinary essay, "No Religion Is an Island."[2] In it, he discusses the question of how Jews should relate to others after the Shoah, especially to Christians. Christian teaching for centuries had portrayed "the Jews" as tools of the devil who killed the Son of God and became an accursed people. Undoubtedly this set the stage for racist Nazi antisemitism, as Cardinal Walter Kasper has written:

> The history of Jewish-Christian relations is complex and difficult. In addition to some better times, as when bishops took Jews under their protection against pogroms by mobs, there were dark times that have been especially impressed upon the collective Jewish consciousness. The Shoah, the

---

2. Abraham Joshua Heschel, "No Religion Is an Island," *Union Seminary Quarterly Review* 21, no. 2 (1966): 117–34.

state-sponsored organized murder of approximately six million European Jews, based on primitive racial ideology, is the absolute low point in this history. The Holocaust cannot be attributed to Christianity as such, since it also had clear anti-Christian features. However, centuries-old Christian theological anti-Judaism contributed as well, encouraging a widespread antipathy for Jews, so that ideologically and racially motivated antisemitism could prevail in this terrible way, and resistance against the outrageous inhuman brutality did not achieve the breadth and clarity that one should have expected.[3]

There had been little or no true dialogue between Jews and Christians for many long years. What conversations occurred were verbal conflicts. Read in this light, Heschel's essay is extraordinary. He offered a new perspective based upon the demands of the present day and of history. At the beginning of his article he writes:

> I speak as a member of a congregation whose founder was Abraham, and the name of my rabbi is Moses.
> I speak as a person who was able to leave Warsaw, the city in which I was born, just six weeks before the disaster began. My destination was New York, it would have been Auschwitz or Treblinka. I am a brand plucked from the fire, in which my people were burned to death. I am a brand plucked from the fire of an altar of Satan on which millions of human lives were exterminated to evil's greater glory....
> I speak as a person who is convinced that the fate of the Jewish people and the fate of the Hebrew Bible are intertwined. The recognition of our status as Jews, the

---

3. Walter Cardinal Kasper, "Foreword," in *Christ Jesus and the Jewish People Today: New Explorations of Theological Relationships*, ed. P.A. Cunningham et al. (Grand Rapids, MI: Gregorian and Biblical Press, 2011).

legitimacy of our survival, is only possible in a world in which the God of Abraham is revered. Nazism in its very roots was a rebellion against the Bible, against the God of Abraham. Realizing that it was Christianity that implanted attachment to the God of Abraham and involvement with the Hebrew Bible in the hearts of Western man, Nazism resolved that it must both exterminate the Jews and eliminate Christianity, and bring about instead a revival of Teutonic paganism. Nazism has suffered a defeat, but the process of eliminating the Bible from the consciousness of the Western world goes on. It is on the issue of saving the radiance of the Hebrew Bible in the minds of man that Jews and Christians are called upon to work together. None of us can do it alone. Both of us must realize that in our age antisemitism is anti-Christianity and that anti-Christianity is antisemitism. Man is never as open to fellowship as he is in moments of misery.[4]

Heschel goes on to write:

The religions of the world are no more self-sufficient, no more independent, no more isolated than individuals or nations. Energies, experiences and ideas that come to life outside the boundaries of a particular religion or all religions continue to challenge and to affect every religion. Horizons are wider, dangers are greater.... *No religion is an island.* We are all involved with one another.[5]

Heschel understood that a new human reality must be built if humanity wants to avoid future disasters like the Second World War. The only certain way to avoid new Holocausts is not to put our

---

4. Heschel, "No Religion Is an Island," 117–18.
5. Ibid., 119.

trust in weapons and violence, but to rely instead on spiritual and ethical resources.

Heschel's essay "No Religion Is an Island"—which was his inaugural lesson as the Harry Emerson Fosdick Visiting Professor at the Union Theological Seminary—had an extraordinary impact on many people. Books, articles, conferences, and studies were devoted to it. And it inspired me as well to become committed to interfaith dialogue.

In Argentina, some opportunities for interfaith dialogue were developed by certain individuals in the 1950s, several years before *Nostra Aetate*. A kaleidoscope of Argentinean priests, rabbis, and laypeople began many interpersonal dialogues that produced sincere friendships. All kind of activities were developed, even a television program named *Mesa de Credos* (The Table of Creeds). Priests and ministers from different Christian denominations sat around a table together with rabbis while a moderator led them in a discussion of various topics together. Certain Catholic preachers in Argentina in the 1950s still delivered antisemitic and hateful sermons. However, during the 1970s, the spirit of *Nostra Aetate* gave great energy to institutions that promoted dialogue, including to some bishops who labored with great devotion and courage to establish solid ties with their Jewish neighbors. In the Seminario Rabínico Latinoamericano as well as in the *Lamroth Hakol* and *Benei Tikva* congregations where I had served as a rabbi since the early 1970s, interfaith dialogue was a priority activity.

Bishops Ernesto Segura, Jorge Mejía, Justo Laguna, and Estanislao Karlik, among many others, made clear commitments to the teachings of the Second Vatican Council generally and *Nostra Aetate* in particular. But it was the then Archbishop of Buenos Aires, Jorge Mario Bergoglio, who later became Pope Francis, who made the greatest strides in interfaith dialogue, working with me and other Jewish colleagues. He and I wrote a book of dialogues studying many subjects, which had never been done before. We discussed, for example, the attitude of Pope Pius XII during the Shoah, the years of oppression and corruption during the military regime in Argentina, the pedophilia crisis in the Church, and so on.

We recorded thirty-one programs of dialogues for the Buenos Aires archdiocesan television channel. He wrote a foreword for a book that I wrote, and I was chosen by him to write the foreword to his authorized biography. In his role as the Chancellor of the Pontificia Universidad Católica Argentina, he advocated for the bestowal of an honorary doctoral degree on me for my contributions to the culture of the city. This act marked a turning point in the history of Argentinean Church in its relations with Jews.

Now that he is the Pope, we continue to work together. I was part of the Vatican delegation that accompanied the Holy Father in his visit to the Holy Land, and I assisted in arranging the ceremony at which an olive tree of peace was planted in the Vatican gardens by the presidents of Israel and Palestine.

In other words, walking the path of dialogue together as Jews and Christians has already begun. My friend Francis has called it "our journey of friendship." Recently, Orthodox Jews who were hesitant to participate in an active and dynamic way in interreligious dialogue have become more involved. Different groups of Orthodox rabbis and rabbinical associations have produced meaningful declarations such as "To Do the Will of Our Father in Heaven: Toward a Partnership between Jews and Christians," published by the Center for Jewish-Christian Understanding and Cooperation, and the statement "Between Jerusalem and Rome: Reflections on Fifty Years of *Nostra Aetate*," formally approved by the Conference of European Rabbis, the Rabbinical Council of America, and the Chief Rabbinate of Israel.

Many dialogue groups around the world used the book Jorge Bergoglio and I wrote as a basis for conversation. It has proven helpful here in the United States as well, where many dialogical initiatives have existed for years, including at the Institute for Jewish-Catholic Relations of Saint Joseph's University, founded in 1967, where I am currently serving as University Professor.

In Argentina, we worked together with Muslim people and with adherents of other religions as well. Although the dialogue between Jews and Christians is unique—since they were literally brothers in their beginnings—Muslims are also closely related to Judaism and Christianity. This point is one of the central topics that the Pope has been addressing in recent years.

Pope Francis became very close to the Grand Imam of al-Azhar University in Cairo, Ahmad el-Tayeb, the highest academic authority of the Sunnis, and collaborated with him on some important declarations and statements. They organized two Global Peace conferences, the first in Cairo, on April 27–28, 2017, and the second in Abu Dhabi on February 2–3, 2019. I was invited to both gatherings. At the second, I participated with other rabbinical colleagues from around the world. Undoubtedly, it was Pope Francis who promoted a Jewish presence at those conferences. Moreover, I was invited as a Guest of Honor, at the insistence of the Holy Father, for the Third Summit of Christian-Muslim Religious Leaders on December 2–4, 2014, in Rome. Pope Francis has taken special care to involve Jewish representatives in these dialogical events, as a sign and model for the way that this dialogue must be conducted.

At the recent conference in Abu Dhabi, Pope Francis and the Grand Imam Ahmad el-Tayeb signed a "Declaration on Human Fraternity for World Peace and Living Together." Among other things, it says:

> We resolutely declare that religions must never incite war, hateful attitudes, hostility and extremism, nor must they incite violence or the shedding of blood. These tragic realities are the consequence of a deviation from religious teachings. They result from a political manipulation of religions and from interpretations made by religious groups who, in the course of history, have taken advantage of the power of religious sentiment in the hearts of men and women in order to make them act in a way that has nothing to do with the truth of religion. This is done for the purpose of achieving objectives that are political, economic, worldly and short-sighted. We thus call upon all concerned to stop using religions to incite hatred, violence,

> extremism and blind fanaticism, and to refrain from using the name of God to justify acts of murder, exile, terrorism and oppression. We ask this on the basis of our common belief in God who did not create men and women to be killed or to fight one another, nor to be tortured or humiliated in their lives and circumstances. God, the Almighty, has no need to be defended by anyone and does not want His name to be used to terrorize people.[6]

Grand Imam el-Tayeb is the one of the foremost leaders in the Sunni branch of Islam; 90 percent of the world's Muslims belong to this denomination. There is little need for much explanation of the importance of this document. That religion cannot be used as a tool for violence and hate is one of the central points of the statement. Now it depends on the respective commitments by the signatories of the document to transform its spirit into reality. It is clear that the mere existence of this declaration will not per se suddenly bring about a world of peace, but it will nonetheless serve for the future as a benchmark to show the way ahead and the goal to achieve.

As I mentioned earlier, I was part of the official Vatican delegation that accompanied Pope Francis on his visit to the Holy Land in 2014. He left a deep vision of peace in the region, symbolized by the embrace of both of us with our Muslim friend, Omar Abboud, at the Western Wall.

A few months after that pilgrimage, on July 8, 2014, a new armed conflict broke out that ended on August 26. Feelings of disappointment overwhelmed me. On July 30, in the heat of that painful conflict, I wrote to Francis by email:

> I am distressed about the suffering of millions of people in multiple conflicts around the world amid a petty and insensitive global political reality. There is no progress,

---

6. See https://press.vatican.va/content/salastampa/en/bollettino/pubblico/2019/02/04/190204f.html

the world remains the same. The centenary of the beginning of the First World War is remembered these days, but humanity does not learn from its lessons. Let us look for intelligent paths to make a mark, so that hope does not die, that sometime, in some future, our dream will be transformed into reality.

In many media, including the *Vatican Insider*, I have responded to the question of whether we have failed in our efforts. My answer was always: on the contrary, in these critical moments the importance of the dialogue that we have nurtured becomes even clearer.

His emailed reply to me on August 4 was:

> Thank you very much for your note. I agree about the "critical moments." Only unfailing prayer and trust in the Lord will suffice. The seed of peace, once sown, will not be destroyed. You just have to wait for the time that that will favor its sprouting and growth with prayer and the commandment of love.

This is the way that Francis proposes for interfaith dialogue: to work together in order to transmit a clear, mature, and balanced message of peace in the midst of the cacophony of hate and destruction that assault people day after day.

Just this past March 4 [2020], Francis announced that, in one year, the archives of the papacy of Pius XII will be opened for research and analysis. With this action, he fulfills his words in a dialogue we had in 2010 that was included in the book we published together, entitled *On Heaven and Earth*.[7] I expressed to him my doubts about Pius XII and his attitude of silence during the

---

7. Pope Francis and Abraham Skorka, *On Heaven and Earth: Pope Francis on Faith, Family, and the Church in the Twenty-First Century* (New York: Image Books, 2013).

Shoah. His answer was: we must search and know the truth. The way forward in the dialogue must have the truth as one of its central pillars.

The first times I met with Bergoglio were in the Cathedral of Buenos Aires, where I used to be invited by the different presidents of Argentina as one of the representatives of the Jewish religion to the *Te Deum* services in honor of the independence days, May 25 and July 9. In his homilies at those ceremonies, he used to criticize harshly the negative aspects of Argentinean society. The president of the nation and the members of the cabinet, as well as many members of the government, judges from the Supreme Court, and others heard his demands for social justice, equity, and mercy. When the ceremonies were finished and we shook hands I used to tell him: "You spoke in a prophetic way. The prophets used to cry for justice and mercy in front of the leaders of the people of Israel. That's what you did here." In addition to truth, the way forward in the dialogue must have this other necessary element: spiritual audacity.

Rabbi Heschel's spiritual work was based on his belief that prophetic inspiration did not cease with the deaths of Haggai, Zechariah, and Malachi. The Sages of the Talmud (Sanhedrin 11a) affirmed this, too: the prophetic challenge has continued in some way from generation to generation. One of Heschel's posthumous books is titled *Prophetic Inspiration after the Prophets*.[8] In it, we find two articles in Hebrew that he had published in 1945 and 1950, which are now translated into English. At the end of the first of them, entitled "Prophetic Inspiration in the Middle Ages (Until the Time of Maimonides)," he writes:

> One cannot grasp the innermost thought of the holy men of Israel without remembering that in their eyes,

---

8. Abraham Joshua Heschel, *Prophetic Inspiration after the Prophets: Maimonides and other Medieval Authorities*, ed. Morris M. Faierstein (Hoboken, NJ: Ktav, 1996).

prophetic inspiration hovered over human reason, and, at times, heaven and earth would meet and kiss. They believed that the divine voice which issued from Horeb was not stilled thereafter. "These commandments the Lord spoke in a great voice to your whole assembly on the mountain out of the fire, the cloud and the thick mist, then he said no more" (Deuteronomy 5:19). *Onkelos* translated this (and so the Targum Jonathan), "it—the great voice—has not ceased from speaking."[9]

This voice was heard by Heschel, and through him and others of his generation, by many others after them. It is the voice of the God of Justice and Mercy, through which He dialogued with Moses, Isaiah, Jeremiah, Ezekiel, Maimonides, Baal Shem Tov, and Heschel. The Voice that seeks to dialogue with us also intends for us to dialogue with each other. We are able to do so today as never before. It is our responsibility to the God who dialogues with us to do so.

Bibliography

Cunningham, P. A., et al. *Christ Jesus and the Jewish People Today: New Explorations of Theological Relationships*. Grand Rapids, MI: Gregorian and Biblical Press, 2011.

Francis, Pope, and Skorka, Abraham. *On Heaven and Earth: Pope Francis on Faith, Family, and the Church in the Twenty-First Century*. New York: Image Books, 2013.

Heschel, Abraham Joshua. "No Religion Is an Island." *Union Seminary Quarterly Review* 21, no. 2 (1966): 117–34.

———. *Prophetic Inspiration after the Prophets: Maimonides and Other Medieval Authorities*, edited by Morris M. Faierstein. Hoboken, NJ: Ktav, 1996.

---

9. Ibid., 67.

Chapter Three

READING QUR'ANIC VERSES ON OTHER RELIGIONS: MODERN EXEGETICAL APPROACHES

Mun'im Sirry

Several passages in the Qur'an can be read as criticizing various Jewish and Christian beliefs and practices, and seem to influence Muslim discourses about "the other" even today. Of course, there are other groups of passages in the Qur'an that seem to show sympathetic attitudes towards and extend salvific promise to others. These seemingly tolerant passages of the Qur'an have been much discussed, in order to provide the scriptural ground for interreligious dialogue in the modern context. This essay discusses those passages of the Qur'an that criticize other religions both in terms of doctrines and social interactions. The significance of this study lies in the fact that this essay will offer nuanced interpretations of those passages of the Muslim scripture that have often been used by radical extremist Muslims to justify their violent actions. Of course, this does not mean that "violent texts" will automatically lead to "violent acts." There is a host of complex factors that transform what D. Andrew Kille calls a "toxic text" into violence. No straight line can be drawn from the text to violent behavior. In his article "The Bible Made Me Do It," Kille writes, "we must recognize that texts do not 'do' anything in themselves. It is only in the dynamic encounter between the text and a specific reader, in a specific community, in a particular historical and cultural context that individuals engage, interpret, internalize and ultimately act on those texts."[1] It is, therefore, instructive to examine to what extent the violent text can be read non-violently for non-violent interactions. In a time when the world is becoming less tolerant,[2] the need for this kind of exploration is more obvious than ever.

Two questions form the main concern of this essay: To what extent have these Qur'anic criticisms of other religions been interpreted differently in light of ideas of religious plurality in the modern context? Also, how has the modern context shaped Muslim understandings of those difficult passages? In this essay, modern Qur'an commentaries written by twentieth-century Muslims, comprising Arab and non-Arab, Sunnī, and Shīʿī, are analyzed. The basic criterion for selecting these particular exegetical works (*tafsīr*) is that they are not only influential in their times and places, but also represent various trends in the project of rethinking Islam in the modern context. This essay begins with an examination of the polemical context of the Qur'an and the nature of its criticisms of adherents to other religions, especially Christians. It then looks at exegetical problems facing Muslim scholars, in order to make sense of those polemical passages, for the sake of non-polemical interactions in the modern world. Some hermeneutical strategies employed by modern Muslims in their exegetical enterprise will also be highlighted. The essay concludes with a brief reflection on how modern Muslims have wrestled with these difficult issues, in order to derive practical guidance from the Qur'an in the modern context.

---

1. D. Andrew Kille, "'The Bible Made Me Do It': Text, Interpretation and Violence," in *The Destructive Power of Religion*, ed. J. H. Ellens (Westport, CT: Praeger-Greenwood, 2004), 9.
2. According to *Freedom House*, a US-based research think-tank, over the past 13 years, global freedom is in decline. For more details, see https://freedomhouse.org/report/freedom-world/freedom-world-2019/democracy-in-retreat.

Qur'anic Criticism and Its Context

How much can we know about the historical context of the formation of the Qur'anic text? There are at least two approaches to this question. On the one hand, some scholars contend that the Qur'an does not offer information about its own "history" or its connection with historical events of its time. "It tells us very little about the events of Muhammad's career," says Michael Cook.[3] Along these lines, Andrew Rippin argues that the Qur'an "is remarkably bereft of immediate historical, geographical and political tags. The text asserts little connection to a contemporary social world beyond a number of generalized facets of society."[4] This lack of internal historical evidence in the Qur'an, including the rarity of references to events of Muhammad's life within the text, has led some scholars to question the chronology of the Qur'an, preferring instead to read it independently of the biography of Muhammad.[5] Their basic contention is that many of the supposedly historical events leading to the revelation of the Qur'an are exegetical in nature. They are purportedly designed to *explain* the Qur'an, and thus reflect "a general desire to historicize the text of the Qur'an in order to prove constantly that God really did reveal His book to humanity on earth."[6] As an alternative, these scholars propose to read the Qur'an

---

3. Michael Cook, *Muhammad* (Oxford: Oxford University Press, 1983), 69.
4. Andrew Rippin, "The Construction of the Arabian Historical Context in Muslim Interpretation of the Qur'an," in *Aims, Methods and Contexts of Qur'anic Exegesis*, ed. Karen Bauer (Oxford: Oxford University Press, 2013), 174.
5. For a review of the rich scholarly discussion on this issue, see Gabriel Said Reynolds, *The Qur'an and Its Biblical Subtext* (London: Routledge, 2010), 3–22; see also, idem, "Le problème de la chronologie du Coran," *Arabica* 58 (2011): 477–502.
6. Andrew Rippin, "The Function of Asbāb al-Nuzūl in Qur'anic Exegesis," *Bulletin of the School of Oriental and African Studies* 51, no. 1 (1988): 2.

in light of the broader context of Jewish and Christian traditions in the Late Antique Near East.[7]

On the other hand, some scholars look at the Qur'an as "accompanying and documenting the historical process of the emergence of the early Muslim community."[8] Alford Welch argues that "the Qur'an is a historical document that reflects the prophetic career of Muhammad and responds constantly to the specific needs and problems of the emerging Muslim community."[9] This methodology, much refined, can be traced back to the nineteenth-century German scholar Theodor Nöldeke, who proposed a chronological reading of the Qur'an that presumes that the history and meaning of the text are to be understood in light of Muhammad's prophetic mission in Mecca and Medina.[10]

It therefore seems that scholars have developed two approaches to reading the Qur'anic text. On the one hand, some claim that, in order to understand what the sacred text means to say, we should read it in light of its engagement with biblical and para-biblical literature. Others argue that, if we wish to understand the Qur'an as it has been perceived by Muslims, then we should consult the biography

---

7. The British scholar John Wansbrough advocates this approach in his seminal books, *Qur'anic Studies: Sources and Methods of Scriptural Interpretation* (London: Oxford University Press, 1977), and *The Sectarian Milieu: Content and Composition of Islamic Salvation History* (Oxford: Oxford University Press, 1978).

8. Angelika Neuwirth, "Negotiating Justice: A Pre-Canonical Reading of the Qur'anic Creation Accounts," *Journal of Qur'anic Studies* 1 (2000): 26.

9. Alford T. Welch, "Introduction: Qur'anic Studies—Problems and Prospects," *Journal of the American Academy of Religion*: [Thematic Issue] 47, no. 4 (1979): 626.

10. Theodor Nöldeke, *Geschichte des Qorans* (Göttingen: Verlag der Dieterichschen Buchhandlung, 1860). For an English translation, see idem, Friedrich Schwally, Gotthelf Bergsträßer, and Otto Pretzl, *The History of the Qur'an*, ed. and trans. Wolfgang H. Behn (Leiden: Brill, 2013). For a detailed discussion of Nöldeke's approach, see Emmanuelle Stefanidis, "The Qur'an Made Linear: A Study of the Geschichte des Qorâns' Chronological Reordering," *Journal of Qur'anic Studies* 10, no. 2 (2008): 1–22.

of the Prophet (*sīra*) and other post-Qur'anic literature. However, these two approaches might not be as mutually exclusive as they are sometimes understood. Looking at the Qur'an's polemical passages from a chronological perspective—which takes into consideration a variety of different encounters between Muhammad and other religious communities—can be useful in understanding why the text contains various, sometimes conflicting, types of criticism. At the same time, however, I do not think that chronology should be viewed as the only possible reading. Reading the Qur'an in light of its conversation with biblical sources is not only possible, but also instructive. Even if we accept that Muhammad received his prophetic message from God alone, without any assistance from teachers or other people's scriptures and prophetic legends, the same issue surfaces in a different form: How could his audience in the early seventh-century Ḥijāz have possibly understood the Qur'an's highly allusive and often obscure references to Abraham, Moses, Jesus, and other prophets without some familiarity with Biblical materials?

In what follows, I will first show the usefulness of reading the Qur'an against the background of the Prophet's encounters with members of other religions, and then discuss the limits of such a reading. During the supposedly Meccan period, the Qur'an seems to speak of Jews and Christians in positive terms, calling them "the People of the Book" (*ahl al-kitāb*). The use of this honorific title has led some scholars like Richard Bell to conclude that, "during the whole of the Meccan period of his activity Muhammad's attitude to the People of the Book, which must be taken as including both Jews and Christians…was consistently friendly."[11] The Qur'an encourages those who doubt the truth of Muhammad's message to consult scriptures revealed before him (e.g., Q 10:94, 16:43, 21:7). We are also told that "those to whom We have given the Scripture

---

11. Richard Bell, *The Origin of Islam in Its Christian Environment* (London: Macmillan, 1926), 147.

rejoice in what has been revealed to you" (Q 13:36).[12] It is worth noting that the terms *Naṣārā* (when referring to Christians) and *Yahūd* and/or *Hūd* (Jews) are used only in Medinan Suras, which can be read as reflecting the absence of an immediate concern of Muhammad with them in Mecca.

The question of why the Meccan revelations refer to Jews and Christians as those who supported and confirmed the truth of Muhammad's message is subject to discussion. S. D. Goitein, for instance, argues that Jews and Christians at Mecca did regard Muhammad with high esteem.[13] However, the problem, as rightly noted by Fazlur Rahman, is that it is difficult to establish conclusively the presence of a significant number of Jews and Christians at Mecca. Therefore, Rahman contends that the Meccan allusions to the People of the Book are based on theoretical assumptions about what the Jews and Christians *should* be like and about how they *might* be expected to behave, rather than on concrete encounters with specific people, as at Medina.[14]

The Medinan Qur'an seems to be overwhelmed by its encounters with Jews and Christians. We also notice a shift in the language of the text. Whereas in the Meccan period Qur'anic references to the People of the Book are rather neutral or even positive, Medinan verses are marked by an increasingly polemical discourse. From the early Medinan period onward, there emerged a kind of competition for authority with the People of the Book. For example, the Muslim scripture begins questioning the association of Jews and Christians with Abraham, a crucial figure in religious history.

---

12. For the translation of the Qur'anic verses throughout this essay, I have used M.A.S. Abdel Haleem, *The Qur'an: A New Translation* (Oxford: Oxford University Press, 2004), with a few modifications where I deem necessary, for the purpose of my own presentation of the Qur'anic text.

13. S.D. Goitein, "The Concept of Mankind in Islam," in *History and the Idea of Mankind*, ed. W. Warren Wagar (Albuquerque: University of New Mexico Press, 1971), 81.

14. Fazlur Rahman, *Islam* (Chicago: University of Chicago Press, 1979), 26.

"Abraham was neither a Jew nor a Christian," the Qurʾan claims, "rather, he is a *ḥanīfī muslim*" (Q 3:67).[15] In this verse, Abraham is claimed as a prophet who prefigured the faith of Muhammad and his followers, rather than that of the Jews and Christians. To this point, G.R. Hawting writes, "Abraham is used in order to distinguish an emerging religious group from its rivals who also claimed a special link with the patriarch."[16]

Perhaps the use of polemical language in the Qurʾan can best be understood as a reaction to the repudiation of, and opposition to, Muhammad's message. In other words, the Qurʾan sometimes articulates its response in discourteous language aimed against older religious communities that were trying to bring about the demise of the religion that the text represents. In this context, the Qurʾan utilizes polemical language sharply to define the identity of the community of the believers in different phases of their development. In her study of the Qurʾanic presentation of Mary (Maryam) and Jesus (ʿĪsā) in the Meccan *Sūrat Maryam* (Q 19) and the Medinan *Sūrat Āl ʿImrān* (Q 3), Angelika Neuwirth contends that the Qurʾan revises itself due to different contexts. She concludes that *Sūrat Maryam* was remodeled on *Sūrat Āl ʿImrān* to fit into more polemical environments in Medina. Such a re-reading of Mary and Jesus from the new perspective of *Sūrat Āl ʿImrān*, Neuwirth argues, "serves a 'political' purpose: to disempower the predominant Jewish tradition represented by "Āl Ibrāhīm," whose weighty superiority, in terms of scriptural authority, had to be counter-balanced."[17]

---

15. For a detailed discussion on the meaning of *ḥanīf* in the Qurʾan, see Mun'im Sirry, "The Early Development of the Qurʾanic Ḥanīf," *Journal of Semitic Studies* 56, no. 2 (2011): 349–70.

16. G.R. Hawting, "The Religion of Abraham and Islam," in *Abraham, the Nations and the Hagarites*, eds. Martin Goodman, George H. van Kooten, and J.T.A.G.M. van Ruiten (Leiden: Brill, 2010), 495.

17. Angelika Neuwirth, "Debating Christian and Jewish Traditions: Embodied Antagonism in Sūrat Āl ʿImrān (Q 3:1–62)," in *Studien zur Semitistik und Arabistik: Festschrift für Hartmut Bobzin zum 60. Geburtstag*, eds. Otto

It can be argued that the Qur'an's polemics against Jews reaches the point where they were juxtaposed with those who associated others with God (*alladhīna ashrakū*) and regarded as the most hostile people to the believers (Q 5:82). Even when dealing with Jesus, the Medinan passages are governed by polemics against Jews. For instance, Jews were accused of killing prophets sent forth before Muhammad. This topic has recently been tackled by Hawting.[18] As for the Jewish claim that they have killed Jesus, the Qur'an rejects it as follows:

> And for their unbelief and their uttering against Mary a mighty calumny; and for their saying, "We killed the Messiah, Jesus son of Mary, the Messenger of God"—they did not kill him, neither crucified him, but so it was only made to appear to them. Those who are at variance concerning him surely are in doubt regarding him; they have no knowledge of him, except the following of conjecture. Indeed, they did not kill him. (Q 4:156–57)

Although this passage has often been understood to support the argument that the Qur'an rejects the crucifixion of Jesus, a careful reading of the precise wording suggests that it is not directed against Christian belief. The anti-Jewish tone of these verses should not be overlooked—what is ultimately denied is the Jewish contention that the crucifixion has been a victory for them. Of course, there

---

Jastrow, Shabo Talay, and Herta Hafenrichter (Wiesbaden: Harrassowitz Verlag, 2008), 282. See also idem, "The House of Abraham and the House of Amram: Genealogy, Patriarchal Authority, and Exegetical Professionalism," in *The Qur'an in Context: Historical and Literary Investigations into the Qur'anic Milieu*, eds. Angelika Neuwirth, Nicolai Sinai, and Michel Marx (Leiden: Brill, 2010), 499–531.

18. G.R. Hawting, "'Killing the Prophets and Stoning the Messengers': Two Themes in the Qur'an and Their Background," in *The Qur'an's Reformation of Judaism and Christianity: Return to the Origins*, ed. Holger Zellentin, 303–17 (London: Routledge, 2019).

are passages criticizing Christian belief directly, which may reflect Muhammad's increased contact with Christians in the final years of the Medinan period. However, we should not think of Qur'anic criticisms of Judaism and Christianity primarily in chronological terms, implying that the earlier Medinan passages reflect conflict with the Jews whereas the latter passages exclusively focus on the Christians. This is one example of the limits of a chronological reading, which assumes that there is a fine line between early and later Medinan revelations. This does not seem to be the case. Instead, there is a certain amount of overlap between them. Some verses critical of Christian belief may date from the same time as passages attacking the Jews of Medina. Likewise, in the latest phase of revelation, the depiction of Jesus can still serve the purpose of polemics against Jewish opponents. Nevertheless, from the later Medinan verses, we learn that the Qur'an portrays Jesus and Mary as being at the heart of a theological controversy, especially in reprimanding the Christians for their attitude toward the divinity of Jesus.

The text also contains passages that specifically criticize Christians for their false beliefs and conduct. For instance, in two places (Q 5:17, 72) the Qur'an states: *la-qad kafara'lladhīna qālū inna'llāha huwa'l-masīḥu'bnu Maryam* ("Those who say, 'God is the Messiah, the son of Mary,' are defying the truth"). Other passages seem to criticize the Christian doctrine of the Trinity, such as Qur'an 4:171, but also 5:73: "Those people who say that God is the third of three (*thālithu thalāthatin*) are defying [the truth]." In Qur'an 5:116, Jesus himself speaks out to disown the errors of Christians. When questioned by God as to whether he told people to take him and Mary "as two gods, apart from God," Jesus insists: "I would never say what I had no right to." One may infer from these last two verses that the Qur'anic understanding of the Trinity consists of God, Jesus, and Mary, rather than the Father, Son, and Holy Spirit. What is, therefore, being criticized in the Qur'an? Why does the Qur'an seem to include Mary as one of the three persons of the Trinity? Does the Qur'anic understanding of the Trinity oppose a truly Christian concept of God, or does it reflect rather a heretical teaching?

These questions are difficult to answer through chronological readings. In addition, what seems interesting is that, in spite of its criticisms of these theological issues, the Qur'an refers to Christians as "the closest in affection towards the believers" (Q 5:82). It goes on to say that among Christians are "people devoted to learning and ascetics; these people are not given to arrogance." Moreover, the Muslim scripture extends its salvific promise to other religious communities, including Jews and Christians. Qur'an 2:62 says: "The [Muslim] believers, the Jews, the Christians, and the Sabians—all those who believe in God and the Last Day and do good—will have their reward with their Lord. No fear for them, nor shall they grieve." Here we can see that the main criteria for salvation are (1) belief in God and the Day of Judgment, and (2) doing good deeds. According to the traditional understanding, this verse is considered as early Medinan and is repeated almost verbatim in Qur'an 5:69. Interestingly, Sura 5 is regarded as being among the last to be revealed in Medina. The fact that such "ecumenical" verses occur at the beginning and end of Muhammad's prophetic career at Medina means that "neither the words nor the purport of these two identical verses were abrogated."[19]

There are other passages in the Qur'an that seem to support and celebrate the idea of religious plurality. One of the most frequently cited such verses is Qur'an 5:48, especially the second part: "We have assigned a law and a path to each one of you. If God had so willed, He would have made you a single community, but He wanted to test you through that which He has given you, so race to do good." The notion of tolerance in this passage is arresting in the breadth of its assertion that religious diversity should not only be tolerated, but also is necessarily good. In fact, many modern

---

19. Mahmoud Ayoub, "The Qur'an and Religious Pluralism," in *Islam and Global Dialogue: Religious Pluralism and the Pursuit of Peace*, ed. Roger Boase (Burlington, VT: Ashgate, 2005), 277.

Muslim scholars consider this verse as a virtual manifesto of the Qur'anic vision of religious pluralism. They maintain that the Qur'an presents religious pluralism as a divine mystery that must be accepted as a given in order to allow for smooth communal relations in public life.[20]

It should be noted, however, that when we look at classical and medieval *tafsīrs*, we find that these passages are not understood to support the idea of religious diversity. The commentators find ways to interpret them to mean the opposite—some, for instance, argued that these inclusive passages should be understood as referring to pre-Islamic communities or those who believed in the prophethood of Muhammad. Some also claimed that the seemingly inclusive passages above (among other similar verses) have been abrogated by the more exclusive ones.[21]

Exegetical Problems

Belonging to the exclusive passages are those Qur'anic verses that criticize the religious beliefs of others, which are believed to have been revealed in Medina in order to establish an exclusivist theology among Muhammad's nascent community of believers. The challenge facing modern Muslim exegetes is twofold. First, how are we to understand the Qur'an's unorthodox view of other religions? As mentioned earlier, it is difficult to ascertain what is being criticized in the Qur'an. For instance, the Muslim scripture

---

20. For a discussion of Q 5:48, see Sirry, Mun'im, "'Compete with One Another in Good Works': Exegesis of Qur'an Verse 5.48 and Contemporary Muslim Discourses on Religious Pluralism," *Islam and Christian-Muslim Relations* 20, no. 4 (2009): 423–38.

21. For a detailed discussion on how this identical passage has been understood in the *tafsīr* tradition, see Sirry, Mun'im, "The Qur'an, Salvation and the Beauty of the Other," in *Finding Beauty in the Other: Theological Reflections across Religious Traditions*, eds. Peter Casarella and Mun'im Sirry, 189–210 (New York: Crossroad, 2019).

seems to present Christian doctrines that Christians themselves do not believe. Second, how are we to reinterpret the Qur'anic criticisms of other religious traditions, which seem contrary to the modern sense that others' religious beliefs must be tolerated and respected? In modern societies, the notion of religious tolerance has generally been accepted and has become more or less axiomatic. As Michael Cook rightly notes, "Indeed it would be considered ill-mannered and parochial to refer to the religious views of others as *false* and one's own as *true*; for those fully educated into the elite culture of Western society, the very notion of absolute truth in matters of religion sounds hopelessly out of date."[22] Thus, the exclusivist and polemical passages of the Qur'an should be understood in light of this modern concern.

Indeed, some modern Muslims strive to reinterpret those difficult passages (1) to vindicate the Qur'an of possible misapprehension and (2) to promote peaceful coexistence. Through an examination of a few examples of Qur'anic criticisms, both doctrinal and social aspects, we will next elucidate these two exegetical problems. Let us begin with Muslim interpretations of the Qur'anic passages dealing with Christian doctrines, paying particular attention to how they attempt to make sense of the Qur'anic criticisms in the modern context. The Syrian scholar Jamāl al-Dīn al-Qāsimī (d. 1914), for instance, was aware of the Qur'an's unorthodox understanding of the Trinitarian doctrine. Since Christians do not believe that Mary is a member of the Trinity, the Syrian scholar associates such a doctrine with a specific group (*firqa*) of Christians called "Collyridians" who said that there were three gods: the Father, the Son, and Mary. In his exegesis of Qur'an 5:116, he mentions this unorthodox teaching, saying, "It is possible that this matter was written in their manuscripts (*nusakh*) and therefore the Qur'an de-

---

22. Michael Cook, *The Koran: A Very Short Introduction* (Oxford: Oxford University Press, 2000), 33.

nied it."²³ Al-Qāsimī also cites the *Kitāb ʿilm al-Yaqīn*, which refers to a Christian sect called the "Maryamiyyūn."²⁴ To further support his view, he argues that even the historian Ibn Isḥāq (d. 150/767) in his *Sīra* also affirms that, among the Christians of Najrān who visited the Prophet, there were some who said "Jesus is God," others who said "He is the son of God," and still others who said "He is the third of three," namely God, Jesus, and Mary—thus, Qurʾan 5:73 was revealed in response to all of their statements.²⁵ Therefore, al-Qāsimī glosses the phrase "God is the third of three" in Qurʾan 5:73 as follows: "One of the three gods; it means, one of them, namely God, Mary, and Jesus."²⁶ Similarly, in his interpretation of Qurʾan 4:171, the phrase "Do not say: Three!" is glossed, "three gods: God, the Messiah, and Mary."²⁷

Al-Qāsimī's reference to Collyridians has become the standard explanation of the Qurʾan's unorthodox view on the Trinity. A few decades after al-Qāsimī, in 1965, the British scholar Geoffrey Parrinder writes, "It is more likely that it is heretical doctrines that are denied in the Qurʾan, and orthodox Christians should agree with most of its statements."²⁸ According to Parrinder:

> The Collyridians, an Arabian female sect of the fourth century, offered to Mary cakes of bread (*collyrida*), as they had done to the great earth mother in pagan times. Epiphanius, who opposed this heresy, said that the Trinity must be worshipped, but Mary must not be worshipped.

---

23. Jamāl al-Dīn al-Qāsimī, *Maḥāsin al-Taʾwīl* (17 vols.; Cairo: Maktabat Īsā al-Bābī al-Ḥalabī, 1957), vol. 5, 1,765.
24. Ibid., vol. 6, 2,098. I have not been able to ascertain the author of this book, because there are many books with the same title.
25. Ibid., vol. 6, 1,922.
26. Ibid.
27. Ibid., vol. 2, 1,764.
28. Edward Geoffrey Parrinder, *Jesus in the Qurʾān* (New York: Barnes & Noble, 1965), 133.

The Qur'an may well be directed against this heresy. It gives its support against Mariolatry, while at the same time it recognizes the importance of Mary as the vessel chosen by God for the birth of his Christ.[29]

In a similar vein, when referring to the Qur'anic verses mentioned above, Timothy George asserts that "what is rejected in the Qur'an itself is not the proper Christian doctrine of the Trinity, but rather a heretical belief in three gods."[30]

The problem is that the information about this Christian sect is only recorded by St. Epiphanius of Salamis (d. 403) who denounced the cult as "foolish, crazy idolatry and the work of the devil."[31] St. Epiphanius describes the Collyridians as a group of women, first in Thrace and Scythia and then Arabia, who "prepare a certain carriage with a square seat and spread out fine linens over it on a special day of the year, and they put forth a bread and offer it in the name of Mary, and they all partake of the bread."[32] Some modern scholars, like Michael P. Carroll, downplay the importance of this sect, saying that "if anything, the lack of references to the Collyridians in the early literature on heresy suggests that they were an

---

29. Ibid.
30. Timothy George, *Is the Father of Jesus the God of Muhammad?* (Grand Rapids, MI: Zondervan, 2002), 59.
31. Stephen Benko translates St. Epiphanius's description of a Collyridian ceremony as follows: "For some women decorate a carriage or a square chair by covering it with fine linen, and on a certain definite day of the year [on certain days] they set forth bread and offer it as sacrifice in the name of Mary" (see Benko, *The Virgin Goddess: Studies in the Pagan and Christian Roots of Mariology* [Leiden: E.J. Brill, 1993], 171).
32. Cited by Stephen Shoemaker, "The Cult of the Virgin in the Fourth Century: A Fresh Look at Some Old and New Sources," in *Origins of the Cult of the Virgin Mary*, ed. Chris Maunder (London: Burns & Oates, 2008), 76–77.

obscure sect of no great importance."³³ According to Stephen Shoemaker, St. Epiphanius's attack on the Collyridians' practices can be understood within a broader critique of the veneration of saints. Of course, Epiphanius exaggerates in his critique to such an extent that he smears his opponents with the charge of replacing God with Mary. Shoemaker has argued persuasively that "it is by no means clear that this widely held opinion of the Kollyridians represents an accurate understanding of their beliefs and practices."³⁴

In part due to the problematic nature of historical sources, some scholars have begun to scrutinize the Qur'an's purported references to Christian heretical groups or teachings. It is not at all impossible that the Qur'anic accusation that Christians claim Mary as God can be understood as a rhetorical statement to polemicize against their beliefs and practices. In more recent scholarship of the Qur'an, as represented by the works of Sidney Griffith and Gabriel Said Reynolds, there is a shift from the "heretical explanation" to the emphasis on the rhetoric of the Qur'an. When the Qur'an claims that Christians said, "God is Jesus the son of Mary" (Q 5:17) or "God is the third of three" (Q 5:73), these should be understood as polemical statements. The Qur'an is aware that Christians do not say this. In the words of Griffith:

> The Qur'an's seeming misstatement, rhetorically speaking, should therefore not be thought to be a mistake, but rather a polemically inspired caricature, the purpose of which is to highlight in Islamic terms the absurdity, and therefore the wrongness, of the Christian belief, from an Islamic perspective.³⁵

---

33. Michael P. Carroll, *The Cult of the Virgin Mary: Psychological Origins* (Princeton: Princeton University Press, 1986), 44–45.
34. Shoemaker, "The Cult of the Virgin," 77.
35. Sidney Griffith, "Al-Naṣārā in the Qur'an: A Hermeneutical Reflection," in *New Perspectives on the Qur'an: The Qur'an in Its Historical Context 2*, ed. Gabriel Said Reynolds (London: Routledge, 2011), 311.

Elsewhere Griffith contends that "the Qur'an's seeming espousal of a position earlier owned by some Jewish Christians hardly constitutes evidence for the actual presence of one or another of these long-gone communities in its seventh-century Arabian milieu."[36] Along these same lines, Reynolds persuasively argues that in Qur'anic passages involving Christianity, we should look for the text's creative use of rhetoric, and not for the influence of Christian heretics.[37] This is a significant development in the critical study of the Qur'an, because it implies that the assumption that the Ḥijāz had been the home of Jewish and Christian heresies is no longer defensible, nor does such a criticism mean that the Qur'an has misapprehended Christian beliefs.[38] Instead, understood within its sectarian milieu (to use Wansbrough's term) the Qur'an's message might be understood as reflecting polemical hyperbole. Even if one were to insist that the Qur'an means to pick out Jewish Christian heresies in some way, we may still ask: Why does the text generalize its criticism as being addressed to Christians as a whole? In his *The Qur'ān's Legal Culture*, Holger Zellentin makes the interesting observation that, rather than assuming "Judeo-Christianity" as being an independent heretical group, it is more likely "that Judeo-Christianity constituted an integral part of various forms of Judaism and Christianity throughout Late Antiquity, as evidenced

---

36. Sidney Griffith, *The Bible in Arabic: The Scriptures of the People of the Book* (Princeton: Princeton University Press, 2013), 37.
37. Gabriel Said Reynolds, "On the Qur'an and Christian Heresies," in *The Qur'an's Reformation Judaism and Christianity: Return to the Origins*, ed. Holger Zellentin, 318–32 (London: Routledge, 2019).
38. The argument that the Ḥijāz was the home of Jewish and Christian heresies is based on the assumption of the remoteness of Mecca at the time of Muhammad. This assumption has been severely questioned by scholars, and it is therefore more convincing to argue that Arabia was not as isolated as has been generally assumed. For a detailed study of this, see Robert Hoyland, *Arabia and the Arabs: From the Bronze Age to the Coming of Islam* (New York: Routledge, 2001); also Suliman Basher, *Arabs and Others in Early Islam* (Princeton: Darwin, 1997).

by the explicit statements of the Didascalia and by the preservation of its heritage in the Qur'an."[39]

There is no question that associating the Qur'anic criticism with specific heretical groups poses a serious exegetical problem. First, the Qur'an does not refer to particular teachings or groups. Rather, it uses general terms when addressing Christians. Second, given that the Collyridians do not exist any longer, are those passages still relevant today? Indeed, the challenge for modern Muslim scholars is how to make the Qur'anic text of the seventh-century Ḥijāz relevant for all times and places (*ṣāliḥ li-kull zamān wa-makān*). One may ask, can the Qur'an's criticisms transcend its context?

Some Muslims strive to demonstrate the accuracy of the Qur'an's claims today, even though the actual adversary might have disappeared from the historical stage. The Indonesian exegete Haji Abdul Malik Karim Amrullah, known as Hamka (d. 1981), and the Iranian scholar Muhammad Husayn Ṭabāṭabā'ī (d. 1981), for instance, argue that veneration of Mary continues to be commonly practiced by certain Catholic churches. Hamka makes mention of the Armenian and Coptic Churches as examples of those Christians who worship Mary. He claims that "in addition to the belief of the Trinity, the Eastern and Western Churches, especially Orthodox, Greek Catholic, and Roman Catholic, have elevated Mary to the status of a god, to whom they pray, ask for blessing and healing, and offer various kinds of worship."[40] For Hamka, the Christian belief in what is generally known as "Marian apparitions" is a form of such veneration.[41] He also alludes to an

---

39. Holger Zellentin, *The Qur'an's Legal Culture: The Didascalia Apostolorum as a Point of Departure* (Tübingen: Möhr Siebeck, 2013), 26.
40. Hamka (Haji Abdul Malik Karim Amrullah), *Tafsir al-Azhar* (30 vols.; Jakarta: Pembimbing Massa, 1967), vol. 7, 90.
41. Ibid. The word "apparition" comes from the late Latin word "apparitio," which means "appearance" or "presence." An apparition refers to the sudden appearance of a supernatural entity, which directly manifests itself to a human individual or group. Within a Catholic context, it could be the appearance of any supernatural figure. In *A Catholic Dictionary*, apparition

interesting phenomenon in Indonesia where most Catholics keep a statue of Mary in their house and regard it with high esteem. He then concludes: "As a result, in addition to the belief of One God in three Persons (the Trinity), they [Catholics] also take Mary as a goddess. However, this additional belief has been rejected by the Protestants."[42]

Ṭabaṭabā'ī rejects the idea that the Qur'an understands Mary as a part of the Trinity (*thalātha*). He distinguishes between taking Mary as a god and believing in her divinity. Taking someone as a god is applicable to submitting to her/him with humility. The Qur'an claims that Christians take Mary (*ittakhadhū*) as a goddess, not that they believe her to be a goddess. The Iranian Shī'ī exegete offers an elaborate discussion of this issue, as some people have found it hard to explain Qur'an 5:116 because the Christians do not believe in the divinity of the Virgin Mary. When the Qur'an says that Christians have taken Christ and his mother as gods besides Allah, Ṭabaṭabā'ī claims that "taking" is not the same thing as naming: taking them as gods occurs when Christians worship them, even if they do not explicitly call them gods. "And that is what happens in their case," says Ṭabaṭabā'ī. We are told that he first came to know that the Christians indeed worshipped Mary when he read a book titled *al-Sawā'ī* from among the books of the Greek Orthodox Church, which he saw in a monastery called Dayr al-Tilmīdh. Ṭabaṭabā'ī then says, "The Catholics declare it openly and

---

is defined as "the name sometimes reserved for certain kinds of supernatural vision, namely, those that are bodily or visibly, as is often used for the manifestation of Our Lady of Lourdes, of St Michael on Monte Gargano, etc." (see "Apparition," in *A Catholic Dictionary*, ed. Donald Attwater [New York: Macmillan, 1961], 30). As for the Catholic Church's position on this issue, one Catholic scholar says: "The Church accepts the authenticity of a supernatural apparition only with great circumspection. She requires that the facts, which she submits to a severe examination, should in themselves be striking and also insists on waiting before passing judgment." (See Louis Lochet, *Apparitions of Our Lady* [New York: Herder and Herder, 1960], 30.)

42. Hamka, *Tafsir al-Azhar*, vol. 7, 90.

take pride in it."⁴³ He also refers to the Jesuit magazine *al-Mashriq* (No. 9), published in Beirut in 1904, which is decorated with pictures of Mary and colored designs. In its seventh-year edition, which was designed as a souvenir to celebrate the Golden Jubilee at the end of the fifth year since the announcement made by Pope Pius IX that the Virgin Mary had become pregnant without pollution of sin, the editor-in-chief of this magazine, Louis Cheikho, wrote an article entitled "*'Aqīdat al-ḥabl bi-lā danas fī'l-kanā'is al-sharqiyyah*" (The Doctrine of the Immaculate Conception in the Eastern Churches) in which he explicitly says that "the worship by the Armenian Church of the chaste Virgin, the Mother of God, is certainly a well-known affair (*la-amr mashhūr*)."⁴⁴ He also writes: "The Coptic Church is distinguished by its worship of the Blessed Virgin, the Mother of God."⁴⁵

For his part, Hamka understands Qur'anic criticism directed against Christians as an exhortation extending to all people, including even Muslims. When explaining the Qur'an's rejection of the divinity of Jesus, he claims that this warning does in fact apply to all people, not only to Christians who believe in the divine sonship of Jesus, but also to those who regard their "holy men" (*Orang Suci*) and priests like God, venerate them, and ask them for blessing (*berkat*) and intercession (*syafa'at*). Moreover, Hamka asserts that the warning also applies to Muslims who venerate the so-called saints (*wali*) and sacred places (*tempat keramat*) by asking them to give blessings, instead of asking God—on the Day of Judgment, he claims, those saints and sacred places will not be able to offer them any help.⁴⁶ It is worth noting the extent to which Hamka attempts to "indigenize" the meaning of the Qur'an to fit into the

---

43. Muḥammad Ḥusayn Ṭabaṭabā'ī, *al-Mīzān fī Tafsīr al-Qur'ān* (21 vols.; Beirut: Mu'assasat al-a'lāmī li'l-maṭbū'āt, 1980), vol. 7, 244.
44. Ibid. Cf. Louis Cheikho, "'Aqīda al-ḥabl bi-lā danas fī'l-kanā'is al-sharqiyya," *al-Mashriq* 9 (1904): 399.
45. Ṭabaṭabā'ī, *al-Mīzān*, vol. 7, 403.
46. Ibid., vol. 7, 305.

Indonesian experience. It is a common practice in Indonesia that Muslims go to the shrines or gravesites of Sufis, seeking blessings and intercession. In his interpretation of Qur'an 4:73, which warns Christians about their excessive attitude towards Jesus (*lā taghlū fī dīnikum*), Hamka contends that such a reminder is also applicable to Muslims, as the Prophet Muhammad is reported to have said: "Do not elevate me like Christians elevated the son of Mary. Instead, I am but His servant and Messenger."[47]

Of course, one may argue that the central idea at the heart of the Christian teaching is not that Jesus was elevated to a divine status, but rather that God descends to earth and incarnates in human flesh. However, Hamka's point is simply to broaden the Qur'anic message and transcend the context to make it applicable to Muslims as well. It is not uncommon for the modern Muslim exegetes examined in this study to extend the Qur'anic criticism of Jews and Christians to Muslims also—this even includes the text's references to the divisions and differences among the People of the Book. The Qur'an records rivalries and divisions among them: "Those who were given the Scripture disagreed out of rivalry, only after they had been given knowledge—if anyone denies God's revelation, God is swift to take account" (Q 3:19). Positioning himself as a religious reformer of the modern time, Egyptian scholar Muḥammad Rashīd Riḍā (d. 1935) reminds Muslims that "it is necessary for us not to forget about differences and conflicts that have afflicted us."[48] While explicating the Qur'anic text dealing with Christians, he warns Muslims of the danger of falling into rivalry and sectarianism—which has caused division and schism

---

47. Hamka, *Tafsir al-Azhar*, vol. 6, 75.
48. Rashīd Riḍā, *Tafsīr al-Manār*, 3rd ed. (12 vols.; Cairo: Dār al-Manār, 1947), vol. 3, 259. For a further discussion of Riḍā's view, see Farid Esack, *Qur'an, Liberation and Pluralism: An Islamic Perspective of Interreligious Solidarity against Oppression* (Oxford: Oneworld, 1997), 127–34. See also, for comparison, Mohammad Hassan Khalil, *Islam and the Fate of Others: The Salvation Question* (Oxford: Oxford University Press, 2012), 113–16.

in the history of Christianity—and he cites several passages of the Qur'an that stress the importance of unity.

In some cases, Riḍā explicates the Qur'anic criticism of Christian doctrines by referring to Western scholarship. Of course, he was not the first to do this. The nineteenth-century Indian polemicist Rahmatullah al-Kayrānawī (d. 1890) exploited higher Biblical criticism in order to argue against the authenticity of the Bible.[49] Along these lines, Riḍā makes use of ninetieth-century Western scholars' critiques of the Trinity, including Thomas Maurice's *Indian Antiquities* (1794–1800) and Thomas William Doane's *Bible Myths and Their Parallels in Other Religions* (1882), which ascribes a pagan origin to the doctrine. The latter author is cited as saying:

> If we turn to India we shall find that one of the most prominent features in the Indian theology is the doctrine of a divine triad, governing all things. This triad is called *Tri-murti*—from the Sanskrit word *tri* (three) and *murti* (form)—and consists of Brahma, Vishnu and Shiva. It is an *inseparable* unity, though three in form.[50]

Riḍā also refers to James Bonwick's *Egyptian Belief and Modern Thought* (1878) and Godfrey Higgins's *Anacalypsis* (1836), concluding that "as for the paganistic nature of this doctrine, European scholars have explained in detail and provided many examples to show the ancient traces in this doctrine."[51] With these references

---

49. For a discussion on this, see Christine Schirrmacher, "The Influence of Higher Bible Criticism on Muslim Apologetics in the Nineteenth Century," *Muslim Perceptions of Other Religions*, ed. Jacques Waardenburg (Oxford: Oxford University Press, 1999), 270–79.
50. Riḍā, *Tafsīr al-manār*, vol. 6, 88. Cf. Thomas William Doane, *Bible Myths and Their Parallels in Other Religions: Being a Comparison of the Old and New Testament Myths and Miracles with Those of Heathen Nations of Antiquity, Considering also Their Origin and Meaning* (New York: The Truth Seeker Company, 1882). 369.
51. Riḍā, *Tafsīr al-manār*, vol. 6, 88.

to Western scholarship, Riḍā attempts to prove the veracity of the Qur'anic criticism on the basis of the testimony from the insiders' (Christian) views.

The way Riḍā approaches the Qur'anic criticism of Christian doctrines is heavily influenced by his polemics against Christian missionaries. Soon after he moved to Egypt, Riḍā published a series of articles in his journal *al-Manār* responding to missionary works, which were later published as a book entitled *Shubuhāt al-Naṣārā wa-ḥujaj al-Islām (Christian Criticisms and Islamic Proofs).*[52] As has been noted by Ignaz Goldziher, Christian missionary activities and their polemical writings against Islam "produced a forceful reaction in *al-Manār.*"[53] Charles Adams argues that Riḍā placed particular emphasis on "counteracting the activities of Christian missions in Muslim lands" in *al-Manār,*[54] and also founded the *Jamʿiyyat al-daʿwah wa'l-irshād* (the Society of Propaganda and Guidance). Of all modern Muslim exegetes whose *tafsīr*s are examined in this study, Riḍā is perhaps the most polemical in his approach to Qur'anic criticisms.

Context and Applicability

In the rest of this essay, we turn our attention to the social aspect of the Qur'an's criticism. As with doctrinal issues, here too the Qur'an displays an ambivalent attitude towards the other. On one hand, parts of the text clearly support religious freedom and

---

52. For a discussion and translation of this work, see Simon A. Wood, *Christian Criticisms, Islamic Proofs: Rashīd Riḍā's Modernist Defense of Islam* (Oxford: OneWorld, 2008).
53. Ignaz Goldziher, *Die Richtungen der islamischen Koranauslegung* (Leiden: E.J. Brill, 1920), 342; idem, *Schools of Koranic Commentators*, trans. Wolfgang H. Behn (Wiesbaden: Harrassowitz Verlag, 2006), 215.
54. Charles Adams, *Islam and Modernism in Egypt: A Study of the Modern Reform Movement Inaugurated by Muhammad ʿAbduh* (New York: Russell & Russell, 1968), 196.

encourage a tolerant approach towards other traditions. Perhaps the most oft-cited verses on this issue are, "There will be no compulsion in religion" (Q 2:265), and "To you your religion and to me mine" (Q 190:5). On the other hand, the Qur'an sometimes promotes an exclusivist position and even stipulates discriminatory treatments of the other. Traditionally, these conflicting views are resolved through the theory of abrogation (*naskh*)[55] and occasions of revelation (*asbāb al-nuzūl*). However, as will become clear later, modern Muslim approaches to these two hermeneutical tools are quite nuanced.

In his *al-Nāsikh wa'l-Mansūkh*, Abū Ja'far al-Naḥḥās (d. 338/950) includes several ecumenical passages that he claims have been abrogated by later revelations. Interestingly, most modern Muslim exegetes examined in this study present an ambiguous attitude towards the supersessionist approach, in order to avoid the impression that the Qur'an includes contradictory statements. Hamka, for instance, strongly rejects the common assumption that exclusive passages like Qur'an 3:85 have abrogated 2:62. While 3:85 claims that Islam is the only true path to salvation ("Whoever desires a religion other than *islām*, it shall not be accepted from him"), the latter extends the salvific promise to other religions. Hamka's argument is twofold. First, the meaning of *islām* in Qur'an 3:85 is an inclusive *islām*, which is the religion of all prophets. Even if one accepts the exclusive meaning of *islām*, this verse does not abrogate Qur'an 2:62 because the real meaning of "*islām*" includes submission to God, faith in the hereafter, and the performance of good deeds. Second, this verse preaches the idea of inclusivity and not exclusivity. Hamka further argues:

> If it is stated that Q. 2:62 has been abrogated by 3:85, that would encourage fanaticism—claiming for them-

---

55. *Naskh*, or abrogation, is a legal strategy by which a verse of the Qur'an revealed earlier is considered to have been superseded or abrogated by a later revelation, thereby becoming inactive.

selves an Islam even though they never practice it, and claiming Paradise only for themselves. However, if we understand the two verses as supporting one another, then the gate of *daʿwa* ("preaching") is always open, and the status of Islam as a religion of purity (*agama fitra*) can be maintained.[56]

The generic sense of *al-islām* as a form of submission is also emphasized by Ṭabaṭabāʾī. For him, *islām* is the *dīn* that God revealed to all prophets throughout the ages. He acknowledges some differences in the *sharīʿa*s of prophets, but the essence is identical—namely, submission and obedience to God, a message that had been delivered by all the prophets. "The differences among these *sharīʿa*s in perfection and deficiency," he asserts, "do not imply contradiction or exclusion, or superiority of one over the others. They are all one in that they are manifestations of submission and obedience to God in all that He demanded from His servants, as conveyed by His Prophets."[57] Ṭabaṭabāʾī then concludes:

> It is clear from the preceding that what is intended is that the true faith, which is with God and in His presence, is one sacred law (*sharīʿa*) that differs only in the degree [of comprehensiveness and perfection] in accordance with the different capacities of the different communities. In essence, however, it is one, one in the form which God has implanted it in humankind in their original state (*fitra*) of pure faith.[58]

---

56. Hamka, *Tafsir al-Azhar*, vol. 1, 187.
57. Ibid., vol. 3, 120–21.
58. Ibid., vol. 3, 121.

With this understanding, Ṭabaṭabā'ī sees no contradiction between Qur'an 2:62 and 3:85, and therefore there is no need for the theory of *naskh*. In his exegesis of 2:62, the learned Shī'ī scholar asserts:

> At the gate of bliss no importance will be attached to names and titles, for example, whether a group is called "the believers," or a faction "those who are Jews," or a party "Sabians," or others "the Christians." The only important thing is belief in God and the Last Day and doing good.[59]

Hamka's and Ṭabaṭabā'ī's reluctance to appeal to *naskh* is understandable because even the proponents of this theory disagreed among themselves about which verse of the Qur'an abrogated which. Another strategy employed by Muslim exegetes to address the Qur'an's conflicting attitudes is to refer to the occasions of revelation (*asbāb al-nuzūl*), a specific genre in the *tafsīr* tradition that is intended to provide historical contexts for revelations, so that Muslims might understand the circumstances in which certain passages were revealed. Yet, again, there have been some disagreements concerning the precise context of a particular verse. Oftentimes, scholars mention more than one occasion for the same verse. Therefore, Ṭabaṭabā'ī calls into question the whole corpus of *asbāb al-nuzūl* as historically spurious. For the Iranian scholar:

> These reports [of its occasion of revelation], like most of the narratives giving theoretical reasons, are in fact mere attempts to fit some occurrences to a verse, and then claim that it was revealed for this reason. These are merely theoretical reasons; the verse most probably does have general application.[60]

---

59. Ṭabaṭabā'ī, *al-Mīzān*, vol. 6, 67.
60. Ibid., vol. 5, 285.

However, some modern Muslims find it useful to situate key Qur'anic criticisms within a certain historical context, in order to restrict its general applicability. This is especially true with regard to Qur'anic references to aspects of social interaction. When it comes to Qur'an 5:51, for instance, which prohibits Muslims from taking Jews and Christians as *awliyā'* (variably translated as "leaders," "guardians," "friends," "allies," and "protectors"), modern Muslims emphasize the hostile environment that formed the backdrop against which the verse was revealed. This verse says, "You who believe, do not take Jews and Christians as *awliyā'*, they are *awliyā'* to one another."[61] Commenting on this verse, Riḍā does not seem to be primarily concerned with the possible various meanings of the term *awliyā'*. Rather, his main focus is to understand the prohibition within a certain context by bringing a significant number of *asbāb al-nuzūl* narratives into discussion. From the outset, Riḍā realizes the problems associated with the fact that two or more different *asbāb al-nuzūl* can be related to one verse, and, therefore, he devises a theoretical framework to harmonize those conflicting narratives.

Riḍā distinguishes between two types of *asbāb al-nuzūl*: general (*sabab ʿāmm*) and specific (*sabab khāṣṣ*). In the case of Qur'an 5:51, the *sabab ʿāmm* can be found in the hostile surroundings of the Muslim community, especially among three Jewish tribes in Medina, namely Banū Qaynuqāʿ, Banū Naḍīr, and Banū Qurayẓah. The Prophet had attempted to live in peace with them by making

---

61. The prohibition of taking non-believers as *awliyā'* occurs several times in the Qur'ān with different identification of non-believers. While Q 5:51 refers explicitly to *al-Yahūd* ("Jews") and *al-Naṣārā* ("Christians"), in three occurrences (Q 3:28, 4:139, and 4:144) the Qur'an simply refers to *al-kuffār* ("unbelievers"). Elsewhere the prohibition applies to "those who took your religion as a subject of mockery and entertainment" (Q 5:57); "your fathers and brothers" (Q 9:23); "other than God" (Q 13:16, 29:41, 39:3, and 42:9); and "My enemy and your enemy" (Q 6:1). As expected, modern Muslim exegetes devote more detailed discussion to the first occurrence of this prohibition in Q 3:28 than its occurrence in other verses.

a pact, Riḍā claims, but they breached the pact and conspired to kill him. It is against the background of such a hostile environment that the prohibition of befriending (*muwālā*) the People of the Book should be understood.[62] With regard to the latter (the *sabab khāṣṣ*), Riḍā mentions different, conflicting narratives, without judging on their authenticity—a practice that is common among earlier *mufassirūn* such as Ibn Jarīr al-Ṭabarī (d. 310/923), who concluded that there is no evidence for the authenticity of any of these stories to the exclusion of the others. It can be safely assumed that the verse relates to a hypocrite (*munāfiq*) who did not want to give up his friendship with Jews or Christians for fear of losing their protection. In any case, al-Ṭabarī argues, the verse should be interpreted according to its evidence and general meaning, not with specific reference to any occasion of revelation.[63] Riḍā, on the other hand, argues that the verse should be understood within the general context of its revelation, namely the hostile environment. Thus, the prohibition of taking the unbelievers as *awliyāʾ* (however this term is to be understood) only applies to this particular circumstance, in which they waged war against the Prophet or against the believers, and when they were the ones who showed enmity. He argues that Muhammad only ever fought against those who conspired to kill him.

Ṭabāṭabāʾī rejects the political connotation of the term *awliyāʾ*, arguing that such a meaning cannot be gleaned from the internal evidence in the Qurʾan, but rather from the external sources—namely the *asbāb al-nuzūl*. As discussed above, Ṭabāṭabāʾī expresses his skeptical attitude towards the historicity of the *asbāb al-nuzūl* narratives and claims that there is no indication in the Qurʾan to justify such a political-military connotation of *awliyāʾ*. This does not mean, however, that he supports the idea that this interdiction

---

62. Riḍā, *Tafsīr al-Manār*, vol. 6, 424.
63. Muhammad b. Jarīr al-Ṭabarī, *Jāmiʿ al-Bayān fī Taʾwīl āy al-Qurʾān* (30 vols.; Cairo: Muṣṭafā al-Bābī al-Ḥalabī, 1954–1957), vol. 10, 399. Al-Ṭabarī says, "*faʾl-ṣawāb an yaḥkum li-ẓāhir al-tanzīl biʾl-ʿumūm ʿalā mā ʿamma.*"

is related to all kinds of interreligious relations. On the basis of the text's internal evidence, he goes to great lengths to insist that a personal dimension, that is, "affectionate closeness," is the essence of its meaning.[64] Although the root *w-l-y* denotes authority to manage something (i.e., guardianship), Ṭabāṭabā'ī argues that "the word has been used—with increasing frequency—in the context of love and affection; if two people love each other, each feels free to look after the other's affairs as love empowers the beloved to manage the affairs, and influence the life, of the lover."[65] What is prevented is not taking Jews and Christians as political leaders, but as friends. Thus, taking the unbelievers as *awliyā'* means establishing a psychological rapport with them to the extent that such an affectionate closeness would taint the believer's vision and adversely affect his thoughts and character.[66] Recognizing that this is a less tolerant reading, he supports his contention with several lines of debate. In particular, he refutes an understanding of *wilāyah/walāyah* in terms of help or contractual alliance, as suggested by some *mufassirūn*.[67]

---

64. For a brief discussion of Ṭabāṭabā'ī's view, see Jane McAuliffe, "Christians in the Qur'an and Tafsīr," in *Muslim Perceptions of Other Religions*, ed. Jacques Waardenburg (Oxford: Oxford University Press, 1999), 111–12; and Esack, *Qur'an, Liberation and Pluralism*, 183.

65. Ṭabāṭabā'ī, *al-Mīzān*, vol. 3, 151.

66. Ibid.

67. According to Ṭabāṭabā'ī, some *mufassirūn* oppose interpreting *wilāya* as "love" and "affection" because it is not supported by the *asbāb al-nuzūl*. Instead, various narratives of the context of the revelation of Q 5:51 seem to support the idea that the verse forbids entering into a covenant and *wilāya* of mutual help between the Muslims, on the one hand, and the Jews and the Christians, on the other. However, the tendency of some *mufassirūn* to bring the context of revelation into discussion is rejected by Ṭabāṭabā'ī, who argues that the narratives of the *asbāb al-nuzūl* are contradictory and do not present a single meaning that can be relied upon. For Ṭabāṭabā'ī, those narratives are not only weak but also "merely attempts to apply historical events to the Qur'anic verses which appear to have some relevance to them." Even if we accept the authenticity of those narratives, he contends, such historical

It seems clear that there is a tendency among modern Muslim exegetes to limit the polemical content of the Qur'an either by looking at the internal textual evidence or by recourse to the *asbāb al-nuzūl*. It should also be noted that Muslim scholars do not present a coherent view on the political rights of non-Muslims. While advocating the idea that Muslims should not appoint Jews or Christians as political leaders, Riḍā allows for non-Muslim *dhimmī*s[68] to be appointed to public office. He rejects the views of earlier scholars such as al-Zamakhsharī (d. 538/1144) and al-Bayḍāwī (d. 685/1286) who prohibit non-Muslims from becoming public officers in Islamic lands. Both exegetes narrate a story in which the second caliph, 'bit b. al-Khaṭṭāb, asked Abū Mūsā al-Ash'arī to dismiss his Christian secretary by referring to Qur'an 5:51.

Riḍā disagrees with both al-Zamakhsharī and al-Bayḍāwī, arguing that the appointment of non-Muslims to public office has been a long-established state policy, from the early Islamic state to modern times. He tells a personal story that took place during his visit to Dār al-Funūn in Istanbul in 1909. One of the teachers there taught the meaning of Qur'an 5:51 by referring to al-Bayḍāwī, and a student stood up and asked: If the case was as al-Bayḍāwī said, why does the state sometimes appoint Jews and Christians as ministers, senators, parliamentarians, or civil servants? We are told that the teacher was scared to death, because if he said something against the constitution he could be severely punished. In that situation, Riḍā asked the teacher if he could respond to the student. In Riḍā's own words, "I explained that *wilāyah* in the verse is about the *wilāyah* of helping (*wilāyat al-naṣra*) and the verse does not ban the employment of non-Muslim *dhimmī*s. The student was satisfied

---

events cannot particularize nor restrict the generality of a Qur'anic verse, otherwise "the Qur'an would have died with the death of those about whom such verses were revealed." See Ṭabaṭabā'ī, *al-Mīzān*, vol. 3, 151.

68. "*Dhimmī*" refers to non-Muslims whose religious beliefs qualify them for legal protection under Islamic rule, including permission to continue practicing their religion, in exchange for a penalty tax, called *jizya*.

with my explanation, so too other listeners. The teacher also looked happy."⁶⁹ Riḍā's point is that there is nothing wrong with the appointment of non-Muslims to public office, let alone mutual friendship and collaboration with them, as long as they are not fighting or conspiring against Muslims. Why then did he opt for the political connotation of *awliyā*'?

While the narratives of the *asbāb al-nuzūl* have been effectively employed by some modern exegetes to restrict the general applicability of certain passages in the modern context, there is another tendency among them to contextualize the Qur'anic discourse within the text itself. The contemporary Indonesian exegete Muhammad Quraish Shihab (b. 1944), for instance, looks closely at the Qur'an's internal textual evidence to argue that the text does not specifically prohibit Muslims from taking Jews and Christians as *awliyā*'. For Shihab, such a prohibition is not only directed at Jews and Christians. He argues that Qur'an 5:51 does not pertain to Jews and Christians only, nor to all Jews and Christians, but that it rather means all those who behave in the negative way depicted in 5:51–53 and the preceding passages of the text. Although Qur'an 5:12–50 describes the negative behaviors of specific Jews and Christians, Shihab does not associate the prohibition with those specific Jews and Christians, but rather he looks at the negative behaviors as the main reasons for their being prohibited as the *awliyā*' of the believers. He, therefore, concludes that whoever behaves like those specific Jews and Christians should be prevented from being *awliyā*'.⁷⁰

It seems clear, then, that modern Muslim scholars have developed several exegetical tools that allow them to limit the applicability of polemical passages in the Qur'an. Although their source of knowledge of other religions is primarily the Qur'an, rather than the religious traditions of others, they did incorporate the "spirit" of the modern time into their exegetical works. It is important to look

---

69. Ibid., vol. 3, 429.
70. M. Quraysh Shihab, *Tafsir al-Mishbah* (15 vols.; Jakarta: Lentera, 2001), vol. 3, 113.

at these commentaries as reflecting modern attempts to read the Qur'an interreligiously because, as Khalid Abou El Fadl has argued, "the meaning of the text is often only as moral as its reader. If the reader is intolerant, hateful, or oppressive, so will be the interpretation of the text."[71] Of course, to some extent, modern Muslim exegetes rely on traditional sources. However, their interpretations are also shaped by their own personal viewpoints as well as the contexts in which they live and interact.

Concluding Remarks

From the above discussion, it can be inferred that modern Muslim scholars seek to emphasize the need to make the Qur'an function within society and history rather than stand outside it. For them, it is the book of guidance for their everyday life and thus maintains a special status in personal and social matters alike. This requires sustainable interpretation and reinterpretation to make the Qur'an relevant in all times and places. In fact, one of the common characteristics of religious scriptures is the unceasing process of reinterpretation that they generate by absorbing the demand of time with new ethics and thought-paradigms. This is particularly true for Muslims who believe that revelation ceased after the death of Muhammad in the seventh century. Another dimension of the necessity of interpretation and reinterpretation is the fact that the Qur'an does not provide detailed instructions and regulations for how to live an Islamic life. How can this text be a source of their religious belief and practice? The task of an interpreter is not only to discover the meaning of the text, but also to transform it into a "living Qur'an." As the Italian scholar Massimo Campanini has pointed out:

---

71. Khalid Abou El Fadl, *The Place of Tolerance in Islam* (Boston, MA: Beacon Press, 2002), 23.

> The most original part of modern Qur'anic exegesis, leaving aside the more traditionalist and conservative or the more strictly philosophical interpretations, has been directed at discovering the Qur'an's practical dimension, which is to say its function in modifying the structure of social reality and revolutionizing human relations.[72]

This kind of wrestling with the seventh-century religious text is evident in the ways that the scholars discussed in this essay endeavor to reinterpret those Qur'anic passages that have often been viewed as an obstacle to peaceful coexistence or non-polemical interactions among different religious communities in the modern context. It must be noted that these commentaries were not written for a Western audience, but rather for their fellow Muslims to seek practical guidance from their sacred scripture in their interactions with people of other religions. They seem to approach the Qur'an with a twofold purpose in mind: namely, to build a religious society on the basis of the divine teaching as well as to contribute to the betterment of the world in which religious tolerance is seen as a key. The modern Muslim exegetes whose works are examined in this essay experienced various distinct challenges during both the colonial and post-colonial periods, and they set out to chart an exegetical enterprise by which to support religious reform (*al-iṣlāḥ al-dīnī*) within the community and religious harmony (*al-tasāmuḥ al-dīnī*) with others.

Although the historical and social contexts in which *tafsīr* emerged have been overlooked in the current scholarship, this essay has demonstrated that modern concerns and local contexts have shaped, and have been shaped by, Muslim understandings of and approaches to the Qur'an. Certainly, the Qur'an is not an easy text to read, and each interpreter brings to it an apparatus for interpretation. As ʿAlī b. Abī Ṭālib is reported to have said, "This Qur'an

---

72. Massimo Campanini, *The Qur'an: Modern Muslim Interpretations*, trans. Caroline Higgitt (New York: Routledge, 2011), 4.

is only lines inscribed between two covers; it does not speak with the tongue. Only human beings can speak on its behalf [*al-Qur'ān bayna duffatai al-mushaf lā yanthiq bi-lisānin, wa-innamā yanthiqu bihī'l-rijāl*]."⁷³ 'Alī was well aware that the Qur'an is a polyvalent text, and the relation between a text and its interpreter is dialectic in nature in the sense that the former is open to a variety of interpretations in various contexts while the latter is shaped and influenced by the text that he/she reads and other factors that have informed his or her philosophical consciousness. In other words, interpretation of a text is built on (to use Gadamer's words) the fusion of horizons. For Gadamer, "Understanding is essentially an effective historical event."⁷⁴ Thus, the socio-historical context of modern interpretation of the Qur'an should not be discounted.

Faced with increasingly pluralistic societies in modern times, Muslim exegetes have addressed difficult questions affecting Muslim attitudes toward other religions. Some of the key polemical Qur'anic references to Judaism and Christianity are undoubtedly responsible for the development of a Muslim theology of the "other," and it is therefore understandable that modern Muslim exegetes have struggled to re-contextualize the Qur'an in light of modern realities. In a time when prejudices, hatred, violence, and distortion are so common, the need to revisit elements of our scriptural tradition is more obvious than ever. Modern *tafsīr*—like classical and medieval Qur'an exegesis—is not merely a theoretical explication of the words of God, independent of the social realities in which it emerged, but is rather an undertaking embedded in a specific socio-historical context. As has been discussed in this essay, modern Muslim approaches to Qur'anic criticism demonstrate a ground-level awareness of these challenges, and offer the potential

---

73. Cited by Carl W. Ernst, *How to Read the Qur'an: A New Guide with Selected Translations* (Chapel Hill: University of North Carolina Press, 2011), 63.
74. Hans Georg Gadamer, *Truth and Method*, trans. Joel Weinsheimer and Donald Marshall (New York: Continuum, 1989), 300.

to reframe these difficult issues as opportunities for peaceful interreligious relations. To what extent they have been successful is yet another question.

Bibliography

Al-Ṭabarī, Muḥammad b. Jarīr. *Jāmiʿ al-Bayān fī Taʾwīl Āy al-Qurʾān*. 30 vols. Cairo: Muṣṭafā al-Bābī al-Ḥalabī, 1954–1957.

Campanini, Massimo. *The Qurʾan: Modern Muslim Interpretations*, translated by Caroline Higgitt. New York: Routledge, 2011.

Esack, Farid. *Qurʾan, Liberation and Pluralism: an Islamic Perspective of Interreligious Solidarity against Oppression*. Oxford: Oneworld, 1997.

Goldziher, Ignaz. *Schools of Koranic Commentators*, translated by Wolfgang H. Behn. Wiesbaden: Harrassowitz Verlag, 2006.

Hamka (Haji Abdul Malik Karim Amrullah). *Tafsīr al-Azhar*. 30 vols. Jakarta: Pembimbing Massa, 1967.

McAuliffe, Jane. "Christians in the Qurʾan and Tafsīr." In *Muslim Perceptions of Other Religions*, edited by Jacques Waardenburg, 106–21. Oxford: Oxford University Press, 1999.

Neuwirth, Angelika. "The House of Abraham and the House of Amram: Genealogy, Patriarchal Authority, and Exegetical Professionalism." In *The Qurʾan in Context: Historical and Literary Investigations into the Qurʾanic Milieu*, edited by Angelika Neuwirth, Nicolai Sinai, and Michel Marx, 499–531. Leiden: Brill, 2010.

Nöldeke, Theodor, Friedrich Schwally, Gotthelf Bergsträßer, and Otto Pretzl. *The History of the Qurʾan*, edited and translated by Wolfgang H. Behn. Leiden: Brill, 2013.

al-Qāsimī, Jamāl al-Dīn. *Maḥāsin al-Taʾwīl*. 17 vols. Cairo: Maktabat Īsā al-Bābī al-Ḥalabī, 1957.

Reynolds, Gabriel Said. "On the Qurʾan and Christian Heresies." In *The Qurʾan's Reformation Judaism and Christianity: Return to the Origins*, edited by Holger Zellentin, 318–32. London: Routledge, 2019.

Riḍā, Rashīd. *Tafsīr al-Manār*. 3rd ed. 12 vols. Cairo: Dār al-Manār, 1947.

Rippin, Andrew, "The Function of Asbāb al-Nuzūl in Qur'anic Exegesis." *Bulletin of the School of Oriental and African Studies* 51, no. 1 (1988): 1–20.
Shihab, M. Quraysh. *Tafsir al-Mishbah.* 15 vols. Jakarta: Lentera, 2001.
Sirry, Mun'im. "'Compete with One Another in Good Works': Exegesis of Qur'an Verse 5.48 and Contemporary Muslim Discourses on Religious Pluralism." *Islam and Christian-Muslim Relations* 20, no. 4 (2009): 423–38.
Ṭabaṭabā'ī, Muḥammad Ḥusayn. *al-Mīzān fī Tafsīr al-Qur'ān.* 21 vols. Beirut: Mu'assasat al-a'lāmī li'l-maṭbū'āt, 1980.

Chapter Four

SCRIPTURE SPEAKING ABOUT ITSELF: THE SELF-REFERENTIALITY OF THE QUR'AN AND CHRISTIAN-MUSLIM DIALOGUE

David Marshall

"This is the scripture in which there is no doubt" (Q 2:2). In a prime location, almost the very beginning of the Qur'an, in the second verse of the second sura, preceded only by a brief prayer in Sura 1—so at a moment when we might expect a defining theme to be stated—the Qur'an does what it will often do: it speaks about itself, and canonizes itself: "This is the scripture in which there is no doubt."

In this essay I shall discuss some further examples of how the Qur'an repeatedly and emphatically speaks about itself and canonizes itself as scripture (*kitāb*). I shall then turn to the Bible, in which we find very little that resembles this distinctively self-conscious and self-referential quality of the Qur'an. I shall then explore several related contrasts in the beliefs and practices of Muslims and Christians regarding their scriptures. The underlying suggestion throughout is that a clear grasp of these significant contrasts will help Muslims and Christians to engage in dialogue that takes difference seriously.

First, however, we should note the different approaches to this subject within confessional Islamic scholarship and Western academic scholarship carried out largely by non-Muslims. In a nutshell: while in recent years non-Muslims have written a great deal about the self-referentiality of the Qur'an, Muslims appear hardly to do so at all.[1] Typical of the former category is Stefan Wild's suggestion that the Qur'an is "the most...self-referential holy text known in the history of world religions,"[2] a point that William A. Graham elaborates in some illuminating comments, worth citing extensively, on the distinctive character of the Qur'an, when seen in a wider religious and historical context:

> Typically, the other sacred texts of the world's religions that we call "scriptures" were not written with any similar consciousness [such as we find in the Qur'an] of belonging themselves to a category of texts called "scripture." Most if not all great scriptural texts other than the Qur'an are unconscious of being even potentially "scripture," for "scripture" or any analogous concept is usually a category developed ex post facto and then applied to a text or texts that a community has experienced as sacred, and consequently given special treatment. Thus the Vedic texts of India do not speak about themselves as *śruti*, nor the Jewish

---

1. The fact that there are many Muslim scholars of the Qur'an working in Western academic contexts, and engaging with non-Muslim approaches to the Qur'an, indicates that this contrast is not absolute. For example, Mehdi Azaiez mentions the self-referentiality of the Qur'an in his essay, "Le contre-discours coranique," in *Le Coran: Nouvelles Approches* (Paris: CNRS Éditions, 2013), 270. This is, however, precisely in a volume focusing on "new approaches" to the Qur'an, and Azaiez draws on non-Muslim scholarship. Especially in relation to pre-modern Islamic scholarship, therefore, my observation remains valid.
2. Stefan Wild, "'We have sent down to thee the book with the truth ...': Spatial and Temporal Implications of the Qur'anic Concepts of nuzūl, tanzīl and 'inzāl," in *The Qur'ān as Text*, ed. Stefan Wild (Leiden: Brill, 1996), 137–53. (This passage at 140.)

or Christian Bible about itself as "scripture" (although the Christian New Testament does treat the earlier Hebrew scriptures as scripturally authoritative); it is rather later generations and their texts that recognize them as "scripture." The texts of the religious prophet Mani are possibly one pre-qur'anic exception to this...and of course some later Buddhist sutras such as the Lotus Sutra present themselves as the word of the Buddha (*buddhavacana*); but there seems to be no major scriptural text before the Qur'an that uses a generic concept of "scripture" as a category to which it also claims to belong.

The Qur'an, for its part, is self-consciously explicit about its own function as scripture, *kitāb,* and about being the latest, culminating revelation in a long line of scriptural revelations from the lord of all beings to previous prophets and their peoples.[3]

Perhaps the most influential publication in this field has been Daniel A. Madigan's fascinating and provocative study *The Qur'an's Self-Image.*[4] He argues that the Qur'an's self-designation as *kitāb* cannot mean (as Muslims have generally assumed) that the Qur'an understands itself as a fixed corpus, because, crucially, it uses such language of itself long before it was written down and its boundaries were defined. Madigan points to the complexities lurking here when he asks: "What is this *kitāb* about which the *kitāb* is always speaking? What is the recitation [*qur'ān*] about which

---

3. William A. Graham, "Scripture and the Qur'ān," *Encyclopaedia of the Qur'ān,* Vol. 4 (Leiden: Brill, 2004), 558–69. (This passage at 560–61.)

4. Daniel A. Madigan, *The Qur'ān's Self-Image: Writing and Authority in Islam's Scripture* (Princeton: Princeton University Press, 2001). Note also Madigan's related *Encyclopaedia of the Qur'ān* articles on "Book," Vol. 1 (Leiden: Brill, 2001) 242–51, and "Revelation and Inspiration," Vol. 4 (Leiden: Brill, 2004), 437–48. A more recent major publication in this field is Anne-Sylvie Boisliveau, *Le Coran par lui-même* (Leiden: Brill, 2014).

verses are constantly recited?"⁵ His proposal is that the Qur'an's usages of the term *kitāb* indicate that it signifies not "a book" but rather processes of divine engagement with the world, characterized by flexibility, responsiveness, and open-endedness. Madigan notes that the implications of his analysis go beyond the merely academic: it is "dangerous" when *kitāb* comes to mean "something as static and fixed as a book." If the Qur'an itself does not license such a "circumscribed conception of divine guidance," then there is clear support here for Muslim accounts of revelation that are less confined and static, more flexible and dynamic, and so able to justify broadly progressive contemporary interpretations of Islam.⁶

Other recent studies of Qur'anic self-referentiality have taken different approaches. Nicolai Sinai, for example, is critical of Madigan on a few points and addresses some different aspects of the phenomenon. In particular, Sinai asks why the Qur'an has this unique character, and argues persuasively that a diachronic approach to the Qur'an illuminates this question. He suggests that the earliest passages of the Qur'an show no traces of self-referentiality, which in fact evolves gradually as "a strategy of self-authorization" in relation to audiences opposed to the Qur'anic message.⁷

When we turn from such non-Muslim studies to Muslim scholarship, the contrast is striking. While writing this essay, I surveyed a selection of both classical and modern commentaries on Qur'an 2:2 (the text cited at the start of this essay), and I found in them no apparent interest in the self-referential character of the Qur'an. As mentioned earlier (see n. 1), some contemporary Muslim scholars have begun to engage with the work of Madigan and others, but it is notable

---

5. Madigan, *Self-Image*, 62. Wild writes in similar vein that in the Qur'an "the maze of reflexivities is dense" (Stefan Wild, "Why Self-Referentiality?" in *Self-Referentiality in the Qur'ān*, ed. Stefan Wild [Wiesbaden: Harrasowitz Verlag, 2006], 1–23, this passage at 15).
6. Madigan, *Self-Image*, 191.
7. Nicolai Sinai, "Qur'ānic Self-Referentiality as a Strategy of Self-Authorization" in *Self-Referentiality*, ed. Wild, 103–34.

that this discussion arose within non-Muslim scholarship, while for the great mass of Muslim scholarship (certainly in pre-modern and more traditional forms) the self-referentiality of the Qur'an, even if it is noted, simply does not appear to be worth mentioning.

This observation reflects a fundamental difference between Muslim and non-Muslim Qur'anic scholarship. Despite all the variety and disagreements within Muslim scholarship, on the one hand, and within non-Muslim on the other, there is a basic contrast between the believing Muslim approach to the Qur'an as divine revelation and non-Muslim approaches, which, by definition, do not share that starting point. The non-Muslim, studying the Qur'an in the wider sweep of the history of religions, may be struck by the solemn self-attestation that is so pervasive a feature of the Qur'an, and may regard this as an interesting phenomenon to investigate. To the Muslim, in contrast, the same phenomenon (if noticed at all) would appear as entirely in keeping with what the Qur'an is understood to be. What could be more natural than that God, the speaker of the words of the Qur'an, should repeatedly and solemnly tell its human recipients (who all too often need persuading of this) that the words they are hearing are divine revelation? Why should this need comment? The self-referentiality of the Qur'an appears to be part of the familiar, encircling environment in which Muslims live and think, an entirely unsurprising correlate of the fundamental convictions about the Qur'an that ground Muslim identity.

To speak of the self-referentiality of the Qur'an is, in simpler terms, to say that it is a scripture that is about itself. The Qur'an is not only about itself: it speaks often of God's creation, for example, and it could also be objected that the Qur'an is fundamentally about God. But to say that the Qur'an is fundamentally about God and that the Qur'an is fundamentally about itself are not ultimately competing claims, because the Qur'an is, in its own account, what God is saying, what God is revealing. And the Qur'an constantly focuses on the drama of the divine-human encounter, at the heart of which is the sending of divine revelation and the contrasting ways in which believers and unbelievers respectively accept and reject it.

The self-referentiality of the Qur'an is present not only in passages where it speaks about itself explicitly (to which we shall turn in a moment). For example, the Qur'an contains many stories of messengers of generations before Muhammad speaking God's message and being rejected by unbelievers. These stories are, at one level, speaking of the past, but they do so to provide a context in sacred history for the crisis in Muhammad's present brought about by his proclamation of the Qur'an and the generally hostile reception given to it. So although these stories do not name Muhammad or the Qur'an, they are in a sense all about the Qur'an and the drama of its proclamation by Muhammad. By speaking of Noah preaching God's message in his day, for example, the Qur'an is talking about itself, grounding itself in the history of God's dealings with the world, and warning those who do not take it seriously.[8]

This kind of implicit self-referentiality that pervades the Qur'an could be compared to the mass of an iceberg below sea level. However, the tip of the iceberg, consisting of those frequent passages where self-referentiality is explicit, is itself an unmissable presence. Wild identifies types of explicitly self-referential passages, including definitions of how revelation takes place (e.g., Q 42:51–3) and responses to hostile questioning (e.g., Q 25:32–3). Often, these responses state what the Qur'an is *not*. For example: "This is the speech of an honored messenger, not the words of a poet…nor the words of a soothsayer…. This is a message sent down from the Lord of the Worlds" (Q 69:40–4).[9] Also of note is that the Qur'an contains

---

8. See, for example, the narratives about Noah in Suras 11, 26, and 71 for parallels between Noah's proclamation in the past and Muhammad's proclamation of the Qur'an in his present context. On this understanding of such passages, see David Marshall, *God, Muhammad and the Unbelievers: A Qur'anic Study* (Richmond: Curzon, 1999).

9. Wild, "Why Self-Referentiality?," 7–8. In the passage cited here, the Qur'an insists that it is not poetry, a category mistake which it frequently rejects, both because this is one way of explaining the Qur'an as being of other than divine origin, and also because of a perception of poets as fundamentally frivolous. See, e.g., Q 26:224–26.

a wide range of terms with which it designates itself. As well as *qurʾān* itself (recitation), other terms include *kitāb* (scripture), *tanzīl* (sending down, revelation), *dhikr* (remembrance, reminder), and *furqān* (translated as variously as "criterion" and "salvation").[10] This cluster of alternating self-designations conveys a rich aura of multifarious functions and complex identity, as well as a robust, assertive, and at times mysterious sense of self in the Qurʾan.

Another significant type of self-referential passage, on which I shall focus particularly, is located strategically at the beginning of suras. Wild notes that about a third of the Qurʾan's 114 Suras start with such a passage, and Sinai rightly emphasizes that this is a "privileged locus for self-referential comments," a setting where they are guaranteed to achieve maximum impact.[11] The passage with which I began this essay is perhaps the most familiar example of this genre: "This is the scripture in which there is no doubt, guidance for the godfearing…" (Q 2:2a). In virtually its first words, the Qurʾan here canonizes itself as scripture with a ringing assurance that allows for no doubt, before moving, characteristically, to an account of the contrasting responses of believers and unbelievers.[12] The opening passage of Sura 3 proclaims first that there is no god but God and then immediately affirms that God has sent down upon Muhammad the *kitāb*. Here, the preceding history of earlier scriptures, the Torah and Gospel, is also affirmed. This is a vital part of the Qurʾan's account of itself and its veracity: it is not the first *kitāb* but has been preceded by scriptures sent down by God upon Muhammad's precursors as prophets and bearers of scriptures, notably Moses and

---

10. Stefan Wild, "Self-Referentiality," in *The Qurʾan: An Encyclopedia*, ed. Oliver Leaman (London: Routledge, 2006), 576–79, at 576.
11. Wild, "Why Self-Referentiality?' 10. Sinai, "Qurʾānic self-referentiality," 116.
12. There is not space here to discuss the question of whether this verse should be translated "*This* is the scripture…" or "*That* is the scripture…." The latter translation can be taken as implying a reference to *umm al-kitāb*, the heavenly book of which the Qurʾan is a faithful rendition. Either way, the essential self-referentiality of the Qurʾan is not fundamentally altered.

Jesus. The Qur'an functions as confirmation (*musaddiq*) of these earlier scriptures and final authority (*muhaymin*) over them (3:2-4; 5:44–48). Another important aspect of the Qur'an's self-description occurs at the start of Sura 12, which emphasizes the specific language in which the Qur'an has been revealed: "These are the verses of the *kitāb* that makes things clear—We have sent it down as an Arabic Qur'an so that you may understand" (Q 12:1).

If we now turn to the Bible, the contrast is striking. As we have seen, to ask what the Qur'an says about itself proves to be a meaningful question, relatively easily answered. Certainly, there are developments in the Qur'an, different emphases and styles and some changes in policy across its different periods and contexts, but it is also a remarkably consistent, univocal, and self-aware text. For Muslims, this is because every word of it is spoken by God, but non-Muslim readers also recognize that this is a scripture with a forceful, coherent sense of self (even if scholars like Madigan suggest some deeper complexities). To address the question of the Bible's account of itself is, by contrast, a much more difficult matter. We must reckon with the Bible's provenance over many centuries and through many authors, not to mention questions such as what exactly is in the Biblical canon and how many, if any, Biblical authors knew that what they were writing would come to be canonized as scripture. As one Biblical scholar observes, the Hebrew Bible "does not even know that it is the Hebrew Bible. As a document, it displays an astonishing lack of textual self-consciousness."[13]

Although some might therefore be tempted to dismiss the inquiry "What does the Bible say about itself?" with the brusque put-down, "Question does not compute," the Bible does, in fact, contain moments of self-referentiality, although on a different scale and of a quite different character from what we find in the Qur'an. Certainly, there is nothing in the Bible quite like the self-referential, self-canonizing utterances that pervade the Qur'an, especially at the

---

13. Jacques Berlinerblau, *The Secular Bible: Why Nonbelievers Must Take Religion Seriously* (Cambridge: Cambridge University Press, 2005), 28.

opening of Suras. Indeed, the differences between the Bible and the Qur'an are such that, although self-referentiality is a useful concept in analysis of the Qur'an, it is not the best term to use in discussing the Bible. At the time of writing, an Internet search for "self-referentiality in the Bible" did not indicate any scholarly work using this terminology.

However, if we widen our frame of reference, we will recognize that there is a great deal of intra-scriptural conversation within the Bible. This much more diffuse form of self-referentiality is likely to be discussed in terms of intertextuality. Throughout the New Testament, it is apparent that the first Christians constantly related the story of Jesus and the experience of the early churches to the Old Testament scriptures. The very first pages of the New Testament give perhaps the most obvious examples of this, with Matthew's Gospel repeatedly noting that events in the life of Jesus occurred to fulfill what was written in the scriptures (e.g., Mat 1:22–3; 2:4–6, 14–15, 17–18; 3:1–3). In addition to explicit citation of this kind, there is also a constant pattern of allusion to Old Testament texts throughout the New Testament, with different authors echoing the scriptures in various ways.[14] There are also processes of intra-scriptural interaction within the Old Testament, for example the re-telling in Chronicles of the narratives of the earlier books of Samuel and Kings, or echoes of earlier prophets in Joel (e.g., 2:32; 3:16, 18).[15] An example of cross-reference within the New Testament occurs at 2 Peter 3:15–16, which mentions the challenges in reading the letters of "our beloved brother Paul." But although 2 Peter appears to regard Paul's letters as belonging to the category of "scripture," we cannot assume that

---

14. See Richard B. Hays, *Echoes of Scripture in the Letters of Paul* (New Haven: Yale University Press, 1989), and *Echoes of Scripture in the Gospels* (Waco: Baylor University Press, 2016).
15. John Day, "Prophecy," in *It Is Written: Scripture Citing Scripture. Essays in Honour of Barnabas Lindars SSF*, eds. Barnabas Lindars, D.A. Carson, and H.G.M. Williamson (Cambridge: Cambridge University Press, 1988), 39–55; the discussion of Joel is at 49.

the writer saw his own letter as scripture, so to speak here of "intra-scriptural reference" would only make sense retrospectively, from a position after the canonization of all the New Testament documents. Indeed, although biblical authors occasionally comment on what they are doing, as at the opening of Luke's Gospel, prospective self-canonization of the explicit kind found throughout the Qur'an is a quite different phenomenon.[16]

Mentioning the opening of Luke's Gospel suggests an illuminating comparative study of the opening of Qur'anic Suras and of the books of the New Testament. Focusing here chiefly on the canonical Gospels, we find at the beginning of Matthew and John clear indications that the story that they will tell relates back to the book of Genesis and the start of the whole scriptural canon. Matthew

---

16. For some examples of self-referentiality in the New Testament, and comparisons with the Qur'an, see Wild, "Why Self-Referentiality?," 17–19. For a conservative Evangelical discussion of this theme, see Wayne A. Grudem, "Scripture's Self-Attestation and the Problem of Formulating a Doctrine of Scripture," in *Scripture and Truth*, eds. D.A. Carson and John D. Woodbridge (Grand Rapids, MI: Baker Book House, 1992), 19–59. Grudem bases his account of the Bible as the Word of God for Christians today on what the Old Testament says about "God's word(s)" and what the New Testament authors say about "the Old Testament text and … the emerging New Testament writings" (19). It is striking that although Grudem puts great emphasis on the elements of self-attestation in the Bible, he also notes that we cannot be entirely clear about what is being referred to at such moments. In a significant passage he acknowledges this complexity: "But were the New Testament writings thought [by their authors] to be God's words in the same sense as the Old Testament writings? Using only the data of the New Testament itself, we are in a situation analogous to that which arose within the Old Testament: It is possible to show that *some* of the New Testament writings are thought to be God's words, but one cannot prove conclusively that all of the New Testament writings were so regarded, at least not by using the data of the New Testament alone" (45, cf. 36). For the purposes of this essay, it is important to note that even with as conservative a Christian approach to the Bible as Grudem represents, there has to be an admission of the limited and somewhat unclear nature of Biblical self-attestation. On any honest account, this is a very different phenomenon from the self-referentiality of the Qur'an.

begins by tracing the genealogy of Jesus back to Abraham, while John 1:1, "In the beginning was the Word," clearly evokes the creation narrative starting at Genesis 1:1. Mark's opening makes explicit reference to Isaiah as well as also citing Malachi and possibly alluding to Exodus. However, although such intra-scriptural reference is clearly present, and might suggest (particularly in Matthew and John) an incipient impulse towards canonical status, there is nothing in the opening of the Gospels to suggest that these documents present themselves as the place of revelation where we encounter God. Rather, they all introduce themselves as accounts of the story of Jesus Christ, who, in himself, is the place of revelation where we encounter God. Unlike the Qur'an, the Gospels are not about themselves; they point not to themselves but to the presence and action of God in Jesus Christ. The declaration in John's prologue that in Jesus "the Word became flesh" (1:14) is perhaps the most decisive indication that, for the New Testament witnesses, scripture—however important—is not the ultimate form of God's self-revelation. While affirming earlier prophetic testimony, the opening of the Letter to the Hebrews is similar to John's prologue in its insistence that the fullness of divine self-revelation is given in the coming of God's Son: "Long ago God spoke to our ancestors in many and various ways by the prophets, but in these last days he has spoken to us by a Son" (1:1–2).

Two more comments should be made on this complex Bible-Qur'an comparison. First, a fuller discussion would need to explore the fact that, within the range of literature in the Bible, and the range of types of authorial and editorial presence and claim, there are moments that could be seen as in some ways analogous to Qur'anic self-canonization. Examples include the opening of Deuteronomy: "These are the words that Moses spoke…just as the Lord commanded him" (1:1–3); the frequent prophetic claim, "The Lord says…"; and the warning at the end of Revelation (22:18–19) against adding to or taking away from "the words of the prophecy of this book."

Second, and balancing that first point, nothing has made its way into the biblical canon that has quite the character of the direct claim confronting us constantly in the Qur'an, telling us that *this*, the words you are hearing or reading *now*, is the locus of divine revelation. The mingling of references to divine and human agency underlying the scriptures is a frequent feature of the Bible that is quite alien to the Qur'an. Note, for example, how the Book of Jeremiah juxtaposes opening references to "the words of Jeremiah" (1:1) and the coming to him of "the word of the Lord" (1:4). The Biblical account of God writing the commandments with his finger on the tablets of the covenant (Exod 31:18; 32:10; 34:1; Deut 5:22) might seem to contradict this argument. This is possibly the nearest analogy in the Bible to a Qur'anic model of revelation. Even here, however, it is the stone tablets themselves, not the words of scripture, that were the numinous locus of divine presence and power, to be preserved in the ark of the covenant. The words of scripture are themselves at one remove from the original moment of divine revelation. The underlying point is that although the emerging body of scripture is, with the passage of time, and especially in the New Testament period, an increasingly significant theme, nevertheless these scriptures are not fundamentally preoccupied with themselves, but with what they are saying about God and the world. In the diffuse sense mentioned above, the Bible certainly contains scriptural self-referentiality, but the simple claim that the Bible points to itself needs a great deal of qualification if it is to say anything at all illuminating about its complex subject matter. In contrast, although of course the Qur'an is also concerned with what it is saying about God, it is, for that very reason, because of its understanding of revelation, its self-understanding as God's *ipsissima verba*, directly self-referential and emphatically concerned with its own authority and the need for human beings to acknowledge this. The Qur'an therefore, understandably, points to itself continually.

Let us now extend this discussion to explore how the contrasts noted so far between the Qur'an and the Bible in relation to self-referentiality (or lack thereof) are part of wider contrasting patterns in how Muslims and Christians understand what their scriptures are, and how, in a variety of ways, Muslims and Christians relate to their scriptures. It should also be noted that it is assumed here that there is a logical priority and centrality to the self-referentiality of the Qur'an that allows us appropriately to see it as that which underlies and generates the other phenomena that we will now explore. It is because the Qur'an is the kind of scripture that we have seen it to be, repeatedly affirming itself as the ultimate expression of God's communication with humankind, that Muslims think about it and relate to it in the ways that will now be mentioned.

First, in repeatedly challenging unbelievers to produce anything comparable to it (Q 2:23–24; 10:38; 11:13; 17:88), another example of Qur'anic self-referentiality not found in the Bible, the Qur'an lays the basis for the doctrine of its inimitability (*i'jāz*) which came to be developed in the Muslim tradition. This doctrine holds that the inability of human beings to imitate the Qur'an is evidence that it can only be accounted for as arising from divine revelation. Navid Kermani explores some of the ways in which Muslims have understood *i'jāz*, offering a fascinating account of traditions illustrating Muslim convictions about the beauty and power of the divine language of the Qur'an.[17] Kermani, incidentally, emphasizes that he regards as "trivial" the question of the factuality of the stories he tells; his concern is with "cultural memory," with what these often extraordinary stories tell us about what the Qur'an has come to mean for Muslims, regardless of whether or not they are taken literally.[18] For example, many significant figures in the earliest Muslim community are said to have been converted simply by the sound of the Qur'an. Note that in such narratives it is not (at least initially) the message of the Qur'an, but merely its sound, its inimitable Arabic language, that converts. A well-known story of this kind concerns the conversion of 'Umar, who later became caliph.[19] Even more striking is the genre of stories about "*qatlā al-qur'ān*,"

---

17. Navid Kermani, *God Is Beautiful: The Aesthetic Experience of the Quran* (Cambridge: Polity Press, 2015).
18. Ibid., 3.
19. Ibid., 16–18.

those who were slain by hearing the Qur'an. On this subject the theologian al-Tha'labi wrote a whole book, documenting cases of slaying by the Qur'an as signs of God's mercy. To be killed by the Qur'an is, in this understanding, a supreme blessing, equivalent to martyrdom, and so to become a model of mystical Islamic piety.[20]

Kermani makes several perceptive comparisons between Islamic and Christian beliefs about scripture and he rightly observes that in Christianity there is virtually no tradition, as in Islam, of finding sacred power in the beauty of scriptural language. The Christian tradition may include narratives of conversion or spiritual awakening through the impact of scripture (Augustine of Hippo, Martin Luther, and John Wesley come to mind), but the emphasis here is always on the message of scripture, that to which it refers, not any claim about the beauty of its language. The idea of being slain by scripture is simply unparalleled in Christianity. If anything, Christians have problematized the idea that the language of scripture is in itself beautiful. Kermani notes the concept of *sermo humilis*, which holds that "just as Jesus Christ humbled himself in becoming human, the language of the Bible is likewise intentionally without splendour in order not to distract attention from its content."[21]

Earlier, we noted briefly that an aspect of the self-referentiality of the Qur'an is its emphasis that it is an Arabic scripture (e.g., 12:2). This relates to the question of translating the Qur'an, because an aspect of the Islamic account of the miraculous inimitability of the Qur'an is that this applies only to the Arabic original and not to any translation. Especially in recent times, translation of the Qur'an has come to be accepted, and even commended, as a way of promoting better understanding of its message, but translations are never understood to be the Qur'an itself. Translations are not the revelation at the heart of Islam, and cannot replace the Arabic original, particularly in liturgical practice but also in serious study of the faith. For

---

20. Ibid., 303–11.
21. Ibid., 188.

Christians, in contrast, the translatability of scripture was axiomatic from the beginning, as evidenced in the translation of the words of Jesus before they even found their way into scripture, and also in the earlier precedent of the translation of the Hebrew scriptures into Greek in the Septuagint, which was itself regarded as scripture, even though a translation. There is no evidence that early Christians were concerned that their human activity of translation introduced distance between themselves and the revealed datum at the heart of their faith. In the Old and New Testaments there is only passing reference to the Hebrew or Greek in which they were written, and no theological significance is ascribed to these languages.[22]

It is particularly illuminating to compare what account Islamic and Christian traditions reveal about the attitudes of the earliest believing communities to the preservation and transmission of the words spoken, respectively, by Muhammad and Jesus. For the Islamic tradition, it is of fundamental importance that the precise Arabic words received as divine revelation by Muhammad and recited by him were accurately memorized, transmitted, and in due course written down and collected as the Qur'an by his followers.[23] Among the first Christians the situation seems to have been quite different. There is no evidence that they ever thought about Jesus as early Muslims did about Muhammad. The locus of divine revelation

---

22. Stefan Wild, "An Arabic Recitation: The Meta-Linguistics of Qur'ānic Revelation," in *Self-Referentiality*, ed. Wild, 135–57. Wild notes (at 136) that the Biblical text "in no way connects its divine origin with the Hebrew language and it is only in post-Biblical times that Jewish scholars started calling Hebrew *leshon ha-qodesh* ('the holy language')."

23. Muslims distinguish between the words that came to Muhammad as divine revelation, which have been collected as the Qur'an, and other words spoken by him. Although Muhammad's utterances outside the Qur'an have been the object of enormous attention by Muslims, and, in the form of hadith literature (collections of traditions concerning sayings and deeds of Muhammad), have shaped much in Islamic belief and practice, human error and even fabrication in the transmission of some of them are freely acknowledged. This recognition is not seen as undermining the securely preserved revealed foundations of Islam in the Qur'an.

was never understood to be the *ipsissima verba* of Jesus, the precise words and indeed syllables uttered by him in a particular language. A striking illustration of this, the few exceptions that prove the rule, are the isolated fragments of Aramaic preserved in the Gospel accounts of sayings of Jesus. Perhaps these were preserved because of the particularly dramatic or poignant episodes which they recall, such as Jesus's raising to life of Jairus's daughter with the words "*Talitha cum*" ("Little girl, get up," Mar 5:41) and his healing of a deaf and dumb man with the one word "*Ephphatha*" ("be opened," Mar 7:34). Also of note is the defining significance of Jesus addressing God as "*Abba*" ("Father," Mar 14:36), which was to prove so important for Christian theology and prayer (e.g., Rom 8:15; Gal 4:6). The fact that these Aramaic fragments are the rare exception, not the norm, indicates clearly that at least the compilers of the Gospels, presumably following the lead of the first disciples of Jesus, did not believe that they were tasked with preserving the very words he had spoken in their original form. This is not to say that the words that Jesus spoke were a matter of indifference. The Gospels record such sayings as, "My words will not pass away" (Mat 24:35), and "The words that I have spoken to you are spirit and life" (Joh 6:63). The words of Jesus mattered greatly, and were preserved and pondered, but the impetus to translate them into other languages was irresistible, and it appears that the process of translation was not felt to occasion any loss. The essence of what God was giving the world in Jesus was not words in a particular language, but the Word made flesh.

There are many other comparisons that could be made here between how Muslims and Christians, respectively, understand and relate to the Qur'an and the Bible. Space permits only a brief reference to the examples mentioned below. The cumulative picture created by these diverse examples offers a broad illustration of how the self-understanding and self-presentation of the Qur'an as the primary revelatory datum offered by God to humankind naturally leads to Muslim bearings towards it that differ significantly from Christian bearings towards the Bible:

- Whereas for Islam's foundational narrative it has been important to emphasize the perfect preservation and sharp demarcation of a scriptural canon with no disputed gray areas or evidence of scribal tampering, the mainstream of the Christian tradition has not seen the credibility of its faith as depending on similar claims about the textual history of the Bible. There is an important contrast here between two accounts of human agency within divine revelation: for Islam, human agency is essentially limited to faithful transmission and accurate collection of divine words, whereas for Christianity, human agents are more fully engaged in the authorship, transmission, and canonization of the scriptures.
- A major process of theological debate within early Islam led to the affirmation of the Qur'an as eternal and uncreated, which became the orthodox Sunni position. After processes of theological debate in early Christianity, the Creeds affirmed the Son of God, not the Bible, as eternal and uncreated.W
- The memorization of the whole Qur'an is a widespread practice among Muslims, a common achievement among children of pre-teen years, and almost a requirement of a serious Muslim scholar. Memorization of sections of the Bible is valued in some Christian traditions, but never on a scale approaching anywhere near the Qur'an memorization practiced by Muslims.
- The revelation of the Qur'an is celebrated during Ramadan as a key point in the Islamic liturgical year, while the major Christian festivals, notably Christmas and Easter, are focused on Christ, not the Bible.
- The contrasting approaches of Islam and Christianity to the translation of scripture generate different experiences for Muslims and Christians of the relationship of their vernacular languages not only to scripture but also to prayer. Although prayer in their vernacular languages is possible for Muslims, for example in the form of optional additional prayers (*du'ā'*), the prayers that Muslims are required

to perform five times daily (*salāt*), which are the defining form of Islamic prayer, are based extensively on the Qur'an and must be recited in Arabic, whether or not this is understood. While it is of course easy to point to the requirement, in the wide sweep of Christian history, to pray in a non-vernacular language such as Latin, the theological basis for such a requirement is much less secure in Christianity than in Islam. Particularly in recent decades, it has become the established practice of the great majority of the world's Christians to pray in their mother tongue.

- The Qur'an is central in Islamic art, notably in calligraphy and Qur'an recitation, while the place of the Bible in Christian art is distinctly secondary to that of Christ.
- Muslims observe practices that show respect for the Qur'an as a physical presence, including regulations governing where the Qur'an is placed and the bodily purity required before handling it. While there are some analogies to these practices in certain Christian traditions, particularly in liturgical contexts, there are many Christian traditions in which no such practice is taught at all.[24]

The cumulative effect of the points covered in this essay has, I hope, made it clear that Christians and Muslims who are committed to dialogue with each other will need to take very seriously not only the differences in the contents of their scriptures but also the profoundly different ways in which they think about what they mean by the very term "scripture." Taking the self-referentiality

---

24. On many of the points listed here, there is considerable convergence between Orthodox Jewish and Muslim beliefs and practices, for example in relation to the eternity and uncreatedness of scripture, the liturgical celebration of God's giving of scripture, and how copies of the scriptures are to be treated physically. That Christianity is the "odd one out" in such matters must ultimately be explained by the way its Christological focus necessitates a comparatively modest theological and devotional place for the Bible. Scripture, in other words, is de-centered by the Incarnation.

of the Qur'an as a starting point helps to show how very different the Qur'an and the Bible are in their foundational sense of self (or indeed lack thereof, for the most part, in the Bible). The fact that in the Bible there is very little that parallels at all closely the self-referential character of the Qur'an is an insight that takes us into core aspects of Islam and Christianity that are worked out in a further range of contrasting beliefs and practices, some of which have been explored here. It is now also worth noting briefly how what has been discussed here underlies the fundamental orientations of Muslims and Christians to each other's scriptures: Muslim approaches to the Bible and Christian approaches to the Qur'an.

Muslim approaches to the Bible are diverse.[25] More negative approaches hold that contradictions between the Bible and the Qur'an arise from the alteration by Jews and Christians of the actual text of the scriptures revealed by God before the Qur'an to Moses and Jesus. More positive approaches are willing to accept the text of the Bible largely as it is, but believe that Jews and Christians have misinterpreted the meaning of their scriptures and so fail to recognize their fulfillment in the final and perfect scripture, the Qur'an. While this diversity must be noted, it is also important to grasp how, across the spectrum of Muslim approaches, there is a fundamental sense of something having gone wrong, either in the text of the Bible itself, or at least in how Christians read it. The Qur'an is the perfect scripture and as such is the criterion in the light of which all other scriptures are to be assessed (Q 5:48). The Bible that Christians read today is a very different phenomenon from the Qur'an, and quite apart from the ways in which it differs from the Qur'an (notably about Jesus), it is also significant that Christians think about the Bible, relate to it, and even handle it, in

---

25. For the roots of this diversity in the complex material on Christianity in the Qur'an, see David Marshall, "Christianity in the Qur'an," in *Islamic Interpretations of Christianity*, ed. Lloyd Ridgeon (Richmond, UK: Curzon, 2001), 3–29, and "Heavenly Religion or Unbelief? Muslim Perspectives on Christianity," *Anvil* 23:2 (2006): 89–100.

ways quite unlike how Muslims approach the Qur'an. Christians may be known by Muslims as "People of the Scripture" (*ahl al-kitāb*), but in many ways the Bible in its present form does not look like an authentic scripture, nor do Christians seem to approach it as one might expect of possessors of a true scripture.

So even though the pre-Qur'anic revealed scriptures do indeed feature significantly in Islam's account of its place in sacred history (e.g., Q 2:285), so that Muslims, especially when emphasizing their commonalities with Christians, insist that they recognize all past scriptures, this theoretical affirmation tends not to be accompanied by actual positive engagement with the Bible by Muslims. While it is true that to varying degrees Muslim exegetes have drawn on biblical material to provide a fuller understanding of Qur'anic narratives, it is, on the other hand, especially significant that the Bible does not have the function in Islamic liturgy played by the Old Testament in Christian liturgy.

Turning to Christian responses to the Qur'an, the points made in this essay indicate the difficulty involved in affirming a "message" that the Qur'an is "about" (such as a non-specific sense of reverence for God or of moral responsibility) and considering this separately from the Qur'an's claims about itself. This is probably more difficult for Christians in relation to the Qur'an than any other scripture, precisely because of the Qur'an's insistent foregrounding of itself and its own divine authority. This makes it hard for Christians to affirm selected congenial Qur'anic themes while ignoring what is arguably the Qur'an's core concern, namely to be accepted as the ultimate revelation from God. Relatedly, both because of the explicit rejection by the Qur'an of belief in the Incarnation, and also because of the Qur'an's implicit correction of this error with its own account of itself as that which God has sent down for the guidance (if not the redemption) of humankind, it is difficult for Christians to give a positive theological response to the proposal that God has retreated from incarnational engagement with the world to a modus operandi focused principally on scriptural revelation. This explains why, when Christians seek to give a positive account of Islam, they often tend to avoid mentioning the Qur'an and instead focus on areas of some commonality such as social ethics and devotional practice, as, for example, in the comments on Muslims in the Vatican II document *Nostra Aetate*.[26]

It has perhaps become a cliché (but, if so, a helpful cliché) to point out in Christian-Muslim dialogue that the position of theological centrality held by the Qur'an in Islam is held in Christianity not by the Bible but by Christ. Pursuing that point further, we might suggest that the only real analogy in Christianity to the self-referentiality of the Qur'an is the self-referentiality of Jesus, notably in the "I am" sayings in John's Gospel, though also in the other Gospels and in Revelation.[27] But taking the Qur'an-Christ parallelism as noted, I will conclude with a different, though closely related, observation, concerning the relationship between scripture and community.

In both the Qur'an itself and also the traditional narrative that Islam tells of its own origins, scripture precedes and creates community. Through Muhammad, God reveals scripture, and the community of believers comes into being around it. In contrast, for the Christian faith, God is revealed in Jesus Christ, and in and around Jesus God establishes a new community. Jesus is not the bearer of a scripture, and it is only many years later that the Christian community generates new scriptures.[28] Yes, these Jewish believers in Jesus already had their Hebrew scriptures, but in those scriptures the same principle applies. Abraham is called to be the

---

26. See David Marshall, "Roman Catholic Approaches to the Qur'an since Vatican II," *Islam and Christian-Muslim Relations* 25:1 (2014): 89–100.

27. E.g., "I am the light of the world" (Joh 8:12, and the following discussion of Jesus' testifying about himself); see also Mat 12:6, 41, 42 and Rev 1:17–18.

28. "It is surely a fact of inexhaustible significance that what our Lord left behind him was not a book, nor a creed, nor a system of thought, nor a rule of life, but a visible community." Lesslie Newbigin, *The Household of God: Lectures on the Nature of the Church* (London: SCM, 1953), 27; see also 61, where the contrast with Islam is made explicit.

beginning of a new community long before any scriptures emerge. The people of Israel predate the Hebrew scriptures.[29]

The relationship between scripture and community and their respective authority is a complex matter; there is a spectrum of forms of that relationship within both Christianity and Islam. Noting that complexity, I nevertheless venture a concluding observation, as at least one key factor to bear in mind as we seek to understand the phenomena explored in this essay: In Islam scripture comes first, and community emerges around it; in Christianity community comes first, and scripture emerges within it.

Bibliography

Boisliveau, Anne-Sylvie. *Le Coran par lui-même*. Leiden: Brill, 2014.

Graham, William A. "Scripture and the Qurʾān." In *Encyclopaedia of the Qurʾān*, Vol. 4. Leiden: Brill, 2004.

Hays, Richard B. *Echoes of Scripture in the Gospels*. Waco: Baylor University Press, 2016.

———, *Echoes of Scripture in the Letters of Paul*. New Haven: Yale University Press, 1989.

Kermani, Navid. *God Is Beautiful: The Aesthetic Experience of the Quran*. Cambridge: Polity Press, 2015.

Madigan, Daniel A. *The Qurʾān's Self-image: Writing and Authority in Islam's Scripture*. Princeton: Princeton University Press, 2001.

Wild, Stefan. "Self-Referentiality." In *The Qurʾan: An Encyclopedia*, edited by Oliver Leaman. London: Routledge, 2006.

———. ed. *Self-Referentiality in the Qurʾān*. Wiesbaden: Harrasowitz Verlag, 2006.

---

29. François Jourdan refers to the Bible as the "human-divine fruit of the Covenant": "À la différence du Coran, descendu du ciel du Livre-Mère, la Bible n'est pas descendue du ciel: elle est le fruit humano-divin de l'Alliance." *Dieu des chrétiens, Dieu des musulmans: des repères pour comprendre* (Paris: L'Oeuvre, 2008), 118.

Chapter Five

THE BEST OF SCHEMERS: DIVINE PLOTTING IN THE BIBLE AND THE QUR'AN

Gabriel Said Reynolds

In November 2018 the Italian conference of bishops approved a change of the Our Father prayer for liturgical purposes. "Non ci indurre in tentazione" (roughly equivalent to the English: "Do not lead us into temptation") became "non abbandonarci alla tentazione" ("Do not abandon us to temptation"). This change in translation followed a similar, earlier change (2017) in France, whereby "Ne nous soumets pas à la tentation" became "Ne nous laisse pas entrer en tentation."

The change in the Italian "Our Father" was prompted in part by a December 2017 Italian television broadcast of a conversation between Pope Francis and an Italian prison chaplain in which they discussed the "Our Father" prayer line by line. Regarding the line "non ci indurre in tentazione" the holy father commented: "I'm the one who falls. But it's not [God] who pushes me into temptation to see how I fall. No, a father does not do this. A father helps us up immediately." The pope continued: "The one who leads us into temptation is Satan, that's Satan's job."[1] In response, some English-language news outlets promptly posted stories about the Pope seeking to "change" the Our

---

1. https://www.americamagazine.org/faith/2017/12/08/pope-francis-suggests-translation-change-our-father. For Italian coverage of the interview see https://www.lastampa.it/2017/12/05/vaticaninsider/ita/news/il-papa-a-tv-per-il-

Father (which had already gone through many changes in English, and other languages, through the centuries).

In fact, the Pope's theological instincts are not out of line with the New Testament. The Greek words of Christ in Matthew 6:13 are *kai mē eisenegkēs hēmas eis peirasmon*. The key words therein are *eisenegkēs*, meaning "to carry" or "lead" "into," and *peirasmon*, meaning a "trial" or a "temptation." Together they could suggest God's actively leading one into temptation. However, they could also suggest God's simply permitting situations in which temptation (from Satan, oneself, or others) might take place (through His passive, but not active, will). This, it seems, is precisely the holy father's point (note that in the Pope's native Spanish the standard translation already excused God from tempting: "no nos dejes caer en tentación"). This reading would match the sentiment we find in the letter of James: "Never, when you are being put to the test, say, 'God is tempting me'; God cannot be tempted by evil, and he does not put anybody to the test. Everyone is put to the test by being attracted and seduced by that person's own wrong desire" (Jas 1:13–14).[2] God, according to James, does not "put anybody to the test" or cause them to fall. Yet other Biblical texts suggest that God can scheme against those who have already fallen and actively oppose God. In other words, the God of the Bible may not be a tempter, but He can be a plotter. In this paper I would like to highlight a few Biblical passages involving divine trickery, and then explore how this notion is picked up and expanded, first by certain Church

---

padre-nostro-non-dio-a-indurci-in-tentazione-ma-satana-GjZiYodbCdH-3GqqAYYDTGO/pagina.html.

2. This and subsequent Biblical quotations are taken from the New Jerusalem Bible (NJB). More support for the Pope's reading is found with 1 Corinthians 10:13: "None of the trials which have come upon you is more than a human being can stand. You can trust that God will not let you be put to the test beyond your strength, but with any trial will also provide a way out by enabling you to put up with it." For the references to these two passages I am indebted to the insights of Fr. Thomas Stegman, quoted in the *America* article above (see n. 1).

Fathers, and eventually by the Qur'an. As we will see, the Qur'an not only emphasizes God's ability to scheme against, and trick, His opponents, but it also gives vivid examples thereof.

Divine Trickery in the Bible

Biblical allusions to divine trickery generally involve God's ability to undo, or to reverse, the schemes of wicked people. In 1 Corinthians 3:19, Paul, reflecting on the foolishness of those who, counting themselves wise, failed to recognize the Christ, declares: "For the wisdom of this world is folly with God. For it is written, 'He catches the wise in their craftiness (panourgia).'" Here Paul means to highlight the larger divine plan of salvation with its culmination in a messiah who died on the cross as a sacrificial offering (and to discourage followers of Christ from boasting in their own wisdom). One could even suggest (more on this below) that the Christian kerygma itself turns on a sort of divine trickery: the world was waiting for a messiah who would rule, not one who would suffer and die. Yet God chose to save humanity in this way so that those who trust in their own "wise" expectations might be confounded, and those who trust in God might be saved.

Intriguingly, in this verse Paul quotes Job 5:13, thereby implying that there is nothing new in God's confounding those who consider themselves wise. In Job the line at hand is part of an address by Job's friend Eliphaz on divine justice. According to the Hebrew text the verse reads: "He traps the crafty in the snare of their own trickery [Hb. *'ōrem*], throws the plans of the cunning into disarray."

The notion of God's "trapping" those who count themselves wise in the Hebrew Bible / Old Testament is vividly portrayed in the story of Moses's confrontation with Pharaoh. God uses Pharaoh's stubborn heart against him, and indeed repeatedly hardens Pharaoh's heart. All of this leads inexorably to the final plague, and to the destruction of the Egyptian army at the Sea of Reeds. In Exodus 14:4 (cf. Exod 14:17–18), just before the Egyptian army sets out in pursuit of the Israelites, God explains to Moses why He is hardening the heart of Pharaoh one last time: "And I will harden Pharaoh's heart, and he will pursue them and I will get glory over Pharaoh and all his host; and the Egyptians shall know that I am the LORD" (Exod 14:4). Thus, the miracle at the sea appears to be the culmination of a divine plot—a plot meant for the glorification of Israel's God.

A still more vivid example of God's plotting in the Hebrew Bible / Old Testament involves the unfaithful king Ahab of the northern kingdom. In 1 Kings (another version of the story is found in 2 Chronicles 18) God places a "lying spirit" into the mouth of the prophets in order to trick King Ahab into going into a battle, which will be his doom. The passage begins with the prophet Micaiah's vision of God's presiding in His heavenly court and asking who will execute a scheme against Ahab. It ends with one of the angels (a "spirit") volunteering to fulfill the command by deceiving the prophets:

> And Micaiah said, "Therefore hear the word of the LORD: I saw the LORD sitting on his throne, and all the host of heaven standing beside him on his right hand and on his left; and the LORD said, 'Who will entice Ahab, that he may go up and fall at Ramothgilead?'
>
> "And one said one thing, and another said another. Then a spirit came forward and stood before the LORD, saying, 'I will entice him.'
>
> "And the LORD said to him, 'By what means?'
>
> "And he said, 'I will go forth, and will be a lying spirit in the mouth of all his prophets.'
>
> "And he said, 'You are to entice him, and you shall succeed; go forth and do so.'" (1 Ki 22:20–23; cf. 2 Ch 18:18–21)

One possible parallel in the New Testament to this unfolding of divine scheming is the very scenario of the crucifixion. Here, however, the nemesis of God is not Pharaoh or Ahab, nor any human,

The Best of Schemers

but rather the devil himself. There are some suggestions in the New Testament that the devil played an active role in the killing of Jesus. The Gospels of John and Luke speaks of Satan's "entering into" Judas (Joh 13:27; cf. Joh 13:2; Luk 22:3) before Judas goes out and betrays Jesus.

Yet Satan does not have the last word. Unlike Adam and Eve, who thought of their own glorification (and deification), Jesus is faithful and follows the Father's will to drink the cup prepared for him. Through this act of obedience—that is, by making himself a sacrificial victim—Jesus outwitted and defeated Satan: "Since therefore the children share in flesh and blood, he himself likewise partook of the same nature, that through death he might destroy him who has the power of death, that is, the devil, and deliver all those who through fear of death were subject to lifelong bondage" (Heb 2:14–15).

Divine Trickery and the Church Fathers

This manner of looking at the crucifixion, namely as a sort of scheme that fools the devil, is suggested by the Church Father Origen (d. 254). Origen seems to arrive at this conclusion on the basis of Jesus's description of himself as a "ransom" ("The Son of man came not to be served but to serve, and to give his life as a ransom for many." Mat 20:28; Mar 10:45). Origen reflects: "To whom did he give his life a ransom for many? Assuredly not to God, could it then be to the Evil One? For [the Evil One] was holding fast until the ransom should be given to him, even the life of Jesus; being deceived with the idea that he could have dominion over it."[3] Thus (in this articulation, at least), deception has a place in Origen's understanding of the crucifixion. The devil thought that he would

---

3. Origen, *On Matthew*, 16:8.

receive the life of Jesus in exchange for the lives of his followers. Little did he know that Jesus would not remain dead!

The notion of divine trickery also appears in the thought of John Chrysostom (d. 409). Before he became Archbishop of Constantinople, around the year 388, John preached a series of sermons in Antioch on Lazarus and the rich man (or "Dives," Luke 16). In one of these sermons, John turns to the Old Testament story of Joseph. He explains how God uses the evil plot of Joseph's brothers (who first throw him in a well and then sell him as a slave to traders headed for Egypt) for the good of Joseph (and of the brothers):

> So because they tried to kill him, for this very reason they knew his dreams. What then? Did they become agents of all the good things which were coming to him and of that eminence of his? Not at all. For their part they plotted to hand him over to death, distress, slavery, and the worst of evil fates; but God who is skillful in devising good used the wickedness of the plotters for the credit of him whom they had plotted to sell.[4]

John thus makes God "skillful in devising," language which, as we will see, is close to that of the Qur'an.

For his part, John's contemporary, Gregory of Nyssa (d. 395), develops the notion of the incarnation as a scheme that defeats the devil. In his *Address on Religious Instruction*, or *Great Catechism*, Gregory argues that the devil thought Christ to be a mere human. Thinking that he could lock up Christ in the prison of death, he was willing to offer the souls of the rest of humanity for the soul of this one, perfect human. Little did he know that Christ was divine, and that the prison of death could not constrain him. Thus, God used Satan's own way, the way of deceit, against him:

---

[4]. St. John Chrysostom, *On Wealth and Poverty*, trans. Catharine P. Roth (Crestwood, NY: St. Vladimir's Seminary Press, 1981), 92. I am grateful to Prof. Brandon Peterson for this reference.

He who first deceived man by the bait of pleasure is himself deceived by the camouflage of human nature. But the purpose of the action changes it into something good. For the one practiced deceit to ruin our nature; but the other, being at one just and good and wise, made use of a deceitful device to save the one who had been ruined. And by so doing, he had benefited, not only the one who had perished, but also the one who had brought us to ruin. For when death came into contact with life, darkness with light, corruption with incorruption, the worse of these things disappeared into a state of nonexistence, to the profit of him who was freed from these evils.[5]

As Rowan Greer puts it in his study on Gregory, the devil "took the human bait" and "was caught by the fishhook of Christ's divinity."[6] It is, of course, worth noting that Gregory (like John Chrysostom before him) insists that God uses deceit for a good purpose.

Divine Trickery in the Qur'an

The Church Fathers were not alone in advancing an understanding of the crucifixion that involved divine trickery. Centuries later, Muslim scholars would describe a trick that unfolded with the crucifixion, yet in this case the victim of the trick is not the devil. Many Muslim exegetes tell a narrative about the crucifixion according to which someone else was made to look like Jesus (various versions of this narrative disagree over who this was). This "substitute" was

---

5. Gregory of Nyssa, *Oratio Catechetica* 26 (Library of Christian Classics 3:303; *Gregorii Nysseni Opera* 3.4:57–60); cf. Morwenna Ludlow, *Gregory of Nyssa, Ancient and (Post)modern* (Oxford: Oxford University Press, 2007), 108–19.
6. R. Greer and W. Smith, *One Path for All: Gregory of Nyssa on the Christian Life and Human Destiny* (Eugene, OR: Cascade, 2015), 224.

seized by the Jews who were pursuing Jesus and crucified, while Jesus himself ascended to heaven, body and soul. In order to offer an example of this narrative, and for simplicity's sake, we might relate the short version found in the late Qur'an commentary known as *Tafsīr al-Jalālayn* of Jalāl al-Dīn al-Maḥallī (d. 864/1459) and Jalāl al-Dīn al-Suyūṭī (d. 911/1505):

> And they, the disbelievers among the Children of Israel, schemed, against Jesus, by assigning someone to assassinate him; and God schemed, by casting the likeness of Jesus onto the person who intended to kill him, and so they killed him, while Jesus was raised up into heaven; and God is the best of schemers.[7]

According to the report of *Tafsīr al-Jalālayn*, the very man who was sent to kill Jesus was the one transformed into his likeness and killed. In other words, God played a trick. Thereby He executed justice by taking the life of the one who sought His prophet's life.

The last phrase in the report above betrays the origin (in part, at least) of the idea that a trick unfolded on the day of the crucifixion. The description of God as "best of schemers" (Ar. *khayru l-mākirīn*) is a quotation of Qur'an 3:54. In this verse, which follows a description of the birth and the miracles of Jesus, the Qur'an declares: "Then they schemed, and God schemed, and God is the best of schemers."[8]

Although the nature of God's "scheme" (Ar. *makr*) is not clear in Sura 3, most interpreters (like al-Maḥallī and al-Suyūṭī) connect this verse with a passage in the next Sura, the only place in the entire Qur'an with a reference to the crucifixion of Jesus. In Sura 4:157, the Qur'an quotes the Israelites as follows: "And for their saying, 'We

---

7. *Tafsīr al-Jalālayn*, trans. F. Hamza (Louisville, KY: Fons Vitae, 2008), 62.
8. My translation. Other Qur'an translations are according to Qara'i as found in G.S. Reynolds, *The Qur'an and the Bible* (New Haven: Yale University Press, 2018).

killed the Messiah, Jesus son of Mary, the apostle of God'—though they did not kill him nor crucify him, but so it was made to appear to them." The declaration here that the Israelites did not kill or crucify Jesus seems to be clear. What caused interpreters headaches is the expression that comes next, rendered here as "so it was made to appear to them" (Ar. *shubbiha la-hum*). What exactly was made to appear to the Israelites on the day of the crucifixion?

The most common explanation of this ambiguous Arabic phrase is that *Jesus* was made to appear to the Israelites. *Someone else* (according to *Tafsīr al-Jalālayn*, his would-be assassin) was given the form and likeness of Jesus. It was this person who was crucified in the place of Jesus (while Jesus himself ascended into heaven, escaping death). The Israelites looked up on the cross and saw this "substitute" who *appeared to them* as though he were Jesus. They thought that they were killing the right man, but Jesus had slipped through their fingers. Some traditions relate that he was taken up to heaven through a hole in the roof of the house where he and the disciples were staying.

As with many such reports found in Qur'anic commentaries, reports on the crucifixion seem to have been generated principally through speculation on the Qur'anic text. And as the Qur'anic verse in question does not offer clear details, it is no surprise to find different sorts of scenarios meant to explain what took place on the day of the crucifixion. For example, the Qur'an commentator Abū al-Qāsim al-Zamakhsharī (d. 538/1144) offers a narrative that disagrees with that of *Tafsīr al-Jalālayn*. According to this narrative, it was not Jesus's enemy but his *friend* who died. One of Jesus's disciples offers his life in place of Jesus: "Jesus said [to his companions], 'Who would like to have my likeness cast on him, to be killed and crucified, and to enter paradise?' One of them said, 'I would.' [Jesus's] likeness was cast on him and he was killed and crucified."[9]

---

9. Al-Zamakhsharī, *Al-Kashshāf ʿan ḥaqāʾiq ghawāmiḍ al-tanzīl* (Beirut: Dār al-Kitāb al-ʿArabī, 1947), 1:587.

Certain variants of this tradition identify this "volunteer" as the apostle Peter.

In any case, all of this brings us back to Qur'an 3:54 (the verse which speaks of God as the "best schemer"). The story of Jesus' crucifixion offered to interpreters a perfect explanation of the divine "scheme" referred to in that verse. According to their logic the Israelites sought to plot against God by killing Jesus. God, however, outwitted them by taking Jesus directly into heaven, and tricked them by changing someone else into his likeness. The Spanish Muslim Abū ʿAbdallāh Muḥammad al-Qurṭubī (d. 671/1273) describes God's "scheme" in Qur'an 3:54 as "the casting of the likeness of Jesus onto another, and the raising of Jesus to Himself."[10]

In the exegetical imagination, this dramatic scenario involving a threat on the life of Christ is parallel to a threat on the life of Muhammad many centuries later. Qur'an 8:30 has God declare to Muhammad: "When the faithless plotted against (*yamkuru*) you to take *you* captive, or to kill or expel *you*—they schemed (*yamkurūna*) and God schemed (*yamkuru*), and God is the best of schemers (*khayru l-mākirīn*)." Much like commentary on Qur'an 3:54, commentary on this verse (cf. Q 12:102, which involves a plot against Joseph) typically involves a story elaborating a plot, this time against Muhammad. In the exegetical and biographical literature, God intervenes to save his Prophet—although Muhammad is not taken to heaven, but simply out of Mecca, to Medina. *Tafsīr al-Jalālayn*, for example, relates the following:

---

10. Abū ʿAbdallāh Muḥammad b. Aḥmad al-Qurṭubī, *al-Jāmiʿ li-aḥkām al-Qurʾān*, ed. ʿAbd al-Razzāq al-Mahdī (Beirut: Dār al-Kitāb al-ʿArabī, 1433/2012), 4:99. Al-Zamakhsharī, in his commentary on the version of the narrative which has Jesus' betrayer killed, emphasizes the poetic justice of the whole scenario. "God schemed," he explains, "by raising Jesus into heaven while He cast his likeness onto the one who sought to assassinate [Jesus], so that [this one] was killed." Al-Zamakhsharī, 1:366. It is this scenario that lies behind the Islamic doctrine that Jesus is still alive in heaven, waiting to descend at the end of time.

> And, remember, O Muhammad, when the disbelievers—who had gathered to discuss your affair at the council assembly—were plotting against you, to confine you, to chain you up and imprison you, or slay you—all of them [acting as] assassins of one man—or to expel you, from Mecca, and they were plotting, against you, and God was plotting, against them, by devising a way [out] for you, when He revealed to you what they had devised and commanded you to leave [Mecca]; and God is the best of those who plot, the most knowledgeable among them about it.[11]

The plots against Jesus and Muhammad are not the only places where the Qur'an develops the theme of divine trickery, and the term in Qur'an 3:54 and 8:30 for "scheming" or "tricking" (from Arabic *makr*) is not the only term used for divine deception in the Qur'an.

In Sura 4, the Qur'an relates, "The hypocrites seek to deceive (*yukhādi'ūna*) God, but it is He who deceives (*khādi'uhum*) them" (Q 4:142a; the verse goes on to explain that the hypocrites make a show of praying but are not in fact mindful of God). Here the Qur'an has God involved in the same activity as the hypocrites (cf. Q 2:9, which has the unbelievers seek, and fail, to deceive God and Q 8:62, which has them seek to deceive the Prophet Muhammad). They employ "deception" (Ar. *khidā'*), and He employs deception (*khidā'*). He is not above deception; He is simply better at deceiving. This is not far from John Chrysotom's reflection on how God responded to the plot of Joseph's brothers with his own plot.

Similar to the term *khidā'* in the Qur'an is the concept of *ighwā'* ("seduction," "temptation," "leading astray"). In Qur'an 11:34 Noah declares to his opponents that God could lead them astray (*yughwiyakum*). In a narrative that appears in seven different Suras, God

---

11. *Tafsīr al-Jalālayn*, 187; For the Arabic see Marwān Siwār, ed. (Beirut: Dār al-Jīl, 1410/1995), 180.

commands the angels to bow down before Adam. They all do so except for the devil (Ar. *iblīs*, from Greek *diabolos*), who is punished by being cast out of heaven. The devil responds by accusing God of deception (*ighwā'*), and declaring that he will accordingly deceive humans: "He said, 'My Lord! As You have deceived me (*aghwaytanī*), I will surely adorn [evil] for them on the earth, and I will surely deceive them (*ughwiyannahum*), all except Your dedicated servants among them'" (Q 15:39–40).[12] Thus, whereas God and the unbelievers or hypocrites both employ *khidāʿ*, God and the devil (if we are to believe the devil) both employ *ighwā'*. The difference is that God leads astray the devil, and the devil leads astray believers.

Closely related to those Qurʾanic passages that speak of both God and Satan "leading astray" are those that speak of how God and Satan "adorn" or "decorate" (the verb is *zayyana*) bad works to make them look good. In the passage cited above (Q 15:39) the devil explains that he will "adorn [evil] (*uzayyinanna*)" among humans. This promise plays out in Qur'an 6:43. Here, the divine voice of the Qur'an asks why the unbelievers did not turn to God, and then gives the answer: "Then why did they not entreat when Our punishment overtook them! But their hearts had hardened and Satan had made what they had been doing seem decorous (*zayyana*) to them."

God can carry out this act of "adorning" or "decorating" evil as well. In Qur'an 27:4 it is God who declares: "As for those who do not believe in the Hereafter, We have made their deeds seem decorous (*zayyannā*) to them, and so they are bewildered." In this case, Satan and God seem to have the same object. Satan confuses the "hard-hearted" unbelievers by making their evil deeds seem good. God too (in Q 27:4) confuses the unbelievers (those who deny the afterlife) by doing the same.

The notion of making one's bad deeds seem good (*tazyīn*) is connected to another description of God's trickery in the Qur'an.

---

12. Modified translation of Qara'i.

The Best of Schemers

The point of *tazyīn* is that sinners or unbelievers do not recognize the error of their ways and consequently are subject to punishment. Elsewhere the Qur'an speaks of God giving a "respite" to the unbelievers to the same effect.[13] Thinking that everything is fine, they continue in their sinful ways and are subject to punishment. This plays out in Qur'an 7:182–83 where God describes this "respite" as his "artifice" (Ar. *kayd*):

> As for those who impugn Our signs, We will draw them imperceptibly [into ruin], whence they do not know. And I will grant them respite, for My devising (*kaydī*) is indeed sure.

Two other passages are similar, Qur'an 68:44–45:

> So leave Me with those who deny this discourse. We will draw them imperceptibly [into ruin] whence they do not know. I will grant them respite, for My devising (*kaydī*) is indeed sure.

And Qur'an 86:15–17:

> They are indeed devising a stratagem (*yakīdūna kaydan*), and I [too] am devising a plan (*akīdu kaydan*). So respite the faithless; give them a gentle respite.

It is hard to escape the impression that the Qur'an's author has developed the notion of a "respite" (that ends in the destruction of the sinners and unbelievers) as a way of explaining why bad

---

13. The term that appears in the first two passages quoted below for "respite" is from the root *m-l-y*, in the fourth form (e.g. *umlī* in Q 7:183). See A.A. Ambros and S. Prochazka, *Concise Dictionary of Koranic Arabic* (Wiesbaden: Reichert, 2004), 259. The term that appears in the third passage is from the root *m-h-l*.

things are not happening to bad people. It is a way of assuring the Qur'an's audience that their opponents will indeed by punished, in God's own time. This notion is developed a bit further in Qur'an 3:178: "Let the faithless not suppose that the respite We grant them is good for their souls: We give them respite only that they may increase in sin, and there is a humiliating punishment for them." The idea of this latter verse seems to be that God *intentionally* withdraws his punishment from the unbelievers. His goal in doing so, however, is not to show mercy. He does this precisely so that the faithless with fall deeper into their faithlessness. Thereby they will sin even more, and accordingly merit divine punishment even more greatly.

Something similar is found in Qur'an 19:75 where we find a declaration that God will even afford a "respite" to wrongdoers so that they can be around when a punishment will come upon them (or the apocalyptic Hour arrives): "Whoever abides in error, the All-beneficent shall prolong his respite until they sight what they have been promised: either punishment or the Hour. Then they will know whose position is worse, and whose host is weaker." Thus, God may actually show patience towards unbelievers. However, He does this not out of mercy, but as part of a larger plan to enact vengeance against them.

This idea did not pass the classical Muslim interpreters by— they called this notion *istidrāj* and they used it to explain why good things might happen to unbelievers.[14] Literally, *istidrāj* means "to be led by degrees" or "steps." The term itself is found in a verbal form (*nastadriju*) in Qur'an 7:182 (cf. Q 68:44), rendered above as "We will draw them imperceptibly [into ruin]" (trans. Qara'i) but could be rendered more literally, as in the translation of Arberry, as "We will draw them on little by little."

---

14. See for example Qurṭubī (4:99), who defines God's *makr* as *istidrājuhu li-ʿibādihi min ḥaythu lā yaʿlamūn* [His *istidrāj* for His servants in a way that they do not comprehend].

For many classical scholars, *istidrāj* exceeds a "respite," or God's withholding of punishment. They speculated that, at times, God actually gives good things to unbelievers in order that they may not realize the error of their ways and repent.[15]

The doctrine of *istidrāj* seems to be fundamentally a "theodicy." A theodicy usually explains why bad things happen to good people—why, for example, an innocent child might be afflicted with a disease. Here it is the other way around—the notion of *istidrāj* is used to explain why good things happen to bad people. The answer is that God is setting these bad people up for their punishment.

Elsewhere the Qur'an puts God's plotting against the unbelievers in even more dramatic language. In Sura 89, after reminding its audience of the way God has destroyed earlier peoples, the Qur'an declares simply: "Your Lord is indeed in ambush (*mirṣād*)" (Q 89:14).

It should be noted, however, that not all Muslim interpreters were satisfied with the possibility of divine trickery. After a discussion of the opinions of different grammarians on the precise meaning of *makr*, and of different traditions on the crucifixion, the philosophically minded scholar Fakhr al-Dīn al-Rāzī (d. 606/1209) concludes: "*Makr* is an expression of deceiving and seeking evil, and it is impossible to speak of God's deceiving."[16] He then explains that God's *makr* is different—the Qur'an means thereby only that God punishes those who are guilty of evil. *Makr* is nothing but *jazā'*, "recompense."[17]

---

15. Al-Zamakhsharī explains *nastadrijuhum* in Q 7:182 as "We shall gradually draw them closer to that which will destroy them and double their punishment." Al-Zamakhsharī, 2:182.

16. Fakhr al-Dīn al-Rāzī, *Mafātīḥ al-ghayb*, ed. Muḥammad Bayḍūn (Beirut: Dār al-Kutub al-'Ilmiyya, 1421), 8:59; Cf. M.M. Ayoub, *The Qur'an and Its Interpreters* (Albany: State University of New York Press, 1992), 2:167. Qurṭubī defines *makr* as "trickery and deception": *al-iḥtiyāl wa-l-khidā'*. Qurṭubī, 4:99.

17. Fakhr al-Dīn al-Rāzī, 8:59. Qurṭubī attributes to the grammarian al-Zujjāj (d. 311/924) the view that God's *makr* is simply the recompense given to unbelievers for their own *makr*. See Qurṭubī, 4:99.

But others disagreed. Qurṭubī reports that some scholars numbered "best of schemers" (*khayru l-mākirīn*) among God's ninety-nine beautiful names. And he reports that the Prophet Muhammad used to pray: "O God, scheme for me, and do not scheme against me!"[18]

The "Green Man" of the Qur'an

This prayer suggests that God does not only deceive unbelievers and sinners, but could, at least in theory, deceive a believer, or even a prophet. Yet the Qur'anic examples of divine trickery generally suggest that God schemes in order to defend the faithful and defeat their opponents. As the Qur'an declares in Sura 3, God is the "ally of the believers."[19] In the two places where the Qur'an describes God as "best of schemers" (*khayru l-mākirīn*), He employs *makr* in order to defend a Prophet, either Jesus (Q 3:54) or Muhammad (Q 8:30).[20]

The point of these verses seems to be ultimately about God's sovereignty. God always defeats His opponents, although His method of doing so may vary. On occasion, as in the famous "punishment stories" of the Qur'an, He obliterates entire cities or civilizations. Muslim believers, however, should not expect that their opponents will always be destroyed. For on other occasions, God works through plots and ruses that may seem surprising until they are fully achieved.

This lesson of God's surprising tactics is taught in the Qur'an through the story of a mysterious "servant" of God to whom Is-

---

18. See Ayoub, *The Qur'an and Its Interpreters*, 2:166; Qurṭubī 4:98–99, ad 3:54; also al-Zamakhsharī, 1:366.
19. *walīy al-muʾminīn*. See Q 3:68.
20. While this phrase does not appear in Q 12:102, the Joseph story in this Sura (as in Genesis, as we have seen, with John Chrysostom) redounds to God's intervention on behalf of Joseph. When the brothers plotted against Joseph, God used their evil plot to execute a greater, good plot.

lamic tradition has given the name Khiḍr, or "green man." In Sura 18, a figure named Moses (apparently the Prophet Moses, although this identification can be problematic) and his companion meet the green man or "servant" of God: "[There] they found one of Our servants whom We had granted mercy from Ourselves and taught him knowledge from Our own" (Q 18:65).

As this introduction to the narrative suggests, the green man is distinguished by knowledge. Moses apparently senses this, as he asks to accompany the green man, and to learn from him. The green man, however, warns him in the following way: "Indeed, you cannot have patience with me! And how can you have patience about something you do not comprehend?" (Q 18:67–68).

What unfolds thereafter vindicates the prediction of the green man. As Moses follows him, the green man proceeds on a journey during which he carries out a number of apparently illogical, and immoral, acts. First he makes a hole in a boat, apparently ruining it (v. 71). Next he finds a young boy and kills him (v. 74). Finally, when they come to a town of inhospitable people, he rebuilds a wall of their city that had fallen into ruin (v. 77). Moses grows increasingly exasperated by the green man's actions, and the latter finally agrees to give an explanation for them before the two part ways. He made a hole in the boat because it belonged to poor fishermen and a king was about to seize it. He killed the boy because he was going to grow up to be troublesome and a burden on his pious parents. He fixed the wall because below it lay a treasure that belonged to two orphans, and in this way he preserved it for them.

The whole story is challenging for Muslim interpreters because it seems to present a prophet, Moses, as a disciple to the green man, who is never described as a prophet. Moreover, Moses seems to be a poor disciple. While he initially promises to be patient, he cannot bear to witness the actions of the green man, and is thoroughly rebuked by the latter for failing to keep his promise.

For our purposes, however, what is most important is how the story of the green man is a way for the Qur'an to teach a lesson about the surprising means by which God achieves his purposes.

The green man, described simply as God's servant who has been given divine knowledge, seems to exemplify the way that God works in the world. His actions appear to be illogical and immoral, but they are all part of a plan to bring forth good in the end. They are all a sort of scheme, or *makr*. The green man seems to be hurting the owners of the boat, but he is helping them. He seems to be acting immorally towards the boy he has killed, but thereby he is acting morally to his parents. He appears to be helping the inhospitable inhabitants of the town by fixing their wall, but he is really helping the two orphans. Appearances do not match reality. God, through the green man, acts in surprising, even deceptive ways. The logic of all of this is not immediately apparent—it is only revealed to Moses at the end of the journey.[21]

In other words, unbelievers and wrongdoers might pursue self-serving plots. God, however, will foil their plot with a counter-plot that cannot be foiled. In Sura 7 the Qur'an, addressing the towns that God has destroyed, asks the following question: "Do they feel secure from Allah's devising? No one feels secure from Allah's devising except the people who are losers" (Q 7:99).

The People of the Sabbath

Elsewhere in Sura 7 the Qur'an describes how a people (apparently Jews) who fail to keep the Sabbath are punished by God by being transformed into apes:

> Ask them about the town that was situated on the seaside, when they violated the Sabbath, when their fish would come to them on the Sabbath day, visibly on the

---

21. The idea that this account might be thought of under the category of divine trickery was suggested to me by Jacob Kildoo. On the possible subtexts for this account in Jewish and Christian tradition, see Reynolds, *The Qur'an and the Bible*, 465.

shore, but on days when they were not keeping Sabbath they would not come to them. Thus did We test them because of the transgressions they used to commit.... So when they forgot what they had been reminded of, We delivered those who forbade evil [conduct] and seized the wrongdoers with a terrible punishment because of the transgressions they used to commit. When they defied [the command pertaining to] what they were forbidden from, We said to them, "Be you spurned apes." (Q 7:163, 165–66)

The logic of this account is as follows: the people of a certain town by the sea (most Muslim classical scholars identify this town as Ayla, a town near the modern day Jordanian city of Aqaba on the Red Sea) were sinners. God tests them by having fish come to them when they are not allowed to fish—on the Sabbath—while having the fish disappear on the other days of the week, when they are allowed to fish. Sure enough, the people fail the test by collecting fish on the Sabbath. For this God curses them in an unusual way, by turning them into apes.

This account is close to a narrative in the Talmud about a people who were caught fishing on the Sabbath. They were declared outcasts and eventually renounced Judaism.[22] However, the Qur'an's interest in the "People of the Sabbath" story is certainly not to encourage its audience to keep the Sabbath. Nowhere does the

---

22. B. Qiddushin 72a. The notion that God would transform people into animals as a punishment may be connected to another tradition in the Talmud (b. Sanhedrin 109a), which has some of the conspirators guilty of building the tower of Babel turned into apes (among other creatures). "They split up into three parties. One said, 'Let us ascend and dwell there'; the second said, 'Let us ascend and serve idols'; and the third said, 'Let us ascend and wage war [with God].' The party which proposed, 'Let us ascend, and dwell there'—the Lord scattered them; the one that said, 'Let us ascend and wage war' were turned to *apes*, spirits, devils, and night-demons" (b. Sanhedrin 109a). Trans.: *The Soncino Talmud* (London: Soncino, 1961).

Qur'an make keeping the Sabbath a religious responsibility (see Q 16:124). In fact, the Muslim day of prayer is Friday, not Saturday, and Friday for Muslims is a day of prayer but not of rest (the notion of God's resting on the seventh day after creation, to which Sabbath observance is linked, is not found in the Qur'an). Instead, this story is meant to inspire fear of a God who is capable of stratagems. It is notable that the story of the "People of the Sabbath" has God set a trap for the evildoers: God arranges for fish to appear visibly to them, as though to tempt them, on the Sabbath. On the other days of the week, the days when it is permitted for them to work, the fish do not appear at all! The "People of the Sabbath" cannot withstand the temptation. They are trapped by God's trick much as their fish are caught in nets. They already are in the habit of committing transgressions (v. 163) and so they commit one more by collecting fish on the Sabbath. For this they are changed into animals.

Conclusion

What are we to make of all of this? The Qur'an speaks almost incessantly of the mercy of God. Every Sura but one begins with the invocation, "In the name of God the merciful, the benevolent." If the God of the Qur'an is merciful, why would He lead further astray those who are already lost, instead of guiding them home? The Qur'an simply never answers this question. But perhaps this is the wrong question to ask of a scripture. The Japanese scholar Toshihiko Izutsu declares to this effect: "The standpoint of the Koran is not that of pure logic."[23] The standpoint of the Qur'an instead, I would suggest, is paraenesis, a desire to convert its audience.

Some Muslim interpreters, however, insisted on trying to solve the theological enigmas in the Qur'an. This is the case with the

---

23. Toshiko Izutsu, *God and Man in the Koran: Semantics of the Koranic Weltanschauung* (Tokyo: Keio Institute of Cultural and Linguistic Studies, 1964), 142.

Mu'tazilite al-Zamakhsharī in his discussion of the way that the Qur'an speaks of God "sealing" hearts, as in Sura 2: "As for the faithless, it is the same to them whether *you* warn them or do not warn them, they will not have faith. Allah has set a seal on their hearts and their hearing, and there is a blindfold on their sight, and there is a great punishment for them" (Q 2:6–7). Just as the notion of God making Pharaoh's heart heavy has caused trouble among Jewish and Christian interpreters of Exodus, so the notion of God sealing hearts has caused trouble among Muslim interpreters of the Qur'an. In his effort to argue against the apparent meaning of this passage, which has God seal both "hearts" and "hearing," al-Zamakhsharī comes up with a variety of possible alternative meanings:

- Perhaps "sealing" here refers only to an innate disposition of unbelief.
- Perhaps "sealing" is used figuratively. Perhaps it is like how people say "the mountain torrent has flown away with someone" when a person has died or "the condor bird has flown away with someone" when a person is absent for a long time.
- Perhaps it is Satan or unbelievers themselves who have "sealed" their hearts.

Al-Zamakhsharī explains: "Since it is God who has granted to them the ability and the possibility (to do so), the sealing (of the heart) is ascribed to Him."[24] While not everyone was convinced by al-Zamakhsharī (in the 7th/13th century a gloss was written on his work by the Ash'arite Ibn al-Munayyir [d. 683/1284] in order to do away with such interpretations), his perspective nevertheless shows

---

24. On al-Zamakhsharī's discussion see Helmut Gätje, *The Qur'an and Its Exegesis: Selected Texts with Classical and Modern Muslim Interpretations*, trans. Alford T. Welch (London: Routledge, 1976), 222; or the original Arabic: al-Zamakhsharī, 1:49–52.

that there are strategies to interpret the Qur'an in a way that does away with divine trickery and divine vengeance.

Still other elements of Islamic tradition emphasized God's ability to "plot." The mystical exegete Sahl al-Tustarī (d. 283/896) tells a story in which the Qur'anic prophet named Luqmān (not known in the Bible) once counseled his son, "Have hope in God without feeling secure from His ruse (*makr*) and fear God without despairing of his mercy. [His son] responded [by asking], 'How can I do that when I only have one heart?' He replied: 'O my son, the believer has two hearts, one with which he carries hope in God and the other with which he fears Him.'"[25]

The disposition recommended by Luqmān falls in line nicely with the standard Ash'arite Sunni creeds, which insist that believers are neither to despair of heaven nor to be sure of it. The reason for this is simple: "Certainty (of Paradise) and despair both turn people away from the religion."[26] The Qur'an, one might say, is hoping for just this disposition with its rhetoric and examples of divine trickery. By developing this biblical motif of trickery, as did certain Church Fathers before it, the Qur'an is concerned with exhortation. The Qur'an means for its audience never to feel secure from God's scheming, and thereby to live in pious fear of their creator and judge.

---

25. Sahl al-Tustarī, *Tafsīr*, trans. A. and A. Keeler (Louisville, KY: Fons Vitae, 2011), 138, on Q 24:37.

26. "We hope for Paradise for the believers who do good, but we are not certain of it, and do not bear witness to them (as having attained it). We seek forgiveness for their evil deeds and we fear for them, but we do not despair of them. Certainty (of Paradise) and despair both turn people away from the religion, and the way of truth…lies between them." From the creed of the Ash'arite al-Ṭaḥāwī (d. 321/933). See W. Montgomery Watt, *Islamic Creeds* (Edinburgh: Edinburgh University Press, 1994), 52.

Bibliography

Al-Maḥallī, Jalāl al-Dīn, and al-Suyūṭī, Jalāl al-Dīn. *Tafsīr al-Jalālayn*, translated by Feras Hamza. Louisville, KY: Fons Vitae, 2008.

Al-Qurṭubī, Abū 'Abdallāh Muḥammad b. Aḥmad. *al-Jāmi' li-aḥkām al-Qur'ān*, edited by 'Abd al-Razzāq al-Mahdī. Beirut: Dār al-Kitāb al-'Arabī, 1433/2012.

Al-Zamakhsharī, Abū al-Qāsim Maḥmūd. *Al-Kashshāf 'an ḥaqā'iq ghawāmiḍ al-tanzīl*. Beirut: Dār al-Kitāb al-'Arabī, 1947.

Ayoub, Mahmoud. *The Qur'an and Its Interpreters*. Albany: State University of New York Press, 1992.

Chrysostom, St. John. *On Wealth and Poverty*, translated by Catharine P. Roth. Crestwood, NY: St. Vladimir's Seminary Press, 1981.

Gätje, Helmut. *The Qur'an and Its Exegesis: Selected Texts with Classical and Modern Muslim Interpretations*, translated by Alford T. Welch. London: Routledge, 1976.

Greer, Rowan, and Smith, J. Warren. *One Path for All: Gregory of Nyssa on the Christian Life and Human Destiny*. Eugene, OR: Cascade, 2015.

Izutsu, Toshiko. *God and Man in the Koran: Semantics of the Koranic Weltanschauung*. Tokyo: Keio Institute of Cultural and Linguistic Studies, 1964.

Reynolds, Gabriel Said. *The Qur'an and the Bible*. New Haven: Yale University Press, 2018.

Chapter Six

"IN THEM YE HAVE BENEFITS FOR A TERM APPOINTED" (Q 22:33): A GIRARDIAN PERSPECTIVE ON THE ORIGIN OF ISLAM

Martino Diez

René Girard passed away on November 4, 2015.[1] Nine days after, Paris was shaken by the Bataclan attacks. If the temporal closeness of the two events is certainly a coincidence,[2] the connection between Girard's life-long research on the roots of violence and the jihadist phenomenon is no accident. The French thinker has indeed laid down the foundations for a new appreciation of the "sacrificial logic" inherent to contemporary jihadism, a logic that makes this phenomenon radically different from the institution of jihad

---

1. An earlier version of this paper was prepared, in French, for the conference *Foi et violence: un enchaînement fatal?*, organized by the Faith and Culture Observatory of the French Bishops' Conference (December 2, 2017) and is now published in the collective volume, *Foi et violence: un enchaînement fatal?* (Paris: Cerf, 2018), 92–105. Qur'anic verses are taken from A.J. Arberry's translation. For the Bible, the New Revised Standard Version Catholic Edition is used.

2. This proximity is the starting point of the touching homage composed by Benoît Chantre, *Les derniers jours de René Girard* (Paris: Grasset, 2016).

in classical Islam.³ The *système Girard*⁴ is thus a unique tool both to decipher the outburst of Islamist terrorism, as he himself began to perceive in his last book *Achever Clausewitz* (2007),⁵ and at the same time to conceptualize the mimetic rivalry between jihadists and anti-Islamic groups, which is becoming increasingly conspicuous.

Yet to reduce Girard's reflection to an acute diagnosis of contemporary terrorism, of all colors and sorts, would mean to miss the best in it. In this contribution I argue that his insights can help scholars better to understand the context wherein Islam first saw the light, as well as some of its rites. At the same time, I suggest that his thought may offer several clues to Christian theologians willing to speculate about the place and function of Islam in God's salvific plan, a thorny issue which is—so to speak—the elephant in the room in every serious Christian-Muslim dialogue (at least from the Christian side). I do not claim that Girard's theory fully answers this vexed question. But I do believe that it allows us to come back to it with major gains in terms of both method and content.

Girard's System:
An Act in a Drama, Not the Whole Play

Before embarking on my attempt to demonstrate this double assertion, a premise is nevertheless required. Girard was not a theologian.

---

3. The suffix *-ism* in jihadism is exactly meant to identify this "form of martyr-based salvational Islam that [holds] to the revolutionary ideal of martyrdom = redemption" (David Cook, "The Routinization of Martyrdom Operations," *Oasis*, December 20, 2017, http://www.oasiscenter.eu/en/suicide-bombings-and-martyrdom-in-islam-4). The same is true for the couple Islam/Islamism (where the -ism conveys the concept of the modern state).
4. A stimulating retrospective of Girard's intellectual itinerary can be found in Benoît Chantre, "The Voice of Prophets," *Oasis* 19 (June 2014): 13–17.
5. (Paris: Flammarion, 2011); 1st ed: (Carnets Nord, 2007), especially the Epilogue, 353–62.

His first book, *Mensonge romantique et vérité romanesque* (1961), was about literary criticism. By analyzing several novels he came to the conclusion that "man is not able to desire on his own: he needs a third party that points him out the object of his own desire."[6] This is the core of Girard's mimetic theory, which has recently seen significant confirmation in the discovery of mirror neurons. His subsequent major book, *La violence et le sacré* (1972), applies this discovery no longer to a set of novels, but to human civilizations as a whole, presenting the sacred as the mechanism devised by human beings to avoid the explosion of mimetic desire within their societies. This gruesome mechanism works through the arbitrary designation of a scapegoat, which is lynched and then deified.

At this point, Girard had already re-converted to Christianity, rediscovering the figure of the Crucified Christ who, taking sides with the victims instead of the murderers, demystifies the archaic religions—a response to Nietzsche's criticism of Christianity as a religion of the weak. His new creed, however, was only revealed in *Des choses cachées depuis la fondation du monde* (1978). Due to this existential itinerary, Girard passed, without mediation, from the anthropological to the theological level. And here lies, in my opinion, the main difficulty with his system. For, whereas his description of the mechanisms of violence likely constitutes a major advance in human sciences, Girard does not seem to differentiate sufficiently, on the theological level, between the status of humanity after the Fall and in God's original plan. The sacred that he analyzes is the sacred of religions, devised in order to overcome the abyss that is by now separating man from God. The mechanism of desire that he unmasks is, in fact, the very structure of sin: "But at the beginning it was not so" (Matt 19:8). Not at the end, either.

Even in our present state, the "yes" of God foreruns—*primerea* as Pope Francis likes to say—the "no" of the world. This explains why, when an act of charity forces us out of the circle of mimetic

---

6. René Girard, *Mensonge romantique et vérité romanesque* (Paris: Grasset, 1961), Preface.

desire, we experience a paradoxical feeling: on the one hand, the irruption of something completely new—the Grace of the utterly Other—but on the other hand, an unbelievable conformity with the most intimate fabric of our desires—our religious sense (this is why, after all, we perceive tragedies to be tragic!). In other words, Girard ponders over the central act of a drama, whose prologue and epilogue are played on another stage, as Hans Urs von Balthasar so compellingly expressed in his *Theodramatik*.[7]

Girard's readers are usually shocked by his apocalypticism, which is bound to his belief that he had unveiled, like a new Hegel, the secret dynamic underlying history. In a way, this is an accurate remark, since the French thinker seems to have trouble figuring out a positive role for the "intermediate time" between the paschal event and the *parousia*. But it is probably his anthropological pessimism that mostly calls for a correction, or at least an integration, as he himself endeavored to accomplish by recognizing the possibility of a "good mimetic desire," albeit utterly dependent on Grace.[8] Finally, it should be recalled that in the Paschal mystery Jesus acts not only as the victim, but also as the priest, thereby instituting a new form of priesthood and cult (cf. Heb 7:27).[9] I would therefore suggest that we treat his theory as the central act in a much larger, trans-historical drama, sketched by Gregory of Nyssa. Unlike Girard, the Cappadocian Father, while acknowledging desire as the

---

7. Cf. especially his criticism of Girard in *Theo-Drama: Theological Dramatic Theory*, Vol. IV: *The Action* (San Francisco: Ignatius Press, 1994), 299.
8. Cf. Girard, "The Goodness of Mimetic Desire," in *The Girard Reader*, ed. James G. Williams (New York: Crossroad Herder, 1996), 62–65. This "aggiornamento" was actually inspired by the reading of von Balthasar's criticism as well as by the works of the Italian philosopher Giuseppe Fornari, including *Fra Dioniso e Cristo: La sapienza sacrificale greca e la civiltà occidentale* (Bologna: Pitagora Editrice, 2001).
9. As one Paschal hymn summarized it, "Christ the victim, Christ the priest" ("At the Lamb's High Feast We Sing," v. 8; this is the English translation of the sixth-century Ambrosian hymn "Ad coenam Agni providi").

driving force of human life, also describes its transfiguration in an appeased contemplation.[10]

Arabia on the Verge of Islam: A Society Haunted by Violence

After this (hopefully not too) long theoretical premise, let us turn first to the context wherein Islam presumably saw the light. I assume, without being able to discuss this point further in this contribution, that Islam was effectively born in seventh-century Arabia and that the Qur'an preserves an echo of Muhammad's preaching, although it may contain some earlier or later fragments.[11] I also believe, adopting what Gregor Schoeler calls a "critical" (as opposed to "hypercritical") approach, that we do not have to discard the Islamic sources, not least for the good reason that, as Michael Lecker once wrote: "While ethnological studies and the literatures of the conquered people can provide confirmation of certain details, the

---

10. Cf. Hans Urs von Balthasar, *Présence et pensée: Essai sur la philosophie religieuse de Grégoire de Nysse* (Paris: Beauchesne, 1988 [first published 1942]). It is striking to observe the complementarity between the trajectories of Gregory of Nyssa and René Girard. The latter intervenes at the exact point where the former remains caught in the neo-Platonic cage, namely when discussing the anthropological effects of the original sin and the role of sexuality.
11. The issue can be discussed in two directions, "downhill" and "uphill," in relation to the presumed lifespan of Muhammad. Thanks to some recent paleographic discoveries we know that the Qur'anic text was fixed at latest by 'Abd al-Mālik's reign (685–705). For sure, there is a big difference whether it was canonized in 'Uthmān's time (r. 644–56), as the Islamic tradition has it, or under the Umayyads, since here "decades counts as centuries," as Mohammad Ali Amir-Moezzi has rightly argued (*Le Coran silencieux et le Coran parlant* [Paris: CNRS Éditions, 2011]). On the other hand, the Qur'an may well contain materials older than Muhammad, especially of a liturgical-narrative nature, but only a "founding figure" like Muhammad can, in my opinion, explain the extent of the changes the Arab tribes brought about in the late-antique Levant and far beyond it.

backbone of future research will remain the Islamic literature, for which there is no real alternative."[12]

Now, Central Arabia seems to have been shaken, on the eve of Islam, by a "sacrificial crisis." This notion is defined by Girard as follows:

> A *crisis of differences*, i.e. of the whole cultural order... When religion breaks down, it is not only physical security that is immediately threatened, but the cultural order itself. Institutions lose their vitality; the armor of society crumbles and falls apart. Erosion of values, though slow at the beginning, soon accelerates. The whole culture is at risk of collapsing and it does collapse one day as a castle of cards.[13]

This description seems to fit what we know, broad and large, about Arab society in Muhammad's time. Unlike prominent scholars such as Gerald Hawting, I maintain the hypothesis that Mecca and Central Arabia were at that time still largely pagan, with cults turning around sacrificial offerings and the veneration of the Kaʿba sanctuary. Although familiar with the biblical universe—as the Qur'an itself amply testifies—the inhabitants of Mecca had not adhered to a distinct form of Judaism or Christianity. This hypothesis is factually possible, as even inside the Roman-Byzantine Empire there were still significant pagan remnants. One thinks here of Procopius's remarks on Justinian's disastrous religious policy in his *Secret History*[14] or the missionary activities of John of

---

12. *Muslims, Jews and Pagans: Studies on Early Islamic Medina* (Leiden; New York: Brill, 1995), XIII.
13. René Girard, *La violence et le sacré* (Paris: Pluriel, 2014), 77–78.
14. Procopius of Caesarea, *Secret History*, XI 26. Also, Procopius, *VI, The Anecdota or Secret History*. Greek text with an English translation by H.B. Dewing, Loeb Classical Library (London-Cambridge, MA: Heinemann-Harvard University Press, 1935), XI 24–34, pp. 137–141.

Ephesus in Asia Minor,[15] to give just two examples. This potentiality, which in itself is not a proof, is further substantiated by certain Qur'anic hints at heathen practices, especially in Qur'an 6:136–40 and 5:97–104, and by the originally pagan rites of Islamic pilgrimage, which could hardly have been invented from scratch.

At the same time, the primary reason behind the widespread suspicion regarding these Arab pagans is the strangeness of their beliefs—or, more precisely, the curious modernness of their beliefs. As the Qur'an attests, their creed boils down to this simple statement: "There is nothing but our present life; we die, and we live, and nothing but Time destroys us" (Q 45:24). In short, they appear no longer to believe in the religion that they practice (which is, incidentally, another way to define a sacrificial crisis). As a result, they are increasingly obsessed with the cycle of vengeance and vendetta, which they no longer control.

Rather than dismissing Qur'an 45:24 as a polemical passage, it is tempting to read this verse as a side effect of the growing prestige of Christianity and Judaism in the Arabian Peninsula. These religions were eroding the foundations of paganism, but had not yet succeeded in taking its place, either because they were only marginally interested in proselytism (as was the case with Judaism, which could at any rate boast a significant number of Arab converts) or because they had not gone yet through a sufficient inculturation process, as was the case with the different Christian confessions. This had resulted, according to many scholars, in the creation of syncretic forms of religiosity[16] of an unstable nature.

---

15. John of Ephesus, *The Third Part of the Ecclesiastical History of John Bishop of Ephesus*. Now first translated from the original Syriac by R. Payne Smith (Oxford: At the University Press, 1860), III 36, pp. 229–32.

16. See for instance the discussion in Nicolai Sinai, *The Qur'an: A Historical-Critical Introduction* (Edinburgh: Edinburgh University Press, 2017), 65–72: "It stands to reason…that the Qur'anic Associators worshipped ancient Arabian deities yet felt free to reinterpret and supplement their ancestral rites by concepts and ideas adopted from the Jewish and Christian traditions that were increasingly seeping into the Arabian interior" (p. 70).

A second point: according to Girard, a sacrificial crisis usually leads to the sudden birth of tragedy as a form of art.[17] Here again the parallel with Arabia is striking. Medieval philologists have actually transmitted a large set of pre-Islamic poems, which seem to arise out of nothing. Although these poems (Arabic *qaṣāʾid*, singular *qaṣīda*) are partially forged, they are likely to preserve some authentic stock. On the whole, they present two interesting features: from one side, they display an almost complete absence of religious references. If Montgomery Watt used to characterize them, with some exaggeration, as a form of a "tribal humanism," the French Arabist Pierre Larcher writes in a more measured way: "[This poetry] is focused on man, in the sense that God and even the gods are absent from it: on the other hand, you come across rites every now and then, a part of which was recuperated by Islam."[18]

While the meaning of most verses in these poems is established, it is hard to discern the sense of their enchainment. Ancient philologists, most famously Ibn Qutayba (d. 889), proposed to see in these compositions a panegyric aim, but this description actually applies only to a part of the production and seems to fit more poems dating from the Umayyad age than pre-Islamic odes.[19]

Faced with this difficulty, modern research has started, from the 1970s onwards, to explore new modes of analysis, employing anthropological categories. Scholars such as Andras Hamori,[20] Stefan

---

I do not share, however, Sinai's persuasion that syncretism was perceived as a coherent belief system by those "inhabiting" it.

17. In fact, as we know, authentic tragedy only appears in very specific cultural turns (Classical Greece, Shakespeare…), although it can be imitated as a literary exercise also in other epochs (Seneca, Foscolo, Manzoni, etc.).
18. Pierre Larcher, *"Actualité de la poésie préislamique,"* conversation with Martino Diez. *Oasis*, December 28, 2016, http://www.oasiscenter.eu/fr/actualite-de-la-poesie-preislamique.
19. Renate Jacobi, "The Camel-Section of the Panegyrical Ode," *Journal of Arabic Literature* 13 (1982): 1–22.
20. *On the Art of Medieval Arabic Literature* (Princeton: Princeton University Press, 1974).

Sperl,[21] and Suzanne Pinckney Stetkevych[22] have all stressed the fundamental role played by Time/Destiny (*dahr*) in these odes and the battle that the hero—usually the lyrical ego—fights against it before recovering (or not recovering) his position in the tribal society. But it is Muhammad Mustafa Badawi that took the decisive step, openly defining the pre-Islamic *qaṣīda* as "[a] ritual more akin to Greek tragedy, a re-enactment in recital of the common values of the tribe, with similar cathartic effects."[23] One can observe the same mythological shift also in Larcher, currently one of the most knowledgeable scholars on pre-Islamic poetry:[24]

> The more I translate these poems, the more I come to believe that this poetry and its associated "stories" transmit the mythology of the Arabs much more than their history. Unfortunately in the Islamic world, which has not had its hermeneutical revolution, theology has killed mythology. And as far as Arabists are concerned, they lack the audacity or, more simply, the skills necessary to perform it.[25]

It would be easy to accumulate other quotations, but the core point is by now sufficiently clear: Pre-Islamic poetry converges with Qur'anic data to convey the impression that Central Arabia was

---

21. *Mannerism in Arabic Poetry* (Cambridge: Cambridge University Press, 1989).
22. Among others: *The Mute Immortals Speak: Pre-Islamic Poetry and Poetics of Ritual* (Ithaca, NY: Cornell University Press, 1993).
23. Muhammad Mustafa Badawi, "From Primary to Secondary Qasidas: Thoughts on the Development of Classical Arabic Poetry," *Journal of Arabic Literature* 1 (1980): 7.
24. Cf. my review of Larcher's volume *Le Cédrat, la jument et la goule* (Arles: Sindbad-Actes Sud, 2016), in *Arabica* 64 (2017): 785–87.
25. Larcher, "*Actualité de la poésie préislamique.*"

experiencing an alarming erosion of its institutions, which threatened to give way to unfettered violence.

This crisis was further amplified by the extra-Arabic political context, marked by endless wars between Persians and Byzantines. The reverse of Roman armies from the reign of Phocas (r. 602–10) onwards left a deep impression on people, as proved by the flourishing of apocalyptic writing.[26]

The Return of Sacrifices

If this was the situation in seventh-century Arabia, it is striking to observe the reinstatement, in Islam, of a certain sacrificial order. This cannot be by mere chance. Whatever one may think of the nature and the evolution of Muhammad's preaching, the religion that finally came out of Medina and quickly spread in a torn and exhausted Middle East exhibits, according to several testimonies close to the events, distinct sacrificial traits.[27]

---

26. Cf. Stephen J. Shoemaker, *The Apocalypse of Empire: Imperial Eschatology in Late Antiquity and Early Islam* (Philadelphia: University of Pennsylvania Press, 2018).

27. For instance, in the disputation of the monk of Beth Ḥālē (late 8th century?), the Arab notable, when asked, "What faith of Abraham do you desire for us, and what are his commandments that you wish us to perform," replies: "*Circumcision and sacrifice* [emphasis mine], because he received them from God." Cf. Robert G. Hoyland, *Seeing Islam as Others Saw It* (Princeton: Darwin Press, 1997), 470, n.51. The disputation is now available in full Syriac edition with parallel English translation by David G.K. Taylor, "The Disputation between a Muslim and a Monk of Bēt Ḥālē: Syriac Text and Annotated English Translation," in *Christsein in der islamischen Welt: Festschrift für Martin Tamcke zum 60. Geburtstag*, eds. Sidney Griffith and Sven Grebenstein (Wiesbaden: Harrassowitz Verlag, 2015), 187–242. The relevant passage corresponds to paragraphs 13 to 15 of his edition. Taylor buttresses through several arguments for a late 8th–early 9th century date, roughly half a century after Hoyland's tentative dating to 720 CE. Nevertheless, the text, insomuch as it reflects a set of standard controversy topics pre-dating the Abbasid age, retains great historical value.

Let us consider first of all the pilgrimage and its rites. As a famous hadith teaches: "Pilgrimage is ʿArafa."²⁸ ʿArafa here refers to a prayer station that is performed on the ninth day of the month of pilgrimage (*dhū-l-ḥijja*), followed, on the next day, by the immolation of sacrificial victims (*al-aḍḥā*) in Mina. This ceremony spills from the Meccan sanctuary all over the Islamic world. As the hadith makes clear, for the pilgrimage to be valid, it is necessary to arrive at ʿArafa at least a few minutes before the dawn of the tenth day of *dhū-l-ḥijja* and take part in the immolation of animals. Whatever comes before can be compensated for later, but not what happens from ʿArafa onwards. A narrator of the hadith, Wakīʿ Ibn al-Jarrāḥ (d. 812–13), comments that "[t]his hadith is the mother of all ritual prescriptions (*umm al-manāsik*)."²⁹

All of these rites are performed in the memory of Abraham and the quasi-sacrifice of his son, identified by most prominent Islamic exegetes as Ishmael (although his name is not explicitly given in the Qurʾan). It is on the model of Abraham that pilgrims implore divine mercy, and the animal that they immolate takes the place of the patriarch's spared son. It is perhaps instructive to add that Abraham is here understood as the founder of Islam, since the new faith is not defined in the Qurʾan as "the religion of Muhammad" (a detail that escapes many) but rather as "the creed of Abraham" (cf. Q 6:161).

---

28. Al-Tirmidhī, Abū ʿĪsā Muḥammad, *Sunan*, ed. Maḥmūd Muḥammad Maḥmūd Ḥasan Naṣṣār (Bayrūt: Dār al-Kutub al-ʿilmiyya, 2017). *Kitāb al-Hajj, bāb mā jāʾ fī-man adrak al-imām bi-Jamʿ fa-qad adrak al-ḥajj*, nn. 889–91, vol. 2, 51. "On the authority of ʿAbd al-Raḥmān Ibn Yaʿmar. Some people from Najd came to the Messenger of God while he was in ʿArafa and asked him [whether their pilgrimage was still valid]. The Messenger of God called a herald and made him proclaim: 'Pilgrimage is ʿArafa. Whoever arrives on the night of Jamʿ [the night spent in Muzdalifa] before the rising of the sun, he has caught pilgrimage.'" The same hadith can be found in Aḥmad Ibn Ḥanbal, Ibn Māja, al-Nasāʾī, and Abū Dāwūd.

29. Al-Tirmidhī, *Sunan*, n. 890, vol. 2, 52.

Pilgrimage is in rupture with ordinary life. Pilgrims assume a sacred state (*iḥrām*) the very moment they enter the *ḥaram*, the space that God has reserved to Himself. This is a numinous place, fraught with perils, and it can easily turn from sacred to cursed/forbidden, from *ḥaram* to *ḥarām*; the toppling is only one vowel away. The polysemy *ḥaram-ḥarām* is not surprising at all, as it is found in most ancient cultures. Even in Latin, *sacer* means at the same time "sacred" and "cursed." This semantic sphere presides also over alimentary prohibitions and the rules of purity related to prayer, as well as the institution of *zakāt*.[30] In itself, the notion of *ḥaram* seems to hark back to a pre-Islamic layer: in the Qur'an, for instance, the sacredness of the Meccan temple is acknowledged as a matter of fact: "Let them [the Quraysh] serve the Lord of this House" (Q 106:3). This sacredness is, however, interpreted and understood in a new way, in relation to Abraham.

In fact, the reactivation of the sacrificial logic might well explain other practices, such as the offering of a victim (*'aqīqa*) on the seventh day after the birth of a child, circumcision (both, at any rate, absent from the Qur'anic text), and in general the often-remarked affinity between Judaism and Islam. It could also account for the attraction that Jews initially felt towards Muhammad's movement, if we are here to believe early Christian sources.[31]

The reactivation of sacrifices and rituals goes hand in hand with the institutionalization of jihad or militancy. Here one can fully measure the distance from contemporary jihadism. Far from taking

---

30. As Fred Donner argues, the term in the Qur'an is likely to mean "purification" (of wealth), including but not limited to the legal alms—see *Muhammad and the Believers: At the Origins of Islam* (Cambridge; London: Harvard University Press, 2010), 63; also Suliman Bashear, "On the Origins and Development of the Meaning of *Zakāt* in Islam," *Arabica* 40 (1993): 84–113.

31. Donner's fascinating thesis about the "ecumenical" nature of the movement of the Believers goes in a similar direction, although he adds to the Jews a group of non-Trinitarian Christians whose exact size and nature remain hard to determine.

on a sacrificial sense, jihad in the Arabian context is actually a form of canalization of violence, which should in principle work as a way to expel it from the newly formed polity, since by now "whoso slays a believer willfully, his recompense is Gehenna, therein dwelling forever" (Q 4:93). This point seems to me capital for an honest and serene evaluation of the institution of jihad, which is, in our day, the object of very different, even contradictory, explanations and practices. On the one hand, a simple reading of the Qur'anic text shows well that jihad is related, albeit not exclusively, to the state of violence.[32] On the other hand, it should not be overlooked that the aim of the Qur'an is not to produce violence, but to contain it, to dam and rationalize it by directing it outside the group.[33] This of course does not solve the issue of the relations to the "outside," but shows its rationale, its *niyya*, to use an Islamic term.

The newly formed community, by separating from impurity, can now hope to have expelled violence from its midst, especially thanks to the institutions of sacrifice and jihad. It can hope to have overcome the crisis by which it had been haunted. And this is not the least factor in explaining its success.

It could be objected that this reconstruction relies too heavily on Islamic sources. But it is not difficult to counter this criticism. Robert Hoyland, the great expert of non-Islamic testimonies on the origins of Islam, summarizes his findings in these terms:

---

32. Souleiman Mourad, who has long been working on this subject, considers that "[t]he recent advocacy that jihad in Islam means internal struggle is disingenuous to say the least" (*The Mosaic of Islam: A Conversation with Perry Anderson* [London; Brooklyn, NY: Verso, 2016], 43).

33. On this point contemporary "liberal" Muslims such as Asma Afsaruddin (*Striving in the Path of God: Jihad and Martyrdom in Islamic Thought* [Oxford: Oxford University Press, 2003]) are perfectly right. The great question, which is outside the scope of the present discussion, is therefore whether jihad can be assimilated to defensive warfare, considering that it arose as a reaction to the hostility of Meccan pagans. By contrast, wholly "pacifist" or "spiritualist" interpretations of this institution, though laudable, are in my opinion doomed to fail.

Non-Muslim writers of the first century AH attest that [the faith that came to be known as Islam] was strictly monotheistic (Sebeos, John bar Penkaye, Anastasius of Sinai) and iconoclastic (anti-Jewish polemicists, Germanus); that its adherents had a sanctuary, their "House of God" (Bar Penkaye), of Abrahamic association (Chronicler of Khuzistan, Jacob of Edessa), called the Ka'ba (Jacob of Edessa), towards which they prayed (Jacob of Edessa) and at which they sacrificed (Anastasius of Sinai) and reverenced a stone (Anastasius of Sinai, Germanus); and also that they followed Muḥammad (Thomas the Presbyter, Sebeos, Chronicler of Khuzistan), who was their "guide" and "instructor" (Bar Penkaye), whose "tradition" and "laws" they fiercely upheld (Bar Penkaye) and who prescribed for them abstinence from carrion, wine, falsehood and fornication.[34]

Our hypothesis does not require more than this.

The Contestation of Sacrifices

Could Islam then be understood as a mere return to the old sacrificial order? Things are not so easy. The Qur'an does not only endorse ancient rites; it also entails a sharp critique of them.

First and foremost, the sacrifice that Islam commemorates is actually a missed sacrifice. Abraham is ordered not to touch the victim, his son, but instead to substitute him with a ram. Surat al-Ṣaffāt declares: "We ransomed him [Abraham's son] with a mighty sacrifice" (Q 37:107).[35] This substitution is utterly Girardian in nature, but it also marks, in the Bible, the beginning of the process of

---

34. Hoyland, *Seeing Islam as Others Saw It*, 549.
35. I would like to thank Gabriel Said Reynolds for pointing me to this reference.

demystification of violence. And for exactly this reason, the episode was read in Christian theology as a prefiguration of the paschal mystery, with Isaac acting as a type of Christ, as in the sequence of the Corpus Christi *Lauda Sion Salvatorem*, composed by Thomas Aquinas: *In figuris praesignatur, cum Isaac immolatur: agnus paschae deputatur: datur manna patribus* ("Shewn in Isaac's dedication / In the manna's preparation / In the Paschal immolation / In old types pre-signified").

Secondly, the Qur'an is also aware of the Old Testament polemics against the inanity of animal sacrifices. One has only to read a passage of the 22nd Sura, which bears the title—not a fortuitous coincidence—"Sura of the Pilgrimage":

> And the beasts of sacrifice—We have appointed them for you as among God's waymarks; therein is good for you. So mention God's Name over them, standing in ranks; then, when their flanks collapse, eat of them and feed the beggar and the suppliant. So We have subjected them to you; haply you will be thankful. The flesh of them shall not reach God, neither their blood, but godliness from you shall reach Him…. (Q 22:36–37)

Denise Masson, in her French translation of the Qur'an, puts verse 37 in relation to Amos 5:22–25:

> 22 Even though you offer me your burnt offerings and grain offerings, I will not accept them;
> and the offerings of well-being of your fatted animals
> I will not look upon.
> 23 Take away from me the noise of your songs;
> I will not listen to the melody of your harps.
> 24 But let justice roll down like waters,
> and righteousness like an ever-flowing stream.
> 25 Did you bring to me sacrifices and offerings the forty years in the wilderness, O house of Israel?

Gabriel Said Reynolds, for his part, adds other relevant biblical passages: Isaiah 1:11, Jeremiah 6:20, Micah 6:6–7, 1 Samuel 15:22, and Matthew 9:13.[36]

As a result of this Qur'anic contestation (or at least relativization), the rites of sacrifice, while integrated into the fabric of Sunni Islam, are also depotentiated and transformed mainly into acts of social justice, by which the poor and the needy receive their share of the animal victims.[37]

Moreover, not only does the Qur'anic God, in His omnipotence, not need human offerings, but He can also dispense with the acts of worship that he has commanded to mankind. In a way that is deeply reminiscent of the Old Testament oracles, the text states: "I have not created jinn and mankind except to serve Me. I desire of them no provision, neither do I desire that they should feed Me. Surely God is the All-Provider, the Possessor of Strength, the Ever-Sure" (Q 51:56–58).

As a third element, if the pair *harām-halāl* structures the Qur'anic perception of reality and space (including the *qibla* or direction of prayer), the text also gives voice to a critique of legalism, again echoing some Old Testament prophets (e.g. Mic 6:8): "It is not piety, that you turn your faces to the East and to the West. True piety is this: to believe in God, and the Last Day, the angels, the Book and the Prophets, to give of one's substance, however

---

36. Gabriel Said Reynolds, *The Qur'an and the Bible: Text and Commentary*, (New Haven, CT: Yale University Press, 2018), 528.
37. Personal communication by Adnane Mokrani to the author. Q 22:28 teaches "when their flanks collapse, eat of them and feed the beggar and the suppliant." The *Sunna* specifies to share the victims in three thirds, for the family, the relatives, and the poor, respectively. The details vary according to the juridical schools. Ideally, nothing must be left. "'Alī said: The Prophet offered 100 animals in sacrifice and ordered me to take care of their flesh and I distributed it, of their ornaments and I distributed them and of their skins and I distributed them" (al-Bukhārī, *Ṣaḥīḥ, Kitāb al-ḥajj, bāb yutaṣaddaq bi-jilāl al-budn* [Dār Ṣādir, Bayrūt s.d., n. 1718, p. 299]).

cherished [but perhaps 'in love of Him' is here a better rendering], to kinsmen, and orphans" (Q 2:177a).

Lastly, the great problem with jihad is, from the very start, how to define the frontiers of the community, outside of which violence must be "thrown." Leaving aside the question of pagans, what is to be done with the gray zone occupied by the "People of Scripture," (*ahl al-kitāb*) who enjoy an intermediate state between believers and unbelievers? The Qur'anic text is torn on this point between an inclusivist and an exclusivist approach and only the legal device of abrogation was able to instill here some measure of order, but at the cost of creating a theological problem thornier than the juridical issues it is meant to settle. Yet, more importantly, how does one decide where Islam begins and where it ends? Where does the dividing line pass between the "inside" and the "outside" of the *umma*? Here lies the conceptual origin of *takfīr* (lit. "declaring somebody an unbeliever"), a practice which today has gained a new, troubling relevance. It is through *takfīr* that competing groups of Muslims first engaged in armed confrontation. This state of affairs is testified by the Qur'an itself, when it speaks of "two parties of believers" in conflict (Q 49:9), the point being here the use of the term "believer" to define *both* of them.[38]

These traumatic events, which constitute the background of most Sunni political thought,[39] reveal the weakness of the sacrificial solution. The wound of *fitna* ("scandal," "division," the technical term, of Qur'anic ascendency, used by Muslims to designate civil wars) can always re-open, even in our day.[40]

The result is therefore a precarious balance. And it might not be otherwise, insofar as Islam comes, *historically*, after the rupture

---

38. *Wa-in ṭā'ifatāni min a l-mu'minīna 'qtatalū, fa-aṣliḥū bayna-humā.*
39. According to Leïla Babès this thought ends being stuck, due to the memory of civil wars, in the deadlock of an "anarcho-theocracy" (*L'utopie de l'Islam: La religion contre l'état* [Paris: Armand Colin, 2013]).
40. Gilles Kepel significantly entitled one of his books *Fitna: guerre au cœur de l'Islam* (Paris: Gallimard, 2004).

with the logic of sacred violence prepared by prophetic Judaism and fulfilled by Christ, although it is *anthropologically* situated before it.[41] In its effort to achieve a reform that reaches back to the source of monotheism, Islam encounters the Bible and at the same time clashes with it. More precisely, it comes across the Bible as a source of inspiration, but also as a barrier preventing the return to the pure sacred of archaic religions, to the age of ignorance or *jāhiliyya* (which we might also translate as *"méconnaissance"* to use the Girardian term)—hence the acceptance of both sacrifice and its critique, the stress on purity rules and their relativization, and the practice of jihad and its backfiring on the community.[42]

This consideration leads me to add a final cursory remark on a much-debated issue—namely essentialism. In principle, I am not among those who consider this term as a kind of academic insult. As Rémi Brague observed with sarcasm, the patron saint of the guild of philosophers, Socrates, used to spend his time looking after the essence of things (virtue, courage, justice, etc.), and it was exactly this that set him apart from the sophists. Therefore I do not see any inherent evil in looking for the essence of phenomena, however difficult this may be.

At the same time, as Francesca Aran Murphy has observed, quoting von Balthasar, "Christians have no theological reason, no reason within their faith, to insist that any religion other than Christianity has a permanent essence or nature."[43] I am not able to say whether this point may apply to other world religions, but, as far as Islam is concerned, I believe that it hits the target. If what precedes is not totally devoid of sense, Islam's essence, if we still

---

41. An application of the theory of relativity to human sciences would be most helpful in this respect.
42. This dynamic could also be used as a framework to evaluate the significance of Ḥusayn's sacrifice in Shi'ism.
43. Francesca Aran Murphy, "It Is Written in the Book," *First Things*, Sept. 7, 2017, https://www.firstthings.com/web-exclusives/2017/09/it-is-written-in-the-book.

want to use the word, seems actually to be a dialectical tension between a "before" and an "after." This would account for the great variations we can empirically observe in the ways of being a Muslim, today as well as in the past.

"For a Term Appointed":
Making Sense of Religious Difference

Heading towards my conclusion, I wish to make a last point which is much more hypothetical and risky than what precedes, and which I am ready to abandon if it proves to be theologically untenable. The question now becomes the following: Can the proposed reading of the formative stages of Islam offer some insights into the already evoked question of Islam's theological status in relation to Christianity? There is actually a theme in the Qur'an which recurs time and again and which, to the best of my knowledge, has not caught much scholarly attention—it is the theme of difference. In several verses, the idea is put forth that mankind originally formed an *undifferentiated* whole. Divergences would have arisen at a later stage and they would have led to a (mimetic) confrontation. As Qur'an 10:19 famously affirms: "Mankind were only one nation, then they fell into variance."[44] Incidentally, this verse would have delighted Girard, who built his theory on a reading of the great texts of humanity. It is highly significant that the famous exegete Muḥammad Ibn Jarīr al-Ṭabarī (d. 923), in his commentary on this verse, elliptically hints at the story of Cain and Abel.[45] And yet, the verse continues: "But for a word (Ar. *kalima*) that preceded from thy Lord, it had been decided between them already touching their

---

44. *Mā kāna l-nāsu illā ummatan wāḥidatan fa-'khtalafū*.
45. *Tafsīr al-Ṭabarī (Jāmiʿ al-Bayān ʿan Taʾwīl Āy al-Qurʾān)*, eds. ʿAbd Allāh Ibn ʿAbd al-Muḥsin al-Turkī et al. (Al-Qāhira: Dār Hajr, 2001), XII, 143. The longest discussion in al-Ṭabarī about the possible nature of this "one nation" is to be found in the comment on 2:213 (III, 620–35).

differences (*wa-law kalimatun sabaqat min Rabbi-ka, la-quḍiya bayna-hum fīmā fīhi yakhtalifūn*)." The expression at the end of this verse, "it had been decided between them already touching their differences," recurs elsewhere in the Qur'an in similar forms. It is always left vague and is usually translated something like "the divergence would have been adjudicated." But the verb *qaḍā* (*quḍiya* in the passive form) also contains the idea of suppressing the difference, of abolishing it altogether. Thus, according to this passage, divergence would have been settled and unanimity recovered (in other words, the sacrificial crisis would have come to an end and people would no longer be at variance), if not for "a word that preceded from thy Lord."

What word? While the text is silent on this point, commentators, on the basis of Qur'an 11:118,[46] have developed the idea of a decree by which God keeps people in their different religions and communities until the Judgment Day. For instance, the popular sixteenth-century *Tafsīr al-Jalālayn* paraphrases Qur'an 10:19 (quoted above) as follows:

> "Mankind were only one nation," belonging to one religion, which is Islam, from Adam until Noah or from Abraham's epoch until 'Amr Ibn Luḥayy [the mythic founder of polytheism in Mecca], "then they fell into variance" because some people kept faith and others disbelieved. "But for a word that preceded from thy Lord" to the effect of postponing the reward until the Day of Resurrection, "it had been decided between them already," i.e. between the people of this world, "touching their differences" in faith matters, through the punishment of unbelievers.[47]

---

46. "Had thy Lord willed, He would have made mankind one nation; but they continue in their differences."
47. *Tafsīr al-Jalālayn*, Q 10:19.

This is already a stimulating proposition. Building on it, the idea that religious differences are willed by God is indeed very often invoked in contemporary Islamic approaches to interreligious dialogue, especially if paired with an inclusivist approach which admits salvation also for some groups of non-Muslims—the latter however being a perspective alien to medieval commentators such as the *Jalālayn*.[48] Along these lines, the Qur'anic phrase made its way into a passage of the document *Human Fraternity* signed by Pope Francis and the Grand Imam of al-Azhar, Ahmad al-Tayyeb, in Abu Dhabi on February 4, 2019.[49]

Staying within the Qur'anic horizon, however, it is possible to move even further than this exegesis by recalling that in the Islamic Scripture, the *Kalima* that precedes from the Lord is actually the Christ (cf. Q 3:45 and 4:171).[50] It is he who prevents people from indulging in the "bad unanimity" that they always try to re-create by uniting against a designated scapegoat. According to Girard, Christ's choice to identify with the victim rather than the murderers demystifies the sacred and, precisely because it exposes the mechanism of ritual violence, destroys the very foundations of archaic religion. Mimetic conflict is thus brought to its paroxysm, since it can no longer be appeased by the sacrifice of an innocent victim. "Do not think that I have come to bring peace on earth;

---

48. Literally, "the two Jalāls," namely Jalāl al-Dīn al-Maḥallī (d. 1459) and Jalāl al-Dīn al-Suyūṭī (d. 1505).

49. The document can be found on the Vatican site: https://w2.vatican.va/content/francesco/en/travels/2019/outside/documents/papa-francesco_20190204_documento-fratellanza-umana.html. The passage in question is the following: "The pluralism and the diversity of religions, colour, sex, race and language are willed by God in His wisdom, through which He created human beings."

50. It is easy to discern two meanings of *kalima* in the Qur'an: a human word, as in Q 3:64, the famous "common word" that Muslims and People of the Scripture are called to share, and a word of heavenly origin, a *Kalima* with a capital K, so to say, i.e., the Christ.

I have not come to bring peace, but a sword" (Matt 10:34) is the Gospel passage Girard liked to quote on this respect.

If the *Kalima*-Christ identification holds true, then it is worth asking whether Islam could be understood, from a Christian perspective, as a partial return to the sacrificial order, which *delays* the outburst of violence, unmasked, once and for all, by the "Word that preceded from thy Lord." In other words, it could be thought to perform a function of containment. And it is perhaps not accidental that this partial reactivation of the sacrificial order took place during the reign of Heraclius, when the church was seriously running the risk of being swallowed by the machine of an imperial propaganda seeking to sanctify warfare[51] religiously and directly entering the realm of dogma (monothelitist crisis).

Still, in the same Sura of the Pilgrimage it can be read: "In them ye have benefits for a term appointed (*ilā ajalin musamman*)" (Q 22:33).[52] "Them" here refers to *sha'ā'ir Allāh* ("symbols" or perhaps "rituals" of God) in the previous verse, and is most probably an allusion to the sacrificial beasts, mentioned only a few verses later, in Qur'an 22:36, using the technical term *budn*. Here again commentators are in doubt as to how to interpret the "term appointed." After relating various exegetical options, al-Ṭabarī steps in in the first person and explains that the "term appointed" refers to the end of the pilgrimage period ("until the circumambulation of the House for some, the conclusion of pilgrimage for others or the exit from the *ḥaram* according to others"[53]), after which life returns to

---

51. In this respect, I profited from an exchange with Tommaso Tesei. See his "Heraclius' War Propaganda and the Qur'ān's Promise of Reward for Dying in Battle," *Studia Islamica* 114 (2019): 219–47.
52. Here I prefer Yusuf Ali's translation to Arberry's: "There are things therein profitable to you unto a stated term." But it is only a matter of taste; the meaning does not change.
53. *Tafsīr al-Ṭabarī*, XVI, 547.

normal.⁵⁴ But again, could this verse not serve to announce the provisional character of the sacrificial order that Islam comes to reinstate?

If what precedes has some plausibility, we have to take a final step and ask what the current shift from jihad to jihadism may indicate. There are indeed indications that the function of containment performed by jihad is no longer operative in contemporary Muslim societies, due to the breaking apart of the coherent edifice that classical Islam had erected. In abstract terms, this consideration leaves two ways open: either Girard's apocalypticism, or the possible birth of new configurations, doctrines, and institutions within the Islamic world, performing the function once assured by jihad.

Leaving for God to determine the when and how of the end of history, it seems safe to concentrate on the second hypothesis. Within this framework, one can expect these new Islamic configurations to engage in a dialogue with other religious traditions, and especially with contemporary Catholic thought⁵⁵ and magisterium, both marked by an explicit renunciation of the logic of sacred violence. To a certain extent, this encounter, also stirred by the testimony of many common Christians in vulnerable areas such as the Middle East, is already happening. It may represent a major development for the future.

---

54. It is worth noting that no animal sacrifices are performed during the 'umra, the "lesser pilgrimage."

55. See the 2014 document of the International Theological Commission, *God the Trinity and the Unity of Humanity: Christian Monotheism and Its Opposition to Violence*, especially the conclusion, n# 97–100. Italian original: http://www.vatican.va/roman_curia/congregations/cfaith/cti_documents/rc_cti_20140117_monoteismo-cristiano_it.html. Unfortunately, only a summary of the document is available in English.

Bibliography

Balthasar, Hans Urs von. *Présence et pensée: Essai sur la philosophie religieuse de Grégoire de Nysse*. Paris: Beauchesne, 1988.

Donner, Fred. *Muhammad and the Believers: At the Origins of Islam*. Cambridge; London: Harvard University Press, 2010.

Girard, René. *Achever Clausewitz*. Paris: Flammarion, 2011.

———. *La violence et le sacré*. Paris: Pluriel, 2014 (original edition: Grasset et Fasquelle, 1972).

Hamori, Andras. *On the Art of Medieval Arabic Literature*. Princeton: Princeton University Press, 1974.

Hoyland, Robert G. *Seeing Islam as Others Saw It*. Princeton: Darwin Press, 1997.

Larcher, Pierre. "Actualité de la poésie préislamique," conversation with Martino Diez. *Oasis,* December 28, 2016, http://www.oasiscenter.eu/fr/actualite-de-la-poesie-preislamique.

Reynolds, Gabriel Said. *The Qur'an and the Bible: Text and Commentary*. New Haven, CT: Yale University Press, 2018.

Sinai, Nicolai. *The Qur'an: A Historical-Critical Introduction*. Edinburgh: Edinburgh University Press, 2017.

Chapter Seven

TOWARDS A COMMUNION OF ALL THINGS BEYOND ANTHROPOCENTRISM AND BIOCENTRISM: A CATHOLIC-CONFUCIAN DIALOGUE ON SOCIAL JUSTICE AND ECOLOGY

Anselm Min

I propose to conduct a dialogue between Catholicism and Confucianism on social justice and ecology.[1] The Catholic side will be represented by Pope Francis's encyclical *Laudato Si'* and relevant aspects of the Catholic tradition. The encyclical is the most recent development and synthesis of Catholic social doctrine in its most authoritative form. The Confucian side will be drawn from the classical tradition of Confucius, Mencius, and Neo-Confucianism. I will proceed in three parts. First, I will present the four central themes of *Laudato Si*, along with some analysis. These themes include: (1) anthropocentrism and the technocratic paradigm as the fundamental source of the ecological crisis; (2) the cosmic solidarity of all things

---

1. This is a revised version of a paper originally presented at the conference on "Christian-Confucian Dialogue and the Church's Mission in Asia" sponsored by the Vatican's International Center for Mission and Formation (CIAM) and held in Rome, December 3–7, 2018.

in the triune God and the interconnectedness of humanity and nature; (3) the praxis of political love for the common good; and (4) the cultivation of simplicity as the ecological virtue. Second, I will discuss four Confucian themes that are directly parallel to these: (1) the absolute primacy of the *dao* or *li* of heaven (天道, 天理), (2) the unity of heaven and humanity (*tianrenhei*, 天人合一) as a central metaphysical insight, (3) the politics of *minben* (民本主義), or government for the people, and (4) the life of the *junzi*, or the authentic person as model of simplicity. Finally, I will provide a brief dialogue between the two traditions on these parallels and their implications, highlighting five points of profound affinity as deserving full exploration in future dialogue.

Laudato Si' *and Its Fundamental Themes*

In this first major papal encyclical devoted to the theme of ecology, Pope Francis does four things. He first presents a diagnosis of the ecological crisis, locating its roots in anthropocentrism and the technological paradigm with which human beings seek to dominate all things. He then pleads for a radically new way of looking at the universe and the place of humanity in that universe where all things are interconnected and interdependent in a universal communion of all things in God. Next, he goes on to highlight the praxis of political love for the common good as a concrete approach to remedying the ecological crisis. Finally, he ends with suggestions for an ecological spirituality based on a cosmic solidarity of all things in God and a simplicity of life, freed from the entangling temptations of greed and power. One distinctive characteristic of the encyclical is its insistence on the inseparability of ecology and social justice, of our responsibility toward both nature and one another.

I. Anthropocentrism, the Technocratic Paradigm, and the Ecological Crisis

For Pope Francis, the root of our present ecological crisis lies in anthropocentrism—our refusal to recognize anything as higher than ourselves, our own desires and interests, and our assertion of an unlimited freedom to exploit and dominate all things according to such desires and interests, with no respect for the intrinsic integrity or value of anything other than our desires. By taking this posture, we reduce the being of all things to nothing more than their utility to us. For this purpose, we utilize all the modern advances in science and technology, and apply the technocratic paradigm as the privileged epistemological paradigm in looking at the world. This paradigm dominates our economics and politics alike. Its ultimate goal is neither the profit nor the well-being of humanity, but the wielding of power over all things, the mastery of nature, for which we violate and sacrifice the integrity of both human life and of ecosystems. It is clearly a one-sided view of the world, but in the contemporary addiction to specialization it has also become the key to the very meaning of existence, ignoring all other aspects of life. It reduces nature to mere raw material to be exploited, with no intrinsic dignity. Technocratic anthropocentrism is "a Promethean vision of mastery over the world" (116).[2] The dominance of technocratic anthropocentrism in all areas of life means that the ecological crisis is not a partial crisis, limited to a particular dimension of life, nor simply one crisis among others. Rather, it is a total crisis of humanity as such and cannot be resolved by technological solutions alone. Instead, what is needed is a fundamental rethinking of our relation to one another and to all of nature. What we need is a "bold cultural revolution," a radically

---

2. The references in parentheses in this section dealing with the encyclical are to the paragraph numbers. The text of the encyclical is found online at: http://w2.vatican.va/content/francesco/encyclicals/documents/papa-francesco_2015052.

new way of looking at reality without the "unrestrained delusions of grandeur" (114).[3]

II. The Cosmic Solidarity of All Things in the Triune God

The "bold cultural revolution" just mentioned consists in liberating ourselves from an atomistic, mechanical view of the world as something to be dominated and converted to cultivate an interconnected and interdependent view of the world, wherein each part maintains its own unique structure and dignity to be respected while also standing in harmonious interrelationship to all other parts of creation—where the whole of the world points beyond itself to bear witness to the beauty, truth, and goodness of the creator whose trace and image it bears.

Human beings are also a part of nature, drawing their sustenance from interaction with it. Nature is the common "home" of all humanity. When we hurt nature, we hurt ourselves. It is a misinterpretation and abuse of scripture to use the references in the book of Genesis (1:28) to human beings being created in the image of God and having dominion over all things in creation as a justification for exploiting nature and destroying its delicate balance, in order to satisfy the ever-expanding human desires for goods. The point of this scriptural teaching is to highlight human responsibility for taking proper care of things in nature, always with full respect for the structure and dignity of things as created by God, not to legitimize unbridled freedom to tyrannize over them in a ruthless exploitation of resources. God, not human beings, is the ultimate purpose of all things. By the same token, however, this recognition of human beings' status as part of, not master over, nature does not mean that human persons are reducible to simply one being among others, nor to one object among others without any uniqueness, as biocentrism tends to think. The interconnectedness

---

3. See also paras. 6, 67–69, 104, 106–12, 115, 122, 155, 224.

of all things does not mean that everything exists on the same level. Human beings are truly part of nature but also a unique part that bears responsibility for guarding its integrity. Human persons transcend the level of physics and biology due to their capacity to enter into dialogue with God and others, to reason, invent, interpret, and create art. We must overcome the contemporary "obsession" among certain ecologists to deny this uniqueness to human beings. To deny the uniqueness of the human person and his responsibility for nature is paradoxically to legitimize the arbitrary use of human freedom to abuse and destroy nature (15, 81, 83, 98).

The world is an interconnected web of relationships wherein nothing exists in isolation nor is self-sufficient, where everything participates in everything else in various ways, where everything depends on other things for its own integrity and completion, where service to others is essential to one's own integrity. Indeed our relationships with one another as fellow humans are not separable from our relations with non-human creatures in the world. When we damage and deplete natural resources to make some of us rich, the suffering falls on the poor in society who bear a disproportionate amount of that suffering. Social justice for the poor and marginalized and ecological justice for the preservation of the integrity of nature go inseparably together. The cry of the poor and the cry of the earth must be heard together. It is inconsistent to bewail the trafficking of endangered species while remaining indifferent to human trafficking. There cannot be a renewal of our relation to nature without a renewal of humanity, no ecology without an adequate anthropology.[4]

It is essential here to return to theological basics in order both to appreciate the gravity of the ecological crises and to undertake the "bold cultural revolution" or the radical change in our way of looking at the world. The God who saves and liberates us, it must be remembered, is also the God who creates the world. The world

---

4. See paras. 15, 16, 49, 71, 78, 79, 81, 83, 90, 91, 118.

belongs to God, not to us, and is given to us as a gift that belongs to everyone, not as a windfall for the powerful to exploit with an absolute dominion, thereby usurping the place of God. When God creates all things, God creates each thing with its own intrinsic nature, value, and autonomy, which we must respect in taking care of God's creation. Respect for God's creation means respect for "the message contained in the structures of nature itself" (116), for its laws and the delicate equilibrium that exists among creatures. As creatures, things in the world reflect something of God's own infinite wisdom and goodness, which makes them a constant source of wonder and awe. Nature is not only the locus of God's revelation through which God speaks to us, but also the locus of God's presence. The Holy Spirit, the Spirit of life, dwells in every living creature and calls us into relationship with him. Through the Incarnation, Christ has taken into himself this whole material world and is intimately present to each being. In fact, each creature bears in itself a Trinitarian structure and dynamism. As subsistent relations, the triune God creates the world as a web of relationships in which creatures tend to God and to one another, where each becomes more itself in proportion as it relates to others, going out of itself to live in communion with God, others, and all creation. The universal interconnection and interdependence among creatures, theologically speaking, is only the Trinitarian dynamism implanted in them when they were created by God. In God, the identity of the divine persons consists precisely in the relation with one another with whom each shares the totality of his own being, in whom identity is *totally* constituted by relationality and vice versa.[5]

The "bold cultural revolution" to which we are called in the encyclical, then, is this theological sense of "universal communion" (76), or communion with all things in the universe, "a spirituality of that global solidarity which flows from the mystery of the Trinity" (240). It is here that we are called to nurture "that sublime

---

5. See paras. 69, 71, 73, 78, 84, 85, 116, 117, 221.

fraternity with all creation" (221) so radiantly embodied in the life of Saint Francis of Assisi—a compelling model of integral ecology that integrates the concern for nature, justice for the poor, commitment to society, and interior peace (11, 12).

III. The Praxis of Political Love for the Common Good

The interconnected and interdependent nature of all reality also dictates an integral approach to the solution of the ecological crisis based on a comprehensive, unifying vision of reality. We are not faced with two separate crises, environmental and social, but with one complex crisis that is both social and environmental, demanding "an integrated approach to combating poverty, restoring dignity to the excluded, and at the same time protecting nature" (139). It is obvious that implementation of such an integrated approach requires collaboration among agencies of all sorts—from local to central governments to international institutions—to produce appropriate agreements, policies, and actions. It will require counteracting the imperialism of the free market and its priorities, liberating the economy from the technological paradigm, changing the technological models of global development, and freeing politics for integral and interdisciplinary approaches so as to deal appropriately with different aspects of the crises based on a different kind of logic. It will require agreement on systems of government to handle the whole range of the issues bearing on "global commons" and ultimately the establishment of a true world political authority (175). It will require pooling all the resources of human wisdom together wherever that wisdom is found, encouraging dialogue among different sciences as well as between science and religion, for the sake of the common good of all humanity and all creation.[6]

All these are contingent on the formation of "political will" (166) on the regional, national, and global scale, in order to make

---

6. See paras. 189, 190, 194, 197, 201.

effective and wise changes in the traditional ways things are done. Here, it is imperative to spread the recognition that we are living in an interconnected and interdependent world, wherein we have a shared responsibility for both one another and the natural world, our common home. Pope Francis has been stressing that political involvement based on the common good and universal fraternity is an increasingly compelling and indispensable way of practicing charity today. "Love for society and commitment to the common good are outstanding expressions of a charity which affects not only relationships between individuals but also macro-relationships, social, economic and political ones" (231). The "bold cultural revolution" in our way of looking at the world also requires a bold political revolution in our way of acting in the world. Political praxis for the common good (based on the universal communion of all creation in the triune God) constitutes part of that revolution in our age, when radically distorted anthropocentric priorities threaten the integrity of both humanity and creation to the violation of the creative and redeeming love of the triune God.

IV. The Cultivation of Simplicity as the Ecological Virtue

The cosmic solidarity of all creatures in the triune God requires not only the praxis of political love for the sake of the common good, but also the cultivation of a new way of living, a new spirituality, a new set of virtues that will nurture new habits of thinking, desiring, and feeling that are more appropriate to the integral demand of the ecological. Many changes are indeed necessary at many levels, as discussed above, but "it is we human beings above all who need to change" (202). We need to develop new convictions, new attitudes and forms of life for a greater sense of community and communion, which poses a great cultural, spiritual, and educational challenge for the renewal of humanity. That is to say, we need, both as individuals and as communities, a profound conversion of heart to this ecological way of life. This conversion is twofold—a conversion to gratitude and gratuitousness based on the recognition that the world is God's loving gift, which invites us to imitate God's generosity in self-sacrifice and good works, and a conversion to the loving awareness that we are joined to the rest of the universe in "a splendid universal communion, [wherein we are] conscious of the bonds with which the Father has linked us to all beings" (220).

Ecological conversion requires a new lifestyle characterized by responsible simplicity of life based on grateful contemplation of God, concern for the needs of others, and the protection of the environment. It involves liberation from compulsive consumerism that seeks to fill the emptiness of the heart with things but that always fails to do so because our heart longs for something more, something divine (205, 206). It means overcoming the dynamics of dominion and the accumulation of pleasures, finding joy and contentment in what is less, detachment from possession, freedom from the distractions of ever new consumer goods, moderation and sobriety that finds happiness in small things. Freedom from obsession with consumption and detachment from wealth and power are part of the ancient wisdom shared by many religions, which we have to learn to appreciate again in our ecological age. A life of simplicity is paradoxically a way of living life to the fullest because it is no longer dominated by non-essential distractions. Such a life is one of inner peace in harmony with nature, with a restored capacity for appreciating its wonders through the noise, distractions, and glitters of the consumerist world, and above all for contemplating the creator living among us. Without this integrity of human life, there is no integrity of ecosystems. The simple life is a life that breaks with the logic of violence, exploitation, and selfishness. "In the end, a world of exacerbated consumption is at the same time a world which mistreats life in all its forms" (230).[7]

In this ecological conversion, we cannot overestimate the importance of the conversion of the "heart." In a world where everything is connected, concern for the environment must be

---

7. See paras. 144, 195, 203, 204, 205, 206, 207, 208, 211, 214, 222, 223, 224.

joined with a sincere love for fellow human beings, and vice versa. When our "hearts" are truly open to the universal communion of things, they cannot exclude anything and anyone. Our indifference or cruelty toward fellow creatures will sooner or later affect our treatment of our fellow humanity. The reason is that we have "only one heart" (92). The same cruelty to animals will also lead to cruelty to human beings. Peace, justice, and the integrity of creation are "three absolutely connected themes" (92), and they are so connected in a most crucial way in the unity of the human "heart." Ecological conversion requires the conversion of the heart to the universal communion of all things in God.[8]

Parallel Confucian Themes

Are there Confucian themes that may be considered parallel to the four Catholic themes just mentioned?[9] Confucianism and Catholicism are two different religions with different doctrines, histories, and ultimate horizons, and we cannot reasonably expect identity of doctrines between them on all four points. It is possible, however, to discover four themes that *point in the same direction* (even if they are conceptualized differently in different contexts), which can perhaps make dialogue between these two traditions both plausible and fruitful.

---

8. See paras. 91, 205, 226.

9. This section reproduces almost verbatim, with slight modifications, my discussion of Confucianism in "Rethinking Justification by Faith Alone in the Era of Globalization: A Confucian Perspective," in *Journal of Ecumenical Studies* 54:1 (2019): 53–63. Reprinted here with permission of the University of Pennsylvania Press.

I. The Absolute Primacy of the *Dao* or Way of Heaven

As we have seen, the first issue addressed in the aforementioned encyclical in its analysis of the ecological crisis was a critique of its main culprit—namely, the anthropocentrism that underlies the technological paradigm. This paradigm dominates human life today, wreaking havoc on both the integrity of human life and that of the natural world. In this regard, Confucianism is at one with Catholicism: power, wealth, honor, and pleasure are not the highest values. Furthermore, the human will, whether individual or collective, is not the highest law or the ultimate source of what is real, what is good, and what is right. Confucianism is based on the worship of heaven (*tian*, 天) as the ultimate source of all reality, the basis of all order, the ultimate source of all movement and change in the world. The highest imperative of human life is to obey and follow the way (*dao*, 道) and the will or mandate (*ming*, 命) of heaven in all things. The Neo-Confucians developed the symbol of heaven into the triad of *taiji* (太極), *li* (理), and *qi* (氣). *Taiji* is the Great Ultimate from which all things originate. It contains both *li* and *qi*—*li* standing for the ultimate ordering or structuring principle or reason of the world, *qi* for the ultimate principle of vitality and change.[10] *Dao* refers to the order or structure of the world in which heaven manifests its governing will according to its own *li* or reason. Philosophical inquiry, in the proper sense, means investigating precisely this *li* or reason or structure of things as manifestation of the *li* of heaven (*tianli*, 天理). Morality means following the *dao* of heaven (*tiandao*, 天道) that manifests its will or mandate in the nature of things (*xing*, 性), both in the cosmos and in human beings. This *dao* and this *xing* are already *given*, and it is the role of human

---

10. For an analysis of the Neo-Confucian triad of *Taiji, Li,* and *Qi*, and a comparison with the Trinitarian theology of St. Thomas Aquinas, see Anselm K. Min, "The Trinity of Aquinas and the Triad of Zhu Xi: Some Comparative Reflections," in *Word and Spirit: Renewing Christology and Pneumatology in a Globalizing World*, eds. Anselm K. Min and Christoph Schwoebel (Berlin: Walter de Gruyter, 2014), 151–69.

reason to discover and recognize them by reflecting on the human heart (*xin*, 心), not, as in modern Western anthropocentrism, to "constitute" (Kant, Husserl), "produce" (Marx), "construct" (postmodernism), "invent" (Derrida), or "imagine" (Anderson) them. The order of the universe, life and death, wealth and rank, and even the success or failure of the *dao* in history: all of these depend on the will or providence of heaven (12.5, 14.38, 6.8).[11]

It is well known that Confucius was rather reluctant to speak about heaven. However, he did believe that he had received a mission and a power from heaven to teach its *dao* at a time when there was a massive decline in the observance of the *dao* in entire societies. It is this sense of personal mission that also gave him the courage not to fear any human attempts to discredit, hurt, or kill him (7.22, 9.5). He trusted that heaven knew and appreciated what he was doing, even if kings and princes did not (14.37). Human beings can deceive one another but not heaven, who knows and sees all things (9.11, 14.37). He even says that "those who offend against heaven have none to appeal to" (3.13), a clear indication of his personal sense of awe before the moral majesty of heaven. In fact, Confucius says there are three things to be feared and treated with awe: the will of heaven, great persons who are great because they observe the will of heaven, and the words of holy sages (聖賢) who reveal that will (16.8). His reticence about heaven, I believe, is an expression not of his agnosticism but of his profound reverence for its transcendence, which is more an object of silent, reverent contemplation than that of facile and noisy speculation (5.12). That is, his silence was a way of honoring, in the spirit of Gregory of Nyssa, what transcends human speech and thought.[12]

---

11. Heretofore, all references in parentheses, unless indicated otherwise, are from the *Analects* of Confucius.
12. Gregory of Nyssa, *Against Eunomius*, III, 5: "By what name can I describe the incomprehensible? By what speech can I declare the unspeakable? Accordingly, since the deity is too excellent and too lofty to be expressed in words, we have learned to honor in silence what transcends speech and thought."

For Confucianism, the proper role of the human being is to cultivate one's humanity by reflecting on one's heart and one's human nature—with which one is endowed by heaven—and to become a person of virtue (the fulfillment of humanity), especially the virtue of humaneness or *ren* (仁), the root of all virtues. The foremost concern of the authentic person or *junzi* (君子) is to center his life on the will and *dao* of heaven, to meditate on it with great reverence and awe (16.8), to embody it in his own life, and to spread it among fellow human beings in society (15.30). In light of this *dao*, he examines his heart in these regards every day: whether he was loyal (*chung*) (忠) to others, sincere with friends (*xin*) (信), and whether he practiced the lessons of the ancient sages that had been transmitted (1.4). All the Confucian virtues—humaneness (仁), righteousness (義), wisdom (智), reverence (禮), reciprocity (恕), etc.—are ways of fulfilling the *dao* of heaven as manifested in human nature, and thus ways of being truly human. To be moral is the human thing to do for human beings. The virtuous person does the right thing neither because she feels commanded to do so against her human nature (Kant) nor because it will produce the greatest benefit to the greatest number in terms of pleasure and pain (J. S. Mill) nor because we implicitly contract to do so in order to produce certain goods and avoid certain evils (Hobbes, Rawls), but simply because doing so is the fulfilling outflow of our human nature (人性), as endowed by heaven. In short, "the ultimate justification" or foundation for human morality is the *dao* of heaven, not the human will to power, wealth, and pleasure, whether expressed individually or collectively.[13] Confucianism completely rejects modern Western anthropocentrism and its will to dominate and exploit.

---

13. Tu Weiming and Dsaisaku Ikeda, *New Horizons in Eastern Humanism: Buddhism, Confucianism and the Quest for Global Peace* (London: I. B. Tauris, 2011), 109.

II. The Cosmic Unity of Heaven, Earth, and Humanity

The second point expressed in the encyclical is the need for a conversion to a radically different perspective on life, based on the recognition of the interdependence of all things, including a sense of "the universal communion of all things" in the cosmos. In some sense, the ancient Confucian vision of the unity and harmony of heaven, earth, and humanity (*tianrenhei*, 天人合一) or the grand union of all things (*datong*, 大同) seems like a doctrine almost made-to-order for our ecological age. Many think that this is the most significant contribution that Confucianism can make to the global community today.[14] Human beings are not at the center of the universe with the freedom to exploit it at will; they too must subject themselves to the *dao* of that unity. *Tianrenhei* means that there is a universal or cosmic feeling-with or sympathy among all the different beings, stones and rocks, plants, animals, and human beings. Each entity has an internal connection to all other things in terms of certain primordial sympathy or feeling-with. The goal of the *junzi* is to cultivate and realize this unity in his person. All the human virtues of Confucianism are ways of realizing this fundamental unity of the universe.

How is this unity manifested? One of the early Neo-Confucians, Cheng Hao (程顥) (1032–1085), argued that the feeling of cosmic sympathy is the culmination of the virtue of *ren*—the basic human virtue, which abolishes all opposition between self and other by opening the self to the world, regarding oneself as "one body with the universe."[15] One of the human roots of *ren*, according to

---

14. Ibid., 105.

15. Wing-Tsit Chan, *A Source Book in Chinese Philosophy* (Princeton, NJ: Princeton University Press, 1963), 523–24; see also his uncle, Chang Tsai's (1020–1077) (張載) similar declaration: "Heaven is my father and Earth is my mother, and even such a small creature as I finds an intimate place in their midst. Therefore that which fills the universe I regard as my body and that which directs the universe I consider as my nature. All people are my brothers and sisters, and all things are my companions," in ibid., 497.

Mencius, is the capacity to commiserate with others in pain, and it was Wang Yang Ming (王陽明), the sixteenth-century Neo-Confucian (1472–1529), who utilized this concept as an argument for the sympathetic unity of all things, whereby we are "one body with all things." As one cannot help feeling alarm and commiseration when seeing a child about to fall into a well, we cannot help feeling the anguish of unbearability when hearing the cries of birds and animals about to be slaughtered. Likewise, we cannot but feel pity when seeing plants broken and destroyed, as we also feel regret when seeing tiles and stones shattered and crushed. Our sense of commiseration is not limited to our own species or sentient beings; it extends to all things, including plants and stones. These feelings are not the result of deliberate effort, but are something natural and integral to our humanity, part of our "heaven-given nature." We form "one body" with heaven, earth, and all things (天地萬物一體論). We should therefore regard the world as one family and the country as one person. This is how I realize my true humanity, my true human nature. This is what the talk about "regulation of the family," "ordering the state," and "bringing peace to the world" (修身濟家治國平天下) aims at. That is, as Tu Weiming puts it, one's self-realization as a human being must transcend not only one's egoistic but also anthropological structure, and "unless one can realize the nature of all things to form a trinity with Heaven and Earth, one's self-realization cannot be complete."[16] The realization of the unity of heaven and earth is what Confucianism is ultimately about.[17]

---

16. Tu Weiming, *Humanity and Self-Cultivation: Essays in Confucian Thought* (Boston, MA: Cheng & Tsui Company, 1998), 97; also 86.

17. Chan, *A Source Book*, 659–61; *The Philosophy of Wang Yang-Ming*, trans. Frederick Goodrich Henke (Chicago: Open Court, 1916), 204–6. On the anthropocosmic, holistic approach of Confucianism, see Tu Weiming, "A Spiritual Turn in Philosophy: Rethinking the Global Significance of Confucian Humanism," *Journal of Philosophical Research* 37 (2012): 389–401, and "Rooted in Humanity, Extended to Heaven: The 'Anthropocosmic' Vision in Confucian Thought," *Harvard Divinity Bulletin* 36:2 (2008): 58–68.

What, then, is the source of this cosmic feeling of unity with all things? To this question, two metaphysical explanations are generally given. One is the pervasive constitutive presence of *qi* (氣), the vital force responsible for all the changes and movements in the world. All modalities of being are made of *qi* with varying degrees of spirituality, and human life is part of this cosmic flow of *qi* and thus organically connected with rocks, plants, and animals. As Tu Weiming puts it, "All modalities of being are made of *qi*, all things cosmologically share the same consanguinity with us, and are thus our companions."[18] The second metaphysical explanation is the sharing of *li* (理) by all things. The *li* of heaven (*tianli*, 天理) is present in the *li* or nature of things and their movements, and the role of the human being is to investigate this *li* or objective structure of things and conform his actions to it. The human being is to have reverence for this *li* of heaven as he would have piety towards his parents. The *li* or *dao* of heaven comprehends both the natural and the moral order, and it is the human being whose role is to mediate the two.[19]

III. The Politics of *Minben* or Government for the People

The third point highlighted in the encyclical is the compelling need for a politics that will put into effect the universal communion of all things or *tianrenhei*—that is, a politics of the common good with a preferential option for the poor and damaged nature. Here again, Confucianism provides parallel insights pointing in the same direction even though it does not use the same language

---

18. Tu Weiming, "The Continuity of Being: Chinese Visions of Nature," in *Confucianism and Ecology: The Interrelation of Heaven, Earth, and Humans*, eds. Mary Evelyn Tucker and John Berthrong (Cambridge, MA: Harvard University Center for the Study of World Religions, 1998), 116.
19. Joseph A. Adler, "Response and Responsibility: Chou Tun-I and Confucian Resources for Environmental Ethics," in Tucker and Berthrong, 123–42; Tu, *Humanity and Self-Cultivation*, 86–97.

or same concepts. It is peculiar to Confucianism that it has been political from the very beginning; politics is not an afterthought. Both Confucius and Mencius spent all their lives roaming the states of their time and trying to reform society by transforming the politics of power into a politics of virtue. This concern for politics and public affairs is based on the fact that the *dao* of heaven was meant to govern all things, private and public, human and natural, secular and sacred (to use the Western language of duality); the *dao* of heaven limited to a particular sphere of life would not be the true *dao* of heaven.

By the same token, politics means government according to the *dao* of heaven and therefore government by virtue. The art of ruling consists in doing what is right (*cheng*) (正) because what is right has a certain irresistible quality (12.17). It is far better to rule with *dao* and *li* (禮) or rules of propriety in social relations than with laws and threats of punishment. Ruling with virtue arouses a sense of shame among the people and inspires them willingly to pursue what is right, while ruling with laws and punishments will only lead them to fear and to try to avoid punishments but without any sense of shame (2.3). Virtue is more attractive and effective than force (12.19). If the ruler does what is right, all will go well even if he does not give orders; but if he does not do what is right, he will not be obeyed even if he does give orders (13.6). When the ruler loves and observes the rule of propriety, the people will be easy to govern (14.44). The ultimate test of good government, for Confucius, is that it makes the people happy and attracts people from far away (13.16). The Confucian politics of virtue is also a politics of people or popularity in the proper sense of genuine concern for the human needs of the people, and there is a strong confidence that government by virtue is precisely what makes the people happy. The heart of the people (民心) reveals the heart of heaven (天心).

Mencius developed this concept into a theory of *minben* (民本主義) or people first—that the people are the foundations of the state, that the sovereign exists for the people, not the other way around. Of the three things that make up the state, people are the most important, the spirits of the land and grain (guardians of the territory) come second, and the ruler comes last (*Mencius*, 7B14). The way of the true king or *wangdao* (王道), as opposed to the way of the tyrant or *badao* (霸道), is to govern with *ren* and *righteousness*, without which the ruler ceases to be legitimate and can be overthrown. *Ren* (仁) is the dwelling for human beings to rest in, righteousness (義) the right path for them to walk. Seeking what is to one's own interest and profit, like killing the innocent and taking what is not one's own, is the source of all political evil. The virtuous ruler must rise above fame, wealth, and power. Above all, the true ruler seeks to share in the joys and anxieties of the people (與民同樂). All legitimate rule derives from the mandate of heaven, but the mandate of heaven is expressed through the people, their joys and sorrows, the test of whether the ruler is ruling with *ren* and righteousness. Rulers who lose the heart of the people lose their heavenly mandate, justifying their overthrow. True rulers will secure the basic material needs of the people, emphasize good farming policies and fair taxation, and provide people with good moral education, showing a preferential *ren* for the most unfortunate of their time—namely, aged men without wives, aged women without husbands, aged persons without children, and children without parents.[20] It goes without saying that politics must respect the integrity of nature. Just as virtue is an expression of true humanity in accordance with the will of heaven and its *dao*, so the government by virtue is itself part of the larger, cosmic context as determined by that heavenly *dao*. That is to say, government of human beings must be located within the context of *tianrenhei* (天人合一), the cosmic unity or harmony of heaven, earth, and humanity.

---

20. See *Mencius*, 4A10, 7A33, 7A11, 1A2, 1A1, 1A4, 1B8, 1A3, 4A9.

IV. The Life of the *Junzi* as a Model of Simplicity

The last point highlighted in the encyclical is the need for a new spirituality, a new way of living demanded by an ecological conversion to the universal communion of all things in God, and this was called the virtue of simplicity. Simplicity, however, is not a single virtue and is not so listed on either the Christian or the Confucian list of virtues. It is, rather, a composite of many elements: detachment from greed, pleasure, honor, and power; liberation from the distractions and competitiveness of the consumerist world that gives inner peace; freedom from the compulsions of the technocratic paradigm of mastery and domination, which enables us to seek peace and harmony with our fellow creatures, human and non-human; and the spiritual freedom to appreciate the gratuity and givenness of nature and to thank the maker of all things for that gift of existence. Taken as a composite virtue, I am inclined to think that the life of the Confucian *junzi* is a perfect model of simplicity.

The basic reason why the *junzi* models a life of simplicity is that the highest imperative of life is to live according to the *dao* of heaven and to honor that *dao* by cultivating different virtues in different contexts—particularly, the four cardinal virtues of humaneness, righteousness, wisdom, and reverence, as well as the virtue of reciprocity. These virtues are ends in themselves, ways of following the *dao* and realizing our humanity; they are not subject to anything higher or extrinsic, such as profit, honor, wealth, or power. The authentic person also cultivates indifference to and rises above these extrinsic motivations. The life of virtue contains an intrinsic critique of, protection against, and liberation from the distractions and temptations of these worldly values. Cultivating the virtues means educating the *heart* (心); purifying it of all that goes against humaneness; opening it further and further to what is righteous, wise, and reverential to others; and expanding its reciprocal sensibilities to all things. It means being free from the complications and illusions of pursuing power, wealth, and honor in the eyes of the world, and being free enough to enter into oneself and meditate on oneself and all other things in the light of the ultimate end of all things—the *dao* and *li* of heaven. The *junzi*, therefore, does all things simply and unpretentiously without worrying about what others may think.

A Catholic-Confucian Dialogue

This survey of parallel views on the four central issues of the encyclical between Catholicism and Confucianism, I think, sufficiently suggests substantive affinities between the two religions. I would like to close this essay by elaborating five of those affinities that are quite significant for the continuing dialogue of the two.

The first is the common rejection of modern Western anthropocentrism. The human will is not the ultimate norm of human action. The ultimate norm is something that transcends the human will and human reason, individual or collective. It is called heaven and its *dao* and *li* in Confucianism, God and God's eternal law in Catholicism. Of course, these two conceptions of heaven and God are not identical. The Christian God is the creator of all things from nothing, omnipotent, omniscient, and omnipresent, revealing himself in history, a community of triune persons, Father, Son, and the Holy Spirit, one of whom became incarnate in the humanity of Jesus in order to redeem all of humanity and creation. The Confucian "heaven" is not as conceptually developed as the Christian God, and while it is quite true that heaven is not the omnipotent "creator" of the world or a triune God, it is also the ultimate source of the reality of the world and provider of its order and movement, omniscient, omnipresent, and providential, clearly a "personal" being equipped with his own knowledge and will. Despite all the undeniable differences between the two concepts, it is clear that the Confucian heaven is transcendent enough to be considered "divine," and it is no wonder that Catholicism has long adopted "the lord of heaven" as a reference to God and called itself "the religion of the lord of heaven" (*Tianzhu jiao*) (天主教) in both

China and Korea. The very title of the first significant Catholic commentary on Confucianism, *The True Meaning of the Lord of Heaven* (*Tianzhu shiyi*, 天主實義) by Matteo Ricci, is a clear testimony to this. While conceptually different, both conceptions of the divine point in the direction of transcendence. Both religions agree that it is this transcendent being that is the ultimate source of the moral law and moral values, and that it is the duty of human reason and human freedom to discern and observe this moral law. What the Apostle Paul says about God is exactly true of Confucianism: "ever since the creation of the world his invisible nature, namely, his eternal power and deity, has been clearly perceived *in the things that have been made*" (Rom 1:18, emphasis added).

The second affinity to be noted is that both religions agree that the *dao* or will of the divine is manifested through the nature of things (*xing*, 性) as endowed by heaven or God, and that it is the role of human reason to consult this nature of things to determine what is right, what is good, and what is true. Confucianism also stresses the fact that this nature of things is especially found in the primordial tendencies of the human heart (*sin*, 心), which also finds an echo in Paul: God, who "shows no partiality" (Rom 2:11), has his law "written on their hearts" (Rom 2:15). We cannot neglect the similarity between the Confucian emphasis on the "heart" and the same emphasis in the Augustinian and Franciscan traditions of Catholicism. While it is true that Catholicism is a religion of revelation and recognizes divine revelation as a source of knowledge not otherwise available to human reason, it is important to note that both Confucianism and Catholicism also belong to the tradition of natural law or law based on the nature of things as endowed by the divine and to the tradition of virtue ethics based on the cultivation of that nature. For Aquinas, when God creates things, God creates them with their own natures, essences, or *lis* as intrinsic principles of their activity. These natures constitute the natural law or law of nature, which in turn is a participation in and a reflection of the eternal law of God or, in Confucian terminology, the eternal *dao* of heaven. In Trinitarian terms, this eternal law is contained in and "appropriated" to the Logos or *li* of God. These are profound similarities that are not always fully appreciated, and should be the subject of a special dialogue between the two traditions.

The third affinity to note is that between the Confucian unity of heaven, earth, and humanity and the Christian communion of all things in the triune God. Again, I think both traditions point in the same direction in a way distinctive to each. Without using Christian Trinitarian language, Confucianism speaks of the entire universe as "one body" sharing in the universal sympathy or feeling-with, based on the common participation of all things in the primordial *li* and *qi*. It advocates the extension of the compassionate "heart" of *ren* to all things in the universe. Catholicism, on the other hand, mobilizes all the conceptual resources of the theology of the Trinity, and presents a universe whose entities are joined to one another and to God as dynamic reflections of the relating love of the triune God as subsisting relations. All creatures participate in Christ, the "recapitulation" of all things, and in the Holy Spirit, the divine *qi*, whose function is to give life to things precisely by ordering and connecting things to one another and to God on the model of Christ, the divine *li*. For Confucianism, the world is "one body," for Christianity it is so as "the body of Christ." Pope Francis also advocates the opening of our "hearts" to the entire universe.

The fourth affinity to note and further explore is the position of both traditions on the purpose of politics and the care for the marginalized of society. The idea of the public as the realm of politics, and the pursuit of the public interest, public good, or common good as the ultimate justification of politics, have been constants in the Western political tradition since Plato and Aristotle, and Catholicism also belongs to that tradition with appropriate theological modifications and interpretations. The Confucian tradition, as far as I know, has not used the term "common good" as the purpose of politics, but it has always distinguished between what belongs to the sphere of the public (公) and what belongs to that of the private (私), and severely condemned the abuse of the public, official power of the state for the sake of promoting private interests. The ideal public servant has been portrayed as someone who remains incorruptible despite all the temptations to acquire power and wealth for his own family or group, and is devoted to promoting the good of the people as a matter of principle.[21] Catholicism defines the common good as the sum of the basic conditions for decent human life and insists on including, under the impact of recent liberation theology, the preferential option for the marginalized of society. The Confucian tradition, as pointed out earlier, extends the principle of humaneness or compassion (ren, 仁) to a group of people who are considered the most vulnerable by the standard of the family-oriented, agricultural society: aged men without wives, aged women without husbands, aged persons without children, and children without parents. For various historical reasons, Confucianism has been political from the very beginning, and has tried to implement the idea of government by virtue. In Catholicism, by contrast, "political" theology in the sense of the central concern of theology as such is a relatively late phenomenon—even though interest in theological reflection on earthly kingdoms is as ancient as Augustine's *City of God* and Aquinas's treatises on law and kingship. This topic is worthy of further exploration.

Finally, the idea of the simple life also offers a fitting subject of mutual dialogue. Both traditions encourage a life of restraint and moderation because both recognize, with or without a doctrine of original sin, the perennial tendency of the human heart to seek more than what is truly good for them, to seek more than one already has, and to enter into a mutual struggle with one another, in the realm of honor, wealth, pleasure, and power. Restraining and moderating oneself, therefore, has been considered the essential condition for a truly humane life. The four cardinal virtues in the Catholic tradition—temperance, courage, prudence, and justice—are ways of practicing that self-restraint, as are the Confucian four root

---

21. On the importance of the public in ancient Confucian political philosophy, see further Joseph Chan, *Confucian Perfectionism: A Political Philosophy for Modern Times* (Princeton, NJ: Princeton University Press, 2014), 225–31.

virtues—humaneness, righteousness, wisdom, and courteousness. The philosophical conceptualizations and ultimate motivations of these virtues may differ in each tradition, but together, they are requisites for liberation from excessive attachment to pleasure, honor, wealth, and power, the prime source for human tensions and conflicts, and from all the complications and illusions generated by those attachments and tensions. They are requisites for the simple life. Each tradition also adds its own motivations for practicing those virtues to an extraordinary or heroic degree, and each tradition has its own list of exemplars of these virtues called saints and sages.

Concluding Reflections

There is far more to say on the similarities between the two traditions on the relevant points of the encyclical than what I have said, and I can only conclude by saying that the dialogue must be institutionalized so that it may gain in intensity, regularity, thoroughness, and reciprocity. Thus far, to my knowledge, the dialogue between Confucianism and Christianity has been rather sporadic and contingent, depending on the interests of scholars who happen to be specialists. Perhaps it is time that the Church showed as much interest in the Confucian-Christian dialogue as it has recently shown in intra-Christian dialogues with Lutherans, Methodists, Reformed churches, Anglicans, and the Orthodox churches. The Christian-Confucian dialogue is all the more compelling with the churches in East Asia, which has been so thoroughly Confucian for over two millennia. There are two things I would note about this East Asian dialogue.

(1) East Asian churches should take much more seriously than they have the weight of the Confucian tradition in which East Asian Christianity itself has been rooted. Christians may believe in different things than their Confucian friends in their more self-conscious, reflective moments, but in their less self-conscious moments and in their behavior they are more Confucian than

Christian, for good or ill, as many scholars point out. Confucianism is in their very blood, in their very habits of the heart. Recently, both traditions have been heavily challenged and eroded by the avalanche of capitalist materialism and nihilism, but the tradition seems to live on more powerfully than many people suspect. It is crucial, therefore, to examine the cultural residue of Confucianism in the mentality of Christians, to distinguish between what is authentic and what is inauthentic in that residue, and to promote a closer mutual understanding between authentic Confucianism and authentic Christianity to the eventual benefit to both. Without denying the many negative aspects of Confucianism so often stressed by political reformers in China and Korea since the beginning of the last century, I am inclined to argue that there are many positive aspects of that tradition that Catholics can still learn from and incorporate into their own self-understanding. The points of similarity mentioned earlier belong to these positive aspects.

(2) In promoting the dialogue between these two traditions, it is important to remember that both are living traditions. Catholics are very sensitive to this because they have become aware of how their own church has been changing since Vatican II. They are not often aware of the changes that Confucianism is undergoing, at least among the scholars of Confucianism. There has been so much going on in Confucian scholarship, especially during the last several decades, and we have been observing the emergence of what is called New Confucianism. New Confucians have been both updating Confucian doctrines in line with the demands of modern society in the matter of human rights, women's equality, political constitution, and virtue ethics, while also preserving and intensifying the positive aspects of their tradition. It is crucial to understand Confucianism not only in its classic expressions and historical developments but also in its contemporary aggiornamento. From all of the scholarly publications, I get the impression that there is a very vigorous scholarly interest, in both China and the West, in a transforming reappropriation of the Confucian tradition as an alternative to both secular liberal individualism and Western

Christianity. Like all religions, Confucianism is also in the throes of revolutionary changes imposed by globalization. Confucianism, it must be remembered, is not fixed at the stage of its founders like Confucius and Mencius, but has been changing ever since and even more so today.[22] A dialogue between the two traditions must take into account precisely these revolutionary changes going on in the world to make the dialogue relevant for today and to keep it from becoming a conversation among antiquarians.

Bibliography

Chan, Joseph. *Confucian Perfectionism: A Political Philosophy for Modern Times*. Princeton, NJ: Princeton University Press, 2014.

Chan, Wing-Tsit. *A Source Book in Chinese Philosophy*. Princeton, NJ: Princeton University Press, 1963.

Confucianism and Ecology: The Interrelation of Heaven, Earth, and Humans, edited by Mary Evelyn Tucker and John Berthrong. Cambridge, MA: Harvard University Center for the Study of World Religions, 1998.

---

22. For just some examples of modernizing interpretations of Confucianism, see Wm. Theodore de Bary & Tu Weiming (eds.), *Confucianism and Human Rights* (New York: Columbia University Press, 1998); Stephen C. Angle, *Contemporary Confucian Political Philosophy* (Malden, MA: Polity, 2012); Daniel A. Bell (ed.), *Confucian Political Ethics* (Princeton, NJ: Princeton University Press, 2008); Chan, *Confucian Perfectionism*; Tucker and Berthrong (eds.), *Confucianism and Ecology*; Robin R. Wang (ed.), *Chinese Philosophy in an Era of Globalization* (Albany, NY: SUNY Press, 2004); Tze-ki Hon and Kristin Stapleton (eds.), *Confucianism for the Contemporary World: Global Order, Political Plurality, and Social Action* (Albany, NY: SUNY Press, 2017); and Roger T. Ames and Peter D. Hershock (eds.), *Confucianism for a Changing World Cultural Order* (Honolulu: University of Hawaii Press, 2018).

Min, Anselm K. "The Trinity of Aquinas and the Triad of Zhu Xi: Some Comparative Reflections." In *Word and Spirit: Renewing Christology and Pneumatology in a Globalizing World*, edited by Anselm K. Min and Christoph Schwoebel, 151–70. Berlin: Walter de Gruyter, 2014.

Weiming, Tu. *Humanity and Self-Cultivation: Essays in Confucian Thought*. Boston, MA: Cheng & Tsui Company, 1998.

———. "A Spiritual Turn in Philosophy: Rethinking the Global Significance of Confucian Humanism." *Journal of Philosophical Research* 37 (2012): 389–401.

———, and Ikeda, Dsaisaku. *New Horizons in Eastern Humanism: Buddhism, Confucianism, and the Quest for Global Peace*. London: I. B. Tauris, 2011.

AFTERWORD

The Truth Shall Set You Free!
Cardinal Robert Sarah

In the first place, my gratitude and congratulations to Dr. Reynolds and Dr. Casarella for their herculean efforts to bring this marvelous project to fruition. The breadth of the project and the wonderful exchange of views of participants from around the world is an invitation to us all to deepen, once again, our approach to these questions. Indeed, I see this work as a summons to a fresh and newly confident exchange, which flows from the prayer of our Lord himself that all peoples and nations may come to know and love and serve the One True God and Jesus Christ his Son, our Lord, indeed, *ut unum sint!*[1]

Christians and, in particular, those who have dedicated themselves to engage in this work on behalf of the Catholic Church must never set aside the conviction that underlies all subsequent good to be hoped for: *The Truth shall set you free!*[2] For truly, the observation of *Nostra Aetate* is, it seems to me, no less valid today—and perhaps more:

---

1. Cf. Jn 17:21.
2. Jn 8:32.

> Men expect from the various religions answers to the unsolved riddles of the human condition, which today, even as in former times, deeply stir the hearts of men: What is man? What is the meaning, the aim of our life? What is moral good, what is sin? Whence suffering and what purpose does it serve? Which is the road to true happiness? What are death, judgment and retribution after death? What, finally, is that ultimate inexpressible mystery which encompasses our existence: whence do we come, and where are we going?[3]

If I may be bold, the gift that Holy Mother Church has to give to all people of good will is objective and life-changing, for individuals, families (not least of all in my own case!), and societies. Plain and simple, Christianity lifts humanity to new and previously unknown heights. Christian charity in transforming individuals transforms cities—indeed whole societies—and makes them better places to live. Christianity summons us all to greatness, to the perfection of our heavenly Father.[4] It should come as no surprise then that we are "compelled" to proclaim it; indeed, woe to me if I do not preach it![5] In the majesty of the divine plan, God chose us, the baptized, to go forth into the world—yes, us—even with all of our failings, to proclaim "Jesus Christ and him crucified,"[6] and to be the instruments, by our words and by our lives, by which they will hear his voice and come to know, love, and serve him.

It is precisely this conviction that gives full purpose to our exchanges. As Pope St. Paul VI famously proclaimed before the General Assembly of the United Nations, the Church is "an expert

---

3. *Nostra Aetate*, Declaration on the Relation of the Church to Non-Christian Religions, October 28, 1965, para. 1.
4. Cf. Mt 5:48.
5. Cf. 1 Cor 9:16.
6. 1 Cor 2:2.

in humanity."[7] In order, however, for the Church's message to reveal the pristine splendor of Jesus Christ, merciful Lord and Savior of the world, it must ever be presented without retouch, tarnish or effort to "improve" upon it. The Word of God is living and active.[8] Of course, authentic faith must ever be combined with ardent charity. As St. Gregory the Great reminds us: "It is not by faith that you will come to know him, but by love; not by mere conviction, but by action."[9] Zeal absent loving concern for our fellow man is a sort of empty proselytism doomed to fail from the beginning. Authentic dialogue is instead the fruit of intense love of God. "Shine through us, and be so in us, that every soul we come in contact with may feel your presence in our soul.... Let us praise you in the way you love best, by shining on those around us."[10]

My compliments again to the editors and authors of this fine volume. It is my sincere wish that it will be put to good use in the field for years to come.

---

7. Pope St. Paul VI, *Address to the United Nations*, October 4, 1965.
8. Cf. Heb 4:12.
9. Pope St. Gregory the Great, Homily 14, *On the Gospels*.
10. Taken from St. John Henry Newman's prayer, "Radiating Christ."

INDEX

A

Abboud, Omar, 64–65
Abraham: call of, 279–280; covenant with, 172; promise to, 198; Qur'an references of, 228–229; sacrifice of, 315, 318–319
Adams, Charles, 244
Africa. *See also specific countries:* Catholic missionary foundations within, 99–103, 119; Christianity within, 99–103, 124; colonial rule within, 107, 113, 123; evangelization within, 100–101; interreligious dialogue within, 121, 123; Islam within, 98, 103–110; Protestantism within, 116; Protestant missionaries within, 110–117; religions within, 98–99, 117–122; witch-finding movements within, 118; Zanzibar mission, 100, 101
African Independent Churches, 19
African Traditional Religion, 23–24
Ahab (king), 284
al-Kayrānawī, Rahmatullah. *See* Kayrānawī, Rahmatullah al-
al-Maḥallī, Jalāl al-Dīn. *See* Maḥallī, Jalāl al-Dīn al-
al-Naḥḥās, Abū Jaʻfar. *See* Naḥḥās, Abū Jaʻfar al-
al-Qāsimī, Jamāl al-Dīn. *See* Qāsimī, Jamāl al-Dīn al-
al-Qurṭubī, ʻAbdallāh Muḥammad. *See* Qurṭubī, ʻAbdallāh Muḥammad al-
al-Rāzī, Fakhr al-Dīn. *See* Rāzī, Fakhr al-Dīn al-
al-Suyūṭī, Jalāl al-Dīn. *See* Suyūṭī, Jalāl al-Dīn al-
al-Ṭabarī, Ibn Jarīr. *See* Ṭabarī, Ibn Jarīr al-
al-Tustarī, Sahl. *See* Tustarī, Sahl al-
al-Zamakhsharī, Abū al-Qāsim. *See* Zamakhsharī, Abū al-Qāsim al-
Amin, Idi, 109
Amrullah, Haji Abdul Malik Karim (Hamka), 239, 241, 245–246
Anglican Church, 18–19
animals, punishment and, 298–300
Annals of the Propagation of the Faith, 99–100
anthropocentrism, 331–332, 348
antisemitism, 213
apes, punishment and, 298–300
apparition, 239, 239n41
Aquinas, Thomas, 68–69, 319, 349
Arab Christians, theological opposition from, 195–196
Arabia, 309–314
ʻArafa, 315
Arafat, Yasser, 191
Argentina, 48–56, 216–218

B

Babel, 18–20, 34
Badawi, Muhammad Mustafa, 313
Bagamoyo (Tanzania), 101
Balthasar, Hans Urs von, 166, 167, 174, 176, 308
Baltus, Jean François, 77, 78
Baptism, Eucharist, and Ministry (BEM), 148, 149–150
Barth, Karl, 72, 161, 170–171, 175, 176
Bataclan attacks, 305
Bell, Richard, 227
BEM document (Baptism, Eucharist, and Ministry), 148, 149–150
Benedictine missionaries, 108–109
Benedict XVI, xii, 136
Benko, Stephen, 236n31
Bergoglian principles, 47

Index

Bergoglio, Jorge Mario. *See also* Francis (pope): as Archbishop, 61; background of, 48–49, 57; globalization viewpoint of, 64; influence of, 47–48; insights of, 34; obedience viewpoint of, 56; piety viewpoint of, 63; quote of, 53, 54–55, 56; return of, 60–61; speeches of, 221; term use by, 50–51; writings of, 61–62, 63–64, 216, 217
Beschi, Constantine, 74, 79–83, 89–90
Bible: Christian bearings towards, 274–276; divine trickery within, 283–285; intra-scriptural conversation within, 267–270; Islamic viewpoint of, 276–277; memorization of, 275; self-referentiality of, 266–267; translatability of, 273; writing of, 81
Bohr, Niels, 57
bold cultural revolution, 333, 334, 336
Bonwick, James, 243
Borghesi, Massimo, 57
Bouchet, Jean Venance, 74, 76–79, 90
Bouyer, Louis, 167
Brague, Rémi, 322
branches, roots and, 66
Britto, John de, 76
Buber, Martin, 212
Buddhism, 72–73
Buganda, 114

C

Calcutta (India), 87
Campanini, Massimo, 253–254
CAN (Christian Association of Nigeria), 20
canons, revoking of, 204–205
Carroll, Michael P., 236–237
Catholic-Confucian dialogue, 348–352
Catholicism: Africa and, 99–103; Charismatic, 90; common good and, 351; Confucianism and, 348–352; division within, 131; dual covenant position of, 198–199; global, 89–91; India and, 74–79; inter-religious dialogue and, 96–97; Judaism viewpoint of, 185–186, 204–205; Mary veneration viewpoint of, 239–240, 240n41; Protestantism and, 136–137; unity viewpoint of, 132; virtues of, 351–352
Catholic Zionism, 189, 194–195, 196, 204–208
Celli, Claudio Maria, 192
Charismatic Catholicism, 90
Cheikho, Louis, 241
Chieti document, 134–136
Christian Association of Nigeria (CAN), 20
Christianity: Africa and, 99–103, 124; branches of, 66; centrality of, 279; dialogue importance within, 155; division within, 36, 159; gentile, 201; healing of, 83–89; Hinduism and, 82–83, 87; human agency and, 275; identity and, 158; incarnation viewpoint of, 242; India and, 75, 86; Judaism and, 36–37, 158, 174–175; within Nigeria, 23–25; prayer and, 276; Qur'an and, 277–278; role of, 358
Chrysostom, John, 286
Church: divisions within, 150, 173; eschatological unity and, 175–177; Israel and, 162–164, 166–167, 169–170, 177–180; Judaism and, 164–165; mission of, 175–177; primacy within, 133–134; purpose of, xiii–xiv; rivalry within, 20–21; salvation and, 162; schism within, 158; scissions within, 157; social topics and, 150; synodality within, 133–134; unity of, 9
Church Fathers, divine trickery and, 285–287
Church Missionary Society (CMS), 18–19, 110–111
Clooney, Frank, 4
Collyridians, 234–235, 236
Comboni missionaries, 102, 105–106
commiseration, 343
Commission for Religious Relations with the Jews (CRRJ), 186–187, 192–193
common good, 351
communion, 132, 135–136
conflict, prevention of, 212

Confucianism: basis of, 339; Catholicism and, 348–352; changes within, 353–354; erosion of, 353; heart emphasis of, 349; human being role within, 341; themes of, 330, 338–348; unity viewpoint of, 342–344; virtues of, 341, 347, 352
Confucius, 340, 345
Congar, Yves, 132
conscience, morality and, xvi, 68
Consolata missionaries, 108
Cook, Michael, 225, 234
counter-witness, 36, 39
crisis of differences, 310
CRRJ (Commission for Religious Relations with the Jews), 186–187, 192–193
crucifixion, 285–286, 287–291
Cullmann, Oscar, xvn7
cultural integration, 54

D

Dale, Anthony van, 78
Dandoy, Georges, 87
Dao, primacy of, 339–341
D'Costa, Gavin, 6
"Declaration on Human Fraternity for World Peace and Living Together," 218–219
deicide, 185–186
Démann, Paul, 161, 178–179
demons, 78–79
Der Gegensatz (Guardini), 57, 58
Devaux, Théomir, 177
Diary of the Council (Congar), 132
Diez, Martino, 8
differences, respect for, 130
Dilthey, Wilhelm, 58
discipleship, 150
diversity, 12, 33–34, 40, 62
Doane, Thomas William, 243
Driesch, Hans, 58
dual covenant position, 198–199

E

eastern Africa. *See* Africa
Eastern Orthodox, PCPCU and, 133–136
ecology, 330, 331–332, 335, 336–338
ecumenical memory, 145–147, 151, 153–154
ecumenism, xviii, xiv, 9
education, 87
Epiphanius of Salamis, 236
eschatological unity, 175–177
essentialism, 322
Evangelii Gaudium: Bergoglian principles within, 47; ecumenism defined within, xiv; Islam discussion within, xviii; Judaism within, xv; polyhedron within, 34–35, 40; quote within, 130; writing of, xii
evangelization, xii, 36, 100–101, 109, 117
Ezekiel the Tragedian, 202–203

F

Faber, Peter, 45
Fadl, Khalid Abou El, 253
Farrell, Brian, 4–5
Fava, Armand, 99–100
Fernandez, Gonçalo, 90
Ferré, Methol, 49, 51, 52n42
Fessard, Gaston, 59, 60
Figueroa, Marcelo, 61–62
Fontenelle, Bernard Le Bovier de, 78
Foucauld, Charles de, xviii
France, missionaries from, 101, 111
Francis (pope). *See also* Bergoglio, Jorge Mario; polyhedron: ecumenism viewpoint of, xv, 9, 138–140; evangelization and, xii; interfaith dialogue of, 218–219, 220–221; La Sapienza speech by, 45–46; *Laudato Si*, 329–338; naming of, xii; quote of, 33, 34, 37, 38, 40–41, 42, 44–45, 129–130, 139–140, 187n5, 281–282; Reformation commemoration by, 136–137; reformation work of, 132–133; rootedness viewpoint of, 67–68; work of, 218
Francis of Assisi, xii
From Evangelist to Jesuit (Wallace), 86
Fundamental Agreement, 191

G

Gadamer, Hans Georg, 255
Gandhi, Mahatma, 10
Gentile Christianity, 201, 204
George, Timothy, 236

Index

Germany, 107, 108, 111
"The Gifts and the Calling of God are Irrevocable," 186–187, 190, 199, 204
Girard, René, 305, 306–309, 310, 325–326
globalization, 42, 43, 44, 64, 354
God: arbitrariness of, 175; as creator, 333–334, 348; deception of, 291; eternal law of, 349–350; green man and, 296–298; love of, 32–33, 65–70, 359; people of, 163; plotting of, 283–284, 295, 302; reconciliation by, 161–162; respite and, 293–295; Sabbath and, 298–300; as schemer, 296–297; sealing by, 300–301; temptation and, 281–282, 291–292; will of, 68–69
Goitein, S. D., 228
Goldziher, Ignaz, 244
goodness, branches and, 66
Gospel, overview of, xii–xiii
grafting, 165
Graham, William A., 260–261
Great Britain, 107
Greenberg, Irving, 187–188n7
green man (translation from Qu'ran of Khiḍr), 296–298
Greer, Rowan, 287
Gregory of Nyssa, 286–287, 308–309
Gregory the Great, 359
Griffith, Sidney, 237, 238
Grudem, Wayne A., 268n16
Guardini, Romano, 57, 57n49, 58–59
Gutmann, Bruno, 120

H

Hamka (Amrullah, Haji Abdul Malik Karim), 239, 241, 245–246
Hamori, Andras, 312–313
Hao, Cheng, 342
Harthi, Bushiri bin, 107
Hartman, David, 188n7
Hawting, G. R., 229
heaven, Confucianism and, 339–341, 342–344, 348–349
Hebrew Catholics, 205–206, 206n38
Hebrew language, 141–142
Hegel, Georg Wilhelm Friedrich, 54, 55
Heidegger, Martin, 58

Heschel, Abraham: influence of, 212; quote of, 207, 214–215, 221–222; writings of, 213, 216
Higgins, Godfrey, 243
Ḥijāz, 238, 238n38
Hilarion, Siegfried, 108
Hindoo Clairvoyance (Wallace), 86
Hinduism, 74–75, 82–89
Hirudayam, Ignatius, 90
Holocaust. *See* Shoah
Holy Spirit, xiii, 39–41
Hoole, Elijah, 75–76, 81–82
Horbury, William, 203
Horner, Antoine, 100
Hoyland, Robert, 317–318
Huet, Pierre-Daniel, 77
Hull, Ernest, 90
human agency, 275
humanity, original unity of, 168
humility, 29
Husserl, Edmund, 58

I

idolatry, 75, 84–85
India. *See also* Hinduism: Catholicism and, 74–79; Christianity within, 75, 86; demons and, 78–79; interreligious tensions within, 90–91; Judaism within, 73; oracles and, 78, 79; theology of, 243; William Wallace as missionary to, 83
India's Religion of Grace and Christianity Compared and Contrasted (Otto), 72–73
Indonesia, 240, 242
initial schism, 5–6, 159–168
initial unity, 162–168
interreligious dialogue, 96–97, 121, 123
interreligious encounters, 38
Isḥāq, Ibn, 235
Islam. *See also* Qur'an: Abraham and, 315; Africa and, 98, 103–110; Arabia and, 309–314; Bible viewpoint of, 276–277, 322; categorization of, xviiin12; conversion to, 271; extremism of, 123; hostile surroundings within, 248–249; human agency and, 275; jihadism and, 305–306, 306n3, 316–317,

317n32, 321; Nigeria and, 23–25; pilgrimage and, 315; poems prior to, 312–314; prayer within, 275–276; Qur'an bearings of, 274–276; rivalry within, 242–243; sacrifices within, 314–323, 326; saint veneration within, 241; salvation viewpoint of, 245; terrorism and, xvii–xviii, 106n14

Israel: Arab Christian viewpoint of, 195–196; the Church and, 162–164, 166–167, 169–170, 177–180; citizenship within, 206n38; covenantal history of, 162; grafting image and, 165; history of, 193; Jesus and, 175–176; Old Testament statements regarding, 197–198; Peace Agreement for, 191, 192; political recognition of, 191; as promised land, 187; remnant of, 176

Italy, missionaries from, 111–112

Ivereigh, Austen, 50n39, 51–52

Izutsu, Toshihiko, 300

J

Jesus. *See also* God; Holy Spirit: centrality of, 279; as covenant fulfillment, 190; crucifixion of, 285–286, 287–291; divinity of, 286–287; humility of, 272; as a Jew, 200–201; as mediator, 199; obedience of, 285; personhood of, 235; as priest, 308; as ransom, 285–286; self-referentiality of, 7; as a stone, 175–176; unity through, 169; words of, 274

Jewish Catholics, 206n38

Jewish Christians, 204

jihadism, 305–306, 306n3, 316–317, 317n33, 321

Job, 283

Johanns, Pierre, 87

John Paul II (pope), xii, 187n5

Joint International Commission, 134

Joseph, 80

Josephus, 202–203

Judaism: antisemitism of, 213; blindness within, 173–174; Catholicism viewpoint of, 185–186; Christianity and, 36–37, 158, 174–175; the Church and, 164–165; diversity within, 172; dual covenant position of, 198–199; education and, 87; grafting image and, 165; history of, 193; identity and, 170–171; India and, 73; land promise to, 197–198; messianic expectation of, 203–204; New Testament and, 168, 171, 200–204; *Nostra Aetate* and, xv; obedience within, 56–65; promises within, 187, 188–189, 202–203; Rabbinic, 201; salvation viewpoint of, 199; Shoah and, 212–214; theological status of, 193–194; traditions of, 200–201, 203, 204; violence toward, 211

junzi, simplicity and, 347–348

K

kabaka (Uganda), 109

Karlik, Estanislao, 216

Kasper, Walter, 213–214

Kayrānawī, Rahmatullah al-, 243

Kenya, 107, 110–111

Kermani, Navid, 271, 272

Kille, D. Andrew, 223–224

King, Martin Luther, 10

Kinnamon, Michael, 146–147

Kinzer, Mark, 207

kitāb, Qur'an as, 261–262

knots, symbolism of, 61

Kollman, Paul, 4

Kurien, Jacob, 148

L

Laguna, Justo, 216

Larcher, Pierre, 312

La Sapienza, 45–46

Latin America, 48–56, 52n42

Laudato Si' (Francis), 329–338

La violence et le sacré (Girard), 307

Lecker, Michael, 309–310

Leo X, 136

LeRoy, Alexandre, 120

love of God, 32–33, 65–70, 359

Lund (Sweden), 136–137

Index

Lund principle, 131
Lustiger, Jean-Marie, 205–206
Luther, Martin, 72, 136, 137
Lux, Richard, 192

M

Mackay, Alexander, 110
Madigan, Daniel A., 261–262
Maḥallī, Jalāl al-Dīn al-, 288
Mahdism, 106, 106n14
Marcionism, 168
Marguerat, Daniel, 166, 174
Marshall, David, 7
martyrdom, xviii, 115
Mary (mother of Jesus), 234–236, 237, 239–241, 239n41
Maryamiyyūn, 235
Masson, Denise, 319
Maurice, Thomas, 243
mediator, Jesus as, 199
Medinan Qur'an, 228–229
Mejía, Jorge, 216
memorization, Qur'an and Bible comparisons of, 275
memory, 137, 145–147
Mencius, 345–346
Mesonge romantique et vérité romanesque (Girard), 307
Messianic Jews, 206n38, 207
mestizaje, capacity for, 53
Meurin, Leo, 79n12
Micaiah, 284
migration, 44n27
Mill Hill missionaries, 101, 108
Min, Anslem, 8
minben, theory of, 345–346
Ming, Wang Yang, 343
missionaries: Africa and, 99–103, 119; Benedictine, 108–109; colonial rule effects to, 108; Comboni, 102, 105–106; Consolata, 108; counterproductivity of, 86; French, 111; German, 111; Italian, 111–112; Mill Hill, 101, 108; Missionaries of Africa, 101, 105–106, 108–109, 117; Nigeria and, 18–19; predispositions of, 96; Protestant, 110–117; rivalries of, 102–103, 115–116; role of, 96; slavery and, 117; Spiritans, 101, 102; Uganda conflict of, 101, 113–115; undermining by, 120; unity and, 130; Verona Fathers, 102; White Fathers, 101; witch-finding movements of, 118
Missionaries of Africa, 101, 105–106, 108–109, 117
Moltmann, Jürgen, 163–164, 178
morality, conscience and, 68
Moses, 172, 283–284, 297
Mourad, Souleiman, 317n32
Muhammad: divine revelation of, 227, 273–274, 273n23; pact by, 248–249; prayer of, 296; proclamation by, 264; quote of, 242; threat to, 290–291
multipolarity, 42–43
Murphy, Francesca Aran, 322
Muslims. *See* Islam
Mussner, Franz, 175–176
Mutesa, 109–110, 114–115

N

Naḥḥās, Abū Ja'far al-, 245
Namboodiry, Udayan, 86
nature, 332–335, 336, 349–350
Nazis, 211, 215
Neo-Confucianism, 339
Neuwirth, Angelika, 229
Nicodemus, 41
Nigeria, 17, 18–22, 23–26
Nigeria Interreligious Council (NIREC), 26
Nobili, Robert de, 73–76, 89
Nöldeke, Theodor, 226
"No Religion Is an Island" (Heschel), 213, 216
Nostra Aetate, xv, 161, 165, 357–358
"Notes on the Correct Way to Present Jews and Judaism in Preaching and Catechesis in the Roman Catholic Church," 192–195

O

obedience, 56–65
occasions of revelation, 247
Oehmen, Dom Nicholas, 157–158, 176–177
Oesterreicher, John, 163

Old Covenant, xv
Onaiyekan, Cardinal, 2
On Heaven and Earth (Bergoglio and Skorka), 63
oracles, 78, 79
Origen, 285–286
original unity, 168
Otto, Rudolf, 72–73
Our Father prayer, 281–282

P

paganism, 311
Palestinian Liberation Organization, 191
Paraclete, 33
Paris, Bataclan attacks within, 305
Parrinder, Geoffrey, 235–236
Patria Grande, 48–56, 52n42
Paul the apostle: circumcision viewpoint of, 203; division viewpoint of, 173–174; as a Jew, 200–201; writings of, 66, 192, 202, 203, 267–268, 283, 349
Paul VI (pope), xi–xii, 358–359
Pawlikowski, John T., 171–172
PCPCU (Pontifical Council for Promoting Christian Unity), 133–137
peace, xi, xvii
Pentecostal Church, 19–20
people, term use of, 50–51, 50n39
Peronism, 49
Peters, Carl, 106–107
Peterson, Erik, 176–177
Pharaoh, 283–284
Philo, 202–203
pilgrimage, rites of, 315, 316
Pius XII, 216
Podetti, Amelia, 54, 55
poems, pre-Islamic, 312–314
political love, 335–336
political will, 335–336
politics, 344–346, 350–351
polyhedron: globalization and, 43, 44; intercultural encounters of, 41–42; Latin American sources for, 47–56; metaphor of, 3, 31; unity and, 34–35, 56; work of, 40
Pontifical Biblical Commission, 200, 203
Pontifical Council for Promoting Christian Unity (PCPCU), 133–137

prayer, 11, 275–276
pre-dilection, 68–69
primacy, 133–134, 135, 136
Programme for Christian-Muslim Relations in Africa (PROCMURA), 109
Propaganda Fide, 102
prophetic inspiration, 221–222
Protestantism, 110–117, 136–137, 142n4
Przywara, Erich, 59, 59n52, 167

Q

Qāsimī, Jamāl al-Dīn al-, 234–235
Qur'an. *See also* Islam: Abrahamic references within, 228–229; applicability of, 244–253; approaches to, 226–227; Biblical comparison with, 269–270; Christian references within, 227–228, 230–232; Christian viewpoint of, 277–278; chronological reading of, 227, 231; context of, 225–233; criticism within, 225–233; crucifixion references within, 230–231, 287–291; deception viewpoint of, 291; difference theme within, 323–327; divine trickery within, 287–296; exclusivist position of, 245; exegetical problems within, 233–244; "green man" of, 296–298; historical evidence lack within, 225; inimitability of, 271; interpretation challenges of, 254–255; Jewish references within, 227–228, 230–231; killing by , 271–272; as kitāb, 261–262; Mary references within, 240; Medinan, 228–229; memorization of, 275; messenger stories within, 264; Muslim bearings towards, 274–276; non-Muslim study of, 263; occasions of revelation within, 247; polemical passages of, 227, 229, 252–253; religious plurality references within, 232–233; respite passages within, 293–295; Sabbath references to, 298–300; salvation reference within, 232, 245; scriptural beauty viewpoint within , 272; self-canonization of,

Index

265–266; self-referentiality of, 7, 263; social interaction references within, 248–252, 248n61; tolerant passages within, 223, 232–233, 245; Trinity references to, 231, 235–236; violent text within, 223–224
Qurṭubī, ʿAbdallāh Muḥammad al-, 290

R

Rabbinic Judaism, 201
Rabin, Yitzhak, 191
Rahman, Fazlur, 228
Rajamanickam, Savarimuthu, 77
Ramadan, 275
Ravenna Document, 133–134
Rāzī, Fakhr al-Dīn al-, 295
RCM (Roman Catholic Mission), 18–19
Rebora, Clemente, 67
reconciled diversity, 62
reconciliation, 161–162, 168
redemption, 161
Reformation, 80, 136–137
respite, 293–295
reunification, 170
Reynolds, Gabriel Said, 8, 237, 238, 320
Ricci, Matteo, 349
Riḍā, Muḥammad Rashīd, 242, 243–244, 248, 249, 251
Rippin, Andrew, 225
Robert, Marie-Hélène, 5
Roman Catholic Mission (RCM), 18–19
Rome, primacy and, 134, 135
rootedness, 36–37
roots, branches and, 66
Rosen, David, 187
Ruden, Sarah, 141–142

S

Sabbath, 298–300
sacrifices, 314–323, 326
sacrificial crisis, 311, 312
Sages of the Talmud, 221
Saint-Valtier, Cochet de, 77
salvation, 162, 198–199, 232, 245
Samartha, Stanley J., 144, 153–154
Satan, 281–282, 285, 292
schism, 5–6, 158, 159–168
Schoeler, Gregor, 309

scissions, 157
sealing, 300–301
Sebastian, Jayakiran, 5
Second Vatican Council, xi–xii, xviii
Segura, Ernesto, 216
Shihab, Muhammad Quraish, 252
Shoah, 212–214
Shoemaker, Stephen, 237
Siegert, Folker, 164
Simmel, Georg, 58
simplicity, 336–338, 347–348, 351–352
sin, 161, 173, 180
Sinai, Nicolai, 262
Sirry, Mun'im, 7
Skorka, Abraham, 6–7, 13, 61–62, 63–64
slavery, 117
Smith, Edwin, 120
social interaction, 248–252, 248n61
social justice, 333
social memory, 137
solidarity, 46–47, 64
Soulen, R. Kendall, 202
Sperl, Stefan, 313
Spiritans, 101, 102, 104, 108–109, 117
Spivak, Gayatri Chakravorty, 150–151
Stanley, Henry Morton, 114
Stetkevych, Suzanne Pinckney, 313
Suárez, Francisco, 45
Sultanate of Oman (Zanzibar), 103–104, 105
Suyūṭī, Jalāl al-Dīn al-, 288
synodality, 133–134, 136

T

Ṭabarī, Ibn Jarīr al-, 249
Ṭabāṭabāʾī, Muḥammad Ḥusayn: quote of, 241, 246, 247, 250; viewpoint of, 239, 240, 249, 250–251n67
Ṭālib, ʿAlī b. Abī, 254–255
Tamil language, 79
Tanganyika, 101, 107
Tanzania, missions within, 101
Tayeb, Ahmad el-, 218, 219
Taylor, John V., 120
technocratic paradigm, 331–332
Tempāvani (The Unfading Garland) (Beschi), 80, 81–82
temptation, 281–282, 291–292
theodicy, 295

theological supersessionism, 185
Thoma, Clemens, 159
Thomas, M.M., 87–88
Time/Destiny, 313
Torah, 201. *See also* Judaism
Trinity, 231, 235–236, 334, 350
Tsai, Chang, 342n15
Tustarī, Sahl al-, 302

U

Uganda, 101, 107, 109, 113–114, 115–116
UMCA (Universities' Mission to Central Africa), 111
United States, migration viewpoint within, 44n27
unity: accent upon, 170; as agenda, 169; Catholicism viewpoint of, 132; the Church and, 9; commitment to, 180; Confucianism and, 342–344; diversity within, 12, 33–34, 40; eschatological, 175–177; evangelization and, 36; foundations of, 173–174; initial, 162–168; initial schism and, 160–162; Jesus and, 169; missionaries and, 130; necessity of, 21–22; original, 168; polyhedric, 56; redemption and, 161; restoration of, 135–136; sin and, 161; universal, 169–170
universal communion, 334–335
universal unity, 169–170
Universities' Mission to Central Africa (UMCA), 111
Upadhyay, Brahmabandhab, 86–87, 88, 89

V

Verona Fathers, 102
Vētaviḻakkam (Beschi), 80–81
violence, 212, 307, 309–314
virtues, 345, 351–352
vision, minimalist, 171

W

Wallace, William, 74, 83–89, 90
Watt, Montgomery, 312
Way of Heaven, 339–341
WCC (World Council of Churches), 97n4, 138

Weiming, Tu, 343, 344
Welch, Alford, 226
Westcott, Brooke Foss, 83n19
White Fathers, 101
Wild, Stefan, 260, 265
witch-finding movements, 118
World Council of Churches (WCC), 97n4, 138
Wyschogrod, Michael, 201–202, 205–206

X

Xavier, Francis, 71–72

Y

Yodo-Shin-Shu, 72
Younan, Bishop, 136–137

Z

Zamakhsharī, Abū al-Qāsim al-, 289, 290n10
Zamakhsharī, Mu'tazilite al-, 300–301
Zanzibar, 103–105, 106, 107, 111, 112
Zanzibar mission, 100, 101
Zellentin, Holger, 238–239

www.ingramcontent.com/pod-product-compliance
Lightning Source LLC
Chambersburg PA
CBHW030104010526
44116CB00005B/94